CITIES OF SPLENDOUR IN
THE SHAPING OF SEPHARDI HISTORY

THE LITTMAN LIBRARY OF
JEWISH CIVILIZATION

Life Patron
COLETTE LITTMAN

Dedicated to the memory of
LOUIS THOMAS SIDNEY LITTMAN
who founded the Littman Library for the love of God
and as an act of charity in memory of his father
JOSEPH AARON LITTMAN
and to the memory of
ROBERT JOSEPH LITTMAN
who continued what his father Louis had begun
יהא זכרם ברוך

'Get wisdom, get understanding:
Forsake her not and she shall preserve thee'
PROV. 4:5

The Littman Library of Jewish Civilization is a registered UK charity
Registered charity no. 1000784

CITIES OF SPLENDOUR IN THE SHAPING OF SEPHARDI HISTORY

JANE S. GERBER

London
The Littman Library of Jewish Civilization
in association with Liverpool University Press

The Littman Library of Jewish Civilization
Registered office: 14th floor, 33 Cavendish Square, London W1G 0PW

in association with Liverpool University Press
4 Cambridge Street, Liverpool L69 7ZU, UK
www.liverpooluniversitypress.co.uk/littman

Managing Editor: Connie Webber

Distributed in North America by Longleaf Services
116 S Boundary St, Chapel Hill NY 27514, USA

First published in hardback in 2020
First published in paperback in 2025

© *Jane S. Gerber 2020*

All rights reserved.
No part of this publication may be reproduced,
stored in a retrieval system, or transmitted, in any form or by
any means, without the prior permission in writing of
the Littman Library of Jewish Civilization

This book is sold subject to the condition that it shall not, by way
of trade or otherwise, be lent, re-sold, hired out or otherwise circulated
without the publisher's prior consent in any form of binding or cover
other than that in which it is published and without a similar condition
including this condition being imposed on the subsequent purchaser

Catalogue records for this book are available from
the British Library and the Library of Congress

ISBN 978–1–835539–97–2

Publishing co-ordinator: Janet Moth
Copy-editing: Mark Newby
Proof-reading: Andrew Kirk
Indexing: Jeremy Complin
Designed and typeset by Pete Russell, Faringdon, Oxon.

The manufacturer's authorised representative in the EU for product safety is:
Easy Access System Europe, Mustamäe tee 50, 10621 Tallinn, Estonia
https://easproject.com (gpsr.requests@easproject.com)

For
RACHEL, LEORA, ABIGAIL, SHIRA, AMIYA, SHILOH, OREN, LIVIA

*Grandchildren are the crown of their elders, and
the glory of children is their parents.*

Pirkei avot 6: 8; Proverbs 17: 6

*The Littman Library records with gratitude that
publication of this volume has been supported by
a donation in memory of*

PAUL GOODMAN
1875–1949

*Assistant Secretary for fifteen years then
Secretary for thirty-five years of the Sephardi community in London*

*Honorary Secretary for twenty years of the
Portuguese Marranos Committee in London and
frequent visitor to historic centres of the Sephardi diaspora*

*With an old-world courtesy and a deep attachment to
Sephardi rites and ceremonies, he was also well known as a Zionist leader and
as a multilingual scholar and writer promoting academic Jewish studies,
particularly the Sephardi heritage*

*A second donation in support of publications in
Sephardi studies is also gratefully recorded*

CONTENTS

List of Plates	viii
Note on Transliteration	ix
Map of the Sephardi World	x
Introduction	1
1. Poetry and Politics in the Caliphate of Cordoba, 950–1150	7
2. Crossing the Borders of Art and Society: Toledo as a Meeting Place of Cultures, 1150–1350	48
3. The Search for Redemption in Safed, 1500–1600	86
4. The Jews of Venice: Between Toleration and Expulsion, 1516–1648	124
5. Reconstructing Sepharad in Istanbul and Salonica, 1492–1600	171
6. Jewish Life in Amsterdam and the Formation of the Western Sephardi Diaspora, 1579–1700	214
Conclusion	259
Bibliography	263
Index	285

PLATES

▪

between pages 182 and 183

1. 'How a Jewess was near death in childbirth and called on Holy Mary and was delivered at that moment', *Cantigas de Santa Maria*, no. 89 (Spain, c.1280)
2. Jews and Muslims playing dice, *Libro de ajedrez, dados y tablas* (Toledo, 1283)
3. A Jew and a Christian playing chess, *Libro de ajedrez, dados y tablas* (Toledo, 1283)
4. Micrography: carpet page in Mudéjar style, Damascus Keter, Burgos, 1260
5. Temple implements depicted in the Duke of Sussex's Catalan Bible, Catalonia, fourteenth century
6. *Matsah*: Kaufmann Haggadah, Catalonia, fourteenth century
7. Stucco decoration, Alhambra palace, Granada
8. Stucco decoration, Alcazar of Seville
9. Stucco decoration, El Tránsito Synagogue, Toledo
10. Hebrew inscriptions and decorative Mudéjar stucco ornamentation, El Tránsito Synagogue, Toledo
11. Scuola Levantina, Venice
12. Detail of *bimah*, Scuola Levantina, Venice
13. Scuola Grande Spagnola, Venice
14. Bomberg Babylonian Talmud, *Pe'ah* 1a, Venice, 1519–23
15. *Ketubah*: Abraham, son of Abrabanel, to Dona Gracia, daughter of Aaron de Paz, Venice, 1614
16. Emanuel de Witte, *Interior of the Portuguese Synagogue Amsterdam* (1680)
17. Romeyn de Hooghe, *Dedication of the Portuguese Synagogue in Amsterdam* (1675)
18. Romeyn de Hooghe, *Herengracht with the Baron Belmonte House* (c.1700)
19. Jacob van Ruisdael, *The Jewish Cemetery* (1655)
20. Romeyn de Hooghe, *Funeral at the Portuguese Jewish Cemetery in Ouderkerk aan de Amstel* (1680)
21. Salom Italia, portrait of Manasseh ben Israel (1642)
22. Rembrandt van Rijn, portrait of Manasseh ben Israel (1636)

NOTE ON TRANSLITERATION

THE transliteration of Hebrew in this book reflects consideration of the type of book it is, in terms of its content, purpose, and readership. The system adopted therefore reflects a broad approach to transcription, rather than the narrower approaches found in the *Encyclopaedia Judaica* or other systems developed for text-based or linguistic studies. The aim has been to reflect the pronunciation prescribed for modern Hebrew, rather than the spelling or Hebrew word structure, and to do so using conventions that are generally familiar to the English-speaking reader.

In accordance with this approach, no attempt is made to indicate the distinctions between *alef* and *ayin*, *tet* and *taf*, *kaf* and *kuf*, *sin* and *samekh*, since these are not relevant to pronunciation; likewise, the *dagesh* is not indicated except where it affects pronunciation. Following the principle of using conventions familiar to the majority of readers, however, transcriptions that are well established have been retained even when they are not fully consistent with the transliteration system adopted. On similar grounds, the *tsadi* is rendered by 'tz' in such familiar words as barmitzvah. Likewise, the distinction between *ḥet* and *khaf* has been retained, using ḥ for the former and kh for the latter; the associated forms are generally familiar to readers, even if the distinction is not actually borne out in pronunciation, and for the same reason the final *heh* is indicated too. As in Hebrew, no capital letters are used, except that an initial capital has been retained in transliterating titles of published works (for example, *Shulḥan arukh*).

Since no distinction is made between *alef* and *ayin*, they are indicated by an apostrophe only in intervocalic positions where a failure to do so could lead an English-speaking reader to pronounce the vowel-cluster as a diphthong—as, for example, in *ha'ir*—or otherwise mispronounce the word. An apostrophe is also used, for the same reason, to disambiguate the pronunciation of other English vowel clusters, as for example in *mizbe'aḥ*.

The *sheva na* is indicated by an *e*—*perikat ol*, *reshut*—except, again, when established convention dictates otherwise.

The *yod* is represented by *i* when it occurs as a vowel (*bereshit*), by *y* when it occurs as a consonant (*yesodot*), and by *yi* when it occurs as both (*yisra'el*).

Names have generally been left in their familiar forms, even when this is inconsistent with the overall system.

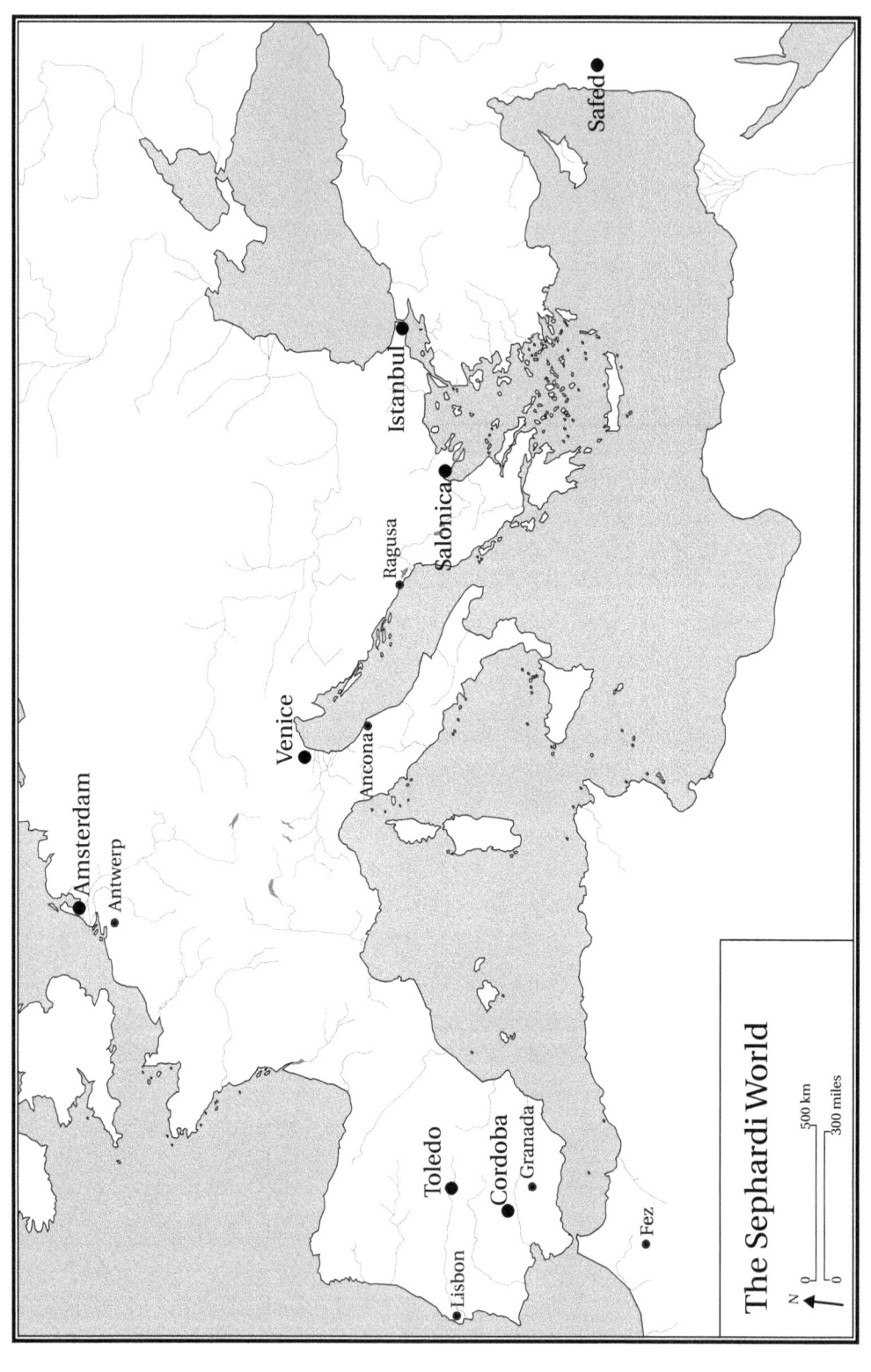

INTRODUCTION

THE SEPHARDIM, one of the two major branches of the Jewish people, were once a familiar sight in cities across the globe. Today their presence has left scarcely a trace beyond placards on streets announcing a former *juderia*, mounted more for purposes of tourism than for the reconstruction of local memory. This book explores the experience of the Sephardim in several major centres of urban civilization. It seeks to understand who they are and how their sojourn in certain cities left its impression upon them and distinguished them from other parts of the Jewish people. While this study assumes that there was no monolithic Sephardi experience nor one prototype of how Sephardim responded to the challenges of living among a variety of cultures, some places had a greater impact on Sephardi identity than others. It also recognizes that being 'Sephardi' means to be connected in some fashion to Spain. Yet most bearers of that designation today never had any contact with Spain, nor did many of their ancestors. The Sephardim include the descendants of Jews who lived in the Iberian peninsula before the Expulsion in 1492 and of Jews who received the refugees from Iberia afterwards. Their identity has been fluid, with new definitions often linked to their new lands of dispersion: their connection to the Iberian peninsula is often to myths of Jewish life in medieval Spain and its association with a golden age of poets, courtiers, and scholars. Special importance is ascribed to their elaborate genealogies and shared history.

As I mentioned more than twenty years ago in the introduction to my book *The Jews of Spain*, the vanished world of Sepharad provides one of the great themes of Jewish history, somewhat analogous to the destruction of the Temple and the Babylonian exile. Yet it is not always clear precisely what Sepharad meant to the Jews 500 years ago when they still lived on Iberian soil, nor what it meant at various historical junctures after they left Spain. Was Sepharad a real or a mythical place? Was it a moment in time? Was it a shared memory of forced conversion and the heroic efforts of the converts to retain a remnant of Jewish observance in the shadow of the Inquisition? Or was it a sense of nobility borne by a courtly and scholarly elite? It was probably some combination of all these elements that lay at the heart of Sephardi identity. The defining moment for the Sephardim was the Expulsion from Spain in 1492, but the memory of a Jewish golden era of creativity and the bitter knowledge of exile form only part of a complex interweaving of history and memory.

Jewish life has been lived on virtually every continent and in countless cities, towns, and villages, evolving over the broadest geographical canvas. However, some places had more influence on the Sephardim than others. While a geographer might regard a place from the point of view of its topographical features or an anthropologist be intrigued by the encounters of Jews with indigenous populations, the historian of the Sephardim can draw upon several sources. I have selected seven cities through which to explore the shaping of Sephardi identity: Cordoba, Toledo, Safed, Venice, Istanbul, Salonica, and Amsterdam. Each is examined from a different vantage point. Significantly, these cities (with the exception of Safed) were also important centres of civilization. The Arabic themes and metric forms in the Hebrew poetry of Andalusia and the artistic calligraphy interwoven into the vegetal motifs on the walls of the fourteenth-century El Tránsito Synagogue of Toledo suggest the artistic sensibilities of the Jews of Spain and their ability to internalize the surrounding cultures and embrace them as their own. Similarly, Sephardi attitudes and identities are mirrored in the illuminated Haggadot of Toledo and in the Spanish synagogue in the ghetto of Venice. Some of this evidence may appear unconventional, but an interdisciplinary methodology provides useful tools for exploring the complexity of the Sephardi experience.

Historians may differ on how to define a Sephardi Jew, but none would question the presence of Jews in Iberian, Ligurian, Anatolian, Italian, and North African cities throughout much of recorded history. They manned the watchtowers and portals when Muslim armies swept into the Iberian peninsula from North Africa in the eighth century; they lived in the interstices of Muslim and Christian civilizations in Toledo during the long era of the Christian Reconquest; they dwelt on the routes of commerce on the distant shores of the eastern and western Mediterranean during the High Middle Ages; they experimented with unique forms of self-government and enjoyed polyphonic music in the segregated ghetto in Venice; and they contemplated the infinite dimensions of exile in the town of Safed in Galilee. When the exiles from Iberia were thrown together in Istanbul and Salonica, they were a fractured and contentious people seeking community after overwhelming tragedy. When the Portuguese Conversos found asylum in the orderly society of Amsterdam, after several generations as Catholics or Marranos, they were hard pressed at times to pioneer as 'new Jews', to retrieve and reshape a forbidden and unfamiliar heritage. The ingredients of Sepharad were, like their bearers, multilingual and cosmopolitan. There was no single prototype of a Sephardi Jewish community. The challenge for the historian is to capture the many contexts in which the life of the Jews from Iberia unfolded without either romanticizing, essentializing, or diluting their fragmented reality.

Like all Jews before the modern era, the Sephardim lived in autonomous communities. However, this did not necessarily mean they were alienated from the people among whom they lived. They were very much at home in the cultures of their adopted lands, filling many roles as merchants, shopkeepers, artisans, physicians, and bankers. At the same time they exhibited great mobility and were members of far-flung family networks. One notable feature of the Sephardim was their multilingualism.

They spoke the languages of their neighbours and had their own dialects among themselves. Knowledge of the native language bound them to their countries of residence, but the shared Jewish languages of Hebrew, Aramaic, and Ladino—a version of medieval Castilian written in Hebrew characters—as well as Spanish or Portuguese bound them to one another.

There is no necessary connection between Jews and cities. Had they been permitted, Jews would undoubtedly have cultivated the land more. However, they were barred from landholding in most of Europe and suffered discriminatory taxes as agriculturalists in the world of Islam. They thus became a quintessentially urban people. Jewish religious requirements also encouraged close settlement in order to have access to their essential social and legal institutions, such as the ritual bath, the synagogue, the ritual slaughterer, the communal oven, and their court of law. The recommended presence of these institutions was spelled out in the Talmud (BT *San.* 17b). Significantly, rabbinic directives on where a scholar should live also included access to a physician and a school for his children. The concentration of Jews in urban settings made them more visible to outsiders, but it also made foreign cultures more accessible to the Jews, since they frequently shared neighbourhoods and economic and social activities with non-Jews. Their identification with urban life and urban economic pursuits contrasted sharply with the predominantly agricultural and rural lives of most populations in human history.

Jewish residential patterns within a city usually depended upon the whim of the local authorities. In Fez and Rabat, the Jewish district adjoined the walls of the royal palace; in Toledo, it was near the main cathedral; in Baghdad, Jews were concentrated in the imperial palace complex at a distance from the main urban population centre. A Jewish residential quarter might sprawl along the banks of a river, such as in the Caribbean settlement of Surinam, or straddle the city walls, as in Toledo. The separate, walled-off ghetto in which Jews were isolated in Venice was a late medieval phenomenon. Even after their physical separation from the general population, the Jews of Venice did not become isolated from the cultural currents of the city.

In Salonica, the Sephardim occupied the commercial heart of the city and its splendid sprawling port district, since the Ottomans had deported the local Greek population, Jewish and Christian, at the time of their conquest in 1430. In Istanbul, they lived in dozens of districts, often moving from one to another in the first century after their arrival. When Portuguese Jews began arriving in Amsterdam in the late sixteenth and early seventeenth centuries, the city was undergoing an ambitious expansion after a long and brutal war with the Habsburgs. The Jews found themselves in a new mercantile centre with immigrants from Flanders and Protestant religious dissidents. Their homes were on land only recently wrested from the seas and a magnet to newcomers of all socio-economic backgrounds. The exiles of 1492 were drawn to Safed in the Land of Israel because of its proximity to the tombs of ancient rabbis and because of the Jewish tradition that the future messianic era would begin in Galilee. Clearly, no single topographical or political circumstances united the Sephardim.

The seven cities discussed here were characterized by cultural hybridity. The Jews of Cordoba formed a heterogeneous community, but so did the Muslims. Different Arab and Berber tribes, newly converted Muslims, Christians, and Jews from all over the Mediterranean jostled in the city's lively markets, drawn by the opportunities of the new caliphate. Toledo's Jewish community was also mixed, including refugees from Andalusia, France, and Germany. The indigenous non-Jewish population was equally diverse. In the ghetto of Venice, Venetian Jews, Jews from several other parts of Italy, refugees from the expulsions from Provence, Spain, and Portugal, and Jews who were permanent residents of the Ottoman empire all rubbed shoulders in the confined space allotted to them. In Istanbul, as many as one hundred congregations from Spain, Portugal, Italy, Asia Minor, and the Balkans, as well as refugees from central Europe, spread out across the city. Even the Portuguese community of Amsterdam ranged across a broad spectrum of belief and disbelief. These factors may account for Sephardi openness to different cultures and diverse currents of thought. Porousness of cultural boundaries distinguished the cities the Sephardim migrated to.

Jewish history is a story of the adaptation of diasporas to the cultures of their surrounding societies. As a minority among other peoples since ancient times, Jews have displayed unusual receptivity to outside cultures while remaining faithful to their essential beliefs and practices, and perhaps the most receptive were the Sephardim. Their leaders were cosmopolitan; the curricula of their schools in Toledo, Salonica, and Amsterdam reflected a breadth of vision that was difficult, if not impossible, to find anywhere in the pre-modern Ashkenazi world.

Three of the cities in this book were Christian, and four Muslim, during the period under consideration. Neither civilization had a monopoly on hospitality or hostility towards its Jewish minority. Some of the cities were also capitals of kingdoms or empires where Sephardim constituted a minority among many minorities. Multi-cultural and multi-ethnic environments tended to be dynamic and advantageous for the Jews. Two of the cities, Toledo and Cordoba, were famed for the significant involvement of Jews in poetry, translation, science, and art before the Expulsion. The other five were centres of Jewish life after the Expulsion where 'the mixed multitudes' from Iberia began to coalesce to become new and different communities. Each of the cities also served as the venue in which a particular dimension of Sephardi Jewry took shape or was expressed in especially intense form.

The book begins in Cordoba in the tenth century, the cradle of Sephardi civilization and a lively regional centre of Arab Islamic culture. By the year 1000 the Jews of Muslim Mediterranean lands were completely Arabized. Jewish merchants and physicians were familiar with the culture of their Muslim peers in ways unimaginable to Jews in the Christian West. The Jews' responses to Muslim assertions of superiority in culture, religion, and pedigree can be found in their refreshingly new and daring Hebrew poetry. Sephardi notions of lineage and poetic talent were born in Cordoba. St Augustine used the city as a metaphor for Paradise; for the Arabs, Cordoba was Paradise itself; for the Sephardim, the whole of Andalusia was later reconceived as Paradise.

The Sephardim fled from Muslim to Christian Spain in the eleventh and twelfth centuries. In Toledo they encountered Ashkenazim fleeing northern Europe. There Sephardi and Ashkenazi cultures, the cultures of Jews from Muslim and Christian realms, entered into dialogue, and memories of Cordoba receded, to be replaced by myths. Foremost among these was a pride in the exalted lineage and aristocratic pedigree of the Sephardim.

The last decade of the fifteenth century marked a seismic change in Jewish history. With the Expulsion from Spain in 1492 and forced conversions in Portugal in 1497, Sephardi Jewry was shattered. Waves of exiles from Spain dispersed throughout the Mediterranean, carrying memories and myths of their sophisticated past as well as heightened anxiety lest they lose their heritage in the upheaval and dispersion. They were forced to explain to themselves their ignoble fates of conversion or flight. Questions of Jewish identity would haunt the survivors. Why had Jewish life in Spain come to such an ignominious end? How were the Jews to repent for their 'misdeeds' which, in most minds, had caused the Expulsion? Did the catastrophe of exile from Sepharad signify that the 'End of Days' was approaching? The turmoil of 1492 was reflected in the development of a mystical doctrine of explosive potential in the city of Safed.

The sixteenth century saw a series of expulsions of Jews in the West. As the Sephardim fled from town to town seeking shelter, their loyalties to Iberian towns and villages dimmed. Most of the refugees moved out of Europe into the expanding Ottoman empire, frequently via Venice. In the newly established ghetto of Venice, the vulnerability of the Sephardim began to be replaced by economic strength and new forms of identity as they exploited the international networks created by the dispersal of their kin. The introduction of printing and the spread of the Jewish book in Venice, Salonica, Istanbul, and Amsterdam provided the most important vehicle for preserving the heritage of Sepharad, of restoring that heritage to Conversos returning to Judaism, and of introducing the Jewish diasporas to one another.

The majority of Spanish Jews arrived in the Ottoman empire in the first half of the sixteenth century. Smaller groups of Conversos followed over the rest of the century. The reconstruction of the Sephardi community in the Ottoman empire, especially in Istanbul and Salonica, forms a vibrant chapter in Jewish history. Energies were focused on rebuilding Jewish institutions and erecting a new edifice using the language and technical skills acquired in Iberia. The Ottoman Jewish communities were lively and fractious. The textile industry in Salonica brought renewal and livelihood to the Sephardim, transforming them into an important economic factor in the empire. Sephardi life in Istanbul highlighted the institutional tensions of internal diversity, while the boycott of Ancona in 1556 revealed the profound fissures within the Sephardi world. By the beginning of the seventeenth century Sephardi heterogeneity in the Ottoman empire, with all its conflicts, was drawing to a close as specific memories of Spain dimmed. The superior numbers of Sephardim, their pride, self-confidence, and affluence, ensured the dominance of their culture, but it was now a very different culture from what the Jews of medieval Iberia had known. As Spain receded ever further in memory, it was preserved and idealized in the Ladino songs and folk wisdom of the Jewish masses.

In Amsterdam in the seventeenth century the descendants of Jews who had undergone forcible conversion to Catholicism in Portugal strove to 'return' to Judaism, a faith they had never known, while complying with the expectations of how a Jewish minority should live in the Protestant city. The Portuguese Jews of Amsterdam expressed an idiosyncratic understanding of Sephardi culture in their art, their synagogues, their leisure activities, and the commissioning of monumental, sculptured tombstones in their cemetery at Ouderkerk. They became pioneers of the western Sephardi diaspora on the continent and in the Atlantic world.

In their long history of living in Spain as Jews and as Jews from Spain elsewhere, the Sephardim excelled in embracing novelty, grappling with contradictions, and exploring syntheses of identity. Just as they knew no geographical boundaries, they also lacked any collective boundaries based on fixed, essential characteristics. Their pride in their lineage could, at times, be overbearing to non-Sephardi Jews. Their sensitivity to languages and their devotion to Hebrew were continuous. At the same time, they showed a remarkable fidelity to the Hispanic dimensions of their heritage. Language and pedigree did not fade, even as the memories of Spain grew dim. The Sephardi past has endured in many forms to inform successive generations, testifying to the vitality of the cultures in which they lived.

CHAPTER ONE

POETRY AND POLITICS IN THE CALIPHATE OF CORDOBA 950–1150

> If we are to call any age golden, it is beyond doubt that age
> which brings forth golden talents.
> MARCILIO FICINO, letter to Paul of Middelburg

THE NAME 'Sepharad' appears once in the Bible in the short prophetic statement, 'The exiles of Jerusalem who are in Sepharad shall inherit the cities of the south' (Obad. 1: 20). As is true of many place names in the Bible, it is not clear what or where Sepharad was, nor is it certain when the Jews of medieval Spain began to consider themselves Sephardi. Being Sephardi, however, is not solely a geographical designation denoting a Jew of Spain, nor is it an exclusively religious or cultural phenomenon. The identification of Sepharad with al-Andalus, or medieval Islamic Spain, and the designation of its inhabitants as Sephardi, first appear in the late eighth or early ninth centuries. By the tenth century the association of Spanish Jewry with the elite exiles of ancient Jerusalem (and the book of Obadiah) was widely accepted. In its literal sense, a Sephardi Jew is one who traces his or her ancestry back to Spain. But more than being from Spain, being Sephardi denotes a particular form of cultural achievement and set of associations and cultural traits.

The distinctive Jewish civilization that emerged in Spain was shaped by the unique coexistence, or *convivencia*, of Jews, Christians, and Muslims on European soil for almost 800 years. *Convivencia* should not, however, be confused with modern notions of tolerance and respect for the other. The Jews of Spain remained a distinctive, subordinate, and vulnerable people under the hegemonies of Christendom and Islam, drawing freely from the cultural vitality of both civilizations while also frequently suffering as the victim of both. At the same time, during their long sojourn on the Iberian peninsula they produced an extraordinary outpouring of Hebrew poetry, engaged in philosophical and scientific enquiry, and crafted a civilization that combined elements of Judaeo-Arabic and Romance cultures. While cultivating many of the same branches of learning that flourished in the Abbasid caliphate of Baghdad, they integrated these sciences and modes of thought into Judaic learning in new and exciting ways in the caliphate of Cordoba and its Muslim successor states. Socially as well, Sephardim have few peers in the annals of pre-modern Jewry. Sepharad produced a galaxy of courtly intellectuals who were equally at home with princes in the corridors of power or among like-minded poets declaiming Hebrew and Arabic verses in verdant gardens. Jewish courtiers rubbed shoulders with royalty, sponsored learning, protected their co-religionists, and delved into philosophy and science.

The uniqueness of Sephardi history and its bearers captured the imagination of nineteenth-century Jewish historians, holding special charms for the founders of modern Jewish historical writing. The Sephardim provided usable models from the Jewish past in the heated discussions on the ability of the Jews to find a place in Western society. The level of Sephardi accomplishment and acculturation, including their use of vernacular languages and the unusual degree of intimacy with their host cultures, were especially useful as ammunition in the battles for the emancipation of the Jews of Europe. Their social networks, cultural exchanges with their neighbours, rich poetry, and broad curriculum of learning all testified to a Jewry that could master the culture of its neighbours and participate in general society. These traits of the Sephardim and the idealization of their history have been united in what has aptly been called the 'Sephardi mystique'. This reconstruction of the Jewish past is a simplification that contains both grains of historical truth and wishful thinking.[1]

Throughout their history Jews have usually responded to the surrounding cultures by adopting, adapting, and transforming elements of them into something new and distinctively their own. When afforded a modicum of freedom and tolerance, Jews have engaged in intensive and prolonged dialogue with the civilizations of their neighbours. Any Jewish culture that did not adapt to new modes of thought would be frozen in an ancient mould. To a large extent, Jewish history is the story of Jewish creative adaptation, replayed in countless cities over the centuries. What distinguishes the story of the Jews in medieval Muslim Spain is the degree of cultural symbiosis they attained. Moreover, the length and intensity of their encounter with the multiple cultures of Spain were unprecedented. Although the boundaries between acculturation and assimilation were blurred in many places and at many times, perhaps nowhere else was the process more thoroughgoing.

Even in its most hospitable moments, however, medieval Muslim Spain was a land of inequality. Jews or Christians were tolerated as autonomous religious and ethnic groups, but it was the toleration by the superior of the inferior, by the overlord of the underling. Under Islam, Jews were defined as *dhimmi*s, 'protected people', who received

---

[1] See Assis, 'Sefarad'; Ray, 'Beyond Tolerance and Persecution'. On the image of medieval Spain among nineteenth-century German Jewish historians, see Schorsch, 'The Myth of Sephardic Supremacy'; Efron, *German Jewry and the Allure of the Sephardic*; see also Gerber, 'Toward an Understanding of the Term "The Golden Age" as a Historical Reality'; on Ottoman Jewry, see Naar, 'Fashioning the "Mother of Israel"'; Stein, 'Sephardic and Middle Eastern Jewries since 1492'.

protection in exchange for submission to a set of humiliating political and social restrictions and discriminatory taxes. Whether Jewish, Berber, *muwallad* (a 'new' Muslim and hence inferior to the 'old' Muslims), or Christian, members of religious or ethnic minorities were frequently barred from participating in significant areas of the economy and the state. At the same time, the various restrictions on Jews were not uniformly imposed. Conditions varied depending upon shifts in political alliances or in the general religiosity of the era and the regime. Moreover, even when social discrimination occurred, it did not preclude cultural sharing. The remarkable influence of Arabic culture on Jewish activities such as the ornamental script decorating the walls of synagogues in Cordoba and Toledo, the shared metaphors and metres of Arabic and Hebrew poetry, or the modes of entertainment at social gatherings are clear symptoms of Iberian Jewish acculturation. These phenomena should not be interpreted as expressions of Jewish appreciation for Muslim toleration: the distinction between suffering social and political disabilities and sharing in the broad cultural currents of society could be, and frequently was, acutely felt. The apprehension of such asymmetry between cultural sharing and social ostracism was one critical factor in shaping Sephardi Jewry. Even at its most comfortable, Sepharad was both diaspora and home: not quite exile, yet not a second Jerusalem either.[2]

Over the centuries, the city of Cordoba has become synonymous with the birth of Sepharad as a definable cultural entity in Jewish history.[3] The era of the caliphate of Cordoba (929–1031) is closely associated with the beginnings of revolutionary experimentation in new forms of Jewish self-expression and new fields of intellectual enquiry. A new Jewish persona, one equally at home in Torah and secular culture, became its standard-bearer. Most of Sephardi Jewry's daring innovations in the manipulation of the Hebrew language or in philosophical and scientific enquiries began during the brief blossoming of the caliphate of Cordoba before it dissolved into a number of equally dazzling statelets. The intellectual and social innovations endured long after the disintegration of the caliphate and the contraction of Muslim rule commenced.

The notion of aristocratic lineage has clung to Sephardi history since medieval times. Sephardi self-consciousness emerged in a society characterized by great heterogeneity. The tumultuous mix of peoples and religions in Muslim Spain was frequently expressed in internecine struggles among different Muslim tribal groups, each rooted in a proud sense of the distinctiveness of its origins in the Near East or among the Berbers of North Africa. Frustrated new Muslims smarted under their inferior status among

---

[2] On assimilation, see G. D. Cohen, 'The Blessing of Assimilation in Jewish History'; on ethnicity and the dynamics of assimilation in Spain, see Glick, *Islamic and Christian Spain in the Early Middle Ages*, 165–93; on acculturation among Ashkenazi Jews, see Malkiel, *Reconstructing Ashkenaz*; Marcus, *The Rituals of Childhood*.

[3] For the efflorescence of political and cultural life in the newly established Muslim caliphate, see Dozy, *Histoire des Musulmanes d'Espagne*, vol. iii; for Cordoba as the site of a new Jewish civilization, see Gerber, *The Jews of Spain*, ch. 2.

the ruling Arabs. The persistence of a sizeable and restive Christian minority contributed to the ethnic hypersensitivity of the medieval Spanish populace. The Jews were not mere spectators to the jockeying for power, prestige, and territory. They too staked out claims of noble origin and antiquity. It is not accidental that special words were devised to denote Arabized Christians who lived in Muslim Spain (Mozarab) and Muslims who lived in Christian Spain (Mudéjar). In this context, the Sephardim emerged as a distinctive Jewish subgroup. Although the Jews drew freely from the majority cultures, internalizing Arabic and later Hispanic cultural expressions, they remained socially marginal. They were strangers to their neighbours even as they engaged in cultural borrowing. Muslim Cordoba and Christian Toledo were critical sites in the ambiguous terrain of creative cultural intermingling that was at the heart of Sephardi self-definition.

The Birth of Sepharad and the Jewish Courtier Tradition

The declaration of the caliphate of Cordoba in 929 by Abd al-Rahman III (912–61) is commonly seen as the beginning of a new era for Muslims and Jews in Spain. However, the act of periodization by historians is an arbitrary one. They seek to demarcate turning points and construct neat categories from a welter of past events. Cultural change, as opposed to political change, is usually a gradual and incremental process. Sephardi cultural identity was long in the making, beginning with the conquest of the Iberian peninsula by the Umayyad caliphate in the eighth century, which set in motion vast demographic, linguistic, and religious shifts. From the early days of Muslim rule, Jews were assigned a distinct role. Although both Christians and Jews were recognized as minority religious groups, the Jews were not adversaries of the Muslims. Indeed, after almost a century of persecution under the Visigoths, the Jews could cautiously greet the arrival of the Muslims with some relief. Those who had practised Judaism in secret as a result of Visigothic persecution at the end of the seventh and beginning of the eighth centuries could now do so openly, and those who had fled to North Africa could return to the Iberian peninsula. According to later Arab chroniclers, Jews were assigned to guard the gates of Cordoba abandoned by fleeing Christians as the Arab armies approached. Such an arrangement, although reported by late and possibly tendentious sources, would be consistent with the methods employed by Muslim armies elsewhere as they pacified conquered territories containing millions of hostile Christians.[4]

---

[4] *Akhbar majmua*, in Stillman, *The Jews of Arab Lands*, 156. Using Jews as guards was commonplace in the Iberian campaigns. Jews adopted a policy of 'wait and see' at the approach of the Muslim armies, while the Christians fled or surrendered. As the Arabs moved northward they tended to leave small garrisons behind, enlisting those elements of the native population that they felt they could trust to secure the rear. See N. Roth, 'The Jews and the Muslim Conquest of Spain'.

The Umayyads chose Cordoba over Toledo or Seville as the seat of their power because of its central location, the fertility of the surrounding countryside, its accessibility to the Muslim south, and, in contrast to the historic cities of Toledo or Seville, its relative indifference to Visigothic Christian traditions. The foundations of Umayyad splendour in Spain were laid enthusiastically by a series of dynamic rulers who established an independent seat of Muslim power in the west. Abd al-Rahman I (756–88), Abd al-Rahman II (822–52), and, above all, Abd al-Rahman III and al-Hakam II (961–76) were responsible for Cordoba's greatness. The emergence of Andalusia and its capital as a great centre of civilization was dramatic. The Arab conquerors imported an array of new crops and introduced a vastly improved system of irrigation, thereby launching an agricultural revolution. With the improvements in agriculture, the population of the region multiplied many times. Population growth and urbanization, in turn, were the catalysts for an exodus from the countryside to the cities and the emergence of new industries requiring both skilled and unskilled workers: metal-working, mining, leather production, textile manufacture, book production, paper-making, iron production, and ivory-carving were only a few of the many new branches of the economy that flourished. Records preserved in the Cairo *geniza*, the storeroom of the Ben Ezra synagogue of Fustat, testify to lively trade from Andalusia to North Africa and the eastern Mediterranean carried on by Jews alongside Muslims and Christians. The North African and Egyptian names of Andalusian Jewish merchants, craftsmen, and scholars (such as al-Fasi and al-Taherti) attest to the steady influx of Jews from North Africa and the heartland of Islam to Iberia, attracted by the promise of economic opportunity on the frontier with Europe.[5]

The city of Cordoba reached its zenith in the 900s. A German nun was moved to exclaim that Cordoba represented 'the majesty and adornment of the world, the wondrous capital . . . radiating in affluence of all earthly blessings'.[6] Descriptions of the city are extravagant. Tenth-century Cordoba reportedly had at least 100,000 inhabitants. Some medieval Arab geographers hyperbolically estimated a population as high as 500,000. It surpassed all other cities in Europe and rivalled Baghdad, Constantinople, and Cairo in size and splendour. According to the Arab chronicler Ibn Hawkal:

The biggest city in Spain is Cordoba, which has no equal in the Maghreb and hardly in Egypt, Syria, or Mesopotamia for the size of its population, its extent, the space occupied by its markets, the cleanliness of its streets, the architecture of its mosques, the number of its baths and caravanserais. Natives of Cordoba who have travelled to Mesopotamia say that it is the same size as one of the divisions of Baghdad.[7]

---

[5] Remie Constable, *Trade and Traders in Muslim Spain*, 52–77, 162–208; Goitein, *A Mediterranean Society*, vol. i: *Economic Foundations*; see also Ashtor, *The Jews of Muslim Spain*, i. 264–90.

[6] Hroswitha of Gandersheim, *Pelagius*, cited in Hillenbrand, '"The Ornament of the World"', 118.

[7] Ibn Hawkal, *Kitab surat al-ard*, 114; see Remie Constable, *Trade and Traders in Muslim Spain*, 79–80, 82, 128, 130, 131; for a different description of Cordoba, see Gerber, *The Jews of Spain*, ch. 2. Historians have generally

By the tenth century Cordoba reputedly boasted 700 mosques and perhaps as many as 3,000 public baths. Its streets were paved, and lights were attached to the outer doors and corners of the houses.[8]

Countless villas dotted the banks of the Guadalquivir river on which the city was situated. Indoor plumbing existed in its luxurious houses. The air of Cordoba was filled with the hum of 5,000 looms weaving silk and brocade. Countless kilns fired the brightly coloured ceramic tiles that were used to line the city's many fountains and reflection pools. In this world of plenty, material richness provided comfort and beauty, as well as enhanced status. Even purely utilitarian objects such as waterspouts were transformed into magnificent sculptures by skilled artists and craftsmen. Nowhere else in Europe could such sophistication be found.

The Arab historian al-Maqqari (1591–1632), in a famous compilation of earlier histories of Andalusia, remarked of the Cordoba of Abd al-Rahman III: 'In four things Cordoba surpasses the capitals of the world. Among these are the bridge over the river and the mosque. These are the first two. The third is Madinat al-Zahra, but the greatest of all things is knowledge: and that is the fourth.'[9] Cordoba's sparkling cultural life was nurtured by an estimated seventy libraries, with the caliph's library alone reportedly stocking 400,000 volumes. Paper-manufacturing was introduced to Spain by traders from the east sometime in the tenth century, with the Spanish town of Jativa emerging as an important centre of paper production. With the introduction of local paper-manufacturing, literacy increased, as did the private possession of manuscripts. In conscious imitation of their rivals in Abbasid Baghdad, the Umayyad princes, more aesthetes than bureaucrats, imported talented architects and scientists from the Near East and North Africa and established schools to translate classical works into Arabic. The famed astronomer Maslama, for instance, joined a circle of scientists under the patronage of the caliph, adapting the astronomical tables of the Middle Eastern astronomer al-Khwarizmi to the meridian of Cordoba in 979. He also translated Ptolemy's *Planosphere* into Arabic as well as composing a treatise on the construction of the astrolabe.

Cordoba was selected by the last surviving member of the Umayyad dynasty as the capital of Islam on the Iberian peninsula in 755 and became the seat of the short-lived caliphate of Cordoba in 929. In keeping with the mores of Muslim potentates, who sought to express their religious devotion through their imperial power, the Umayyads commenced ambitious building programmes. The glory of medieval Cordoba was reflected in its imperial quarter and in the city's great mosque, an architectural gem rivalling in size and beauty the most famous religious monuments in the Islamic

been lavish in their praise of the city, especially Arab historians, for whom the greatness of Cordoba marked a pinnacle of splendour rivalling Baghdad. See also Ashtor, *The Jews of Muslim Spain*, i. 435 nn. 24, 26.

[8] Hillenbrand, '"The Ornament of the World"', 118.
[9] Ahmad ibn Mohammed al-Maqqari, *The Breath of Perfume from the Branch of Green Andalusia*, cited ibid.

heartlands of Syria and Iraq. Its cinnamon-coloured exterior, stark and understated, stood in sharp contrast to a rich interior adorned by an elaborately carved wooden ceiling, enamelled and gilded doors, and geometrically subtle tile work. The interior decoration of the mosque consisted of quranic quotes in graceful Arabic script, with intricate, abstract leaf-scroll patterns derived from Arabic calligraphy sculpted into the capitals of its endless rows of columns. The vast inner spaces of the mosque were illuminated by 4,000 lamps filled with perfumed oil and 300 candelabra constructed from the bronze of the melted-down church bells of the cathedral of Santiago. The mosque was repeatedly enlarged under the Umayyads to accommodate the ever-growing circle of converts to Islam. Not only did it set the pattern for Islamic art in Spain, it also served as a source of inspiration and imitation for synagogue architecture.

The embellishment of Cordoba reached its peak in 936, when Caliph Abd al-Rahman III decided to build a new imperial enclave approximately 7 kilometres from the city, called Madinat al-Zahra. The administrative apparatus of the young caliphate was transferred to the magnificent new palace complex, further distancing the government from the general populace. The complex was reportedly named to honour Abd al-Rahman's favourite concubine, Zahra, although it is possible that it was simply named for her in imitation of the extravagant palatial gift for the legendarily beautiful Shirin from her lover, King Parvis of ancient Persia. It was common for medieval Islamic rulers in Baghdad and Samarra to incorporate ancient Persian practices into their statecraft, and the rivalry of the caliphate of Cordoba with both Fatimids in Egypt and Abbasids in Baghdad was never far removed from the considerations of the ambitious Abd al-Rahman III.

Construction of the colossal project took more than twenty years, employing more than 10,000 workers and 1,000 mules and resulting in an extended economic boom in the city. No expense was spared. The Byzantine emperor had tons of marble sent from North Africa. An army of craftsmen and artisans was recruited to produce and install the 15,000 wooden doors plated with iron or polished bronze. Special attention was accorded to its fantastic gardens, with their many pavilions, walkways, exotic flowers, and the ingenious theatrical waterworks designed for the caliph's amusement. One of the reception halls, for instance, overlooked dramatically placed gardens of exotic plants and fountains; its roof was made of gold and silver, its walls of rare marble. In the middle of the main reception hall a magnificent pearl was suspended, another gift from the Byzantine emperor. The hall had eight doors on each side, formed by marble columns supporting interlaced arches of ebony and gold, inlaid with gold, gems, and mosaics. The caliph delighted in observing the astonishment of his guests as they entered the hall. Ostentation, rarely absent from royal architecture, is always an expression of power.[10]

---

[10] For a detailed description of the gardens of Madinat al-Zahra, see Ruggles, *Gardens, Landscape, and Vision in the Palaces of Islamic Spain*, 67. Only 10 per cent of the vast palace complex has been excavated, but sufficient

In addition to the hundreds of buildings and magnificent gardens, Madinat al-Zahra included a zoo, an aviary, a mint, and enormous fishponds. There was no distinction between architecture exclusively dedicated to the expression of power and that dedicated to the private whims and tastes of the caliph and his entourage. The construction of such an immense complex, from the quarrying of its stones, the transporting of the materials, the planning and organizing of work gangs, to the acquisition of its rich and varied contents, was in itself an expression of power that few contemporaries could match. It is estimated that more than 13,000 household attendants, including jesters and poets, acrobats and musicians, astronomers and astrologers, vied with diplomats and courtiers, royal guests, and hangers-on for the attention and favour of the ruler. Being secluded within the imperial complex added to the aura and mystique of the newly proclaimed caliph and all those who came into contact with him.

Not long after the completion of the palace, the caliphate collapsed in civil war, and the kingdom dissolved into a number of petty, warring statelets, known as *taifas*. Muslim court life dispersed and multiplied in these small Berber and Arab kingdoms. The architects of Madinat al-Zahra quickly found employment in the new courts that sprouted up during the upheavals and political reshufflings of the eleventh century. Each *taifa* possessed its own palace and court ritual, providing a multitude of patrons of culture who competed with one another to surround themselves with talent. The courtly environment of the *taifas* reached its pinnacle in the Alhambra palace in Granada, but there were other centres of culture throughout Andalusia: the greatest Arabic poets hailed from Saragossa and Cordoba. Some of the *taifas*, such as Seville and Almeria, were ruled by accomplished poet-kings. The Umayyad court of Cordoba provided the model on which the *taifas* built their cultural life. If anything, the memory of Medinat al-Zahra was magnified as the last physical traces of it were pillaged, its precious marbles and porphyry picked over to adorn the new palaces of the petty princes. Even in ruins, Cordoba remained the standard for magnificence and princely decorum.

Beautification of the caliph's palace was only one part of Abd al-Rahman III's vision. Any court was expected to be the locus of culture and enlightenment, and Medinat al-Zahra was a host to the arts. Caliphs typically combined the role of warrior with that of collector and connoisseur of fine things. Gifts brought by diplomatic delegates introduced foreign delicacies that also attested to the caliph's refinement. Exotic and rare plants were cultivated for their colours, aromas, culinary or medical uses, or aphrodisiac powers. Caliphal patronage of scientific works included the collection of ancient manuscripts and the sponsorship of translations into Arabic. Cordoba's status as an intellectual centre was a major priority of its tenth-century

evidence has been found to confirm that the reality of the Umayyad court exceeded even its most enthusiastic literary descriptions. It was not a place that commoners ever entered. It was intended to impress international dignitaries and local subjects.

caliphs, especially the bibliophile al-Hakam II. In the rarefied milieu of the Umayyad and *taifa* courts, Jewish courtiers began to appear in the roles of physicians, translators, astronomers, astrologers, musicians, writers, scribes, and secretaries.

The beginning of a new age for the Jews, referred to retrospectively as 'the golden age of Spain', is commonly associated with a physician and courtier in the court of Abd al-Rahman III, Hasdai ibn Shaprut (915–70). His entrance onto the stage of history was described by the medieval Jewish historian Abraham ibn Daud (1089–1164): 'In the days of R. Hasdai the Nasi the bards began to twitter, and in the days of R. Samuel the Nagid [Samuel ibn Nagrela (993–1056)] they burst into song.'[11] Hasdai's life, with its combination of worldliness and piety, poetry and politics, would become paradigmatic for an elite class of Jews in Spain. While Hasdai's role in launching the Jewish cultural revolution in Spain has been repeatedly recalled, his activities have not generally been placed within their Andalusian historical and artistic context nor evaluated from the perspective of the shaping of Sephardi Jewry. According to one Muslim chronicler:

> Hasdai was the first to open for Andalusian Jewry the gates of their science and jurisprudence, chronology, and other subjects. Previously, they had recourse to the Jews of Baghdad in order to learn the law of their faith and in order to adjust the calendar and determine the dates of their holidays . . . .
> When Hasdai became attached to al-Hakam II . . . he was able to procure (through the caliph) the works of the Jews in the East which he desired. Then [Hasdai] taught the Jews of Spain that of which they had previously been ignorant.[12]

This comment links Hasdai to Jewish cultural developments that began in Iraq, the eastern heartland of Islam, were transported by the Jews to North Africa, and ultimately transplanted to Spain. The Jewish culture of the medieval Mediterranean world was deeply responsive to the new linguistic, scientific, and philosophical trends originating in Baghdad. The Mediterranean basin was transformed by the Muslim conquests into one vast cultural unit, Arabic in form and content and increasingly Islamic in religion. The golden-age culture of the Jews of Cordoba drew directly from these broader intellectual trends. Linguistic and talmudic studies spread from the east to mature in the main centres of Jewish learning in Morocco (Fez), Tunisia (Kairouan), and Algeria (Tahert) during the ninth century.

The active role of the courtier as a patron of learning is a central feature of the life of Hasdai. He was the scion of a learned family that had moved to Cordoba from Jaén in eastern Andalusia early in the tenth century.[13] His father reportedly endowed a synagogue and subsidized Jewish scholars in his home town. In accordance with the

---

[11] Ibn Daud, *Sefer ha-Qabbalah*, 150–1.
[12] Said al-Andalusi, *Tabaqat al-Umam*, in Stillman, *The Jews of Arab Lands*, 210.
[13] See Gerber, *The Jews of Spain*, 46–52; Ashtor, *The Jews of Moslem Spain*, i. 155–227; Decter, 'Before Caliphs and Kings', 4–12; on the later courtier tradition, see ibid. 12–28.

customs of the learned classes, the father provided his talented son with tutors in Judaica, mathematics, Hebrew, and Latin. Young Hasdai showed an early aptitude for the sciences, gaining recognition at a young age for his medical skills. Science, and especially medicine, was a standard part of the humanist curriculum for males of the ruling class among the three faith communities in Spain. Hasdai's medical abilities, including his discovery of antidotes for poisons, first brought him to the attention of Abd al-Rahman III and his ministers in the 940s when he was barely 30 years old. He won influential friends for his rediscovery of an ancient compound, theriaca, considered by contemporaries to be effective not only against poisoning but also against jaundice, snakebites, impotence, and the plague. Before long Hasdai was invited to the royal court, presumably to serve as a physician.

Trusted physicians were often appointed to administrative posts. In this fashion, Hasdai's political star began to rise. One position led to another, from dealing with customs revenues to reorganizing cadastral registries. The gratitude of Abd al-Rahman III was in proportion to his need for ever-increasing income to meet his colossal architectural ambitions and military campaigns. Eventually, the ruler appointed Hasdai *nasi* (prince) of the Jewish community as well as finance minister of the state, and entrusted him with sensitive diplomatic negotiations. Personal service to the ruler became the hallmark of the Sephardi grandee.

The court Jew was in many respects a central paradox of pre-modern Jewry.[14] On the one hand, the courtier generally possessed wealth, indeed often conspicuous wealth, and the appearance of power. As a result of his access to ruling circles, he was commonly an honoured member of the Jewish community, often owing his position in the community to the non-Jewish authorities, and his job might include serving as the representative of the Jews on government councils. Holding positions in both the government and the Jewish community enabled him to act as a liaison between the two. Despite his influence, however, the court Jew was ultimately powerless. Subject to the mercurial whims of autocratic rulers, his fate might reverse in a moment, his sudden personal change of fortunes bringing down the entire Jewish community with him. Since court Jews were often associated with the authorities as tax collectors or inspectors, they allowed the ruler to distance himself from unpopular practices. The fall of a patron could lead to retribution against the Jews.

The association of Jews with royal power is recorded in the earliest narratives of the Jewish people. The story of Joseph in the book of Genesis reveals the complex issues raised by the service of Jews in the courts of kings. The link between the courtier's career and the well-being of the Jewish community is spelled out in this early chapter of Jewish history. The courtier Mordechai of ancient Persia is described in the book of

---

[14] On medieval court Jews, see Y. Kaplan, 'Court Jews before the Hofjuden'; Wasserstein, 'Jewish Elites in al-Andalus'.

Esther as a man 'who sat in the king's gate' (Esther 2: 21), his position and power depicted as 'second only to the King Ahasueras, great among the Jews, and popular with the multitude of his brethren' (Esther 10: 3). The jealousy of Mordechai's competitors for royal patronage eventually threatened to overwhelm the Jews of Persia; however, he managed to save the community from destruction.

Nowhere were the connections between the Jewish community, the Jewish courtier class, and the secular and ecclesiastical authorities more complex than in medieval Spain. Perhaps no historical issue, aside from that of the religious identity of the Conversos, is more contested than the question of the cultural identity of the Sephardi courtier. Widely varying assessments of the Jewish courtier's role in Sephardi life abound. Some observers have questioned the courtiers' loyalty to their community and its ancestral traditions, vilifying them for their moral laxity, and citing as proof of their estrangement from tradition their frequently flamboyant lifestyle or high level of acculturation. Others have faulted them for their close relations with heads of state, relations that sometimes redounded to the security of the Jews, but frequently brought the wrath of the masses down upon them. Medieval Sephardi rabbis and moralists warned against becoming too closely associated with the Jewish courtly class. Their excesses are enumerated in the words of the fourteenth-century scholar Menahem ben Aaron ibn Zerah:

I have seen those who walk in the court of our master the king, who shield and protect His nation according to their stature and place. However, because of the unsettled time and because of their desire for luxuries and other unnecessary items, they have declined in their observance of the commandments, particularly those who travel, their servants and those who sit before the king. They abandon prayer and blessings; they ignore the laws of permitted and prohibited food, Shabbat and holidays, laws concerning women and laws of wines, even completely abandoning those laws.[15]

In the assessment of Yitzhak Baer, the court Jews of medieval Christian Spain, educated in rationalist philosophy and prone to religious relativism (which Baer identified as Averroism), were ultimately responsible for leading the community into a moral abyss and apostasy. Ambiguous evidence suggests that some Converso courtiers in late fifteenth-century Spain became so estranged from the values and fate of their community that they were party to the crucial discussions that culminated in the Expulsion of 1492.[16] The sophisticated pleasure-seeker and ruthless, high-handed politician

---

[15] Menahem ben Aaron ibn Zerah, *Tsedah laderekh*, cited in Ray, *The Sephardic Frontier*, 170 n. 46. The institution of concubinage was widespread among Jewish courtiers as well as among Christians and especially Muslims in medieval Spain. For a discussion of sexual immorality among the Sephardi elite, see Assis, 'Sexual Behaviour in Mediaeval Hispano-Jewish Society'.

[16] For two cryptic accounts implicating Conversos in pressing the Catholic Monarchs for the Expulsion, see Marx, 'The Expulsion of the Jews from Spain'.

depicted in Baer's *History of the Jews of Christian Spain* has remained the dominant interpretation of the Jewish courtier of Christian Spain until recently.

However, the favoured position of the Jewish courtier bore much positive cultural and political fruit. Politics and culture were perhaps nowhere more closely interconnected than in medieval Muslim Spain. Hasdai served as a Maecenas of Hebraic culture, launching a poetic revolution that became synonymous with the golden age of Spain. Among his many cultural activities on behalf of the Jews, Hasdai acquired Hebrew books from North Africa and the east, supported the establishment of a yeshiva in Cordoba, and provoked and delighted in the rivalry of the Hebrew poets in his service, some of whom he recruited from North Africa. Once news of the intellectual ferment in Cordoba began to circulate, gifted scholars followed in the footsteps of Jewish artisans and merchants, who were flocking to Spain to seek their fortune. Some of them would find Hasdai a mercurial patron—a typical feature of the courtier—capable of suddenly turning against his erstwhile favourites. Hasdai brutally discarded his secretary, Menahem ibn Saruq, in favour of the newcomer, Dunash ben Labrat, who possessed more 'modern' notions of prosody, and even had his hapless former employee thrown into prison. The relationship between patron and retainer was often riddled with conflict and subject to rumours, conspiracies, and reversals.

Like their Muslim contemporaries of a similar class, Jewish courtiers sponsored soirées of poetry readings, commissioned poetic panegyrics, amassed fine libraries, endowed schools, imported teachers from abroad, and, in the later Middle Ages, also commissioned illuminated manuscripts and endowed beautiful houses of worship. Noted for their refinement and purity of language, Spanish Jewish courtiers subsidized a rarefied culture that percolated downwards and was emulated, if not always unhesitatingly embraced, by the Jewish masses. Unfortunately, although the names of many individual Jewish courtiers in Muslim Spain have been preserved, most remain simply names lacking any additional information. No information on how they were recruited and trained for leadership or got on with their Muslim counterparts has survived.

Jewish courtiers were often in a position to help their co-religionists abroad in the event of threats to their physical or fiscal well-being. During his service as court physician, economic adviser, and administrator in the service of Abd al-Rahman III and al-Hakam II, Hasdai intervened in the cases of the beleaguered Jews in Byzantium, the oppressed Jewish community in the Holy Roman Empire, and the demeaned Jewish leadership of Toulouse. In his letter to the king of the Khazars, Hasdai acknowledged the utility of his presence in the Cordoban court and stressed the correlation between Jewish well-being, divine providence, and the presence of a Jewish intercessor in the caliph's court:

We, indeed, who are the remnant of the captive Israelites, servant of my lord the king, are dwelling peacefully in the land of our sojourning, for our God has not forsaken us, nor has His shadow departed from us. When we had transgressed He brought us into judgment . . . stirred up the minds of those who had been set over the Israelites to appoint collectors of tribute over them, who aggravated the yoke of the Israelites, oppressed them cruelly, humbled them grievously and inflicted great calamities upon them. But when God saw their misery and labour and that they were helpless He led me to present myself before the king, and has graciously turned His heart to me . . . and by this covenant the poor of the flock were exalted to safety, and the hands of the oppressors themselves were relaxed, they refrained from further oppression.[17]

Although impressed by the existence of an independent kingdom of Jews in Khazaria, Hasdai's approach to the Khazar king was almost as an equal, as they were both powerful men, each mindful of his responsibilities to an exiled Jewry. The spectacle of the well-placed Jewish intercessor in the palace, ephemeral as his position may have been, provided a source of consolation to a powerless medieval Jewry, reinforcing its confidence that the 'sceptre had not passed from Judah' and that the taunts of Muslims and Christians that the Jews had been abandoned by God were without substance.

The proliferation of independent Muslim kingdoms following the fall of the caliphate of Cordoba in 1031 did not spell the end of the political role of the court Jew. On the contrary, when the caliphate disintegrated, the proliferation of *taifas* that emerged provided opportunities for many more Jews to rise to positions of power, each sponsoring his own cultural programme and gathering his own personal entourage of hangers-on and literati. In the courts of Seville, Saragosa, Badajoz, Granada, and elsewhere, the tradition of the Jewish courtier was replicated.

Iberia's Muslim rulers were not unique in their cultivation of Jewish courtiers. A small Jewish elite also wielded power in medieval Egypt and North Africa, as well as in the Iranian and central Asian provinces of the Muslim world. The rise of Jews to prominent positions in the Islamic world has often been cited as evidence of a tolerant official policy towards the Jews. Examination of the individual careers of these courtiers and the historical contexts in which they wielded political power reveals that the rise of a Jew to high office was frequently the result of the ethnic or religious isolation of the ruler from the majority of his subjects, not a symptom of special tolerance on the ruler's part. An unpopular ruler, lacking allies from his own tribal group or co-religionists, might turn to a Jewish subject to help him govern his unruly population, entrusting the Jew with the finances or affairs of state. *Raisons d'état* in such instances overrode the strictures of Islamic law. Examples abound of the meteoric rise of Jews in the courts of unpopular or isolated rulers. For instance, a certain Isaac rose in the court of Sultan Mahmud of the Ghaznavid dynasty in Iran, and Ya'qub ibn Killis emerged as vizier when the Shi'ite Fatimids seized power in Sunni Egypt. Similarly, the Karaite banker Abu Sa'd Ibrahim al-Tustari served the Fatimid court in a conspicuous economic position in eleventh-century Egypt. In Fez, Aaron (Haroun) ben Battas

---

[17] 'Hasdai ibn Shaprut's Correspondence with Joseph, King of the Khazars', in *Letters of Jews through the Ages*, i. 98–9. Once doubted by scholars, the genuineness of this correspondence is now widely accepted.

achieved the rank of vizier during the unpopular rule of the Banu Wattas in the fifteenth century. When the Banu Wattas were finally overthrown in 1465, the uprising escalated apparently spontaneously from a response to the assassination of the king and his Jewish adviser to a wholesale attack on the Jewish community and the establishment of the first Moroccan ghetto.[18] Anti-Jewish and anti-dynastic currents melded at an earlier date further east, in central Asia, in the case of Sa'd al-Dawla, chief administrator of the Mongol leader Arghun. When Arghun died in 1291, the Jewish vizier al-Dawla and leading Jewish families of the Mongol state were wiped out, and the rioting against the regime spilled over into a pogrom against the Jewish community. As one chronicler astutely remarked of Sa'd al-Dawla's violent end:

The man who yesterday was an officer and could bind and set free and was arrayed in royal apparel was today swathed in sackcloth and had dirty discolored hands as if he were a dyer and not a scribe, a beggar going round from door to door and not an officer. The trials and wrath which were stirred up against the Jews at this time neither tongue can utter nor pen write down.[19]

The powerful Jewish courtier frequently also held the position of head of the Jewish community (*rais al-yahud* in Arabic, *nasi* or *nagid* in Hebrew). It is not always clear whether he received his appointment to lead the community as a result of his relationship with the authorities or vice versa. In the case of one of the most prominent Jewish courtiers in Spain, the poet, halakhist, statesman, and warrior Samuel ibn Nagrela, his leadership of the Jewish community preceded by more than a decade his elevation from court scribe to the rank of vizier and leader of the armies of the king of Granada, which he obtained in 1027.[20] While Ibn Nagrela's military career is unique in the annals of medieval Jewish history, his elevated social status was not uncommon for a court appointee.

The Sephardi courtier was generally a multi-talented man. His educational training, especially in medicine and the sciences, proved to be the path to administrative and political advancement. Hasdai ibn Shaprut's service among the physicians at Abd al-Rahman III's court opened the door to diplomatic power. Using his medical knowledge and psychological acumen to treat the obesity of Prince Sancho of the Spanish Christian kingdom of León, Hasdai helped consolidate a treaty between the Cordoban caliphate and one of its enemies to the north. It was not uncommon to make discreet use of Jews as diplomats, since the occasional negotiations and alliances that Muslim princes formed with Christian powers could provoke the animosity of the Islamic religious establishment. During the 940s the strategic interests of the Christian emperor

---

[18] See Gerber, *Jewish Society in Fez*, 20–1.

[19] Bar Hebraeus, *The Chronography*, 476; on the fate of Jewish courtiers in Fatimid Egypt and the Mongol state, see Fischel, *Jews in the Economic and Political Life of Medieval Islam*; on the fate of al-Dawla, see Bar Hebraeus, *The Chronography*, 494.

[20] See Ashtor, *The Jews of Moslem Spain*, ii. 41–189; Weinberger, *Samuel ibn Nagrela*; on Jewish elites, see Wasserstein, 'Jewish Elites in al-Andalus'; see also Schirmann, 'Samuel Hanagid'.

of Byzantium, Constantine VII, began to coincide with those of the Cordoban caliphate. Both empires shared common enemies in the Abbasid caliphate in Baghdad and the Shi'ite Fatimid dynasty in North Africa. The Andalusian and Byzantine rulers also shared a personal interest in the arts and sciences. Coincidentally, they were equally unfettered by traditional theological inhibitions that kept Christian and Muslim kingdoms apart. In opening their diplomatic negotiations, however, they needed suitable interlocutors who could be entrusted to conduct delicate diplomatic conversations with discretion. Hasdai's proven gifts as a translator, diplomat, and adviser enabled him to perform this task.

Typically, diplomatic delegations to the caliph in Cordoba would be welcomed with great pomp, including the declamation of poetry specially composed for the occasion and the exchange of valuable gifts, such as exotic animals and plants, exquisite fabrics, and important books. One exceptional gift from the Byzantine emperor, a rare Greek manuscript from the first century by Dioscorides, posed a challenging problem for the caliph. The book in question, *De materia medica*, a classic textbook of pharmacology, was not entirely unknown in Spain since it had been translated into Arabic in Baghdad in the ninth century. But the translation had been so flawed that its remedies were virtually unusable. Since nobody knew Greek in Abd al-Rahman III's court, the eager caliph requested that his Byzantine counterpart dispatch an instructor in Greek to Cordoba. One Nicholas, a monk learned in Greek and Latin, was dispatched from Constantinople. Hasdai formed part of a multi-religious team of translators appointed to work with the Byzantine monk. Nicholas translated from Greek to Latin and Hasdai translated the Latin into Arabic. No longer would medical students in Spain be forced to travel to North Africa or Baghdad for their scientific training now that this crucial text was available locally in Arabic. Perhaps as a result of Hasdai's accomplishment, he was entrusted with several challenging diplomatic assignments involving the Christian kingdoms in the north and the German emperor Otto I (936–73).

In his capacity as diplomat, Hasdai demonstrated another role of the Jewish courtier—protector of his people. Hasdai would customarily enquire about the welfare of beleaguered Jewish communities when he went abroad on diplomatic missions for his caliph. Given his reputation and exalted position, foreign Jews would write to him seeking help, confident that they could rely upon his assistance. He interceded in cases of local persecutions, confiscation of Jewish books, and arrests of Jewish scholars in Byzantium, southern Italy, Germany, and France. His direct appeals to the Byzantine empress Helena in 948 to protest sweeping anti-Jewish measures in the empire were delivered with the approval, or at least the tacit permission, of the caliph. In a separate incident, Hasdai undertook a defence of the Jews of Toulouse who were required to donate 30 pounds of wax for church candles annually and to present this special tax at the cathedral gate at Easter time. As each Jew presented his offering, the bishop would respond with a resounding slap. It is not known whether Hasdai succeeded in having this humiliating ceremony stopped, but the very existence of 'a prince of Israel' in Islamic Spain was seen far and wide by Jews as proof of God's concern for his people. Lauded by Hebrew poets, some no doubt in his pay, Hasdai was perceived by his generation as a providential gift dispatched to protect them.

Hasdai corresponded with Joseph, king of the Khazars, a nomadic Turkic tribe who had wandered for centuries in the central Asian and Crimean region where Byzantine and Muslim borders were constantly shifting in ongoing raids and warfare. By the seventh century the Khazars controlled several cities with mixed Jewish, Muslim, Christian, and pagan populations. During the Byzantine persecutions in the eighth century, the Khazars repeatedly offered refuge to the Jews. The beleaguered King Bulan, finding himself caught between the warring armies of Byzantium and Islam and pressed by both sides to convert, chose quasi-neutrality by formally adopting Judaism in the 740s. By the ninth century Khazaria covered much of southern Russia in a vast area between the Caucasus, the Caspian Sea, the Volga, and the Dnieper.

News of this sovereign Jewish kingdom filtered back to the west through the commercial and diplomatic envoys of the Byzantine emperors, arousing messianic hopes and excitement among European Jews who smarted under the frequent taunts that their exile and impotence were proof of their rejection by God. At the very least, the existence of the Khazar state nurtured Jewish self-esteem. As Hasdai himself confessed in his correspondence with King Joseph: 'We have been cast down from our glory and have nothing to reply when they say daily unto us "Every other people has its kingdom, but of yours there is no memorial on the earth."'[21] Hasdai was moved by news of the existence of the Jewish kingdom to address his royal co-religionist with joy: 'Blessed be the Lord of Israel, who has not left us without a kinsman as defender nor suffered the tribes of Israel to be without an independent kingdom.'[22]

On a more practical level, Hasdai asked King Joseph whether he knew when the exile would end and the Jews be gathered together by the messiah and reconstituted as a nation in the Land of Israel. This query was neither casual nor unusual, especially, it seems, for a Sephardi Jew. During the Middle Ages, the Sephardim repeatedly searched for signs that might help them calculate the date of the messiah's arrival and the end of the exile. Messianic speculation engaged some of the best minds of Spain and, later, of the Sephardi diaspora. Frequently, these messianic yearnings would be channelled into poetry. Sometimes they were translated into quasi-political movements that involved armed uprisings to bring an end to Jewish statelessness and hasten redemption. It has been noted that the Sephardim produced false messiahs with some regularity.[23] Of

---

[21] 'Hasdai ibn Shaprut's Correspondence with Joseph, King of the Khazars', in *Letters of Jews through the Ages*, i. 105. [22] Ibid. 106.

[23] G. D. Cohen, 'Messianic Postures of Ashkenazim and Sephardim'. Cohen emphasizes the political activism of Sephardim as opposed to the quietism of Ashkenazim, and relates these contrasting traits to the

course, the failure of each movement would exacerbate dependency or despondency, but the messianic longings of the Sephardi masses and their leaders could not be long suppressed. Although the king of the Khazars could provide no insight about the coming of the messiah, the mere knowledge of the existence of the autonomous Jewish kingdom provided a consolation of sorts.

At home, Hasdai was bringing about an astonishing change within his own community. Until his ascendancy Andalusian Jews had typically turned to Baghdad's rabbinic scholars (*gaonim*) for instruction and guidance, much as Islamic Spain, despite political rivalry with the Abbasid dynasty, turned east for its religious and cultural leadership. The pre-eminence of the intellectual leaders of Sura and Pumbedita in Iraq as interpreters of Jewish law was a tradition that stretched back hundreds of years to the completion of the Babylonian Talmud. But, with Hasdai at its helm, the Andalusian community entered a new era of independence and cultural autonomy. First, Hasdai actively patronized scholars and founded an academy of learning in Cordoba under the direction of the immigrant scholar Moses ben Hanoch. According to a popular tradition, which circulated during the Middle Ages in Abraham ibn Daud's *Sefer ha-Qabbalah*, Moses ben Hanoch had been ransomed from pirates by Hasdai and his erudition recognized by fellow Jews in Cordoba. Most likely, the account of Moses' ascendancy represented a maturing of the Spanish community, accelerated by the philanthropic and cultural activities undertaken by Hasdai. When, for example, the talmudic academy of Sura in Baghdad was temporarily closed, Hasdai procured its library, ensuring that Andalusian Jews would become less dependent on the east for religious guidance. No longer did they have to ask the Jewish authorities in Baghdad to resolve halakhic issues, waiting months for a reply. In establishing Spain's cultural autonomy, Hasdai drew heavily upon the model of Babylonia, just as his sovereigns Abd al-Rahman III and al-Hakam II drew upon Abbasid models to assert their independence. Still, although some parallels with the Muslims may have been intended, Sephardi assumption of its own cultural path was not merely a reflection of Muslim attitudes to power or culture but a result of internal Jewish developments. For example, Hasdai's authority within the Jewish community of Cordoba was similar to the secular powers of the *rosh hagolah* (exilarch) in the Abbasid capital. In similar fashion, Sephardi religious authority was entrusted to their *rosh yeshivah*, Moses ben Hanoch, a position somewhat akin to that of the Babylonian *gaon*.

Hasdai's role as courtier and rabbi, unlike any prior leadership role exercised by a Jew in Spain, became the subject of community pride and the prototype of Sephardi leadership for subsequent generations. Like other men of his class, whether Muslim, Christian, or Jewish, Hasdai surrounded himself with cultivated and talented people. Support of such talent was considered a mark of quality as well as of power. Soirées in

---

stance of the two Jewries to martyrdom. This dichotomy is challenged by Elisheva Carlebach in *Between Ashkenaz and Sepharad*. See also Chapter 3 below.

the courtier's presence were scintillating affairs. Fathers exhorted their sons, as no doubt Hasdai's father had done to him, to associate with the learned, to tend the poor without a fee, to seek the company of poets, and to write with elegance and erudition. Propagation of rabbinic culture, specifically of talmudic learning, a model initiated by Hasdai, reached its zenith in the career of Samuel ibn Nagrela. Abraham ibn Daud described the geographical extent of his influence:

And he performed [acts of munificence] for Israel in Sefarad and in the Land of the Maghreb and in Ifriqiya and in the land of Egypt, and in Sicily and as far as the Babylonian academies and as far as the Holy City. All Torah scholars in these lands benefited from his wealth. And he acquired many books of sacred writings.[24]

The culture of Muslim and Jewish Cordoba fostered an appreciation of books. Arab historians of Cordoba never fail to mention the numerous expansions of the great mosque of Cordoba paralleled by the equally impressive expansions of the caliphal library. Al-Hakam's library of 400,000 volumes was only one of many in the city, according to Ibn Said:

Córdoba held more books than any other city in al-Andalus, and its inhabitants were the most enthusiastic in caring for their libraries; such collections were regarded as symbols of status and social leadership. Men who had no knowledge whatsoever would make it their business to have a library in their homes; they would be selective in their acquisitions so that they might boast of possessing unica, or copies in the handwriting of a particular calligrapher.[25]

For the Jews as well, possession of books was a sign of proper breeding. The admonitions of Judah ibn Tibbon (1120–c.1190) to his son Samuel in his famous ethical will encapsulate the ethos among learned and affluent Sephardim. In advising his son to follow in the footsteps of his forefathers, the elder Ibn Tibbon enjoins Samuel to respect the books in his possession:

I have assisted thee by providing an extensive library for thy use and have thus relieved thee of the necessity of borrowing books. Most students must wander about to seek books, often without finding them. But thou, thanks to God, lendest and borrowest not. Of many books, thou ownest two or three copies. I have besides procured for thee books on all the sciences. . . . Examine thy Hebrew books at every new moon, the Arabic volumes once in two months, and the bound codices once every quarter. . . . Never refuse to lend books to anyone who has not means to purchase books for himself, but only act thus to those who can be trusted to return the volumes. . . . Cover the bookcases with rugs of fine quality; and preserve them from damp and mice, and from all matter of injury, for thy books are thy good treasure. If thou lendest a volume make a note of it before it leaves thy house, and when it is returned, draw thy pen over the entry. Every Passover and Tabernacles call in all books out on loan.[26]

---

[24] Ibn Daud, *Sefer ha-Qabbalah*, 74.
[25] Ibn Said al-Maghribi, *The Adornments of the West*, cited in Hillenbrand, '"The Ornament of the World"', 120.   [26] 'Judah ibn Tibbon's Letter of Admonition to his Son', in *Letters of Jews through the Ages*, i. 156–65.

Among the most prominent roles of the courtier was that of patron to poets and musicians. Hasdai was the first in a line of courtiers to actively sponsor Hebrew poets. His extensive correspondence was facilitated by the use of secretaries, Menahem ibn Saruq and Dunash ben Labrat, both known for their epistolary and poetic skills. The literary rivalry between these two men apparently delighted Hasdai. Ibn Saruq compiled a dictionary of biblical Hebrew and drafted his ornate correspondence for Hasdai in the Hebrew language. He was a staunch defender of traditional theories of the nature of Hebrew, who made no reference to contemporary, scientific Arabic philological studies. His rival, Dunash ben Labrat from Fez, had studied with Sa'adyah Gaon in Baghdad and was influenced by contemporary innovations in Arabic linguistics and inspired by his teacher to apply these to Hebrew philology. Sa'adyah Gaon was the outstanding Bible translator, exegete, philosophical commentator, and Hebrew philologist and grammarian of his time. His translation of the Bible into Arabic and his rhyming dictionary, the *Agron*, proved useful philosophical and lexicographical tools for Jewish poets in their debates with Muslims over whether Arabic or Hebrew was the language of God, and whether the Quran or the Hebrew Bible contained the actual words of God.

Dunash's arrival in Spain in the 940s was symptomatic of the wider phenomenon of the migration of fresh talent, particularly to Cordoba, armed with the latest philological theories acquired in Baghdad or Kairouan. Dunash quickly assumed a vocal role in the debates between Hebrew and Arabic poets, insisting on a comparative approach to philology and poetry. Dunash's defence of what appeared to be arcane issues, of interest only to scholars and grammarians, concerning the construction of the Hebrew language constituted a defining moment in medieval Jewish cultural history. From these technical linguistic debates Jews drew conclusions about the triliteral structure of Hebrew words. These insights allowed Sephardi intellectuals of the tenth century to engage with the biblical text in novel ways and to use Hebrew for revolutionary poetic ends.[27]

Unfortunately, there is very little surviving information on the role that Jewish women played in the literary revolution in Andalusia. Medieval Jewish women, in general, were minor participants in the written culture. Moreover, the poetic salons conducted in Spain and elsewhere in the Muslim world seem to have been male affairs, replete with young men serving wine at all hours of the night to slightly inebriated poets.[28] However, an astonishing discovery in the Cairo *geniza* by Ezra Fleischer has identified a single poem by Kasmuna, the otherwise unknown wife of Dunash ben

---

[27] Saenz-Badillos, 'Hebrew Philology in Sefarad'; Brann, 'The Arabized Jews'; Drory, *The First Contacts between Jewish and Arabic Literature* (Heb.); ead., 'Literary Contacts and Where to Find Them'; see also Schirmann, 'The Function of the Hebrew Poet'.

[28] The wine party and poetic performance are noted repeatedly by Scheindlin: see *Wine, Women and Death*, 11, 19, 21, 24, 30, 32.

Labrat. It is not clear whether her literary prowess was part of a broader phenomenon of Jewish female literacy or whether, as the wife and daughter of poets, she was an exceptional figure. Writing in lyrical Hebrew she addressed her husband upon his departure on a journey, perhaps in connection with either a private mission or in flight from his mercurial patron. It is the first personal poem in the post-biblical Hebrew canon and one of the few Hebrew poems written by a woman that has been preserved:

> Will her love remember his graceful doe,
> Her only son in her arms as he parted?
> On her left hand he placed a ring from his right,
> On his wrist she placed her bracelet.
>
> As a keepsake she took his mantle from him,
> And he in turn took hers from her.
> He won't settle in the land of Spain,
> Though its prince give him half his kingdom.[29]

Arabization, *'Arabiyya*, and *Shu'ubiyya*

The Arabization of the Jews began soon after the Arabs swept through the Mediterranean world. During the ninth and early tenth centuries Jews in the eastern caliphate and North Africa became almost entirely arabophone, speaking Jewish dialects of the Arabic that became the lingua franca of the Mediterranean Muslim world, while continuing to speak the local languages such as Amarzigh (Berber). Another feature of the Arabization of the Jews was its self-perception of possessing noble pedigree and illustrious lineage. How, precisely, this process occurred requires closer scrutiny of Muslim–Jewish dynamics within the multi-ethnic society of Cordoba.

Sephardi assertions of noble ancestry first made their appearance in Muslim Spain during the ninth century, as the process of Jewish acculturation and Arabization was nearing completion. The Jews of Muslim Spain and the Near East, like other non-Muslims living as minorities in the Islamic world, were especially sensitive to the specific challenge posed by aggressive Arab claims of their noble tribal ancestry and cultural superiority. These claims were buttressed by genealogy, a favourite Arab science. In the complex ethnic mosaic of medieval Andalusia, ethnic identity and ethnic politics lay at the heart of the social structure. At the same time as Spain was undergoing the process of Islamization and Arabization, a great debate raged in the heartland of Islam, known today as the *'arabiyya–shu'ubiyya* controversy, over Arab claims to racial and linguistic superiority. Although all Muslims were theoretically equal, the proponents of *'arabiyya* insisted on the superiority of the Arabic language, of the Arab lands, of the Arab race, and, above all, of descent from the tribe of Muhammad in

---

[29] Kasmuna, 'Will her love remember his graceful doe', cited in Cole, 'Solomon ibn Gabirol', 7; see Fleischer, 'On Dunash ben Labrat, His Wife, and His Son' (Heb.).

Arabia. At the time of this culture war, diverse groups in the Iberian peninsula were converting to Islam and entering the Arab cultural orbit. Special attention was paid to national origins and to pedigrees in the struggle to attain status and privilege. Real and imagined genealogies began to circulate, forming the basis for new social stratifications.

Within the hierarchy of people, religions, and ethnicities in medieval Spain, Arabs were on top, Berbers lower down, and Christians still lower, with Jews somewhere near the bottom (only slightly superior to slaves and eunuchs: the *sakaliba*).[30] An entire cottage industry emerged creating pseudo-genealogies to prove people's 'Arabness' and to conceal Berber origins. These genealogies formed the basis for privileges such as tax exemptions, landholding prerogatives, and access to government positions. So important was Arab tribal ancestry that some of the last rulers in the caliphate of Cordoba even resorted to dyeing their hair and beard in order to fit more neatly the Arab racial stereotype (this was especially difficult since most of the caliphs' mothers were Christian slaves or concubines, and they were thus generally quite fair in complexion and blue-eyed).[31]

Persians and other non-Arabs, the exponents of *shu'ubiyya* in the Abbassid eastern caliphate, responded that while Arabic, the language of the Quran, was undoubtedly superior, the Arabs were not the greatest of peoples. Indeed, they argued, Persians and other non-Arabs surpassed them in science and the humanities.[32] *Shu'ubiyya* propaganda circulated widely in Muslim lands and found a receptive audience among non-Arab Muslims in Spain. The controversy soon spread to Andalusian poetic circles, where classical Arab forms of poetic expression were in the process of being discarded in favour of shorter and simpler poems extolling love, wine, and other secular pleasures. Just as the Persians in the east began to stress the antiquity and superiority of Persian language and history, parallel movements arose in Spain among Christians, Berbers, and Jews. The Christians of Spain revelled in their indigenous, pre-Islamic Visigothic or Roman ancestors; the Jews in their biblical roots.

Although few Jews in Spain converted to Islam, they were not impervious to Arab claims of ethnic and cultural superiority and, in response, sought their own noble ancestry, claiming descent from ancient Judaean priests or royalty. They insisted that their noble ancestry rendered them the most accomplished and socially superior

---

[30] On *'arabiyya* and Jewish reactions to claims of Arab superiority, see Allony, 'The Reaction of Moses ibn Ezra to *'Arabiyya*'; id., 'The Kuzari of R. Judah Halevi in the Light of the *Shu'ubiyya*' (Heb.); on *'arabiyya* in Islamic Iberia, see Larsson, *Ibn Garcia's Shu'ubiyya Letter*; on conversion to Islam and Arabization in Iberia, see Bulliet, *Conversion to Islam in the Medieval Period*. The most important extant source for the debate is Ibn Garcia, *Risala*.   [31] Fierro, *Abd al-Rahman III*, 29.

[32] On the *shu'ubiyya*, see Goldziher, *Muslim Studies*, i. 137–63; Gibb, *Studies on the Civilization of Islam*, 62–73; on *shu'ubiyya* among the Berbers, see M. Shatzmiller, *The Berbers and the Islamic State*, 24. See also Larsson, *Ibn Garcia's Shu'ubiyya Letter*; Ibn Garcia, *Risala*. For an expanded and alternative approach to the question of Jewish genealogical claims of nobility of lineage, see Gerber, 'Pride and Pedigree'.

community of Jews in the diaspora. In keeping with a popular Arab literary genre that praised particular cities and the personality traits of their residents, the Jews of Spain began to link themselves to particular cities in Andalusia, ascribing specific qualities to their inhabitants. Merida, for the Andalusian Jews, was the home of the elite of the Jewish exiles, those of the house of King David; Lucena was a city of poetry and Jewish aristocracy; Cordoba combined social elitism and poetry.

The Sephardi writer and theoretician of Hebrew poetry Moses ibn Ezra (c.1055–c.1138) boasted of his personal descent from ancient Judaean royalty. Samuel ibn Nagrela proclaimed his descent from the ancient Levites, calling himself the King David of his day in his verse; the thirteenth-century biblical commentator David Kimhi (born in Granada although he lived much of his life in Provence) expanded upon the genealogical basis of Sephardi superiority, repeating the tradition that Spanish Jews were descended from ancient Jerusalem nobility while the Jews living in Ashkenaz were descended from less distinguished Jews.[33] However unscientific these claims may have been, they added a measure of prestige to the Jews in the eyes of Muslims and Christians. The phenomenal rise of Jews to positions of influence in the Andalusian kingdoms seemed to confirm Jewish claims of royal lineage. According to Norman Roth, Sephardi assertions of superiority among the Jewish people represented 'a kind of Jewish *shu'ubiyya*', a reaction to claims of supremacy by the Jews of Babylonia, parallel to and imitative of the Muslim responses to Arab claims of hegemony.[34] He has also suggested that Sephardi boasts of noble lineage may have been inspired by Berber assertions of descent from important Arabian tribes in their ongoing rivalry with the Andalusian Arabs.[35]

Arab assertions of superiority were not confined to their ancestry. Alongside lineage, they placed a premium on the mastery of Arabic language and literature. Jews could compete in this arena without compromising their religious scruples. Mastery of Arabic, moreover, was an automatic path to advancement in political circles. The Jews of medieval Muslim Spain were exposed to Arabic language, Arabic poetry, and a full curriculum of Arabic humanities. Samuel ibn Nagrela sent Arabic poems from the battlefield to his sons to perfect their poetry; the ethical wills of dutiful fathers would remind their sons of the importance of mastering Arabic poetry and calligraphy. So immersed were the Jews in Arabic culture that they were inevitably drawn into its controversies, hoping to show the excellence of Hebrew and to underscore the fact that the Jews, too, possessed a language with divine credentials, every bit as supple and subtle as the language of the Arabs. Following in the footsteps of the *shu'ubiyya*, the Jews began to explore Hebrew philology and grammar, to extol the virtues of the

---

[33] On Ibn Nagrela's identification with biblical characters, see Brann, *The Compunctious Poet*, 53–5; see also Ray, 'Images of the Jewish Community in Medieval Iberia'.

[34] N. Roth, 'Jewish Reactions to the *'Arabiyya* and the Renaissance of Hebrew in Spain', 72; Allony, 'The Reaction of Moses ibn Ezra to *'Arabiyya*'.   [35] N. Roth, *Jews, Visigoths and Muslims in Medieval Spain*, 164–5.

language, and to seek to demonstrate its inimitable qualities. They even claimed that the Arabic culture that was so developed and advanced in their day was actually the descendant of an earlier Hebrew high culture, lost as a result of the exile of the Jews from the Land of Israel. Moses ibn Ezra ascribed the excellence of Spanish Hebrew poetry to the origins of the Sephardim in the royal house of King David.[36] The influence on the Hebrew poetic revolution of the Arabs' attitude towards their language cannot be overestimated. To the followers of Muhammad, the exceptional language of the Quran was proof of divine favour. Their case for cultural superiority rested on the claims they put forth for their language:

Whoever loves the Prophet loves the Arabs, and whoever loves the Arabs loves the Arabic language in which the best book was revealed. . . . Whoever God has guided to Islam . . . believes that Muhammad is the best of prophets . . . that the Arabs are the best of peoples . . . and that the Arabic language is the best of languages.[37]

Far from exploring Hebrew as an intellectual exercise, Sephardi poets seem to have responded to the Arab claims to linguistic superiority in a quasi-nationalist fashion. Other motivations were also at play in the great culture wars of medieval Muslim Spain, some of them internal to each community. The study of Hebrew could serve as an effective weapon in answering the challenges of the Jewish sectarian Karaites, who had spread from North Africa to Iberia by the tenth century and were a formidable intellectual force. Regardless of motivation, the end result of this competitive atmosphere was the emergence of the sensitivity to Hebrew language and poetry that characterizes Sephardi civilization.

The Spanish Golden Era and the Hebrew Poetic Revolution

The Jewish civilization that was born in Cordoba was at its most expressive and original in the Hebrew poetry that began to take shape during the decades when the caliphate was at its most radiant. Jews with aspirations to advancement in Arab society consciously set about mastering the Arab curriculum of grammar, poetics, and science through disciplined study. One generation of Jews learned Arabic rhetoric, and their sons, to a remarkable extent, made the language their own. The Jewish consumers of the new Arabic culture emerging in the east and the west included not only scholars and linguists but also an international class of merchants and craftsmen. Poetry was an important leisure activity in all the imperial and commercial centres of the Muslim world before it was practised by Jews, and Jews did not consider the emulation of

---

[36] In the fifth chapter of *Sefer ha'iyunim vehadiyunim*, Moses ibn Ezra develops his theory of the noble genealogy of Sephardi Jews and their special qualities. See also Allony, 'The Reaction of Moses ibn Ezra to 'Arabiyya', 20; Scheindlin, 'Moses ibn Ezra'; id., 'Rabbi Moses ibn Ezra on the Legitimacy of Poetry'.

[37] Abu Mansur al-Thal'alibi, *Fiqh al-Lughra*, cited in Lewis, *The Middle East and the West*, 86.

Arabic culture as particularly radical. They shared many affinities with Muslims, including a common preference for language over image in religious expression. Law was at the heart of both civilizations, and the study of law occupied the best minds of both religious establishments. Moreover, mastery of the huge linguistic reservoir existing in the works of the poets of the pre-Islamic era known as the *jahiliyya* could be comfortably pursued by Jews, since it was grounded in a pagan desert milieu and was unrelated to the religion of Islam. As new economic opportunities unfolded with the general expansion of commerce and personal wealth under Islam, Jews became caught up in the intellectual stimulation and excitement. They were not simply speaking Arabic, but were actually putting its idioms to use in the elaboration of Jewish culture. Knowledge of correct literary Arabic was highly valued, and much Jewish religious and secular literature was produced in Arabic, not Hebrew. Access to the more advanced Arabic scientific and philosophical vocabulary enabled Jews to explore new areas of knowledge that had previously been closed to them. Thus Muslim Spain became the site of exciting Jewish interaction with the aesthetic, rhetorical, and philosophical values of the surrounding Islamic society.

Perhaps the most memorable cultural developments to occur among the Jews in Muslim Spain were in the areas of poetry and Hebrew language. As Hebrew poets began to experiment with Arabic poetics, they produced new forms of Hebrew poetry that lay somewhere between classical Hebrew and Arabic metre. The new poetry was connected with the courtier class of Jews and Muslims, initially in the palace of Madinat al-Zahra and subsequently in the courts of the *taifas*, but it was eagerly shared by all classes of Jewish society. Hebrew verse became ubiquitous in Jewish society: in diplomatic and personal correspondence, in letters of recommendation, in funeral eulogies, or chiselled on the walls of buildings in fine calligraphy as a decorative architectural detail. A poem would be dispatched as an invitation on perfumed stationery; the recipient might read it aloud to the accompaniment of music. The secretaries of courtiers and statesmen were expected not only to write official correspondence in ornate script but also to dash off poems to mark victories on the battlefield, the birth of a prince, or the downfall of a rival. Most patrons of Hebrew poets were themselves learned Hebrew and Arabic versifiers and boon companions to Arab or Berber princes. Facility in poetry was recognized as a means to maintain a position in Muslim courts and Jewish salons. Fame in one context could lead to patronage or popularity in the other, since the two circles were closely connected.

Prior to the revolution in Hebrew poetics in Spain in the tenth century, Hebrew poetry, or at least the portion that has survived, was modelled on the literary conventions of the Bible. It followed accepted conventions and was generally earmarked for a specific place in the liturgy. It lacked rhyme or metre, relying instead upon repetition, or parallelism between stanzas, to underline its message. Perhaps because the prayer book had been standardized by the tenth century under the aegis of the *gaonim* in Baghdad, Jewish poetic talents sought new outlets outside the traditional milieu. Experiments with new poetic content and form began using the pre-Islamic forms, such as the *muwashshah*, a strophic verse consisting of five or six stanzas in classical Arabic and a final couplet in either Judaeo-Arabic or the vernacular language, and the *zajal*, a poem in the Arabic dialect of Andalusia, often with some words of the vernacular.[38]

These poetic forms were undoubtedly startling to their audience, since they were associated with popular street tunes about love and drinking wine. But Arabic motifs and literary conventions were refashioned by the Hebrew poets and interlaced with shared philosophical and scientific concepts and quotations from the Bible. New forms of expression opened the door to new poetic content, a process that was facilitated by the kinship between Arabic and Hebrew. Linguistic precocity and literary gymnastics excited the imagination of Jews well beyond the small elite of ambitious politicians, giving rise to heated debates on the finer points of philology at social gatherings.[39] Before long, the new style of poetry also entered the synagogues, enhancing the old liturgy with novel expressions of worship that have since become part of the patrimony and liturgy of all Jews.[40]

The multilingualism of the Jews of Spain has often been noted. Hebrew poets used Romance languages as well as Hebrew and Arabic, sometimes even within a single poem. Judah Halevi, for example, wrote Hebrew love poems in the *muwashshah* form with final stanzas in the vernacular, thus preserving some of the earliest examples of the medieval language from which Spanish, Catalan, and Portuguese emerged. In other instances, a Sephardi poet might translate a vernacular love poem into Hebrew. Even Aramaic was recruited for poetic purposes: Ibn Nagrela wrote poetry in this ancient language, which had been formally confined to Jewish legal literature for centuries. These activities took place in an atmosphere of curiosity about language in general, with Jewish courtiers, like Hasdai ibn Shaprut, sponsoring the study of comparative linguistics. Knowledge of the grammatical foundations of Hebrew enabled poets to coin new words not found in the Bible. This was essential since, unlike Arabic, Hebrew had not been spoken for over a thousand years and, consequently, had a somewhat limited vocabulary. Like Arabic, however, it is a language in which minute changes in vocalization can produce major changes in meaning. As the Hebrew poets learned more about their linguistic tradition, the influence of the Bible became pervasive. Ibn Nagrela, for instance, composed a poem to his son describing the siege of Lorca whose thirty-one lines contain seventeen biblical allusions. The success of this poetry was only

---

[38] Monroe, 'Zajal and Muwashshah'.

[39] For the ambience of the Jewish salon where verbal pyrotechnics were the order of the day, see G. D. Cohen, introduction to Ibn Daud, *Sefer ha-Qabbalah*.

[40] For an analysis of the application of the new style and content to Jewish liturgical poetry, see Scheindlin's annotations in *The Gazelle*; see also Scheindlin, introduction to Ibn Gabirol, *Vulture in a Cage*.

possible with an audience capable of appreciating such metaphor and allusion. The display of cleverness and wit on the part of the poet was predicated upon the existence of just such a class of Hebrew literati. The combination of a new secular Hebrew poetry with an Andalusian Jewish aristocracy was one of the hallmarks of the Sephardi tradition emerging from the rich cultural melange of Cordoba, Granada, and other Muslim cities in Andalusia.

The new Hebrew poetry was revolutionary in content as well as in form. Its themes reflected the contemporary lifestyle of the Jewish poets and their Arab neighbours. Notwithstanding Islamic injunctions against the consumption of alcohol, the wine feast in a scented garden was a favourite topic for poetic improvisation. It also became a theme in Hebrew. A poem might take flight using any seemingly inconsequential detail of the feast: a joyous description of the rich bouquet and bubbles of a good wine or the magical setting in which the wine was imbibed. The sparkle of the crystal goblet, a cultural and technological innovation of the tenth century, not just its intoxicating contents, was also the subject of the playful new poetry.

Sephardim picked up the frivolous theme of the wine feast with verve, embellishing it with rich biblical allusions and transforming the drinking party and the properties of wine into subject matter for the creation of some quite remarkable verse. The wine theme initially appeared in a poem by Dunash ben Labrat:

> He said: 'Do not sleep.
> Drink vintage wine,
> While henna and lily,
> Myrrh and aloes,
>
> Pomegranates and dates,
> Tamarisks and grapes,
> And pleasant anemones
> Fill the garden rows.
>
> The singers are accompanied
> by cithern and viol,
> The ripple of fountains,
> The murmur of the lute,
>
> All the little birds
> Sing among the leaves,
> In the tall trees,
> Whose boughs are thick with fruit.
>
> The doves are moaning
> As if thinking of music
> And the pigeons answer
> With flute-like tones.

> We shall drink in the gardens
> Surrounded by lilies,
> And with sons of praise
> Ease our weary bones.
>
> We shall eat sweetmeats
> And drink from bowls,
> Pretend we are giants
> And drink from the vats.
>
> I shall go out to the herd
> And kill some fine beasts,
> Both calves and rams,
> All choice and fat,
>
> We shall pour out fine oil,
> Burn woody spices.
> Let us finish our feast
> Before life's last hour!'[41]

Moses ibn Ezra, a master of liturgical poetry and penitential hymns (seliḥot), also left some artful verse containing the wine motif. Thus for example, his poem 'The Coming of Spring' is much more than a simple ode to drink:

> Wintertime has fled like a shadow;
> Its storms and gales have already ceased.
> And the sun, with its own circumscribed law,
> Is full in the Ram, like a king at his feast.
> The hills have put on their turbans of flowers,
> And the plains their garments of herb and grass.
> Let the earth release her scent for our nostrils,
> Pent up in her folds till winter could pass.
> Give me the cup to enthrone my joy,
> And to relieve my heart of its pain.
> And temper its heat only with tears,
> For its angry fire's a-flame.
> Beware of Fate; for all her gifts
> Are the drops of honey in vipers' tongues.
> Deceive your soul with her bounty at morning,
> And await her treachery when the night comes.
> Drink all day long, till the light turns,
> And the sun stamps the silver with its golden seal;
> And all through the night, till she flies like a negress,
> And the hand of the dawn takes hold of her heel.[42]

---

[41] Dunash ben Labrat, 'Reply to an Invitation to a Feast', in *Hebrew Poems from Spain*, 15–16. Reproduced by permission of the Littman Library of Jewish Civilization.

[42] Moses ibn Ezra, 'The Coming of Spring', in *Hebrew Poems from Spain*, 78. Reproduced by permission of the Littman Library of Jewish Civilization.

Every Hebrew poet in Muslim Spain tried his hand at wine poems, some writing entire collections. The poems would often include an opening invitation to the wine party—'O friends, drink with me'—followed by an evocation of the setting of the party —'Turn with me to sit in the perfumed garden'—and ending with the poet ruminating in a quasi-serious manner on the fleeting nature of life and friendship. The site of the poetic gathering in a perfumed garden and the soft sounds of its bubbling fountain and accompanying music were often described. The garden was a favourite of both Hebrew and Arabic poets and was especially rich in associations: of changing seasons and the passage of time, of performance, of stolen moments of romance, a reminder of now-desolate palatial gardens, of the blessings of water whose origins recall a desert civilization. The juxtaposition of levity and solemnity would become an identifiable trait of the poems of many Sephardi intellectuals.

Following the break-up of the Umayyad caliphate at the beginning of the eleventh century, Samuel ibn Nagrela took his knowledge of Arabic etiquette and culture to Granada, where he rose to the position of vizier in the Zirid Berber kingdom. He combined administrative talents with formidable skills in Jewish law and Hebrew poetry. In a probably apocryphal story, his talents as calligrapher first brought him to the attention of the Berber princes. According to his protégé Solomon ibn Gabirol (c.1020–c.1057), Ibn Nagrela's home possessed gardens paved with marble and alabaster, flanked by palms and myrtles, and complemented by a spectacular fountain of lions that spewed water into channels or canals. On the basis of this poetic description of Ibn Nagrela's garden, the statuary in the villa has been linked to the famous statuary of the Court of the Lions at the Alhambra palace:

> And there is a full sea, like unto Solomon's Sea,
> Though not on oxen it stands,
> But there are lions, in phalanx by its rims,
> As though roaring for prey—these whelps
> Whose bellies are wellsprings that spout forth
> Through their mouths floods like streams.
> And there are hinds embedded in the channels,
> Hollowed out as water spouts
> To douse the plants in the beds,
> And upon the lawns to shed clear waters
> Wherewith to freshen the myrtle garden
> They are like clouds sprinkling the treetops.[43]

---

[43] Solomon ibn Gabirol, 'Go forth my friend and friend of the heavenly stars', cited in Bargebuhr, 'The Alhambra Palace of the Eleventh Century', 199; see also Ruggles, *Gardens, Landscape, and Vision in the Palaces of Islamic Spain*, 164. The lions in Ibn Gabirol's poem do not actually support a basin as they do in the Alhambra courtyard.

The image of a lion had several meanings for Hebrew poets: it could evoke the concept of royal privilege or the pastime of the hunt. The lion was traditionally associated with the ancient tribe of Judah and the independent kingdom of Judaea. A literate audience of Jews listening to such poetry would not fail to recognize the biblical allusions.

Even the erudite Samuel ibn Nagrela himself tried his hand at composing wine poems. In some instances the poetry was quite serious in tone, while in others, such as this, the tenor is playful and mocking:

> Friend, lead me through the vineyards, give me wine
> And to the very brim shall joy be mine;
> Perchance the love you pledge me with each cup.
> May rout the troops around my care's ensign.
>
> And if in love for me, eight toasts you drink
> Fourscore the toasts in love for you I link;
> And should I predecease you, friend, select
> Some spot where vineyards twist, my grave to sink.
>
> In grape-juice have my body laved, and take
> With divers spices, grape-pips—These shall make
> All my embalming. Mourn me not, guitar
> And pipe with music's sound shall cheer my wake.
>
> And on the place that shall conceal my mold
> Let not the earth be heaped and rocks be rolled
> To raise a monument: to mark the spot
> Rather a pile of wine-jars, new and old.[44]

In another poem, Ibn Nagrela celebrates a night of drinking as a source of literary inspiration:

> My friend, tell me,
> When shall I pour you my wine?
> The cry of the cock woke me,
> And sleep deserted my eyes.
> Come out and see the morning light
> Like a scarlet thread in the East.
> Make haste, give me a cup,
> Before the dawn starts to rise,
> Of spiced pomegranate juice,
> From the perfumed hand of a girl,
> Who will sing songs. My soul
> Revives and then dies.[45]

---

[44] Samuel ibn Nagrela, 'Friend, Lead Me through the Vineyards', cited in Loewe, *Ibn Gabirol*, 61–2.

[45] Samuel ibn Nagrela, 'An Invitation', in *Hebrew Poems from Spain*, 34. Reproduced by permission of the Littman Library of Jewish Civilization.

Still more frivolous is the following, on drinking wine:

> If you're like me, and want to pour the wine of joy,
> Hear what I have to say.
> I'll teach you pleasure's way, though you don't want to hear,
> You friends of sighs and pain.
> Five things there are that fill the hearts of men with joy,
> And put my grief to flight:
> A pretty girl, a garden, wine, the water's rush
> In a canal, and song.[46]

Or the following, in praise of wine:

> Red in appearance, sweet to the taste,
> Vintage of Spain, yet renowned in the East
> Feeble in the cup, but, once in the brain,
> It rules over heads that cannot rise again.
>
> The mourner, whose blood is mixed with his tears—
> The blood of the grape demolishes his fears.
> Friends, passing the cup from hand to hand,
> Seem to be gambling for a precious diamond.[47]

The following wine poem by Moses ibn Ezra undoubtedly enchanted a learned audience with its clever use of biblical allusions and metaphors:

> Come down to the garden that has donned blue
> And purple and wrapped itself in fine cotton and white
> And a river whose streams are pure
> And never yet fouled by foot or blight
> And the sun of the vine, like fire, blazes and razes
> But is caught up by the goblet, and held there tight
> And the foam on its surface is like drops
> of crystal, or like manna, flaky and light.[48]

The poetry of the Andalusian Jews is steeped in the surrounding Arab culture, but it also demonstrates great ingenuity in its employment of biblical language and imagery. Biblical verses might be quoted, or concealed in arcane allusions and indirect references. An educated Jew participating in the wine-feast would have recognized that the imagery of the 'blue and purple' 'white and fine cotton' was derived from the description of the royal banquet in the book of Esther (1: 6). The foam bubbling on

---

[46] Samuel ibn Nagrela, 'If you're like me, and want to pour the wine of joy', in Scheindlin (ed.), *Wine, Women and Death*, 51. Reproduced by permission of the University of Nebraska Press. Copyright © 1986 by the Jewish Publication Society.

[47] Samuel ibn Nagrela, 'In Praise of Wine', in *Hebrew Poems from Spain*, 33. Reproduced by permission of the Littman Library of Jewish Civilization.

[48] Moses ibn Ezra, 'Derekh el hagan', cited in Bremer, *Judah Halevi and His Circle of Hebrew Poets*, 75.

the rim of the crystal goblet is explicitly flaky and light, but also implicitly cold and white 'like hoarfrost on the ground' (Exod. 16: 14).

The social setting in which it was delivered was an integral part of the poem. It would most likely have been recited or improvised after a leisurely meal to the accompaniment of a lute, while charming young men served goblets of wine. Professional dancers might also enliven the soirée. The resultant mixture of alcohol, perfume, music, dozing, and verse sometimes glistens through the stanzas of the poem. Scintillating conversation on such occasions might focus on politics, literature, or simply the latest gossip in the court, synagogue, or marketplace. Homoerotic themes also formed part of the poetic repertory. At the same time, a tension ran through the poetry and the psyche of some of the poets. Hebrew poets in Spain approached life with a mixture of *joie de vivre* and melancholy: their laughter and playfulness were often tempered by a realization that life was ephemeral and their exilic existence interminable. This realization sometimes broke through during moments of merriment. In the midst of their carousing, the ruins of Jerusalem would be recalled and the humiliation of exile invoked. Thus, in 'Reply to an Invitation to a Feast' quoted above, Dunash ben Labrat revelled in the poet's lush garden, allusions to the Temple service interwoven deftly into his verse, only to conclude with a volte-face of lamentation and melancholy:

> I rebuked him: 'Silence!
> How can you talk so,
> When the Temple, God's footstool,
> Is in the enemy's power?
>
> Your words are foolish.
> You prefer to be idle.
> Your thoughts are worthless.
> You scorn the divine.
>
> You no longer think
> On the law of God,
> You can be happy,
> And there are foxes in Zion.
>
> How can we drink wine?
> How raise our eyes?
> When we are as nothing,
> A race all despise!'[49]

Were Dunash's closing verses genuine, was he merely paying lip-service to piety to please more traditional readers, or was he simply displaying his erudition? It is impossible to know for sure.

Other motifs, such as the spectacle of ruins of abandoned sites of past rendezvous,

---

[49] Dunash ben Labrat, 'Reply to an Invitation to a Feast', in *Hebrew Poems from Spain*, 16. Reproduced by permission of the Littman Library of Jewish Civilization.

seem to be derivative of Arab conventions. The theme of 'paradise lost' reverberated through Arabic poetry in the west, especially after the collapse of the Umayyad caliphate and the destruction of Madinat al-Zahra, and Jews also took up the theme. Thus, the garden and Andalusia are nostalgically recalled by the Arab poet Abu Ishaq ibn Khafaja (d. 1139):

> A garden in al-Andalus has
> Unveiled beauty and a lush scent
>
> The morning glistens from its teeth
> And the night is overshadowed by its scarlet lips.
>
> When the wind blows from the East
> I cry: O how I long for al-Andalus.[50]

The Arabic garden, the site of inspiration and generator of these poems, bore few similarities to other European gardens and is hence largely unfamiliar to Western readers. The French orientalist and convert to Islam, Louis Massignon, has tellingly distinguished the cultural differences between Muslim and Western gardens, and his insights are also applicable to their poetics:

> In our classical garden, which began with the Roman Empire and continued with the Medicis and Louis XIV, the intent is to control the world from a central point of view, with long perspective lines leading to the horizon and great water basins reflecting the distances, all framed by relentlessly pruned trees, leading the eye, little by little, to a sense of conquest of the surrounding land.
>
> By contrast, the Muslim garden's first and foremost idea is to be enclosed and isolated from the outside world; instead of having its focus of attention on the periphery, it is placed in the center. The garden is created by taking a piece of land, 'vivifying' a square section of the desert, into which water is brought. Inside a high enclosing wall, one finds a staggered arrangement of trees and flowers growing close to one another, as one moves from the periphery to the center, and in the center, next to a spraying fountain, is a kiosk. This garden, contrary to the Western garden . . . enables thought to unfold in an atmosphere of relaxation.[51]

The sensual garden setting was only one element of the new Hebrew poetry. Equally important was the musical accompaniment. Unfortunately, no system of musical notation from that time has survived, and the references to music in the poetry are therefore all the more valuable. Even when there were no instruments, the poems were sung. Moses ibn Ezra likens the birds in the trees of the garden to singing girls concealed behind curtains, although it is not known if girls were present at such events.

Other important poetic skills were the ability to improvise on set themes and displays of linguistic virtuosity. Poets would vie in cleverness, creating verses on the spot that retained their meaning whether recited backwards or forwards. Some composed entire poems using only words that started with the same consonant or without

---

[50] Abu Ishaq ibn Khafaja, *Diwan ibn Khafaja*, cited in Brann, 'How Can My Heart Be in the East?', 368.
[51] Louis Massignon, *Testimonies and Reflections*, cited in Cole, 'Solomon ibn Gabirol', 26.

ever using one particular letter of the alphabet. Such skills could win the poet a lifetime pension, provided his patron did not fall out of favour himself in the Arab court.

Ibn Nagrela also wrote poems about the wars he was involved in, in which he led Muslim troops in combat. He conflates the ancient battles of the hosts of Israel with the heated combat of the armies of Granada. In one nocturnal poetic musing at the campsite of his troops, he contemplates his own military victories, not with glee but with the realization of the ultimate vanity of all earthly conquests:

> I bade my troops encamp once at a town
> That enemies had razed in ancient times.
> We pitched our tents and slept upon its site,
> While under us its former masters slept.
> Then to myself I mused: 'Where are the folk
> Who long ago inhabited this place?
> Where are the men who built and those who wreck?
> Where rich, where poor, where slaves, and where the lords?
> Those who begot and those bereft, the sons
> And fathers, mourners, bridegrooms—where are they?
> And generation after generation, born
> As centuries succeeded years of days.
> Upon the face of earth they used to live,
> And yet today they lie within its heart.
> They've changed their palaces for sepulchers;
> They've moved from lovely mansions into dirt.
> But should they lift their heads and leave those graves,
> How easily they'd overwhelm our troops!
> Never forget, my soul, that one day soon
> This mighty host and I will share their doom.[52]

One of Ibn Nagrela's most talented protégés was Solomon ibn Gabirol, best remembered for his deeply religious poetry and his Neoplatonic philosophical treatise *Mekor ḥayim* ('Source of Life'). His philosophical poem 'The Kingly Crown' has earned a most honoured place in Jewish liturgy as part of the High Holiday ritual. Ibn Gabirol's brief life was blighted by physical infirmities and characterized by personal bitterness. He found the social system that required him to pander to his patron's vanity particularly abhorrent. His religious temperament notwithstanding, Ibn Gabirol also tried his hand at wine songs in order to make a living.[53]

Another Hebrew poet, Isaac ibn Khalfun, searched in vain for a patron in Cordoba, and spent years wandering from one court to the next seeking sponsorship and subsidies. His complaints about the miserliness of courtiers became a motif of his poetry,

---

[52] Samuel ibn Nagrela, 'I bade my troops encamp once at a town', in Scheindlin (ed.), *Wine, Women and Death*, 155. Reproduced by permission of the University of Nebraska Press. Copyright © 1986 by the Jewish Publication Society.   [53] See Ibn Gabirol, *Vulture in a Cage*, 151–274.

capturing the general insecurity of the institution of the court poet. The juxtaposition of biblical allusion and frivolous subject matter, such as in the following poem, 'A Present of Cheese', is intentionally startling:

> I invited you, my dearest friend, with joy,
> And heaped upon you favours, as my guest.
> I regarded you as a shield and a buckler
> Against my enemies, a tower of strength, my trust—
> Like a hut in the shade when the sun beats down,
> Like a warm stove in time and frost.
> I remembered you—and may God remember you for good—
> As Elkanah remembered Peninah—with the best.
> And send me a present, a portion of cheese.
> And what's the good of cheese, when I am dry with thirst?[54]

The thwarted lover might also serve as a theme for Ibn Khalfun:

> When desire arouses me, I leap like a
> Deer to see my lady's eyes. And when I
> Come, I find her mother there—and her
> Father and her brother and her uncle!
> I look at her, then quickly turn away,
> As though I were not her beloved. I am
> Afraid of them, and my heart mourns
> For her like the heart of woman bereft
> Of her only son.[55]

Almost any object might become the subject of a poem to show off the poet's use of pure biblical Hebrew or deft turn of phrase. Judah Halevi could not resist composing an ode upon the discovery of his first grey hair:

> When a gray hair appeared all on its own
> Upon my head, I cut it down.
> 'You are the victor now,' it said
> 'But what will you do, once my banners are spread?'[56]

The reflections on an old tattered cloak by Abraham ibn Ezra (1089–1161), an extraordinary polymath whose talents ranged from poet and scientist to biblical exegete, include a remarkable testimony to the prevailing Andalusian interest in science,

---

[54] Isaac ibn Khalfun, 'A Present of Cheese', in *Hebrew Poems from Spain*, 29. Reproduced by permission of the Littman Library of Jewish Civilization.

[55] Isaac ibn Khalfun, 'The Retreat', in *The Penguin Book of Hebrew Verse*, 283. Copyright © T. Carmi, 1981. Reproduced by permission of Penguin Books Ltd.

[56] Judah Halevi, 'The Army of Old Age', in *Hebrew Poems From Spain*, 115. Reproduced by permission of the Littman Library of Jewish Civilization.

especially astronomy. These disparate elements are transformed into a work of beauty that mixes frivolity and solemnity in its surprise ending:

> I have a garment. It is like a sieve
> With which to sift barley or wheat.
> At the dead of night I spread it out like a tent
> And the stars of heaven put through it their light.
> From within it I see the moon and the Pleiades,
> And when it is bright there peeps through Orion.
> I get tired from counting all its holes
> Which seem like the teeth of a saw in profusion.
> A piece of thread, to sew up its rags,
> Both warp and woof would be superfluous.
> If a fly landed on it with all his weight,
> He, like an idiot, would soon grumble and curse.
> My God, make good the repairs which it needs.
> Make a mantle of praise from these tattered weeds.[57]

Jewish poets, like their Arab counterparts, prized improvisation and spontaneity: on one occasion, Ibn Gabirol composed fifteen short poems on the subject of apples. Some of the improvisations were adaptations of familiar Arabic poems. It is difficult to imagine that the following poem was penned by a man who was one of the foremost liturgical poets of medieval times:

> My lord, take this delicacy in your hand.
> Perceive its scent. Forget your longing.
> On both sides it blushes, like a young girl
> At the first touch of my hand on her breast.
> An orphan it is without father or sister,
> And far away from its leafy home.
> When it was plucked, its companions were jealous,
> Envied its journey, and cried aloud:
> 'Bear greetings to your master, Isaac.
> How lucky you are to be kissed by his lips!'[58]

The combinations and juxtapositions in Spanish Hebrew poetry offer a vivid testimony to the facility with which the Jewish poets of Muslim Spain moved between two cultural vocabularies, Arabic and biblical Hebrew, adding a talmudic *bon mot* here and there as well. These ingenious feats delighted those in attendance and increased the general atmosphere of literary competition that engaged the Jewish literati and

---

[57] Abraham ibn Ezra, 'I have a garment', in *Hebrew Poems from Spain*, 124. Reproduced by permission of the Littman Library of Jewish Civilization.

[58] Solomon ibn Gabirol, 'An Apple for Isaac', in *Hebrew Poems from Spain*, 63. Reproduced by permission of the Littman Library of Jewish Civilization. The Isaac in question was probably Ibn Gabirol's patron, Yekutiel ben Isaac ibn Hasan, who was executed in 1039.

commercial elite of Spain. Not all the poems thus composed, of course, were memorable. Some of the panegyrics were patent flattery, composed for a fee, and representing no more than the poets' panderings to the egos of their patrons. Following the pre-Islamic Arabic model of lovelorn speakers in arid deserts, the stereotypes could become hackneyed.

Whether light-hearted verse or puns and riddles, the poetic oeuvre of the Jews in the gardens and salons of Muslim Spain produced a melange of frivolity and religious solemnity: the same poets crafting riddles about scissors, needles, a pen, or a pomegranate also composed some of the most lofty descriptions of the relationship of God to his people that adorn the Jewish prayer book. Laments of hapless suitors were expressed in one breath by the singer who longed in expressive verse for the messianic deliverance of the people of Israel in another. In one instance of this rare combination of talents, Ibn Gabirol transformed mundane wintery imagery through a delicate use of Hebrew. Even translated into English, the poet's dexterity is apparent:

> The winter writes with the ink of its rain and its showers,
> With the nib of its lightning, with the hand of its clouds,
> A message upon the garden, of violet and purple.
> No human being can perform acts such as these.
> And when the earth becomes jealous of the skies,
> It embroiders its garments with flowers like the stars.[59]

The poetry of the golden age of *convivencia* was part of a hedonistic lifestyle that allowed for the coexistence of worldly and religious impulses. For all their enjoyment of their Iberian diaspora, sombre reminders of exile would suddenly break into the poet's merriment. It is not always clear whether this change of mood was a poetic convention or whether it expressed a traditional Jewish response to levity. The theme of exile appears frequently in pre-Islamic poetry in several forms; it could connote the psychological and physical displacement of poets, *al-ghurba al-makaniyya* (exile from a place) and *al-ghurba al-zamaniyya* (exile from time). Hebrew poets were aware of this Arabic trope and combined it with traditional Jewish concepts of exile. In the tenth century they added another dimension—existential exile, *al-ghurba al-ruhiyya* (exile of the spirit) or the exile of the soul within the body introduced by Neoplatonism. Thus the Hebrew poet was mindful of his own state of multiple exiles—political, religious, social, and existential—even while enjoying a wine feast in a luxuriant garden.

The Hebrew poets Samuel ibn Nagrela, Ibn Gabirol, and Moses ibn Ezra, and the Muslim poets Ibn Darraj al-Qastalli (958–1030), Ibn Shuhayd (992–1035), and Ibn Zaydun (1003–70) were all witness to the break-up of the caliphate of Cordoba. Flight became a central concern in their lives and an important metaphor in their poetry. Moses ibn

---

[59] Solomon ibn Gabirol, 'The Writing of Winter', in *Hebrew Poems from Spain*, 65. Reproduced by permission of the Littman Library of Jewish Civilization.

Ezra compared the cultural uprooting of his day to the ancient exiles of his people.[60] Jewish migration from Muslim to Christian Spain became the occasion for melancholy reflections on the ancient separation of the people of Israel from the Land of Israel with the personal malaise of the wandering poet, adrift and insecure in search of a patron, expressive of the collective voice and fate of the medieval Jews.[61] Moses ibn Ezra also employed metaphors of exile to refer to old age and the loss of pleasure. When he finally reached Castile in his flight from Andalusia in 1095, he complained of his displacement—'I have come to the iniquitous domain of a people scorned by God and accursed by man, among savages who love corruption'—comparing this condition to his youth 'in the gardens of truth', the Arabic culture of Granada, as he confronted a fate of being obliged to 'hew, in old age, the wood of forests and folly'.[62] Biblical descriptions of 'the most pleasant of lands' and 'the river of Thy pleasures' describe the poet's years in Granada.[63] The conflation of the individual fate of the poet and the national fate of the people of Israel was not unique to Ibn Ezra. The exiles of 1492 would also see their fate as a reflection of the ancient tragedies of their people, perhaps consciously echoing their medieval poetic heritage in an attempt to understand their plight, in which Spain represented a new Jerusalem now lost.[64]

In 1085 the Muslim ruler of Seville, al-Mu'tamid ibn Abbad, turned for military assistance against his Christian foes to the Berber Almoravid dynasty of Morocco. In exchange for their aid, the Almoravids took over part of Andalusia and soon demanded the implementation of a strict, more puritanical version of Islam, including the application of anti-*dhimmi* legislation against Jews and Christians. This discriminatory policy was spelled out by Muslim jurist Muhammad ibn Abdun of Seville in a legal manual concerning the 'proper' interaction of Muslims, Christians, and Jews in the city's markets. Among the manual's many specific instructions, the author reminds Muslim believers:

A Muslim must not massage a Jew or a Christian nor throw away his refuse nor clean his latrines. The Jew and the Christian are better fitted for such trades, since they are the trades of those who are vile. A Muslim should not attend to the animal of a Jew or of a Christian, nor serve him as a muleteer, nor hold his stirrup. If any Muslim is known to do this, he should be denounced. . . . A garment belonging to a sick man, a Jew, or a Christian must not be sold without indicating its origin. . . . No contractor, policeman, Jew, or Christian may be allowed to dress in the costume of

---

[60] On the use of the term *galut* to denote 'exclusion from the majority culture', see M. R. Cohen, 'Sociability and the Concept of *Galut* in Muslim–Jewish Relations'; Rosenberg, 'Exile and Redemption in Jewish Thought in the Sixteenth Century'; on the literary development of the theme of exile at the time of the Almohads, see Decter, *Iberian Jewish Literature*.

[61] See Alfonso, 'Uses of Exile in Poetic Discourse'.

[62] On the metaphor of forests and landscapes of estrangement, see Decter, *Iberian Jewish Literature*, 12, 19–20, 33–4, 36–7; on the forest as foreign territory in which the poet struggles to survive, yearning for the sophisticated culture he has lost, see ibid. 37.

[63] Ibid. 52.   [64] See Yerushalmi, 'Exile and Expulsion in Jewish History'; Navarro, 'Moses ibn "Ezra"'.

people of position, of a jurist, or of a worthy man. They must, on the contrary, be abhorred and shunned and should not be greeted with the formula 'Peace be with you.' . . . They must have a distinguishing sign by which they are recognized to their shame.[65]

Despite their initial ascetic and reformist tendencies, the Almoravids soon succumbed to the courtly culture and hedonistic ways of Andalusian life. The resulting religious laxity eventually led to another group of puritanical reformists, the Almohads, seizing power among the Berber tribes of North Africa. The Almohads posed a much more serious danger to Jewish existence than the Almoravids. In 1147 they invaded Spain after sweeping through the Maghreb on a wave of fundamentalist terror and a campaign of forced conversion of Jews, setting off a Jewish flight from Muslim Spain. Abraham ibn Ezra, who fled the persecutions, wandering for years in Provence, Italy, and England, enumerates the agonies endured by the Jews of Andalusia and North Africa at the hands of the Almohads and the eclipse of their great centres of learning, specifically mentioning Cordoba and its sages among the victims:

> Woe, for calamity has descended upon Sepharad from the heavens!
> My eyes, my eyes flow with water.
>
> I weep like an ostrich for Lucena,
> Her remnant dwelt innocent and secure,
> Unchanged for a thousand years;
> Then came her day and her people were exiled and she a widow.
>
> I will shave my head and cry bitterly over the exiles from Seville,
> Over her noble men that were slain and their sons enslaved,
> Over refined daughters converted to the foreign faith.
>
> Alas, the city of Cordoba is forsaken, her ruin as vast as the sea!
> Her sages and learned men perished from hunger and thirst.
> Not a single Jew was left in Jaén or Almeria;
> Mallorca and Malaga struggle to survive.
>
> The Jews who remain are a beaten and bleeding wound.
> For this I mourn and learn a dirge and wait with bitter lamentation;
> I shout in my distress: They have vanished like water.[66]

The advent of the Almohads postponed but could not long prevent the fall of one Muslim city after another to reinvigorated Christian forces. A decisive Muslim defeat at Las Navas de Tolosa in 1212, the fall of Cordoba in 1236, and the capitulation of Seville to Ferdinand III in 1248 virtually completed the Catholic Reconquest of Spain. Only a small enclave of Muslims was able to hold out in Granada until 1492. In the course of the long crusade for hegemony on the peninsula, Christian and Muslim societies were

---

[65] Muhammad ibn Abdun of Seville, *Ḥisba Manual*, in *Medieval Iberia*, 175–9.
[66] Abraham ibn Ezra, 'Woe, for calamity has descended upon Sepharad', cited in Decter, *Iberian Jewish Literature*, 149.

each restructured with a new and more militant self-perception and religious identity. Caught in the middle, the Jews began to move out of Andalusia and into Christian Spain. As they scattered, they carried their Andalusian traditions with them. Some refugees wandered for years: Moses Maimonides eventually reached Morocco and ultimately settled in Egypt in 1168. His traumatic experiences under the Almohads would shape his later empathetic epistles to beleaguered Jewries who faced similar choices between conversion and death. Some Jewish refugees, like the Kimhi and Ibn Tibbon families, fled to Provence, introducing Andalusian Jewish culture into southern France. Other victims never found permanent asylum: like the polymath Abraham ibn Ezra, they wandered for years, lingered for a while, and then moved on.

In assessing the place of Cordoba in the shaping of Sephardi civilization several themes emerge. Andalusian Jews were convinced not only of their noble lineage but also of their unique relationship to the Hebrew language. At times this singular devotion to Hebrew was understood to be the result of the Sephardi aristocratic pedigrees. At other times, the Sephardim vaunted their fidelity to *tsaḥut halashon*, the 'purity of the language', as proof of their uniqueness in relation to the Arabs. Guardianship of the Hebrew language, they claimed, had been their special destiny. In the words of Moses ibn Ezra, 'there is no doubt at all that the inhabitants of Jerusalem, from whom we—members of the Spanish exile—are descended, were more knowledgeable in rhetorical eloquence and in rabbinic tradition than the residents of other cities and towns'.[67]

Another characteristic that the Jews of Andalusia acquired in the formative centuries of life in Muslim Spain was a sense of rootedness in a particular place, of belonging to a particular geographical location. This trait evolved in medieval times to become a prominent feature of their psychological make-up. True, many families had resided for hundreds of years in a particular location in other countries, but longevity of residence alone is not an adequate explanation for the unusual manifestations of local patriotism that the Sephardim exhibited. Their attachment to place was also manifest in language differences and ritual nuances. They tended to cling to their memories of Muslim Andalusia precisely because it was such a diverse and exceptional period in Jewish history: similar recollections were romanticized by Muslim poets and immortalized in Arabic poetry. With the passage of time, the Cordoban chapter in Sephardi history became ever more romanticized. Centuries after leaving Muslim Spain, Andalusia and its cultural attitudes continued to occupy an honoured place in Hebrew literature and in Jewish social life. To write in the 'Andalusian style' remained a sign of sophistication long after the courtier class had been debased or discredited.

The Jewish association with Cordoba did not cease with the flight of Maimonides and his family in the wake of the Almohad invasion in the twelfth century. After a semblance of civic order had been restored and persecution had subsided, Jewish life

---

[67] Ibn Ezra, *Kitāb al-Muḥāḍara wa al-Mudhākara*, 29a (ed. Halkin, p. 54).

resumed in the now ruined city on a diminished scale. When Muslim Cordoba fell to King Ferdinand III of Castile in 1236 the Jews were assigned a residential quarter near the cathedral, next to a fish market. The district's main street, known as the Calle de los Judíos, is today's Calle de Maimonides, in memory of the city's most famous Jewish refugee. The names of other streets in the medieval Jewish quarter, such as the Street of the Tanners, the Street of the Pedlars, the Street of the Silk Market, and the Street of the Goldsmiths, suggest the economic continuation of Jewish life in Christian Cordoba on a much more modest scale.

A small, elegant synagogue from medieval times still stands in Cordoba. It is one of the few original historic synagogues to remain in Spain. It consists of a modest hall measuring approximately 21 by 23 feet. Perhaps it served as a private chapel in the Middle Ages. More likely, its diminutive size is a reflection of the new, more restrictive environment that the Jews confronted in Christian Cordoba. In keeping with the policies prevailing at the time of the Reconquest, Jews were permitted to remain as part of the royal effort to encourage the presence of a middle class in the city. Soon after the Reconquest, however, the archdeacon of the city complained about the height of some newly constructed synagogues, and turned to Pope Innocent IV for support in restricting further synagogue construction. In a pastoral letter of 1250, the pope responded to the archdeacon:

We have learned that, despite the prohibition of our dear son, the Archdeacon of the Chapter of Cordoba, the Jews of the province of Cordoba are rashly presuming to build a new synagogue of unnecessary height, thereby scandalizing faithful Christians and causing much harm to the Church of Cordoba, wherefore we have been humbly petitioned mercifully to make this matter Our particular concern. We command your Fraternity by Apostolic letter to enforce the authority of your office against the Jews in this regard, and to do so without the obstacle of appeal. Given at Lyons, on the Ides of April in the Seventh Year.[68]

The diminutive scale of the Cordoba synagogue is probably the result of this ecclesiastical intervention. A few noteworthy features of the synagogue's architectural detail are still visible in its otherwise bare interior. Windows are absent on three of the four walls (the single windowed wall is the southern one). This feature might have been in response to newly imposed restrictions on synagogue construction. Devoid of windows, the exterior of the structure bears no resemblance to a house of worship. Hidden behind a small courtyard, the synagogue would be unlikely to attract attention. One of the most interesting features of the building is the dedicatory Hebrew inscription set in an ornamental panel on the eastern wall, which blends Hebrew and Arabic styles in a single harmonious whole. The result is characteristically Sephardi and reflects the former cultural reality. The few words that are legible read:

---

[68] Innocent IV, pastoral letter, 13 Apr. 1250, cited in Wischnitzer, *The Architecture of the European Synagogue*, 30.

Isaac Menhab, son of the honourable Ephraim, has completed this lesser sanctuary [*mikdash me'at*] and he built it in the year [50]75 [1314/15] as a temporary abode. Hasten, O God, to rebuild Jerusalem.

Like the poetry of the golden age, the dedication of the small synagogue of Cordoba in 1314 suggests the creation of a culture that once bridged the Jewish and Muslim worlds now repeated and reshaped under the hegemony of the Christians in reconquered Cordoba. The courtier-poets and artists once moved easily in the dominant cultures of the peninsula. Their verse reflected an intensity of cross-cultural encounters that would not be repeated until modern times. The Sephardi identification with Cordoba and its courtly secular Arabic culture created a powerful legacy for all Jews, even those who had not directly experienced it.

CHAPTER TWO

CROSSING THE BORDERS OF ART AND SOCIETY: TOLEDO AS A MEETING PLACE OF CULTURES 1150–1350

> And I came to the spread out city
> That was garbed in charm that inspires and displays its adornment
> The tribes went up there, the tribes of the Lord
> She shall put the luminaries to shame with the magnificence of her beauty and splendour
>
> JUDAH AL-HARIZI, *Taḥkemoni*

> Study should always be in beautiful books, pleasant for their beauty and the splendour of their scripts and parchments, with elegant ornament and covers. . . . And the places for study should be desirable, the study halls beautifully built so that people's love and desire for study will increase. . . . It is also obligatory and appropriate to enhance the books of God and to direct oneself to their beauty, splendour, and loveliness. . . . Just as God wished to adorn the place of His sanctuary with gold, silver, and precious stones so is this appropriate for the book which is His sanctuary.
>
> PROFIAT DURAN, *Ma'aseh efod*

TOLEDO was the first Andalusian city to fall to the Christians in 1085. Situated in the heart of Muslim territory, it remained a Christian enclave within a Muslim region for over a century, strategically poised on the shifting political frontier between the two warring civilizations. Located at a cultural crossroads where Christian and Islamic traditions intersected, Toledo's Jews formed an integral part of a city that was defined by diverse languages, cultures, and peoples. The Jews were not immune to the changes that the region was undergoing. They straddled the fluid political borders of Iberia and responded to the cultural transformations among their Muslim and Christian neighbours.

A new Castilian identity slowly emerged out of the embers of Andalusia and the ongoing clashes of the Reconquest. New Jewish identities also developed. With the reconfiguration of political borders, population shifts occurred on a grand scale. A steady stream of Christian immigrants poured into Castile: royal brides for the Castilian princes; crusaders from France en route to the east; middle-class merchants, artisans, and artists eager to find customers and patrons at the seat of Castilian power; and Cluniac monks and enthusiastic members of the mendicant and military orders. The Jews experienced similar population displacements and demographic changes. As Jewish refugees from Andalusia moved northward in the wake of the Almohad persecutions, streams of Ashkenazim in flight from Germany, France, and Provence were simultaneously migrating southward into Spain. The meeting of the two Jewries in thirteenth- and fourteenth-century Toledo marked a critical moment in the shaping of Sephardi Judaism. The arrival of Ashkenazim, especially of Asher ben Yehiel (the Rosh) and his son Jacob ben Asher (c.1270–c.1343), infused Toledo with fresh leadership and the vast erudition of the Tosafists. At the same time, novel mystical texts from Provence and Catalonia captured the hearts of many Spanish Jews. The dramatic clashes between mystical and rationalist approaches to Judaism that erupted as these streams of thought collided wrought new forms of Sephardi identity. Toledo became the meeting place as well as a prime battleground for the many competing social and intellectual currents in Christian and Jewish circles.

The migration of the Jews from Muslim to Christian Spain in the twelfth century did not spell the end of the rich culture that Jews had created in Andalusia. Continuities with the past endured even as new challenges arose. Jews continued to speak Arabic well into the fourteenth century and to cultivate Arabic-inspired arts. These formed an essential part of their identity. Even when poetic and prose works were no longer written in Arabic but in Hebrew or early Castilian, the poetry and prose often retained an Andalusian spirit in its form and content.

Jews were recruited by the victorious Christian powers in the repopulation and reconstruction of the newly conquered territories. While this process was occurring, Western Christendom was simultaneously undergoing fundamental reconsiderations of the place of the Jews in society. Mounting missionary zeal against Jews (and Muslims), accompanied by anti-Jewish legislation, spread from Rome. As Jews entered the Christian towns of Spain they received protective charters, but alliances contracted with local rulers and municipalities could provide only partial protection. The charters frequently represented the fruits of competition among kings, nobles, and even clergy. Treaties were part of the complex web of overlapping and competing power relationships which the Jews were forced to navigate. Jews countered threats against their persons and their beliefs with new polemical and exegetical tools in words and images. The intercession of a Jewish court favourite could curtail a religious disputation or mitigate special tax assessments. But the power of a courtier and his relationship to a particular monarch no more reflected tolerance towards Jews than they had in Cordoba. King Alfonso X (r. 1252–84), for example, exhibited contradictory attitudes towards his Jewish subjects. Nevertheless, Toledo provided a congenial home to the new Sephardi cultural syntheses during the course of his long reign.

One response to the declining position of Jews in Christian Spain is reflected in the iconography of Jewish art that emerged in Toledo. Jewish artists sought to bolster their self-confidence against the mounting legal and exegetical attacks on Judaism through symbols and allusions to midrashic defences and explanations of their tradition. Expressions of self-esteem and messianic confirmation that their exile would not endure for ever were embedded in Hebrew illuminated manuscripts. At the same time Sephardi art expressed a specific sensitivity to the aesthetic expressions and beauty of the cultural milieu. The subtle architectural details and carefully selected inscriptions in the synagogue of courtier Samuel Halevi Abulafia (c.1320–60) are testimonies to a world of ambivalence. As the multilingual Sephardim resumed their familiar role as intermediaries between Muslim and Christian cultures, their artistic sensibilities and translation skills assumed new prominence. Whether in the illumination of Haggadah manuscripts or the decorative details of architecture, the Sephardim responded to the new challenges of the Reconquest and the attacks on their tradition with the artistic vocabularies of the surrounding cultures.

Flight from Muslim to Christian Spain and the Reconquest

Not all Muslims fled the Christian conquest of Toledo: some remained and were permitted to maintain their own culture. The indigenous Toledan Jews were also permitted to remain in their homes. Their numbers were soon augmented by the flood of Jewish refugees seeking asylum from the Almoravid and Almohad rule in Andalusia, and Jews who were attracted by the economic opportunities opening up in the newly conquered Christian territories. One of the first goals of King Alfonso VI (1065–1109) after conquering Toledo was to stabilize the city's population. Joseph Ferrizuel, the king's personal physician, was recognized as the head of the Jewish community. He served the king in several other important capacities, including tax-collector and bailiff. He enjoyed wide political and economic power in Castile, and is recalled in Jewish sources for his role in protecting and representing the Jews before the authorities.[1] His nephew, Solomon ibn Ferrizuel, was also a courtier and was admiringly described by Judah Halevi.[2] Joseph fled to Guadalajara during a bloody attack on the Jews in Toledo in 1108. His considerable estate was confiscated by King Alfonso VII (1126–57) and given to the monastery of San Servando. Solomon was murdered on an official diplomatic mission to Aragon in the same year. The vicissitudes of the Ferrizuel family were part of larger historical developments in which Jewish courtiers continued to serve as envoys to the Muslim courts, exercising conspicuous political power, not only in Castile but particularly in the new territories of Valencia and Andalusia.

The elders (*muqaddamin*) who served as the governing body of the community often owed their power to connections with the Christian authorities and were also

[1] Ray, *The Sephardic Frontier*, 67.   [2] Y. Baer, *A History of the Jews in Christian Spain*, i. 50.

frequently beholden to Jewish courtiers. But royal favour for the few came at a price for the many. It was common for the court Jew to bequeath his political position to a son or other relative. Over time an elite group of Jewish courtiers emerged in Christian Spain. They received exemptions from some taxes and communal obligations in return for their services. They were also not required to wear the discriminatory and distinguishing clothing forced upon the rest of the Jewish community. The assimilated lifestyle of this privileged class frequently assumed the trappings of nobility, leading to deepening alienation and class divisions within the Jewish communities. The history of the Jews in Christian Spain, as it has been reconstructed until recently, is heavily weighted towards the deeds and misdeeds of this small Jewish elite, influenced by Yitzhak Baer's *The Jews of Christian Spain* and its emphasis on the foibles of the courtier class. As in Muslim Spain, the association of Jewish courtiers with unpopular royal authority posed potential dangers. However, the consolidation of Jewish communities during the Reconquest testifies to their skills. At the same time, their ambivalent reputation hovers in the shadows of Sephardi memory.

While it is commonplace to telescope the transplantation of the Jews from Muslim to Christian Spain into one dramatic moment sparked by the Almohad invasion from North Africa in 1147, in actuality the Jews had started abandoning Muslim Spain in the eleventh century in response to the opportunities of the new frontier society. Their migration proceeded over the course of several generations and was, naturally, accompanied by cultural disorientation. Writing from his place of asylum in Toledo, Abraham ibn Daud described the tribulations of the Reconquest. He stresses the role of the courtier Judah ibn Ezra in rescuing Jewish refugees from Almohad persecution, and depicts him in his many roles as head of the Jewish community, *almoxarife* (royal tax-collector) of Alfonso VII, supplier of the king's troops, and 'lord of the king's household'. Ibn Daud explicitly attributes Ibn Ezra's effectiveness to his loyalty to God, his royal connections, and his illustrious ancestry. He also acknowledges the importance of Toledo as a place of asylum:

The rebels against the Berber kingdoms had crossed the sea to Spain having wiped out every remnant of Jews from Tangiers to al-Mahdiyya. . . . They tried to do the same thing in all of the cities of the Ishmaelite kingdom in Spain. . . . When the Jews had heard the report that the rebels were advancing upon them to drive them away from the Lord, God of Israel . . . [they] fled for their lives. Some were taken captive by the Christians, to whom they willingly indentured themselves on condition that they be rescued from Muslim territory. Others fled on foot, naked and barefoot. . . . However, He who prepares the remedy before afflictions [God] put it into the heart of King Alfonso the Emperador to appoint our master and rabbi, R. Judah the Nasi b. Ezra, over Calatrava and to place all the royal provisions in his charge. The latter's forefathers had been among the leaders of Granada, holders of high office and men of influence in every generation. . . . There is a tradition current among the members of the community of Granada that they are descended from the inhabitants of Jerusalem . . . R. Judah the Nasi, his father and uncles . . . all of them are of royal blood and descended of the nobility. . . . Now when this great Nasi, R. Judah, was appointed over

Calatrava, he supervised the passage of the refugees, released those bound in chains and let the oppressed go free by breaking their yoke and undoing their bonds. At his home and at his table, where the refugees found rest, he fed the hungry, provided drink for the thirsty and clothed the naked. Then, providing animals for all the feeble, he had them brought as far as Toledo in great dignity. . . . When all the nation had finished passing over [the border] by means of his help, the King [Alfonso VII] sent him and appointed him lord of his household and ruler over all his possessions.[3]

Each milestone in the victorious battle of the Christians against the Muslims set off new waves of Jewish migration into Christian Spain. In Toledo, Saragossa, and Tortosa, the Christian kings extended economic and political concessions to the Jews, both individually and collectively, in order to induce them to enter the newly conquered and depopulated territories. At the same time, the Muslim intellectual class tended to flee southward to the kingdom of Granada or to North Africa, exhorting the rank and file of their community to follow rather than remain as a Muslim minority under Christian rule. With the departure of the Muslim intellectuals and their followers, the decline of Arabic cultural influence in Spain was only a matter of time. Sporadic Muslim rebellions against Christian domination provoked sharp reprisals in Castile (1264–6) and Aragon (1275–7) and stimulated further emigration. Nevertheless, a strong Muslim presence persisted in Christian Spain, particularly in the rural areas. The victorious Christian warriors chose to retreat to their castles rather than dwell among Muslims and Jews in the newly conquered towns. The Christian authorities introduced a policy of distributing free shops, farms, and administrative positions to Jews as well as to Christians in order to repopulate the conquered territories. Jews were regarded as part of the royal treasure, their tax revenues belonging to the Crown.

The Reconquest was partially religious—to launch a massive offensive against Islamic foes—and partly ethnic—to oust the Arab 'usurpers' from former Visigothic territory. In the course of the protracted battles for domination of the Iberian peninsula, a spirit of intense piety was forged. As Christian knights and clerics streamed into Spain from France to join the battle, they transported anti-Jewish sentiments that were rooted in the soil of northern Europe. For those crusading 'warriors of the faith' who were passing through Spain en route to the east to wage war against the 'infidel', the temptation to attack the Jewish 'infidels' they met on Spanish soil was great. In the heat of crusading fervour, distinctions between one infidel and another were not necessarily made. The influence of the religious orders of Dominicans, Franciscans, and the smaller Cistercians and Benedictines, also grew. As Christian forces that had previously fought against each other united against their shared enemy, new emphases on honour, noble birth, and Christian valour began to emerge, especially in the newly formed

[3] Ibn Daud, *Sefer ha-Qabbalah*, 97–9. On the process of re-establishing Jewish communities and negotiating charters with local authorities, see Barton, *Contested Treasure*; Glick, 'Reading the *Repartimentos*'; Ray, *The Sephardic Frontier*.

Spanish military orders of Calatrava, Alcantara, and Santiago. Thus cultural adaptation and reorientation was only one of the many challenges, and not necessarily the most significant one, that the Jews would confront in the kingdom of Castile. The Jewish–Christian confrontation took many forms in Spain: compulsory religious disputations, aggressive missionary activities, anti-Jewish legislation, and physical attacks on Jews. Jews had to defend themselves against these assaults in writing, in debate, and in art.

At this time, the term 'Sepharadim' begins to appear with some regularity to denote the Jews from Muslim Spain, although a vagueness of nomenclature persisted as Jews adapted to the several kingdoms and cultures of Christian Spain. Nevertheless, a collective memory of a significant and shared religio-cultural legacy from life in the former Muslim realms with its aura of splendour began to emerge.

In accepting the Jewish refugees from Andalusia, Toledo admitted a culturally Arabized Jewish population, reinforcing its own indigenous, Arabized Jewish community. By and large, a mutually beneficial arrangement began to evolve between Christians, Mudéjares, and Sephardim: while the Christians pursued the business of war, Jews and Muslims were left to cultivate the arts of peace, including the reorganization of commerce and industry, the repossession and recultivation of the land, the redrafting of the cadastral registers, and the building of new towns and the repopulation of old ones.[4] Jews were given houses and land that had been vacated by fleeing Muslims. The houses were usually two storeys in height and possessed patios, courtyards, and gardens. In some places, Jews were settled in fortresses to serve as a garrison or assigned other military responsibilities. Abandoned agricultural properties were also distributed to Jews as individuals or as groups.[5]

The traditional division of Jewish history in Spain into a Muslim period of amity and a Christian age of persecution is overly simplistic. The transition from one regime to another followed different paths in different regions of the Iberian peninsula. There were incentives to encourage Jews to settle in many towns and villages spelled out in compilations of laws or charters known as *fueros*. One charter would become the prototype for another, as Jews, counts, clerics, or municipalities, in combination or separately, entered into mutually beneficial relations. The charters also extended the protection of the kings or counts to the Jews in specially designated Jewish neighbourhoods known in Castilian as *juderías*, in Portuguese as *judiarias*, and as *calls* in Catalan.[6] By the thirteenth century, but especially in the fourteenth century, separate neighbourhoods for Jews, Muslims, and Christians coalesced. The separation of Jews from the rest of the population was further buttressed by ecclesiastical decrees, which increased in severity in the course of the thirteenth and fourteenth centuries. In his famous legal collection,

---

[4] See Ray, *The Sephardic Frontier*. [5] Y. Baer, *A History of the Jews in Christian Spain*, i. 113.

[6] Hebrew sources generally refer to the Jewish quarter as *shekhunat yisra'el*, *shekhunat hayehudim*, or *migrash hayehudim* (see Assis, *The Golden Age of Aragonese Jewry*, 199). The Hebrew *kahal kadosh* and the Arabic *al-jama* are the most common designations of the organized Jewish community.

Las siete partidas, Alfonso X permitted Christians to work for Jews, but, among other restrictions, he prohibited Jews from living in the same houses as Christians.[7] Alfonso's measures to segregate the Jews were not enforced during his reign and remained dormant until long after his death. The repeated stipulations that Jews be segregated that appear in various codes and ecclesiastical councils during the thirteenth and fourteenth centuries suggest that they were ignored by successive monarchs.

Some Jewish community leaders, concerned about the negative moral influence that they felt Christians might have on Jews, welcomed the segregation. They condemned the loose morality and rough-and-tumble ethos prevailing in many reconquered areas, especially in the frontier towns, and pointedly denounced the Jewish courtier class and its mores. The rabbis introduced controls on gambling and limitations on the practice of concubinage, and voiced strong disapproval of Jews visiting brothels. Sensing the growing animosity of the general populace towards Jews, the Jewish leadership introduced restrictions on luxurious clothing and ostentatious celebratory events, fearing that too much display, especially by the courtiers and their entourages, would further arouse the enmity of the masses. Most troublesome to the rabbinic leadership was the frequency with which many Jews of all classes resorted to the secular or ecclesiastical courts to adjudicate their affairs. Recourse to the secular courts led inevitably to a breakdown of rabbinic authority and Jewish law. But the repeated exhortations that Jews use only the rabbinic courts and desist from social and sexual relations with Christians met with only limited success. Effective Jewish communal control over individual morality remained a problem until the last days of Jewish life in Spain.[8] Recognition of the many currents of social unrest in Spanish society thus forms an indispensable part of any assessment of the forces that shaped Sephardi identity.

Jewish Population and Jewish Occupations

It is difficult to ascertain how many Jews lived in Toledo at any given time during the Middle Ages. Medieval population estimates, in general, are notoriously inaccurate. It is entirely possible, judging from the area occupied by the Jewish quarter, that the Jews may have constituted as much as 25 per cent of the city's population immediately after the city fell to the Christians in 1085. One index of the size of a Jewish population is the number of synagogues, although this can be misleading, as wealthy individuals commonly possessed private synagogues in their homes, thereby evading restrictive

---

[7] For an analysis of the specific anti-Jewish clauses, see Carpenter, *Alfonso X and the Jews*. The disparity of laws and life was common in the Middle Ages. On the status of Jews in Catalonia, see Klein, *Jews, Christian Society, and Royal Power in Medieval Barcelona*.

[8] On morality in the Jewish community, see Assis, 'Sexual Behaviour in Mediaeval Hispano-Jewish Society'; Y. Baer, *A History of the Jews in Christian Spain*, i. 186–305; ii. 1–94; for Jewish ordinances and sumptuary legislation, see Finkelstein, *Jewish Self-Government in the Middle Ages*.

legislation on new synagogue construction. All synagogues required a regular quorum of ten males in order for worship to take place, so private synagogues were not analogous to the private chapels constructed by Christian nobles in their castles. Fourteen synagogues and schools in Toledo are mentioned by name in an anonymous fourteenth-century dirge composed to memorialize the countrywide pogrom of 1391,[9] and Judah al-Harizi refers to the synagogues of Toledo in his comparison of the city with Jerusalem.[10]

Baer's estimate of approximately 350 Jewish taxpayers in Toledo at the end of the thirteenth century suggests that the city possessed a sizeable Jewish community by medieval European standards, certainly among the largest, if not the largest, in medieval Spain. The Jews were concentrated in their own district known as Rabd al-Yahud or Madinat al-Yahud on a hill in the south-western corner of the city and running down to the River Tagus. This covered about one-tenth of the total area of medieval Toledo. One of the city's walls formed the northern boundary. A gate near the quarter was known as Bab al-Yahud. The southern city wall contained a fortress that was occupied by Jews and popularly known as Qasr al-Yahud, the citadel of the Jews. Jewish occupation and defence of fortresses was not uncommon in medieval Spain. Among the occupations of Jews cited in medieval documents was that of *ballasteros* (crossbowman).[11] In some places, such as Tudela in the northern kingdom of Navarre, the role of Jews as defenders of the city's walls was explicitly spelled out in their charter. Not infrequently, the protected location of the Jewish quarter under the city walls prevented mob violence against Jews from reaching catastrophic proportions. This was the case more than once in Toledo.

As a result of its hilly topography and location on the periphery of the town, the Jewish quarter of Toledo 'was virtually a city in itself'.[12] The names of streets within the quarter, such as the Lane of the Shoemakers and the Street of the Silversmiths, reflected the occupational diversity and artisan status of many of its residents. However, the Jewish quarter was not a ghetto in the sense of an area of compulsory domicile but an area of Jewish preference and perceived safety. Nor were the inhabitants of the quarter exclusively Jewish: Muslims and Christians lived there as well. Jews also possessed shops and storehouses in the centre of the city, the main area of Christian residence and occupation, until they were forced to relinquish them in the fourteenth century. Moneylending did not emerge as the primary Jewish occupation in Christian Spain until the late thirteenth or fourteenth century, when specific anti-Jewish legislation was promulgated, aimed at ousting Jews from most other fields of economic endeavour. Even then, however, moneylending was not an exclusively Jewish occupation. Although barriers to Jewish economic diversity multiplied as the Middle Ages

---

[9] See C. Roth, 'A Hebrew Elegy on the Martyrs of Toledo'.
[10] Al-Harizi, *The Book of Taḥkemoni*, 345–6. See below on the El Tránsito Synagogue as a 'private' synagogue.   [11] Y. Baer, *A History of the Jews in Christian Spain*, i. 113.   [12] Ibid. 79.

progressed, the fact that most Spanish Jews chose to live in the Christian kingdoms rather than follow the retreating Muslim forces to the kingdom of Granada is testimony to their recognition that Christian Spain held the promise of a dynamic, albeit problematic, environment.

With the development of a new tax-gathering bureaucracy, several of the Jewish families who had been prominent in Muslim Spain, such as the Ibn Ezras, Ibn Shoshans, Alfakhars, Halevi Abulafias, and Ibn Zadoks, assumed positions of influence as tax-collectors in Christian kingdoms. They were also able to advance the money necessary to conduct the war against the Muslims, and served as accountants and in other occupations that required fiscal skills and literacy. Jews performed the role of physician at many Christian courts, and Jewish courtiers served in a variety of other capacities in Toledo, including Todros ben Joseph Halevi, adviser to Alfonso X; Solomon ibn Zadok of Toledo, ambassador, treasurer, and collector of tribute from Granada; Abraham al-Barchilon, quartermaster and paymaster to Sancho IV; Yosef de Ecija, treasurer to Alfonso XI; and Samuel Halevi Abulafia, treasurer and tax-collector to Pedro the Cruel. Jewish merchants and administrators also served the Christian military orders, the Knights of Santiago, and the Templars, sometimes receiving land, and even in one instance a castle, in return for their services.[13] As in other conquered cities, the presence of courtiers and royal officials should not obscure the fact that Toledo's Jews remained an economically diverse community, containing rich and poor well into the fourteenth century.

The decline in Jewish economic status in Christian Spain was gradual and initially imperceptible. Each region followed a somewhat different trajectory. Jewish landholding remained a reality in Toledo after the city passed from Muslim to Christian rule: Jews continued to own vineyards, mills, and fields outside the city walls. Moreover, the division between urban and rural residence was not sharply drawn. In some instances, Jews acted as landlords on newly conquered rural lands, raising interesting questions of whether the taxes owed on formerly Christian- or Muslim-owned land, now occupied by Jews, should be remitted to the Church or the Crown. In some places Jews were required to pay their new overlords the same taxes and fees they had formerly paid to their Muslim overlords.[14] As the Middle Ages progressed and emperors and popes contested over who 'possessed the Jews', this competition played out locally in Spain.[15] Despite mounting economic restrictions during the twelfth and thirteenth centuries, the gap between the rich and poor in the Jewish community of Toledo began to widen.[16]

---

[13] Ray, 'The *Reconquista* and the Jews'. On Jewish service to the military orders, see id., *The Sephardic Frontier*, 63, 83; on the castle, see Shideler, *A Medieval Catalan Noble Family*, 205–6.

[14] Y. Baer, *A History of the Jews in Christian Spain*, i. 53.

[15] Baron, 'Plenitude of Apostolic Powers and Medieval Jewish Serfdom'.

[16] Assis, 'Poor and Rich in Jewish Society in Mediterranean Spain' (Heb.), 116. The divide between rich and

Many skills were required to maintain Spain during the centuries of warfare between Muslims and Christians. The tasks of reconstruction were best performed by a literate and loyal urban minority like the Jews. Notaries, surveyors, and mapmakers were all in demand to register and reorganize the lands that had been vacated. The construction of bridges, clearing of roads, and restoration of irrigation canals required the services of engineers as well as labourers. Diplomats and go-betweens were in high demand to contract truces and negotiate new arrangements for local rule. Jews were an integral, yet distinct, part of a frontier society in a state of flux. Thus, a mutually beneficial arrangement seemed to be evolving as Christian rule spread.

Many groups were associated with specific occupations—Jews might rise in court to the position of physician or fiscal adviser, the Genoese were sea captains and military instructors, while Muslims in Castile might serve the court as architects and builders—but such distinctions were only partial. Like the Muslims in Castile, the Jews were also skilled craftsmen and artisans. They excelled as tailors, dyers, weavers, and smiths, as many had in Muslim Spain. Their woven fabrics and woollen goods were coveted in the city's markets, some of which were even managed by Jews.

New intergroup relations emerged as a result of the Reconquest. Jewish courtiers were entrusted with the finances of Catholic religious orders or with Christian religious objects given as surety against loans. Jews were authorized to collect the tribute that the Nasrid kingdom of Granada, though theoretically an independent Muslim state, owed to the kingdom of Castile. The frequent visits to Granada necessary to fulfil these tasks exposed them to Muslim art and architecture, while their close social relations with Christians presented many opportunities to gain familiarity with Christian culture and mores.

Kings and counts, in their self-appointed role of protector of the Jews, often opposed the anti-Jewish ordinances of the ecclesiastical and municipal authorities. Kings also occasionally rescued Jewish communities from mob violence.[17] Foremost among the royal motives in sponsoring Jewish settlement in the kingdom of Castile was the fiscal one. The minting of coins for the new authorities was only one part of the programme of economic reconstruction. The redrafting of cadastral registries and the organization of new markets were also necessary. Rulers required credit for new building projects, and both Jewish and Christian moneylenders appear prominently in the records in this connection. An army of auditors was recruited as new taxes were introduced. As Jewish and Christian tax farmers spread out across the countryside, a cadre of Christian lawyers followed. Laws that had existed under the Visigoths had fallen into abeyance in the intervening centuries of Muslim rule, and some of their

poor has been the subject of scholarly discussions since the appearance of Baer's *History of the Jews in Christian Spain*.

[17] For an example of a revolt against the Crown that targeted the Jews, see Y. Baer, *A History of the Jews in Christian Spain*, i. 43; on protection of Jews from mobs by Ferdinand IV, see ibid. 308–10.

clauses were incorporated into the new order that was established.[18] These codes frequently incorporated new clauses to regulate the status of the Jews.

The Jewish population was directly dependent upon royal patronage and protection, and they were popularly perceived as an extension of royal authority and as royal property. A typical assertion of royal power is emphatically enunciated in a decree pronounced at the *cortes* of Valladolid in 1322:

> All Jews who dwell in all the parts of the kingdom should come to dwell in the royal towns which belong to the king. And that no prince nor baron nor noble nor knight nor baroness nor lady nor any other have a Jew or Jewess nor Jewish quarter, but that all Jews be of the king and dwell in his towns. And if a Jew does not want to come, the magistrates and judges or justices of the towns are to have them do it by force.[19]

Cultural Reconfigurations

Toledo was the site of lively cultural exchanges between Muslims, Christians, and Jews, demonstrating that the borders between the intellectual worlds of Andalusia and Christian Iberia were quite porous. These exchanges commenced alongside the demographic shifts. Perhaps in order to maintain its identity in the face of the mounting influence of north European culture, Christian Toledo cultivated its Arabic elements as an expression of indigenous 'Spanish' culture. The persistence of Muslim culture was also a natural phenomenon in the border zones where Muslim and Christian populations lived alongside one another.[20]

The Jewish culture that had reached its peak during the caliphate of Cordoba and the *taifas* was carried by the refugees into Christian Spain. The memory of Andalusia remained a powerful force, injecting a strong dose of cosmopolitanism into their lives. Although the number of Jews who had had access to the more courtly aspects of Andalusian culture was small, they nevertheless continued to set the tone for the new Jewish community. The initial hope of the Jews was to re-establish Andalusia on safer soil. As Ibn Daud proclaimed, they sought to restore 'the poetry and philosophy, the sciences and the Torah that would display the same harmony on the shores of the Tagus as they had on the Guadalquivir'.[21] Arabic-style poetry persisted as a vital part of Hebrew belles-lettres, and courtiers continued to patronize poets. For some Jews, Andalusia, especially in retrospect, represented sophistication, culture, and worldly

---

[18] Glick, 'Reading the *Repartimientos*'. For a general discussion of the Jews in Toledo, see N. Roth, 'New Light on the Jews of Mozarabic Toledo'; on the violent end of several courtiers, see id., 'Two Jewish Courtiers of Alfonso X called Zag (Isaac)'; Gerber, *The Jews of Spain*, ch. 3.

[19] Ray, *The Sephardic Frontier*, 149. On competition for control over the Jews, see Barton, *Contested Treasure*.

[20] For a lively interdisciplinary discussion of the cultural formation of medieval Toledo, see Dodds, Menocal, and Balbale, *The Arts of Intimacy*. Many of their insights pertaining to Christians and Muslims apply equally to Jews.   [21] Ibn Daud, *Sefer ha-Qabbalah*, 97.

power. For others, however, it was associated with decadence, a culture of forced or unnatural elegance, and a social class that was artificial and excessively rationalistic. The question of what Andalusia was and whether its aristocratic political and cultural standard-bearers reflected the broader Jewish community would provoke major controversy among Jews in Toledo and elsewhere in Spain. Some of this controversy was channelled into the battle over the place of philosophy, and the standing of Maimonides in particular, in Jewish life.[22] Crossing the border from Muslim to Christian Spain, both figuratively and literally, meant breaching the walls that separated the two cultural universes. The meeting of the former ethos of Andalusia and the new cultural environment of Christian Spain posed unusual questions.

Arabic remained the language of choice for Jewish intellectuals in the early years of resettlement in Christian Spain. Even when Hebrew and Castilian superseded Arabic, many Jewish cultural artefacts retained an Andalusian spirit.[23] Given their mastery of several languages and more than one culture, the Jews were especially well suited to play a creative role in the hybrid cultural world that was emerging in Toledo. Their involvement in the cultural and scientific activities at the court of King Alfonso X, known as El Sabio (the Learned or the Wise), constituted an important chapter in the development of general Western culture as well as in the intellectual life of the Sephardim.

The discord and tensions generated by the clash of Graeco-Arabic learning and the cultures of Provençal and French Jewry in the Middle Ages have been generally studied within the framework of the Maimonidean controversy. The meeting of Ashkenazi and Sephardi (specifically Andalusian) traditions in Toledo, though less well known, forms another major chapter in Jewish intellectual and social history. The arrival in Toledo in the late thirteenth century of Jacob ben Asher, a giant of Ashkenazi, or Tosafist, hermeneutics, marks a watershed in the penetration of Ashkenazi thought into Jewish cultural life in Spain. He composed *Arba'ah turim*, one of the most important codifications of talmudic law produced in medieval times. He and his descendants dominated traditional Jewish learning in the kingdom of Castile. At the same time as the place of rationalist thought was being debated in Jewish circles in Provence, Castile was also racked by internal debates on the role of philosophy and rationalism in Jewish life. This development unfolded as a new movement of pietism resonated among circles of kabbalists in Catalonia. The kingdom of Castile was not unaffected by the circulation of Jewish mystical texts, and the new mystical ideas reshaped Sephardi traditions. These major ideological debates have dominated the attention of Jewish scholarship, as they correctly should, but the more modest story of the engagement of

---

[22] Septimus, 'Piety and Power in Thirteenth-Century Catalonia'; id., *Hispano-Jewish Culture in Transition*.

[23] For cultural persistence and cultural memory in the Hebrew poetry and prose of the eleventh to the thirteenth centuries, see Decter, *Iberian Jewish Literature*. Decter employs current literary theory to highlight the Arab and northern European (especially French) motifs in the writings of al-Harizi and Jacob ben Eleazar.

Sephardi translators in the courts of Christian Spain, particularly that of Alfonso X, sheds new light on the place of Toledo's Jews as mediators in the cultural development of western Europe.

Sephardim as Cultural Mediators in the Court of Alfonso X

Toledo is often seen as the city most responsible for the transmission of Islamic scientific knowledge to Christian Europe, although it was not the monopoly of a single city nor the work of one individual. The great age of transmission began under the leadership of Archbishop Raymond of Toledo (1125–51); it flourished in the thirteenth century under the patronage of Archbishop Rodrigo Jiménez de Rada (1208–47) in Toledo; and it reached its apogee in the second half of the thirteenth century under Alfonso X. Burgos and Seville were also important centres of transmission, but Toledo outshone them both, mainly because of its library—which housed thousands of Arabic translations of classical Greek philosophical and scientific works—and the personal interests of Alfonso. Jewish engagement with this cultural transmission was also centred in Toledo.

Toledo's clergy began to engage in translation activities soon after the conquest of the city. Teams of translators were commissioned to translate the Arabic texts into Latin. Islamic learning in science, literature, philosophy, and mathematics spread northward across the borders, contributing to a revival of learning in medieval Europe. The multilingual Jews found a natural niche in this undertaking. Moreover, translation activities were not new to them. Jewish participation in translation projects in Spain went back to the Umayyad court of Cordoba and the *taifas*. Instruction in Greek, Arabic, and Hebrew alongside philosophy, science, rhetoric, and medicine was a standard part of the humanistic Jewish curriculum.[24] Knowledge of Latin was soon added to the linguistic repertoire of Jewish scholars.

King Alfonso was a multifaceted man of enormous intellectual energy and organizing talents, considered by many to be the creator of the Castilian language. In contrast to this exalted position in Spanish history, his place in Sephardi history is contradictory. On the one hand, he was a broad-minded humanist who appreciated the vast library of Arabic knowledge at his disposal. He associated comfortably with learned Jews, recruiting them for service in his court and his treasury. Although he failed to achieve one of his chief goals, succession to the position of Holy Roman Emperor after the death of his cousin Frederick II, he succeeded in transforming Toledo into a

---

[24] For the Jewish curriculum in twelfth-century Toledo, which reveals the interplay of Jewish and Arabic cultural ideals and the humanistic education attained by Jewish men, see 'A Medieval Curriculum of Advanced Jewish and Secular Studies', in Stillman, *The Jews of Arab Lands*, 226–8. Judah ibn Tibbon's ethical will assumes that Jewish physicians would posses a wide-ranging library and have broad intellectual interests ('Judah ibn Tibbon's Letter of Admonition to His Son', in *Letters of Jews through the Ages*, i. 156–65).

metropolis for the transmission of classical culture, cementing his reputation as a cultural titan in Europe. He was also the compiler of one of the most important literary works of medieval Spain, the *Cantigas de Santa Maria*, a collection of hundreds of tales, musical scores, and artistic miniatures in praise of the Virgin Mary. The collection constitutes a work of major literary and social importance in the development of the Castilian language and Spanish culture. However, it is riddled with anti-Jewish imagery. Alfonso was also responsible for the promulgation of the major Castilian law code, *Las siete partidas*, which contains several significant anti-Jewish clauses. He founded a school to teach missionaries to proselytize more effectively among Jews and Muslims, and proselytizing, rather than intellectual curiosity, probably motivated his sponsorship of translations of the Talmud and the Quran into Castilian.

Alfonso's translation team included five Jews, four Spanish Christians, four Italians, and a Muslim convert to Christianity. They generally worked in pairs—usually a Jew who knew both Arabic and the vernacular and a Christian who knew the vernacular and Latin—which transformed the translation process into a sort of medieval colloquium.[25] Abraham ibn Daud collaborated in this fashion with Archdeacon Dominicus Gundissalinus in Toledo on the translation of a portion of the philosophical encyclopedia of Avicenna, and, according to Jacob ben Makhir ibn Tibbon, a similar translation process from Hebrew into Latin took place in Provence:

> Thus begins the treatise of Profait of Marseilles [Jacob ben Makhir] concerning the Quadrant, which he composed for the discovery of whatever might be learned using the Astrolabe—translated from Hebrew into Latin by Magister Armengaud Blaise, following [Profait's] oral instruction, in Montpellier.[26]

The precise extent of Alfonso's involvement in the translations is unclear. The conventional view of him as an active participant, an image that his admirers eagerly disseminated, seems scarcely plausible given his busy military schedule. The introductions to several of the translations attributed to Alfonso claim that he actively engaged in the process and was responsible for the composition of the translation team. His personal interests are also reflected in the choice of texts selected from the wide variety of Arabic and classical works available: some reflect courtly tastes, such as treatises on falconry, hunting, and chess; others are of philosophical and scientific interest, such as treatises on ethics and astronomy; works of secular Arab cultural significance (*adab*, or belles-lettres) are also included. Judah ben Moses Cohen, Alfonso's personal physician who was well versed in several languages, recommended *Libro de las cruces* and *El libro de las juicios de las estrellas* as worthy of translation, two works of astrology, a subject that was of particular interest to Alfonso.[27]

---

[25] For the scientific translations, see Glick, 'Science in Medieval Spain'.
[26] See Stern, *Philosophy and Rabbinic Culture*, 49.
[27] Proctor, 'The Scientific Works of the Court of Alfonso X'.

Alfonso's interest in the translation of Greek and Arabic classics began while he was still the heir apparent. Jews were already involved in this activity. The first known translation executed under his auspices was a scientific book on gems known as the *Lapidary*, or *Lapidario*, commissioned between 1243 and 1250. A later prologue to this work reveals the Jewish involvement in several stages of the translation project:

> And he [Alfonso] obtained it [the Lapidary] from a Jew who held it hidden, who neither wished to make use of it himself nor that any other should profit therefrom. And when he [Alfonso] had this book in his possession, he caused another Jew, who was his physician to read it, and he was called *Yhuda Mosca el menor* and he was learned in the art of astrology and understood well both Arabic and Latin. And when through this Jew his physician he understood the value and great profit which was in the book, he commanded him to translate it from Arabic into the Castilian language.[28]

In a few cases, he required a second translation decades after the first in order to improve its accuracy:

> Master Fernando of Toledo translated this book from Arabic into romance at the command of the most noble king Alfonso . . . in the fourth year that he reigned. And afterwards he commanded Master Bernardo *el Arabico* and Don Abraham his physician [*alfaqui*] to translate it a second time in Burgos better and more completely, in the twenty-sixth year of his reign [AD 1277].[29]

Alfonso was involved in the translations for most of his life, and particularly intensively during the 1250s and again in the 1270s.

Latin was most often the target language of translation since it was the common language of Christian Europe, but Alfonso also insisted that works be translated into Castilian. An intermediate language was also frequently necessary. This was often Hebrew or one of the vernacular languages of the Iberian peninsula (Castilian, Catalan, and Gallego or Portuguese). Here Jews could apply their multilingualism to advantage, translating from the original Arabic into one of the intermediary languages, and the Christian half of the pair could then translate it into Latin. This method of translating entailed a great deal of interaction between the members of the multi-religious and multinational team: difficult terms had to be discussed in order to capture the appropriate nuance. Often new words needed to be invented, particularly scientific, mathematical, and technical terms. A mixture of Arabic, Hebrew, and Latin terms was pressed into service, thereby greatly expanding the vocabulary of Castilian.

Alfonsine translations are frequently literal because of the rudimentary state of the Castilian language and following contemporary norms of translation. But the choice

---

[28] See ibid. 19. The mechanics of translation are also described in N. Roth, 'Jewish Translators at the Court of Alfonso X'; Proctor, *Alfonso X of Castile*, 113–39; Harvey, 'The Alfonsine School of Translators'. Most of the major translators were not Jewish. One of the most important pre-Alfonsine translators, Gerard of Cremona, personally translated or led a group that translated over seventy books from Arabic manuscripts, including the works of Galen, Archimedes, Aristotle, Hippocrates, and the philosophers al-Farabi and al-Kindi.

[29] *Los libros del saber de astronomia*, cited in Proctor, 'The Scientific Works of the Court of Alfonso X', 16; see also N. Roth, 'Jewish Collaborators in Alfonso's Scientific Work.'

of the Castilian vernacular as a final product of the translation team was historically significant. By doing so, Alfonso and his team reached a much wider audience and transformed Castilian into a literary language. The culture of Spain thereby took a great leap forward, as the translations served to increase the rate of literacy in the Castilian-speaking population.

The names of many Jews involved in translation are known. Four of them—Yehuda ben Moses Cohen, Isaac ben Sid, Samuel Halevi, and Master Fernando—are referred to as 'of Toledo'. Isaac ben Sid was a cantor and merchant in Toledo and was learned in astronomy, astrology, architecture, and mathematics. He was responsible for translating treatises on the construction and use of the astrolabe and quadrant. Samuel Halevi served as personal physician to Alfonso's wife, Queen Violante, and accompanied the royal family to Perpignan. He was reportedly in attendance during Alfonso's audience with the pope. Another Jew in the team of translators was Abraham Alfaquim, who served as astronomer and physician to Alfonso and his son Sancho IV, appearing in the royal records in 1293 and 1294. Apparently he was the attending physician at Sancho's death in 1295.

One of the most famous works sponsored by Alfonso became known as the Alfonsine Tables, which could be used to compute the movements of the sun, moon, and planets. They were based on the work of an eleventh-century Cordoban astronomer called al-Zarkali and updated and corrected sometime between 1262 and 1272. The long Castilian introduction includes the authors' solar and lunar observations in Toledo for an entire year. They became the most popular astronomical tables in Europe and were so highly regarded that a copy was presented to the explorer Christopher Columbus by the Portuguese Jewish scientist and courtier Abraham Zacut.

Jewish fascination with astronomy was not a new phenomenon. Like the Muslims, Jews worked extensively in the field both theoretically and practically. Members of both religions were drawn to the study of astronomy since lunar calculations and the observation of astronomical phenomena were essential in the determination of their religious calendar. During Abbasid times, the Arabs had delighted in the construction of astronomical instruments and tables, both for the observation of the stars and for navigational purposes. Many of the Arabs' astronomical theories were buttressed by findings in the mathematical works they had discovered in India and translated in Baghdad. These scientific works circulated in various centres of Islamic learning in Spain and North Africa.

The treatises on astronomy and astrology were of special interest to Alfonso. While the merit of some of the works he selected is questionable, especially the works of astrology, the impact of the Alfonsine Tables alone earned him the epithets 'amador de los sciences et de sabers' ('lover of science and wisdom') and 'rex excelsus qui scientiam diligit' ('the high king who loves science'). As Thomas Glick has pointed out, many of the translations of the scientific works were more than simple translations.

The translations of the *Libro de las estrellas fijas* (a treatise on the armillary sphere) and the *Libro de la alcora* ('Book of the Celestial Sphere') included fresh observations by Isaac ben Sid of lunar eclipses in 1263, 1265, and 1266. These can justifiably be considered updated scientific treatises that constitute important works of medieval astronomy in their own right.[30]

Despite working closely with Jews and relying upon their medical talents, Alfonso harboured many decidedly anti-Jewish attitudes. Perhaps no work has been more closely associated with him, especially in the development of the Spanish language, than the *Cantigas de Santa Maria*. According to Albert Bagby, Alfonso envisaged himself as a 'royal troubadour' or as the Virgin's own troubadour in compiling this work.[31] The negative portrait of Jews that emerges from the *Cantigas* reflects the anti-Jewish stereotyping of medieval Spanish society shared by its cultured king. Those modern scholars who praise Alfonso and point to his relationship with his Jewish translators as proof of a spirit of tolerance in Toledo tend to understate the anti-Jewish material in the *Cantigas* and the atmosphere prevailing in the society of its authors and artists.[32]

Jews in the *Cantigas de Santa Maria*

The *Cantigas de Santa Maria* consists of 420 tales or songs relating to the Virgin Mary that constitute a personal statement of Alfonso's devotion to her. This literary masterpiece includes musical scores and magnificent miniature illustrations. While Alfonso was not the sole author of the work, he probably conceived of its overall design and wrote parts of it. The work has been described as 'the most sumptuous literary artifact' of thirteenth-century Iberia.[33] It is also notable for its use of Castilian.

The *Cantigas* draws upon a corpus of material on Jews and Judaism then circulating in Iberia. Jews appear as protagonists in forty *cantigas*, or approximately a tenth of the material, as well as in numerous incidental or passing references. The scattered references to Jews are wholly gratuitous comments that are interjected in narratives that otherwise contain no Jewish characters or themes. When Jews appear as protagonists, they are portrayed as Christ-killers (in the largest number of references), disparagers of the Virgin and Jesus, maligners of Christianity, traitors and sorcerers, and murderers of Christian children in league with the devil. They are represented as avaricious people

---

[30] Proctor, 'The Scientific Works of the Court of Alfonso X', 92; id., *Alfonso X of Castile*, 113–39; see also Harvey, 'The Alfonsine School of Translators'; N. Roth, 'Two Jewish Courtiers of Alfonso X called Zag (Isaac)'.   [31] Bagby, 'The Jew in the *Cantigas* of Alfonso X, el Sabio'.

[32] For example, this side of Alfonso X is absent from the enthusiastic tributes to the tolerance of Alfonso's Toledo in Dodds, Menocal, and Balbale, *The Arts of Intimacy*.

[33] See Carpenter, 'The Portrayal of the Jew in Alfonso the Learned's Cantigas de Santa Maria'. On Alfonso's authorship and participation, see Snow, 'The Central Rôle of the Troubadour *Persona* of Alfonso X in the *Cantigas de Santa Maria*'; for an analysis of the Jewish references in the *Cantigas*, see Bagby, 'The Jew in the *Cantigas* of Alfonso X, El Sabio'; for samples of the illustrations, see Patton, *Art of Estrangement*.

who are 'saved' from eternal damnation only after recognizing the 'true' faith and converting to Christianity. *Cantiga* 4 recounts the attempts of a Jewish father to kill his son because he has taken Communion with Christian children; *Cantiga* 6 depicts a Jew killing his child in response to the child's praise of the Virgin Mary. Perhaps no representation of Jews is more insidious than *Cantiga* 12, where the Jews are portrayed crucifying the wax image of a Christian child in a re-enactment of the crucifixion, which sparks a pogrom. The Jew in *Cantiga* 34 involved in the theft of an icon of the Virgin is depicted with an enormous nose and a large beard, and appears to be leering as he engages in his evil activity. The illustrations form an integral part of the work and buttress the alleged negative qualities of the Jew embodied in the collected tales. Even when the literary text does not emphasize the nefarious powers of the Jew, the Jew's demonic associations are emphasized in the illustrations, as in those to the tale of Theophilus in *Cantiga* 3. In *Cantiga* 85, a Jew converts to Christianity after the Virgin reveals to him the rewards and punishments of Heaven and Hell. To emphasize the salvific quality of belief in the Christian faith, *Cantiga* 89 sings of the conversion of a Jewish woman who is on the verge of death in childbirth but is saved, along with her infant, after she invokes the Virgin and converts to Christianity (Plate 1).

The *Cantigas* is a classic of medieval literary invention as well as a triumphalist statement of religious faith. Its composition was intended to celebrate Alfonso's victory over the Muslims at Murcia. Its anti-Judaic content is admittedly secondary to its principal objective of spreading the cult of Mary, but, as in other medieval narratives, the Virgin's mercy is juxtaposed to the Jews' malevolence and her power extends to non-Christians as well as Christians. Its intended message is clear: those who honour Mary are saved, while those who reject her are doomed to a terrible fate.

The inclusion of the blood libel in the *Cantigas* attests to the doctrine's growing familiarity and popularity. According to Dwayne Carpenter, the depiction of the desecration of the host in the *Cantigas* was primarily intended to emphasize the mysterious and miraculous nature of the Eucharist.[34] Transubstantiation, a new doctrine promulgated by the Vatican in the thirteenth century, was difficult for the average Christian to understand and accept. By celebrating the wafer and demonizing the Jews, Alfonso assisted in the popularization of one of the most devastating canards in the antisemitic arsenal. In his great legal code, *Las siete partidas*, Alfonso did not repudiate the growing anti-Jewish violence that the doctrines of blood libel and desecration of the host were fomenting. On the contrary, the code required that the veracity of any accusation of Jewish ritual murder or host desecration be determined by the king, the implication being that sometimes the Jews actually did commit such atrocities.[35] Nor did Alfonso repudiate the new ecclesiastical proselytizing campaign, arguing instead

---

[34] Carpenter, *Alfonso X and the Jews*, 64–5. On the general cultural milieu, see Burns (ed.), *Emperor of Culture*.
[35] Carpenter, *Alfonso X and the Jews*.

that conversion of Jews should be accomplished through persuasion and good example, not coercion.

In the illuminations created at Alfonso's court, the depictions of Jews were often contradictory, probably reflecting the daily reality that Jews confronted. On the one hand their features are stereotyped: most Jews are depicted in an antisemitic fashion, recognizable by their distinctive conical headgear and beards. At the same time Jews interacted on a daily basis with Christians in the market and workplace as well as in the court. In one famous manuscript from Alfonso's time, the *Libro de ajedrez, dados y tablas*, the image of the Jewish chess player contrasts strikingly with the courtly mien of the Christian (Plate 3). Another illustration depicts a Jew playing dice with a Muslim in which both figures appear as part of groups of Jews and Muslims, seated together in a courtyard (Plate 2). While the two groups of players are clearly interacting, the positioning of the Jews, as well as their stance and gestures, suggest their inferior status.

In the last years of his rule, Alfonso X turned against his Jewish courtiers. In 1279 he ordered that his Jewish tax-farmers be imprisoned, hanging Don Çag de la Maleha, one of the most talented of them. Not long after that, the Jews were incarcerated in their synagogue in Toledo and forced to pay an exorbitant levy to obtain their release. Whether these hostile actions were sparked by his suspicions that the Jews were involved in intrigues against him is unclear, but they show the ambiguous and unpredictable attitude of the monarch towards his Jewish subjects.

As Christian power consolidated and Islamic rule retreated to a small enclave in the southern kingdom of Granada, official ecclesiastical policies turned increasingly triumphalist. New assaults on the tenets of Judaism, the integrity of the Talmud, and the rabbinic tradition in general were launched in several circles. These attacks constituted an increasingly prominent part of general European culture in the High Middle Ages. Occasional assaults on Jews were accompanied by legislation limiting their economic activities and compelling them to attend Christianizing sermons in their synagogues and to participate in religious disputations. Learned treatises, often composed by converts from Judaism and Islam, offered blistering attacks to aid in the new proselytizing efforts.[36] Papal legislation aimed at separating the Jewish population from Christians and emphasizing their humble and dejected state increased.

Most medieval European monarchs attempted to maintain a balance between adherence to the anti-Jewish demands of the religious authorities and the protection of the Jews as a royal asset. Although the Spanish kings pursued a policy of protecting Jews for longer than many others in Europe, they could not permanently withstand

---

[36] For the role of the disputation in thirteenth-century ecclesiastical policies and the honing of the defences of the Jewish community, see Berger, *The Jewish–Christian Debate in the High Middle Ages*; Chazan, *Barcelona and Beyond*; J. Cohen, *The Friars and the Jews*; id., *Living Letters of the Law*; Lasker, *Jewish Philosophical Polemics against Christianity in the Middle Ages*; for an alternative interpretation of evolving Christian attitudes towards the Jews, see Yuval, *Two Nations in Your Womb*.

ecclesiastical and popular pressure to implement new restrictions on them. A sustained tug of war between popes, kings, municipalities, and nobles over the status of the Jews animated the politics of the High Middle Ages. Thus, for instance, Pope Honorius III became irate when Ferdinand III (1217–52), conqueror of Seville and Cordoba, did not require Jews to wear a special badge and distinctive clothing. When the pope demanded an explanation for the king's disregard of papal instructions, Ferdinand warned that Castilian Jews would flee to Muslim Granada if the humiliating restrictions were enforced. Such an exodus, the king claimed, would be disastrous for the revenues of his kingdom. In this instance, the king prevailed. However, Alfonso X justified the application of discriminatory papal legislation regarding Jews on social grounds:

Whereas in certain provinces of the Church the difference in their clothes sets the Jews and the Saracens apart from the Christians, in certain other lands there has arisen confusion that no differences are noticeable. Thus it sometimes happens that by mistake Christians have intercourse with Jewish or Saracen women, and Jews or Saracens with Christian women. Therefore, lest these people, under cover of an error, find an excuse for the grave sin of such intercourse, we decree that these people of either sex, and in all the Christian lands, and at all times, shall easily be distinguished from the rest of the population by the quality of their clothes.[37]

Alfonso's explanation suggests that Jews were often still indistinguishable from their neighbours in mid-thirteenth-century Castile.

Royal opposition to the implementation of the regulations provided a convenient opportunity to collect special fees from the Jews. Pope Honorius IV set out his cynical reasons for waiving the discriminatory legislation, conceding that compelling Jews to wear distinguishing signs could have a negative impact on the royal coffers. In a letter to the archbishop of Toledo he declared:

On behalf of our dearest son in Christ, Ferdinand, the illustrious King of Castile, as well as on behalf of yourself, we have been informed that the Jews who reside in the Kingdom of Castile are so seriously wrought over that which has been decided with regard to them in the general council in the matter of wearing a sign that some of them choose rather to flee to the Moors than to be burdened with such a sign. Others conspire because of this, and make secret arrangements. As a result, the King, whose income in large measure derives from these very Jews, can hardly raise his expenses, and serious misfortune may befall the Kingdom. Wherefore we have been humbly petitioned on behalf of this King as well as yourself, that our permission be given you to set aside the execution of this edict, since you cannot proceed to its enforcement without great trouble.[38]

The logic of the pope's argument was temporarily accepted. At the same time, Jews were prohibited from wearing costly garments lest they be mistaken, as occasionally occurred, for members of the nobility. The illustrations of distinguishing Jewish headgear and outer garments in the *Cantigas* suggest that discriminatory Jewish dress was

---

[37] *Siete partidas*, cited in Carpenter, *Alfonso X and the Jews*, 99–100.
[38] Pope Honorius VI to Archbishop of Toledo, in Grayzel, *The Church and the Jews in the XIIIth Century*, i. 151.

familiar to observers in Castile by the late thirteenth century. While the Jewish leadership opposed the discriminatory regulations imposed upon them by the government, they simultaneously attempted to restrain and discipline members of their community who comported themselves like royalty, on the grounds that ostentatious clothing was apt to arouse the envy of their neighbours and possibly lead to bloodshed. They further argued that a show of affluence provoked discord within the Jewish community. At the same time, the gap between rich and poor widened. Oppression and humiliation required more subtle responses to buoy the spirits of a proud, yet beleaguered, community.

Hebrew Illuminated Manuscripts as Art and Self-Defence

Some time in the late twelfth or the early thirteenth century, Hebrew illuminated manuscripts began to be commissioned in the Jewish communities of Castile. The earliest known manuscript is an illuminated Bible produced in Toledo, dating from 1197/8. The largest number of illuminations date from thirteenth-century Toledo and fourteenth-century Catalonia. By the late thirteenth century Toledo, and a number of places in Catalonia, were producing spectacular Hebrew illuminated manuscripts. Toledo abounded with artists and copyists, translators and scientists. It remained a brilliant artistic centre until the mid-fourteenth century. The most significant artistic developments occurred among the Jews during the reigns of Ferdinand III and Alfonso X in Castile and under James II (1291–1327), Alfonso VI (1327–36), and Pedro IV (1337) in the united kingdoms of Castile and León. But after the devastating persecutions associated with the Black Death in 1348, the Jewish community of Toledo could no longer afford the same level of artistic production, and fine manuscript production moved to Catalonia.

The Hebrew illuminated manuscript tradition testifies to new social realities in the Jewish community and points to the expansion of a new consumer group of merchants, courtiers, and other literate Jews of means. Illuminated halakhic codices, scientific treatises, the works of Maimonides, and Haggadot were coveted by Jewish scholars and the new elite of tax-farmers. The widening market for luxury items among the Jews was paralleled among the Christians. Christian production of illuminated manuscripts also increased in the thirteenth century to meet the growing demand for books among the military and religious orders, the recently established universities, and a new class of Christian urban consumers. Jewish narrative art began at about the same time that Christian illustrated manuscript art left the precincts of the monastery scriptorium and became a popular art form. Christian scribes generally worked in groups, since wealthy institutions, such as royal courts, cathedrals, or monasteries, were able to support writing workshops. In contrast, Jewish book production tended to be a private affair. Most Hebrew books were commissioned by their users, with scribes and patrons working closely with one another. Sometimes Jewish scribes were commissioned by a wealthy patron to produce a book for a specific occasion, such as a marriage. Like the arts in general, the Hebrew illuminations display a synthesis of artistic and cultural traditions and offer striking evidence of a blending of older Iberian motifs from Muslim Spain with newer motifs from Christian Spain. Illuminated Hebrew manuscripts represent both an appreciation for the aesthetic that is commonly associated with Sephardi civilization and the emerging confidence and talent of the Jews to convert a valued popular medium of artistic expression for their own internal polemical purpose. The illustrations served to emphasize the Jews' unique understanding of their heritage, as a defence against new anti-Jewish attacks, and to counteract the mounting Christological interpretations of Jewish texts.

Two distinctive styles of Hebrew manuscript illustration existed in medieval Toledo: a richly narrative and representational style and an older aniconic or non-figurative Islamic style.[39] The two styles were also present in Spanish Christian art, where the pictorial style was associated with Gothic or French taste and the aniconic style recalled the era of Muslim power. Both styles sometimes even appeared within the same work of art. Christian pictorial models were readily accessible to Jewish scribes as monasteries and the nobility would often deposit their illuminated manuscripts with Jewish moneylenders as collateral for a loan. Jews would thus be able to scrutinize Christian art closely in a safe (i.e. protected and private) setting. But a Jewish scribe did not require the close study of a Christian manuscript in order to learn the symbols and representations of the majority culture. Christian symbols and artistic motifs were ubiquitous: they were frequently displayed publicly on bridges or buildings. As a result, a shared repertoire of biblical pictorial traditions existed among Jews and Christians in Toledo. The use of the artistic vocabulary of the majority culture in a Hebrew illuminated manuscript does not necessarily mean that the artist in question was Christian or an assimilated Jew. Since cross-cultural borrowing and cultural fusion were common phenomena in all the arts in Christian Spain, their appearance among the Jews is not surprising. Jewish artists and craftsmen were also sensitive to the fact that Arabic modes of expression continued to represent sophistication and refinement. Wherever the residents of Toledo gazed, multiple cultural traditions and influences greeted them, whether in a single monument such as a synagogue or church, in an illustrated psalter, or in a luxury object such as an ivory box. This cultural hybridity was the norm rather than the exception. The opulent tastes of the Muslim Nasrid court in Granada also continued to be influential in shaping artistic conceptions and techniques, especially in the cities of Seville and Toledo. According to Jerrilynn Dodds, the blending of the Islamic and the Gothic in one work of art became a trademark of Spanish

---

[39] One famous example of an aniconic or non-representational Bible decoration from thirteenth-century Toledo is the Marseilles Bible by Isaac ben Israel. See Sed-Rajna, 'Hebrew Illuminated Manuscripts from the Iberian Peninsula'; ead., 'Toledo or Burgos?'.

culture.⁴⁰ The fact that Jews in Spain also display this trait in their own arts is another indication of their familiarity with the cultures around them.

The illuminations that Jews commissioned for their Bibles, Haggadot, and other manuscripts were intended solely for internal consumption. They could therefore safely and conveniently provide an effective solace against the increasing attacks on Jews and Judaism. The specific biblical texts selected for illustration were frequently those with midrashic interpretations that had not been appropriated by Church authorities or popular preachers and were consequently devoid of Christological connotations. Some may have had oblique allusions to contemporary polemics that the Jews were constrained from addressing openly and freely. One of the most popular subjects was the Exodus story.

Few illuminated Hebrew manuscripts have survived the ravages of the Middle Ages, and the full range of Jewish artistic expression can consequently only be surmised. Hebrew manuscripts often suffered the same violent fate as their owners or were lost in the periodic confiscations of Hebrew books. Laments over the loss of personal libraries often appear in the introductory remarks by scholars or scribes. Most of the extant Hebrew manuscripts produced in thirteenth-century Toledo were the handiwork of several generations of one family, that of Israel Hasofer. A few colophons from other Spanish centres of manuscript production, such as Saragossa or Barcelona, have also been preserved. Some are fairly elaborate, occasionally even offering unusual personal data, thereby helping to place the Sephardi illuminations within their proper chronological and geographical context.⁴¹

The production of an illuminated manuscript was a complicated process that required a number of different talents, often from different people, with the illustrations added at the final stage. The division between scribe and illuminator was not hard and fast: for some manuscripts they were the same person; for others, the scribe would leave space for the illuminations. It was not uncommon for a Jewish scholar to serve as the scribe of a manuscript while its illustrations were executed in a Christian workshop.⁴² It was once widely assumed that the Jewish patrons of Hebrew illuminated

---

⁴⁰ Dodds, 'The Mudéjar Tradition in Architecture'; ead., 'The Arts of al-Andalus'. For a more extended discussion of the arts and architecture of Toledo in the thirteenth and fourteenth centuries, see Dodds, Menocal, and Balbale, *The Arts of Intimacy*.

⁴¹ It is often difficult to ascertain the identity of those who worked on a manuscript, since personal data, including the names of the scribe, illustrator, donor, or owner, and date and place of copying, were ordinarily placed in a colophon at the end of the codex. Over time the back pages were likely to be lost, taking the information with them. Spanish Jewish scribes frequently obtained commissions outside Spain and, in the process, transported their local customs elsewhere, making identification of the provenance of a manuscript difficult. It is also often difficult to ascertain whether the illuminator of a particular work was Christian or Jewish and whether the illustrator served as scribe as well. The use of distinctive decorative motifs as a 'trademark' was limited to only a few of the known Hebrew scribes, rendering it easier to identify the artist, the scribe, and the manuscript's place and date of composition.

⁴² On the collaboration of Jewish and Christian artists in the production of the famous fourteenth-century

manuscripts commissioned Christian artists since the illustrations of Hebrew works did not bear a distinctive 'Jewish' style. It has also been suggested that Jews were unable to produce representational art as a result of biblical prohibitions. Today it is generally acknowledged that Jewish scribes and illuminators were familiar with Christian manuscripts and freely borrowed from Christian pictorial models that were, in many cases, part of a shared culture.[43]

Traditional Jewish artistic styles, such as the decorative use of tiny Hebrew lettering, known as micrography, were employed to create designs and shapes (Plate 4). Micrography dates back to the production of the Masoretic texts. The earliest surviving examples of micrographic illustrations, dating from the ninth century, were found in the Cairo *geniza*. It was once generally assumed that Jews did not depict the human form, in obedience to the biblical prohibition: 'Thou shall not make unto thee a graven image.... Thou shalt not bow down unto them, nor serve them' (Exod. 20: 4–5). This was more the case among the Ashkenazim than the Sephardim. At least one medieval Ashkenazi artist rendered the human figures in the margins of his manuscript with animal features, such as birds' heads with pronounced beaks (the Bird's Head Haggadah from southern Germany housed in the Israel Museum).[44] This meticulousness is unusual, however; most rabbinic leaders condoned human representations, limiting their prohibition to representations or personifications of God. In his *Mishneh torah*, Maimonides clearly distinguished between two-dimensional art, which was permitted, and three-dimensional art, which was prohibited:

It is forbidden to make images [for the sake of beauty] even though they are not used for idolatry.... This [prohibition] includes even objects of gold and silver which are made only for beauty, lest those who worship idols be misled by them and think they are for purposes of idolatry.... However, this prohibition against fashioning images for beauty applies only to the human form and therefore we do not fashion a human form in wood or plaster or in stone. This holds when the form projects.... However, if the form is sunken, or of a medium like that of images on panels and tablets or those woven in fabric, it is permitted.[45]

Some objects employed in Muslim rituals raised specific questions that were not easily resolved by this Maimonidean distinction. As Jews moved from Muslim to Christian Spain, the question of recycling Muslim artefacts arose. One interesting case is

---

illuminated manuscript of Maimonides' *Moreh nevukhim* housed in Copenhagen, see Sed-Rajna, 'Hebrew Manuscripts of Fourteenth-Century Catalonia'. Her discussion includes consideration of the composition and chronology of this work in relation to a larger group of Christian and Jewish manuscripts. On Menahem Bezalel, the Jewish court physician to Pedro IV who commissioned the work, as well as the probable identity of the artist, Ferrer Bassa, who apparently died in the Black Death in 1348, see Alcoy i Pedros, 'The Artist of the Marginal Decorations of the "Copenhagen Maimonides"'. Menahem also died in 1348, perhaps also as a result of the plague.

[43] Bland, *The Artless Jew*. [44] See M. M. Epstein, *The Medieval Haggadah*, 19–128.
[45] Maimonides, *Mishneh torah*, 'Laws of the Worship of Stars and Their Statutes', 3: 10–11.

recorded in the responsa of Rabbi Asher ben Yehiel (c.1250–1327). The Jews of Toledo enquired about using decorative Muslim prayer rugs as wall hangings in the synagogue. In his reply Asher ben Yehiel demonstrated an unusual degree of knowledge of Muslim ritual, especially for a rabbi who had immigrated to Spain from Germany. His responsum also preserves rare details of medieval synagogue interiors, perhaps alluding to some specific structure in Toledo:

> You inquired about the matter of the small mat which is called *sajjada* in Arabic, on which it is the custom of the Muslims to pray and which bears an image resembling a black weight—whether it is permitted to hang it in the synagogue next to the ark, one on each side, and to pray facing them, even though God forbid that a single Jew should pray with intention toward something forbidden. I inquired about this matter on your behalf and investigated it, and it became clear to me that in Toledo they enacted a prohibition against placing such a mat in the synagogue for seating; certainly it is forbidden to hang it beside the ark. It is said that the black image formed in it is the depiction of the place to which they go [the *ka'aba*] to celebrate in their land [Mecca]. There are also those who say it contains an image . . . and that it is their custom to pray on it and to prostrate on it during prayer. It has also been said to me that the mat is therefore called a *sajjada* because they prostrate on it. And since this is the case, it appears to me that it is forbidden to hang it in the synagogue . . . certainly on either side of the ark. One must remove it from the synagogue so that no trace of it will remain there. Why should we place a thing like this that was prepared for their prayers in our synagogue?[46]

Despite this ruling, the rug apparently remained in use, its problematic depiction of the *ka'aba* modified through the addition of woven flowers. When Asher ben Yehiel's son, Rabbi Judah ben Asher (1270–1349), was called upon to adjudicate the matter anew, he responded: 'Concerning the matter of the small mat about which you asked, I have not seen my father's responsum and I do not know why he prohibited it. If it were because of idolatry, because there may be people who worship it, then it is forbidden for eternity if it comes into the hands of a Jew.'[47]

Aesthetic appreciation was widely acknowledged as one aspect of Mediterranean Jewish worship. Spanish rabbis in particular proclaimed the importance of decorative ritual objects and sacred texts, 'pleasant for their beauty and the splendour of their scripts and parchments'. Art was also a powerful educational tool, particularly in societies where literacy was generally restricted to the males. In addition, art could serve as a propaganda tool or as an ideological weapon with which Jews might defend themselves against the mounting conversionist campaigns they confronted. The illustrations in the Passover Haggadot could serve as precisely such a pedagogical tool for women and children and as a defence mechanism in the increasingly ideological battles being mounted against the Jews. Its illustrations of carefully selected texts with powerful iconography could convey a compelling message in the privacy of one's home.

---

[46] Asher ben Yehiel, responsum, in *Jewish Texts on the Visual Arts*, 48.
[47] Judah ben Asher, responsum, ibid. 49.

'Subversive' illustrations would be safest in a private book, away from the prying eyes of Church authorities, rather than one more widely accessible in the synagogue. As assaults on the Jewish faith intensified during the thirteenth and fourteenth centuries, the book most consistently used for such defensive purposes was the Passover Haggadah.

The ritual recitation of the Exodus story was originally included in the synagogue prayer book and did not emerge as a separate illustrated book until the thirteenth century. Precisely at that time, the art of illumination was developing in the Jewish communities of Germany and Spain; however, only about two dozen manuscripts or fragments of Spanish illuminated Haggadot have survived. The Haggadah is a richly dramatic but relatively short work consisting of blessings, biblical texts, historical narratives, triumphal songs, and rabbinic discussions of the Exodus story from the Mishnah. Over the centuries, Jewish communities have appended their own material, such as folksongs and illustrations, to the original text. One index of the Haggadah's popularity is that it is among the earliest printed Hebrew books (Guadalajara, 1482; Castelmaggiore, 1486) and has repeatedly appeared all over the world with emendations, additions, and original illustrations.[48] Since the materials that can be included in the Haggadah are not rigidly prescribed, new songs and texts continue to be added.

The recounting of God's redemption of the Israelites from slavery that is at the heart of the Passover celebration is meant to be read aloud by participants of all ages. Therefore, the text of the Haggadah is fully vocalized. The high point of the holiday observance is a festive meal (the Seder) during which the story of Israelite slavery, the enumeration of miraculously inflicted plagues upon the stubborn Egyptians, and the hasty departure of the Israelite slaves are recounted and sometimes re-enacted.

The Passover Seder is replete with symbolic food prominently displayed and consumed for pedagogical and commemorative purposes. The Haggadah illustrations often included not only details of the Exodus story but also representations of the elaborate preparations and the gathering around the table. These helped to explain the festival's strict requirements and to instruct Jewish women in the intricacies of the preparations: the rigorous cleaning of the house, the family's ritual search for leaven (ḥamets), the burning of the ḥamets, the cutting of wheat and proper preparation of flour to make the unleavened bread (matsah), the ritual baking of the matsah either at home or in the communal oven, and the purification of eating utensils and the laying out of the Seder table.[49] Many valuable details of the domestic life of the medieval Jews have been preserved in these illustrations, including some rare indications of the gestures that differentiated Sephardi from Ashkenazi rites. Haggadah illustrations also emphasized the shared communal value that all members of the com-

---

[48] See Yerushalmi, *Haggadah and History*, 18.

[49] On the cleaning of the home for Passover, see Metzger and Metzger, *Jewish Life in the Middle Ages*, 99; on the family celebration of the Seder, see ibid. 262; on the communal oven, see ibid. 113.

munity, even the poorest, should have access to the required unleavened bread, with depictions of Jewish notables distributing *matsah* prior to the holiday.[50]

The Passover Seder is a festive, multi-generational family gathering in which the attendees, in their best clothes, sit around a table as if at a royal banquet. The Passover Haggadah is read interactively in a manner somewhat akin to the passion plays performed by Christians in the marketplaces. Regardless of the country, the Seder included *matsah*, *haroset* (fruit, nuts, and wine ground together in a paste to represent the mortar that the Israelite slaves used to build the pyramids for the Egyptian pharaohs), and *maror* (bitter herbs, symbolizing the bitterness of slavery and hard labour). The Seder plate containing the symbolic foods and the wine goblets is prominently illustrated in illuminated Haggadot. Past and present are conflated as each celebrant is instructed to see themselves as having been personally redeemed from Egypt. This annual retelling of the Exodus story elaborates upon the daily emphasis in Jewish liturgy on the miraculous redemption of the Israelites from Egyptian bondage and Jewish hope for divine intervention in human affairs in the context of past redemption. Given the holiday's hopeful message, it is small wonder that its observance grew in popularity as Jewish life became more precarious. Passover offered celebrants consolation in the present with the promise of deliverance in the future.[51]

The Passover celebration is specially designed to engage the interest of children. Thus, for instance, the Sephardim physically re-enact the Exodus in the early part of the meal and Ashkenazi as well as Sephardi Jews open the door for the prophet Elijah at the conclusion of the meal. Certain postures—reclining, leaning to one side, raising a cup of wine—are adopted at designated points in the retelling. The reading of the Haggadah culminates in the utterance of the messianic hope: 'Next year in Jerusalem.' Various hymns, or *piyutim*, are recited after the Seder, emphasizing themes of redemption and God's intervention in history, each addition providing an opportunity for further didactic illustrations.

In the Passover Haggadot Sephardi Jews expressed some of their deepest longings and responses to the new and more hostile environment in which they found themselves. If they adopted motifs that were popular in the broader society, they infused them with their own messages. The central Passover symbols of bread and wine were prominently depicted in the surrounding Christian culture. The new emphasis on the Eucharist in Christian circles might have motivated the Jews to emphasize the Jewish meaning of these objects. By the thirteenth century bread was used in the Communion service to symbolize the body of Christ and wine to symbolize his blood. These and other Christian reinterpretations of biblical imagery were also widely known to Jews. It is probable that the prominent and ornamental depiction of wine and *matsah* in the

[50] For an illustration of a Jewish notable overseeing his servants bearing baskets and trays laden with *matsah* and distributing their contents to the needy, see the Golden Haggadah, ibid. 214.

[51] See Sarna, *Exploring Exodus*; Narkiss, *Hebrew Illuminated Manuscripts*.

illuminated Haggadot was an attempt to emphasize their original Jewish context in the Bible. The avoidance of depicting the paschal lamb, also a central part of the Passover story, was probably due to the long-held Christian interpretation of the sacrificial lamb in Isaiah as Jesus.

Attacks on Jewish texts emanated from many quarters in medieval Europe. Proselytizing sermons, which Jews were forced to attend, included vilification of the Talmud. Disputations on the 'proper' Christological reading of the Bible were foisted upon Jewish leaders by the Dominican friars. Offensive allusions to Jews appeared in passion plays and public processions. Christian interpretations of the Bible were abundantly on display in public art. Jewish responses had to be cautious given the weakness of their position, and Jewish artists required subtle ambiguity to avoid offending the Christian authorities and the populace and yet bolster the faith of the Jews. Since the Passover symbols could be read on multiple levels through pictorial allusions and midrashic interpretations, they could bolster Jewish confidence and optimism in the ancient traditions of God's promise to his covenanted people. These consolatory messages could be entwined, perhaps under some rabbinic direction, in visual form and prudently disseminated through the private medium of the Haggadah. In Haggadah illuminations the artist might even permit himself to express uncensored emotions of anger or vengeance, such as depicting the drowning of the Egyptians at the Red Sea or illustrations of the tenth plague, for example. Moreover, precisely those symbols that had been appropriated by Christian exegesis could be reclaimed by the Jews and lavishly rendered to provide a vigorous assertion of their original Jewish meaning. While the pictorial models of the Hebrew illuminated manuscripts may have been Christian, and some were probably even produced in Christian workshops, they were executed for a Jewish market with Jewish needs in mind.

The Haggadah often included an introductory section containing miniature illustrations of various biblical stories, commencing with the account of Creation or the patriarchal cycle from the book of Genesis. This material was not related to the Passover story but was included with pedagogical purposes in mind. The illustration of biblical texts that had acquired Christological interpretations or that were used by Christian disputants in their proselytizing debates, such as, for example, the sacrifice of Isaac (Gen. 22), was studiously avoided. Instead, biblical allusions to the liberation of the Jews and the rebuilding of the Temple of Jerusalem were used. The Temple was an especially powerful image, as was the menorah; the ram's horn, or *shofar*, herald of the messianic era; the table with the shewbread; and the ark of the covenant. Artists might lavishly illustrate the implements of the Temple of Jerusalem in gold leaf (Plate 5). According to Michael Batterman, such decorations constituted 'sites of subversion', which enabled Jews to privately challenge the majority culture through the inversion of Judaism's most significant symbols.[52]

---

[52] Michael Batterman also compares the *matsah* to a royal seal, a symbol of authority which granted

The round *matsah* was a highly charged symbol akin to the Communion wafer.[53] The use of the host in the Christian Mass in the early thirteenth century was followed by the introduction in 1264 of eucharistic processions on the Feast of Corpus Christi, held annually thereafter in towns and villages throughout Spain. Since the new doctrine of transubstantiation was not readily understood, its popular acceptance as part of Catholic dogma required much official repetition and persuasion on the part of the ecclesiastical authorities. Jewish artists may have had Christian illustrations of the host in mind when they chose to depict a piece of *matsah* prominently in gold leaf or as a heraldic shield in their Haggadah illuminations (Plate 6).

In the Sarajevo Haggadah, which was produced in Barcelona in the fourteenth century, the depiction of the Temple of Jerusalem is accompanied by an overt message of hope drawn from the Bible: 'This Holy Temple, which will be rebuilt soon, in our days.'[54] Medieval Haggadot also included new prayers, such as 'Pour out thy wrath!' in response to the massacre of Jewish communities during the Crusades.[55] The popular pictorial depiction of the 'four sons' in the Haggadah—'the wise son', 'the simpleton', 'the wicked son', and 'the son who doesn't know how to ask questions'—served multiple polemical purposes that were accessible through subtle and not-so-subtle pictorial representations. They were commonly interpreted as four different Jewish responses to the Passover story, but it was also possible to link them to the social reality: the wicked son was represented as a Christian or Muslim knight; the wise son was depicted as a rabbi. Similarly, the Egyptians depicted in hot pursuit of the Israelites at the Red Sea were often recognizably Christian knights.[56] Such representations could have a cathartic effect upon a vulnerable and helpless minority.

The illuminated Haggadah was a response to mounting attacks on Jewish texts through a specifically Jewish understanding of biblical narratives. The iconography presented a visual text that could buttress polemical works such as *Sefer nitsaḥon yashan*,

---

protection to its bearer and was widely used in medieval Spain. Its use was a privilege granted to Jewish courtiers, and it enabled the Jewish community to enact its own ordinances. Denying Jews the right to use the seal was a way to strip them of their authority and force them to use Christian notaries and Christian courts. Batterman, 'The Emergence of the Spanish Illuminated Haggadah Manuscript', 186; see also M. M. Epstein, *Dreams of Subversion in Medieval Jewish Art and Literature*.

[53] See Batterman, 'The Emergence of the Spanish Illuminated Haggadah Manuscript'; id., 'Bread of Affliction, Emblem of Power'. Only in the twentieth century, with the industrial production of *matsah* in the United States, did it become rectangular rather than round. On the spread and elaboration of the blood libel and the association of the Passover *matsah* with the accusation of ritual murder, see Ruben, *Gentile Tales*.

[54] See C. Roth, *The Sarajevo Haggadah*.

[55] See Saperstein, *Moments of Crisis in Jewish–Christian Relations*, 19.

[56] Harris, 'Polemical Images in the Golden Haggadah', 107; Kogman-Appel, 'The Sephardic Picture Cycles and the Rabbinic Tradition'; ead., 'Coping with Christian Pictorial Sources'. Although most of the illuminations discussed are Catalan, they were produced for the same social class in all the centres of Haggadah production.

a verse-by-verse response to Christological interpretations of biblical texts.[57] Lacking a prescribed imagery, the Haggadah was a flexible vehicle capable of reaching all members of the Jewish community and countering the dramatic negative representations of Jews. In addition, for the growing number of Jews in Spain in the fourteenth century who were turning to mystical works such as the Zohar, the illuminated Haggadah provided a resounding celebration of God's love for his people.

Samuel Halevi Abulafia, the El Tránsito Synagogue, and the Hybridity of Jewish Culture

Perhaps no topic has generated more heat than the role of the Jewish courtier in shaping Sephardi life and history. Sephardi pride, since medieval times, has focused on claims of personal descent from 'noble families' who wielded influence with royal authorities. However, according to Yitzhak Baer, it was the courtier class that led the Jewish community of Spain to the brink of destruction. The inscriptions and decorations on the walls of the fourteenth-century El Tránsito Synagogue built by Samuel Halevi Abulafia provide an ambiguous message about the role of the courtier and his status in Toledo's Jewish community.

Samuel Halevi was the quintessential court Jew.[58] He was probably descended from the Abulafia family whose members had provided several generations of courtiers, philosophers, poets, and doctors in Spain. He entered service in the court of Alfonso XI (r. 1312–50) in 1344 as the protégé of Juan Alfonso de Albuquerque, tutor to the heir to the throne, Pedro. He advanced in official circles through his involvement in the heir apparent's intrigues and romances, predominantly related to his royal succession. Halevi eventually attained the powerful position of *tesoro mayor del rey* (chief treasurer) to Pedro I (r. 1350–69) and served effectively in this position from 1353 to 1360, appointing members of his family as his assistants. In this role, Halevi succeeded in collecting vast sums of tax arrears in the kingdom of Castile, through confiscating the estates of recalcitrant nobles, and advancing Pedro's cause. Through these measures Halevi may have gained royal favour, but he also succeeded in alienating himself from the Castilian nobility. One sign of Halevi's power and position of royal confidence is his use of the royal seal. When the issue of succession arose in the 1360s, convulsing the country for almost a decade, one of the complaints of Pedro's rivals was that Pedro was an 'ennobler of Jews and Moors'. In December 1360 Samuel Halevi Abulafia was arrested

---

[57] Berger, *The Jewish–Christian Debate in the High Middle Ages*; see also Chazan, *Medieval Stereotypes*; J. Cohen, *The Friars and the Jews*; id., *Living Letters of the Law*.

[58] On the career of Halevi and the reign of Pedro I, see Estow, *Pedro the Cruel of Castile*, esp. ch. 7; see also López de Ayala, *Crónica del rey don Pedro*. López de Ayala was extremely hostile to Pedro as well as to Halevi, but his chronicle, despite its bias, remains an invaluable source of information.

on charges of corruption, taken to Seville, imprisoned, and tortured to death.[59] It is not clear who denounced him, accusing him of hiding a fortune that rightfully belonged to the monarch and possibly also implicating him in conspiratorial activities against the Crown.[60] As an able tax-collector and loyal supporter of the king and by allying himself with Pedro against the king's illegitimate half-brothers, Halevi was drawn into the murderous dynastic politics of the kingdom of Castile. Pedro's personal role in the betrayal and murder of his Jewish financier is unclear. Halevi's arrest, perhaps coincidentally, occurred four days after the arrest of the archbishop of Toledo on charges of conspiracy.

In 1357 Halevi had dedicated a synagogue in the city of Toledo. It was intended to serve for his personal use and was readily accessible from his luxurious home, which is believed to be the present-day El Greco house and museum nearby. After the Expulsion the synagogue was given to the Order of the Knights of Calatrava, and several of them are buried beneath its floor. The order ceded the building to the Jesuits, and it became the seat of the San Benito order, then, later, a church called El Tránsito de Nuestra Señora. The building was declared a Spanish national monument in 1877 and has since undergone considerable excavation and restoration. Today the Sephardi museum of Toledo is housed in what is believed to have been the women's gallery of the medieval structure.

The walls of the synagogue are richly decorated with stucco panelling, Castilian coats of arms, and interlacing vegetal motifs in the characteristic Mudéjar style that was popular in Toledo. The most noteworthy feature of the synagogue is the exceptionally beautiful Hebrew inscriptions that adorn its four walls in three bands of varying sizes encircling the entire main sanctuary. They are surely the most famous Hebrew inscriptions of the Middle Ages.

The synagogue decoration contains a surprising element that has continued to intrigue historians and has led to a variety of interpretations. Arabic inscriptions, barely visible to the viewer, are located throughout the sanctuary: under one of the rows of large Hebrew inscriptions, in the beams of the carved wooden ceiling, in several cartouches or medallions, and in the women's gallery. The Arabic writing seems to float in and out of the vegetal frieze in which it is entwined. The presence of Arabic inscriptions in a synagogue in Christian Spain begs explanation. Its re-examination within the context of the life of the Jews of Toledo may provide a neglected key to understanding

---

[59] See Taggie, 'Samuel ha-Levi Abulafia and the Hebraic Policy of Pedro I'; Estow, *Pedro the Cruel of Castile*, 155–79.

[60] According to the official chronicler of King Pedro's regime, Halevi's confiscated fortune consisted of 107,000 doubloons; 4,000 silver marks; 125 chests filled with gold, silver, and precious textiles; and 80 Muslim slaves (López de Ayala, *Crónica del rey don Pedro*, 510). This last allegation is probably baseless: it is doubtful whether even the most favoured Jewish courtier would have been permitted to hold such a vast number of slaves. Both Spanish Jewish and Christian legislation prohibited slaveholding by Jews.

the persona of the Jewish courtier and offer some insights into the still contentious issue of the relationship of the Jewish courtier to his king, his co-religionists, and the majority culture.[61]

The Hebrew inscriptions in the synagogue have been the subject of considerable scholarly interest since they were initially recorded in the eighteenth century. In 1905 Rodrigo Amador de los Ríos published a full transcription and Spanish translation and also noted the presence of the inconspicuous Arabic inscriptions, identifying them as quranic. This identification has been generally accepted, partly as a result of the stature of Amador de los Ríos.[62] Only recently has the question of the literal and symbolic meaning of the synagogue's Arabic inscriptions been raised. María Rosa Menocal has suggested that they represent 'positive proof of Jewish gratitude for the Islamic culture of tolerance' in 'a palace of memory of a culture of tolerance'.[63]

The construction of a new synagogue in fourteenth-century Spain, especially one of such beauty, raises several questions. New synagogues were banned by *Las siete partidas* and in the ordinances of numerous regional councils. The prohibition could, however, be overruled through a special dispensation, usually obtained upon payment of a large sum of money to the king. The prohibition might not have been applicable to the construction of synagogues in private homes or if the new one was replacing an old synagogue, and recent archaeological evidence suggests that the El Tránsito Synagogue may have been built on the ruins of a former synagogue dating back to Muslim times. Given the lavish encomia of King Pedro that Halevi inscribed on the synagogue's dedicatory plaque, it is highly likely that the king was party to the erection of this private house of worship.

The El Tránsito Synagogue is a classic example of the Mudéjar style of art and architecture. Although the term evokes intercultural and inter-ethnic relations in Iberia, it is rarely used to refer to Jewish architecture. With the notable exception of Jerrilynn Dodds, most art historians do not mention synagogues when discussing the Mudéjar style, despite the fact that it was the architectural style of three of the four medieval synagogues that have survived in Spain.[64]

One characteristic feature of the Mudéjar style is the inclusion of Arabic and pseudo-Arabic inscriptions, even when the building or object had a clearly Christian religious purpose. This could be either the result of recycling Muslim monuments or

---

[61] For an expanded and different description of the inscriptions in the synagogue and the career of Halevi see Gerber, 'The World of Samuel Halevi'; ead., 'Those Who Walk in the Court of Our Master, the King'.

[62] Amador de los Ríos, *Toledo*.

[63] Menocal, *The Ornament of the World*, 239, 243; cf. ead., 'Culture in the Time of Tolerance'; see also Heydeck, *Inscripciones hebreas de la Sinagoga Toledana de R. Samuel ha-Levi*. Rachel Wischnitzer accepted the Arabic inscriptions as quranic (Wischnitzer, *The Architecture of the European Synagogue*, 35); see also Cantera Burgos and Millas Vallicrosa, *Las inscripciones hebraicas en España*; C. Roth, 'Las inscripciones historica de la Sinagoga del Tránsito de Toledo'. For the most complete and judicious discussion of the inscriptions, see Foster, 'The Writing on the Wall'.   [64] Dodds, 'Mudéjar Tradition and the Synagogues of Medieval Spain'.

the handiwork of Muslim stonemasons, plasterers, and carpenters. These Muslim architects and artisans, it is suggested, would spitefully sneak quranic verses into their designs, confident that their patrons would be unaware of them. Such reasoning is highly unlikely in the case of the El Tránsito Synagogue. Halevi was an exacting and demanding man of the world. He was an efficient businessman who dealt extensively with the Muslim court in Granada and undoubtedly spoke Arabic. Even if he could not read or write it, he would certainly have been able to recognize the script. Recognition of Arabic lettering, even without a reading knowledge of the language, was quite common among Jews in Toledo as late as the fourteenth century.[65] Rather than considering the Arabic script in the synagogue as a political statement about the tolerance of Islam, it is more fruitful to consider the inscriptions in both Hebrew and Arabic as a personal statement by Halevi and an important expression of Sephardi identity.

Inscriptions in medieval buildings served several purposes. The most obvious was providing information on its date of construction, the identity of its patron, or the ruling dynasty. Some inscriptions, such as the ones that appear repeatedly on the walls of the Alhambra palace proclaiming 'Power to our lord Abu Abdallah' or 'There is no victorious one but God', were more political than religious in intent, conspicuously filling the walls in celebration of the power of the ruler of the Nasrid kingdom, Muhammad V (1354–91), and his victory over his Christian foes at Algeciras. Oleg Grabar has convincingly argued that Arabic script could carry meaning regardless of whether it contained a meaningful text.[66] The script is frequently ornate and difficult to decipher, and may sometimes be applied to an object simply for aesthetic effect, the very shape of the letters constituting an art form capable of conveying ideological meanings. In Grabar's view, the Arabic on the walls of the Alhambra falls into this category: it constitutes an audacious and extravagant statement of royal luxury intended to awe the spectator with the power of the Muslim king. Halevi's use of Arabic inscriptions in his private synagogue should be understood within this cultural and theoretical framework.

Many buildings in Christian Spain were decorated with what looked like Arabic inscriptions, but which were devoid of meaning. The script was employed for its decorative value, and its intended effects were fashionable, aesthetic, and even probably political, but not religious. It was associated with luxury and beauty. Use of the Mudéjar style during the boom in church construction accompanying the Reconquest was never intended as a tribute to Islam. On the contrary, it was used precisely because it was understood as a Spanish national style that had arisen during the period of Islamic hegemony over the peninsula. It recorded an era of Iberian greatness. The style was favoured by Spanish Christians in opposition to the new and imported Roman-

[65] Wasserstein, 'Jewish Elites in al-Andalus'.
[66] Grabar, *The Alhambra*; id., *The Mediation of Ornament*, 103; Ecker, *Caliphs and Kings*.

esque and Gothic architecture popular among the clerics and other immigrants streaming into Spain from France.[67] Halevi's commissioning of a building decorated with Arabic calligraphy is probably an assertion of his identification with a Spanish cultural idiom that was already mythologizing its affluent Andalusian past.

In the course of his service to King Pedro, Halevi had ample opportunity to contemplate Islamic architecture. Pedro had grown up in Andalusia and had never lost his taste for Andalusian styles, even after becoming king of Castile. When he renovated his royal complex, the Alcazar of Seville, a former Almohad fortress, Pedro retained many of its Islamic decorative touches and inscriptions. This renovation project occurred between 1353 and 1364, precisely the time that Halevi was constructing his synagogue. The great palace of the Alhambra in the kingdom of Granada was also under renovation at this time. The impressive Mudéjar architecture of the two royal residences was accessible to all highly placed court visitors. As a royal tax-collector, Halevi was a frequent visitor to both the Alcazar of Seville and the Alhambra in Granada. Since the Castilian king Pedro and the Nasrid king Muhammad V were personal friends and frequent allies, it would have been quite natural for them to share architects, artists, and designs. Perhaps their masons and artists also offered advice to the self-confident Jewish courtier who shuttled back and forth between Seville and Granada with his royal account books while preoccupied with his favourite personal project of building a private synagogue adjoining his house. Halevi's official visits to Seville and Granada probably multiplied during the 1350s as the need for a steady flow of money into the royal coffers grew more urgent in the aftermath of the Black Death.

Even the most superficial examination of the walls of the two palaces alongside the synagogue's interior reveals remarkable similarities in design and detail (Plates 7, 8, 9). The scallop-and-diamond designs, the profusion of interlacing leaf-and-vine scrolls, and the prominent role of inscriptions as decorative elements suggest the hand of the same artist. The Mudéjar style of all three edifices was the preferred style of the Castilian nobility. Halevi considered himself Jewish nobility, a prince among princes of the tribe of Levi. If the similarities among the three edifices are obvious, their differences are also telling.

The Arabic calligraphy in the Alhambra and the Alcazar of Seville is profuse, visible, and quite legible: it appears at eye level in public and private areas. In contrast, the Arabic inscriptions in the El Tránsito Synagogue are barely noticeable and scarcely decipherable (Plate 10). They are located on the uppermost part of the synagogue: on its walls, the ceiling, in medallions in the second-floor gallery, and on the entrance lintel of the tribunal area. The epigraphy is densely written in small, semi-cursive, or Kufic, script without any diacritical marks. The absence of diacritical marks immediately

---

[67] See Dodds, 'The Mudéjar Tradition in Architecture'; ead., 'The Arts of al-Andalus'; ead., *Architecture and Ideology in Early Medieval Spain*; ead., *Al-Andalus*.

suggests that the writing was not meant to be read. Significantly, there are no Arabic inscriptions on the eastern wall, the focus of the worshippers' attention since it contains the niche for the ark housing the Torah scrolls, the wall that faces the direction of Jerusalem. The eastern wall of the El Tránsito Synagogue bears the most prominent Hebrew inscriptions containing data on Halevi, his royal mentor, and the date of the dedication of the building.

Arabic script on buildings in Christian Spain is evocative of an Islamic era of dynamism and power. For the fourteenth-century Jews of Spain, it also evoked the memory of an era in which Jews were at ease in their adopted land. In Halevi's day, the Mudéjar style suggested the earthly power of Iberian rulers and their lavish endowments, without any reference to Islam. The style was typically Andalusian, associated in particular with Andalusian palaces. The presence of Arabic, whether at the Alcazar of Seville or in the synagogue, was more important than its content. Arabic calligraphy made a powerful statement of class identity, and, in the El Tránsito Synagogue, it constituted Halevi's proclamation of his identification with the ruling class.

The Hebrew inscriptions in the synagogue, in contrast to the Arabic, are prominent and legible. They refer to Jewish heroes connected with royal power such as King David and King Solomon; the ancient courtier Mordechai, saviour of the Jews of the Persian empire; and Halevi's biblical namesake, the prophet Samuel. The invocation of these figures provides an implicit comparison between the great kings and courtiers of ancient Israel and Halevi. The Hebrew inscription on the right of the Torah niche compares the synagogue lectern, Torah, and lamps to those of the Temple of Solomon in Jerusalem:

> See the sanctuary now consecrated in Israel
> And the house which was built by Samuel
> With a pulpit of wood for reading the law
> With its scrolls and its crowns all for God
> And its lavers and lamps to illuminate
> And its windows like the windows of Ariel.[68]

The inscription to the left of the Torah niche draws parallels between the architectural details of the synagogue and the Temple:

> And its courts for them that cherish the perfect law
> With a seat for each who sits in the shade of God
> And those who see it will almost say it appears
> Like a work that was wrought by Bezalel
> Go ye nations and enter into its gates
> And seek the Lord, for it is a house of God even as Bethel.[69]

---

[68] El Tránsito Synagogue inscription, cited in Omer, *The Synagogue of Samuel Halevy*, 181. For a Spanish translation of the inscriptions, see Cantera Burgos, *Sinagogas españolas*; see also Amador de los Ríos, *Toledo*.

[69] El Tránsito Synagogue inscription, cited in Omer, *The Synagogue of Samuel Halevy*, 177.

Other inscriptions on the eastern wall praise Halevi as a saviour of Israel, 'a noble of nobles' who stands before kings and seeks 'the good of his people'. Verses are skilfully and seamlessly interwoven into the delicately interlacing arabesques on the walls. It is as difficult to separate the decorative scrolls and vines as it is to discern whether the subjects of the enthusiastic praises are ancient Israelite heroes or Pedro and Halevi. The Jewish courtier is transformed into a redeemer, a bulwark, the 'crown and the great man of the Jews. To him peoples come from the ends of the Earth. . . . He is the ruler of the land. The great tamarisk. Fort of strength and greatness . . . a royal diadem. . . . He stands at the head . . . exalted among the exalted of the Levites of God, Samuel Halevi.'[70]

Amidst the encomia to himself, Halevi invokes the name of his king: 'The great king, our shelter and our lord the king Don Pedro. May God aid him, And increase his might and his glory. And guard him as the shepherd of his flock. The king has made him great and exalted him. And raised his throne above all the ministers . . . . He has been to Israel a saviour.' At the conclusion of the prominent, dedicatory plaque Halevi himself is resoundingly praised:

He has saved [us] from [our] enemies and since the day of our exile not one of the Children of Israel has attained to his height. . . . Tree with multiple roots. The great compassionate and righteous man the exalted among the exalted of the Levites.

Rabbi Samuel Halevi, luminary of society, great in observance . . . . The Law and those who learn it. Who restores [crowns as in] the first days and an[cient] years [as in the day] of God's gift. A man [who] added to and increased all the[se] to build a house of prayer for the Lord God of Israel

And built the house and completed it in the year GOOD [for the Jews] [=117] or 5117, 1356/7.[71]

Through carefully selected biblical passages, the power of the courtier and his relationship to his sovereign are underscored. The coats of arms of Castile and León are interspersed between the Hebrew verses and in the friezes (Plate 10). The conspicuous placement of King Pedro's name in the Torah niche's dedicatory plaque reminds the viewer of the courtier's royal sponsor. Association with royal power, the trademark of the courtier and the key to his privileges within the Jewish community, was a haunting and powerful symbol that the Jews of Spain carried in their memories.

The texts that link ancient Israel and the fourteenth-century courtier may also contain another layer of meaning and set of allusions. Perhaps Halevi was referring to another Samuel, also a Levite, Samuel ibn Nagrela. Ibn Nagrela was the most powerful Jewish statesman of medieval times, and his legendary exploits, like his martial poetry, stirred generations of Jews with pride. His reconstruction of the battle of Alfuente was as stirring to the Jews as were the ballads of El Cid to the Christians. Stories of Ibn Nagrela continued to circulate in Spain long after his death. The invocation of Ibn Nagrela was probably not unusual in Granada, particularly at the time that the

[70] El Tránsito Synagogue inscription, cited ibid.   [71] El Tránsito Synagogue inscription, cited ibid.

Alhambra was being constructed. It is possible that the Alhambra was erected on the site of the original villa of the Ibn Nagrela family and that its famed Lion's Court incorporates the stone statuary that originally stood in Ibn Nagrela's garden.[72] If indeed this is the case, Halevi undoubtedly delighted in hearing of the deeds of Samuel ibn Nagrela while he was on official business in Granada.

Other affinities between the eleventh-century Samuel ibn Nagrela and the fourteenth-century Samuel Halevi may have also been present in Halevi's mind. Both vaunted their Levite descent, Ibn Nagrela in his poetry and Halevi on the walls of his synagogue. Ironically, both men indirectly caused widespread destruction to their communities within a decade of their deaths, partially as a result of the enmity they aroused by their personal power and their connection with detested monarchs.

The El Tránsito Synagogue and the status of its patron Halevi are not necessarily signs of Jewish well-being in fourteenth-century Toledo. It is entirely possible that the associations with Ibn Nagrela and the royal palace in Granada held special appeal for the Jews in Toledo precisely because their own status was increasingly precarious. The several associations with royal power that the synagogue and its Arabic and Hebrew inscriptions evoke are problematic to the modern viewer, but do they substantiate Yitzhak Baer's condemnations of the shallow and assimilatory identity of the Spanish Jewish courtier class? Perhaps the decorative inscriptions were intended to conflate the power and affluence of Islamic culture in Spain and the ancient triumphs of Israel in order to fill the Jewish worshipper with optimistic pride. Like the gilded Temple implements in the illuminated manuscripts, the manifold references to the Temple of Jerusalem in the Hebrew inscriptions of the El Tránsito Synagogue recall the many biblical promises that the original Temple would be restored. The synagogue's repetitious mantras—'happiness', 'power', 'beneficence', 'prosperity'—etched in Arabic were the lifeblood of the courtier, embodying his aspirations and his values, as well as the fervent hopes of a declining community.

In the final analysis, the place of the courtier in Sephardi annals remains problematic. Perhaps Samuel Halevi Abulafia suspected that he would be remembered by posterity, if at all, not as a Jewish prince, but as the sponsor and preserver of Toledo's artistic Jewish heritage in the beautiful Mudéjar synagogue he built. Halevi's synagogue inscriptions, like the Haggadah illuminations and the presence of Toledo's Jews at the centre of King Alfonso's translation teams, testify to the complex process of cultural

---

[72] According to Dodds, the opulence of the Alhambra can be seen as a gesture of defiance in the face of the rapid erosion of the power of the Muslims in Spain (Dodds, 'The Arts of al-Andalus', 618). The Alhambra constituted a palace of style that celebrated a culture that was old but still potent. Its countless Arabic inscriptions lauded Muslim military prowess just as that prowess was on the verge of collapse. The complex was completed around 1369, the same year that King Pedro was murdered. The portion of the Alhambra containing the Patio de los Leones was built after El Tránsito's completion and it is therefore difficult to relate the Patio de los Leones meaningfully to Samuel Halevi's visits to the Alhambra.

exchange between the Sephardim and the surrounding society. In their embrace and transformation of the dominant cultures around them the Jews of Toledo demonstrated the extent to which the crossing of cultural borders between Jewish, Muslim, and Christian culture shaped and defined Sephardi history.

CHAPTER THREE

THE SEARCH FOR REDEMPTION IN SAFED
1500–1600

Safed has intimations of eternity. It is a most suitable place in which to penetrate the secrets and profundities of the Torah, for its air is the purest in the Holy Land.

ABRAHAM AZULAI, *Ḥesed le'avraham*

Awake, O drunken ones, for the day comes when a man must cast away his gods of silver, worldly desires, and his gods of gold and lust for power. Go to the Land of Israel.

SOLOMON ALKABETZ, introduction to Joseph Karo, *Magid mesharim*

THE EXPULSIONS from Spain and Portugal in 1492 and 1497 were echoed in Sicily, southern Italy, and Sardinia, as the Jews were driven out of their homes to drift like flotsam from one Mediterranean port to the next, briefly finding refuge in one place only to face expulsion again, moving always towards the east. Expulsion followed expulsion, as Jews from Provence, the papal states, and the Dalmatian coast joined the homeless wanderers choking the routes of the Mediterranean. Within a generation, global Jewish settlement patterns were drastically altered as the Muslim world became home again to hundreds of revitalized or new centres of Jewish life. In this resettlement and reshuffling, two separate branches of the Sephardim were formed. A large and heterogeneous diaspora of Ladino- and Arabic-speaking Jews emerged throughout the eastern Mediterranean and the Balkans. In western Europe, a smaller number of primarily Portuguese-speaking Jews lived openly as Jews in a few places in Italy or as secret Jews (Marranos) in Iberia, the Low Countries, France, and England. While the first group was drawing closer to its Jewish roots and moving slowly towards the creation of a Sephardi diaspora, the second was either searching for its lost identity or growing increasingly estranged from its ancestral traditions.

As the Iberian Jews wended their way eastward they tended to be introspective and melancholy, for the world they knew had collapsed and they saw no relief in sight. Traditional explanations of self-blame and stoic acceptance of suffering alternated with expressions of fury and religious doubts. For Judah Zarco, a Hebrew poet from the island of Rhodes, the trauma of Jewish history caused a temporary loss of faith. Elegies written after 1492 defiantly question the ways of God: 'Alas, our Father, is this the recompense we have sought?' 'Is this the way a father treats his children?' Radical new relationships with God appeared necessary as the old answers no longer sufficed in the face of the expulsions.

Some Jews began to read portents of redemption in their circumstances. God's intervention might be discerned in the welcome that they received at the hands of the Ottoman sultans or it could be inferred from the contest for power between Catholic Europe and the Muslim Turks. Perhaps the fall of Constantinople in 1453 was a sign of the approaching 'End of Days' when the kingdoms of the earth, Gog and Magog, would engage in the great battle of Armageddon that would usher in the messianic era predicted in apocalyptic scenarios in the Bible. Similarly, Martin Luther's challenge to the supremacy of Catholic Rome provided a measure of hope and consolation. Even the discovery of America, it was suggested, could be construed as positive proof that these were indeed messianic times. Letters attesting to the encounters with the lost Ten Tribes of Israel in the jungles of South America quickened hopes. Any unusual event might serve as a portent: according to David Ruderman, an Italian Jew named Isaac Dieulosal saw the appearance of Halley's Comet in 1456 as a sign of the messiah and redemption.[1]

The messianic doctrine in Judaism is a complex one that has been among the most creative and seductive intellectual forces in history. Christianity and Islam both grew out of the matrix of Judaism's messianic traditions, each putting its own original imprint on Jewish notions of a suffering redeemer, a hidden leader, and the cataclysmic end of time. Indeed, the Jewish concept of a suffering redeemer gained new relevance as the central motif of Christianity. The same doctrine was transformed in the person of the hidden imam in Islam, particularly among the Shi'ites. In rabbinic Judaism, in contrast, emphasis on a human redeemer was either submerged or only enigmatically represented and then relegated to the sidelines during the first centuries of the Common Era. Nevertheless, outbursts of messianic enthusiasm could occasionally swell into mass movements, as Jews lost patience with their suffering and sought to accelerate the difficult process of redemption. Charismatic figures might then arise and command a following of hopeful adherents. Counsels of repentance through prayer, quietism, and good works would give way to activism or organized migration to the Land of Israel, where the messiah was expected to appear. The messianic impulse, born in ancient times and usually channelled into the study of texts of an apocalyptic nature, could nevertheless be activated and transformed into organized messianic movements

---

[1] See Ruderman, 'Hope Against Hope', 300; see also Elior, 'Messianic Expectations and Spiritualization of Religious Life in the Sixteenth Century'. Dieulosal's excited reaction was expressed in tandem with the messianic exuberance and anticipation of an Italian Christian, Francesco da Meleto, who was also agitated by the messianic predictions of Spanish Jews in the 1470s. See Y. Baer, 'The Messianic Movement in Spain in the Period of the Expulsion' (Heb.), 63–4.

under extreme conditions. The aftermath of 1492 provided precisely some of these conditions.

Predicting the advent of the messiah was an uncertain pastime, however, condemned by rabbinic leadership throughout much of Jewish history. The study of mystical texts to decipher their encoded clues to the advent of the End of Days had the potential to spin out of control and end in disappointment or even despair. While the messianic doctrine that promised an ultimate redemption of the Jews was always present in Jewish thought, it was ordinarily contained. Its power lay in its very vagueness and its ability to strengthen the resolve of a dispersed and frequently beleaguered people, fortifying them to weather current crises with future hope. But the fifteenth and sixteenth centuries were scarcely normal times: messianic predictions were everywhere. Visions of the apocalypse based on astrological prognostications abounded in late medieval and Renaissance Christian culture as well as in Muslim circles. Several dates had astrological significance for the Jews: 1484, 1500, 1503/4, 1517, 1524, 1530/1 each provided fresh stimulus to Jewish prognosticators of redemption. In Ferrara, the Jewish thinker Abraham Farissol and the eccentric Christian prophet Mercurio da Correggio both mused about the astrological potential of 1484. Spiritual preparation for the apocalypse, regardless of when it might occur, was urgent.

Many biblical texts lent themselves to calculations of the date of the redemption, but few dwelt on the identity of the redeemer. If redemption was a certainty, the redeemer remained enigmatic. Nevertheless, Sephardi and Middle Eastern Jewries have been noted for their penchant for messianic activism and the periodic appearance of colourful messianic pretenders in their midst. Certain junctures of history proved especially tumultuous when external events seemed to augur the impending fulfilment of the messianic age. Seventh- and eighth-century Islam, for instance, was awash with turmoil, and warfare with heterodox movements erupted throughout the eastern provinces. With the Abbasid dynasty fighting for supremacy, entire regions were suffused with apocalyptic excitement in both Muslim and Jewish circles. Similarly, a wave of messianism swept through the Jewish world during the Crusades.[2] These movements were quickly quelled by the co-ordinated opposition of the Jewish authorities and the caliph's troops in Baghdad. Despite the suppression of the various local movements, their impact was temporarily contagious and the aftershocks were felt for decades among disappointed 'believers'.

Jewish mysticism and Jewish messianism were two separate though interrelated movements. Contemplation of the beginning of the world and the origins of humanity are the main concern of Jewish mysticism. Jewish messianism, in contrast, is

---

[2] On Jewish messianic movements during the Crusades, see Mann, 'Messianic Movements during the First Three Crusades' (Heb.); on the general phenomenon of messianism among the Sephardim, see G. D. Cohen, 'Messianic Postures of Ashkenazim and Sephardim'; for an alternative interpretation, see Carlebach, *Between Ashkenaz and Sepharad*.

ineluctably drawn to the end of time. Nevertheless, the techniques for understanding the beginning and the end of time were similar. It was widely accepted by Jewish teachers that the apocalyptic date was encoded in certain biblical texts. Isaiah 2: 2–4, Deuteronomy 30: 1–10, and Amos 9: 9–15, for instance, were believed to be fraught with hidden messianic meanings that begged careful reading. The letters of the Hebrew alphabet might also contain hidden clues revealing the date of redemption. Since each letter of the Hebrew alphabet possesses a numerical equivalent, computations of specific texts took on special significance among mystics. This technique of textual computation, known as gematria, was a favourite means of unlocking the secrets of the Bible and of predicting the eschaton. One messianic date that the method of gematria suggested was 1096. Great trauma and persecution could also be interpreted as a sign of the end. Thus the havoc and destruction wrought by the Crusaders as they passed through Europe and the Middle East en route to Jerusalem during the First Crusade seemed to fulfil the messianic potential of the Hebrew date corresponding to that year. Surely the conjunction of the messianic date and the carnage was charged with meaning. Did the historical events portend the fulfilment of the biblical apocalypse? No one could be certain.

Particular dates in the calendar also occasionally served as catalysts for a messianic movement. The approach of the year 1122, for instance, the half-millennium after Muhammad's flight from Mecca, marking the beginning of the Muslim calendar, was portentous for Muslims. Some believed that the date would herald the beginning of the era of the redemption. Muhammad ibn Tumart (c.1080–c.1128), a Muslim fundamentalist leader in the southern desert region of Morocco, proclaimed a messianic message based on this tradition that also predicted the return of Muhammad on the quincentennial of the Hegira. At the same time, a Jewish messianic pretender, Moses al-Dar'i, appeared in Fez and announced that the Jews would be redeemed on Passover eve. He exhorted the community to hasten to prepare for the event, but Maimonides' father, a judge in Fez, interceded to calm the masses. Although the two movements were probably independently inspired and did not cross the boundaries of the separate faith communities, the atmosphere of expectation was shared.

Jewish messianism has frequently been regarded as a religion of the downtrodden, a cry of hope of simple folk during periods of persecution. Indeed, many of the medieval Jewish messianic pretenders arose among poor villagers in the eastern provinces of the Islamic lands, in Kurdistan or Azerbaijan. Local conditions of social and military turmoil enabled heterodoxy to flourish among all peoples of the region. The credulous Jews in outlying areas were more vulnerable to the appeal of a charismatic leader than the more sophisticated and learned Jews of Baghdad, Kairouan, or Cordoba, but even the urban Jewish population in the heartland of Islam was not immune to messianic agitation. A sober Jewish statesman like the worldly tenth-century courtier of Cordoba, Hasdai ibn Shaprut, longed for indications of the date of the messiah's appearance, begging the king of the Khazars in 948 for any information he might possess on the date of the messiah's advent: 'One more thing I ask of my lord, that he would tell me whether there is among you any computation concerning the final redemption which we have been awaiting so many years, while we went from one captivity to another.'[3] This query was not an idle indulgence in messianic reverie on the part of a cobbler in central Asia but came from an urbane physician in the opulent palace of the most powerful caliph of Cordoba. Medieval Cordoba was the setting in 1105 for the appearance of a shadowy Jewish messianic pretender named Ibn Aryeh.

Messianic speculation, if uncontrolled, could wreak havoc in a community. Reprisals were inevitable as the secular authorities sought to restore order. Moreover, as the date of the anticipated end approached, Jewish enthusiasm would heighten, paralysing the normal flow of economic life. Then, when the date passed with no palpable change in the Jewish condition, the masses would be plunged into despair and become the laughing stock of their neighbours. The example of the Jewish community of Baghdad in 1120/1 is telling. An unnamed daughter of 'Joseph the physician' declared publicly that the prophet Elijah had appeared to her in a dream announcing that the redemption of Israel was imminent. Many Jews were thereupon imprisoned by the authorities and threatened with death. They were ultimately released, but the possible adverse consequences of the messianic ferment were not lost on the Jewish leadership. The Jews had been induced to prepare for their redemption by selling their property, abandoning the marketplace, and engaging in intense prayer accompanied by fasting. On the appointed day of redemption they were urged to ascend to their rooftops where they should wait to be carried to the Holy Land 'on wings of eagles', as predicted in the Bible. This sequence of events ended in fiasco in Baghdad, with grave economic and psychological consequences.[4] Heightened expectations naturally led to deep disappointment.

In more than one instance, women played a conspicuous role in messianic movements. An undated fragment from the Cairo *geniza*, written hastily and in apparent excitement, describes the visions of a pregnant Jewish woman from Catania in Sicily. Her message of the imminent advent of the messiah spread from Jews to Christians. She also included instructions to ambassadors to facilitate the passage of the Jews from Sicily to Jerusalem. The movement spread as far as Spain, where a local bishop refused to allow the Jews to depart until they had relinquished their property (which they agreed to do).[5]

---

[3] See 'Hasdai ibn Shaprut's Correspondence with Joseph, King of the Khazars', in *Letters of Jews through the Ages*, i. 97–115; on Hasdai's leadership, see Chapter 1 above.

[4] See Goitein, 'A Report on Messianic Troubles in Baghdad in 1120–21'; on a messianic movement in Sicily, see Mann, *Texts and Studies in Jewish History and Literature*, i. 34–8; on Solomon Hakohen, a Karaite messianic figure in northern Palestine in 1121, see ibid. ii. 42.

[5] See Mann, *Texts and Studies in Jewish History and Literature*, i. 34–44.

At least eight widely scattered cases of messianism occurred among Jews in Germany, Crete, Morocco, and Kurdistan during the upheavals that accompanied the first three Crusades. These probably represent only a fraction of the actual incidents, randomly saved for posterity through their mention in chronicles or in documents preserved in the Cairo *geniza*. Many similar instances probably passed unrecorded. So great was the yearning for the messiah's advent among the Jews that even Maimonides, the symbol of Jewish rationalism, ventured to offer a date for the advent of the messiah in his *Epistle to Yemen*. In response to the confusion among the Jews in Yemen caused by oppression and calls for conversion to Islam by a false messiah, Maimonides shared an old family tradition that the messiah was going to appear in either 1210 or 1216.[6] His dilemma over how to respond was palpable: how to strengthen the hope of a downtrodden community in crisis, while at the same time discrediting the movement at hand. In offering a specific yet still distant date for the messianic advent, Maimonides walked a fine line. While denouncing the contemporary messianic pretender in Yemen, he simultaneously upheld the validity of the messianic tradition that Jews cherished. In this fashion, he hoped to contain the messianic excitement of his followers while preserving their confidence in the veracity of the tradition. Other Jewish leaders would repeatedly counsel against calculations that might precipitate unrestrained Jewish messianic activism. Like Maimonides, they would hasten to repudiate a movement at hand while upholding the validity of the messianic promise. Maimonides' rational and restrained vision of the nature of the messianic era is carefully conveyed in the concluding words of the *Mishneh torah*:

In that era there will be neither famine nor war, neither jealousy nor strife. Blessings will be abundant, comforts within reach of all. The one preoccupation of all mankind will be to know the Lord. Hence Israelites will be very wise, they will know the things that are now concealed and will attain an understanding of the Creator to the utmost capacity of the human mind, as it is written, 'For the land shall be filled with knowledge of the Lord as the waters cover the sea' (Isaiah 11: 9).[7]

Most occurrences of active messianic enthusiasm passed without incident, and mystical contemplation of the End of Days remained a quietistic intellectual and social phenomenon. The masses customarily contained their impatience, counselled by their rabbis that the quality of waiting was what mattered most in hastening the End of Days. Only during messianic times, they counselled, would a perfect world order be established, the oppression cease, and the ingathering of all Jews in the Land of Israel take place. This utopian vision was usually presented as the climax of an intentionally vague timetable.

---

[6] Maimonides' *Epistle to Yemen* provides an important list of messianic outbursts, primarily in the medieval Muslim world. He found the messianic pretender David Alroy especially impressive: see *Epistle to Yemen*, 90, 123–30.   [7] Maimonides, *Mishneh torah*, 'Laws of Kings and Their Wars', 12: 4–5.

The Expulsion of 1492 created an unpredictable marriage of disparate Jewish messianic and mystical traditions. The Zohar had appeared in Spain in the thirteenth century. It was attributed to the ancient rabbi and martyr Shimon bar Yohai, but internal textual evidence attests to its medieval composition. Its popularity had spread beyond Iberia before 1492, and it was embraced by Jewish scholars in Italy and Byzantium. It continued to command a following in Spain during the fifteenth century. Some of the revolutionary implications of its doctrine of redemption seemed to be just around the corner as Jewish life in the Iberian peninsula sank to new depths. The appearance of a monumental kabbalistic work, the anonymous *Sefer hameshiv*, testifies to the serious engagement of Spanish Jewish scholars in kabbalistic creativity before the Expulsion.[8] The popularity of mysticism among Sephardim and Greek-speaking Jews in the sixteenth century cannot be attributed entirely to the trauma of 1492, although the acceptance of esoteric doctrines by the masses was ignited by it. The Expulsion produced a constellation of unprecedented conditions which proved fertile soil in which mysticism and messianism, usually quite separate traditions, converged. The mysticism that circulated in fifteenth-century Spain was an esoteric and restricted phenomenon. Messianism was another matter entirely.

The official accounts of inquisitorial proceedings testify to the messianic agitation that gripped the Jews of Spain immediately before and after the Expulsion: female Conversos in several rural regions testified to visions of the appearance of the messiah in the late 1400s and early 1500s, setting off waves of excitement. But it was not only rural Jews who were succumbing to messianic fantasies; at the other end of the social spectrum even a sober statesman like Don Isaac Abravanel engaged in the contemplation of the specific date of the anticipated advent of the messiah, speculating that the miraculous event would occur in 1503, or no later than 1531. Even before the Expulsion from Spain he had indulged in messianic interpretations of the Bible. These grew more explicit in the light of the near-apocalyptic events that he experienced in his expulsion from Spain and subsequently from Naples. His 'messianic trilogy', *Ma'ayanei hayeshuah*, a commentary on the book of Daniel written between 1496 and 1497, exuded confidence that the messianic era was at hand:

As for the birth of our righteous messiah, I have no doubt that he was already born before the great Expulsion caused death and destruction for the Jewish diaspora in Spain. . . . For the prophet said: 'Before she labored, she was delivered' [Isa. 66: 7], meaning before the birth pangs of redemption Zion, or the Jewish nation, gave birth to the messianic king. . . . Perhaps in the preceding year [1491], the chief of the shepherds, the anointed of the God of Jacob was born.[9]

---

[8] Scholem, 'On the Knowledge of Kabbalah before the Expulsion' (Heb.), 167; see also Idel, 'Enquiries into the Doctrine of the Book of Meshiv' (Heb.); id., 'Spanish Kabbalah after the Expulsion'.

[9] Abravanel, *Ma'ayanei hayeshuah*, 12.2.7.

In another context, he stated:

> Our righteous messiah will be born among the Jews in the diaspora of Rome, in the midst of Christians.... The messianic king will be born or will reveal himself when the Jews are being expelled from the Roman and Christian lands.... He will be one of those who experience acts of persecution and forced conversion.[10]

A contemporary Jewish historian, Joseph Hakohen, also drew radical messianic conclusions from events he had witnessed or heard about from his émigré parents, incorporating these expectations into his *History of the Kings of France and of the Ottoman Turkish Sultans*.[11]

Concrete expressions of messianism among both Jews and Christians after 1492 were quite varied: a prophetic movement arose in Cordoba between 1499 and 1502;[12] gematria pointed to the years 1496, 1497, or 1507; historical events seemed to validate the conviction, held by an expanding circle of Christians and Jews, that 1500 would usher in the long-anticipated redemption. At this juncture an enigmatic messianic figure appeared among the refugees of Iberia and galvanized the Marranos of Portugal with his messianic message and concrete proposals to bring about an end to Jewish suffering.

David Reubeni and Solomon Molkho

As the Sephardi émigrés reconstituted themselves in Europe, two enigmatic personalities—David Reubeni (d. *c*.1538) and Solomon Molkho (1500/1–32)—tapped into the messianic currents then coursing through the Sephardi diaspora and the Christian and Muslim worlds, setting off ripples of expectation, especially among Conversos. Their careers unfolded in an age of credulity. Reports of distant lands ruled by king-priests such as Prester John or the sightings of the Lost Tribes of Israel were electrifying the people of Europe. Descriptions of novelties encountered by explorers in Asia and America were a source of wonder among diverse audiences in Europe. It would be well into the seventeenth century before Europeans began to sort out fact from fiction as their geographical horizons expanded to embrace new worlds and unfamiliar phenomena. It should therefore come as no surprise that an eccentric figure like Reubeni, with his accounts of his brother's messianic armies in the remote reaches of Africa or Arabia, could gain a hearing among worldly and even scientifically trained Italian Jews.

---

[10] Abravanel, *Yeshuot meshiḥo*, 2.1.2; see Tishby, 'Acute Apocalyptic Messianism', 285 n. 46; Lawee, *Isaac Abarbanel's Stance Toward Tradition*; id., 'The Messianism of Isaac Abarbanel'. Lawee points to the many continuities between Abravanel's pre- and post-1492 outlook and discusses the extent to which the Expulsion was a turning point in his thinking. He questions whether Abravanel believed in his own messianic visions and dates.

[11] Yerushalmi, 'Messianic Impulses in Joseph ha-Kohen'; Tishby, *Messianism in the Time of the Expulsion from Spain and Portugal* (Heb.).   [12] Beinart, 'A Prophesying Movement in Cordova in the Years 1499–1502' (Heb.).

His testimony was no more implausible to the credulous ears of statesmen and homeless Jews than other tales of magic currently circulating in Europe.

Reubeni attracted Jewish attention immediately on his arrival in Venice in 1524. Little is known of his antecedents.[13] Upon arrival he proclaimed that he was an emissary of his brother, King Joseph, ruler of three of the Lost Tribes of Israel that dwelt beyond the mythical River Sambatyon in Habor. Reubeni announced confidently that he was on an important mission to Europe that required audiences with the most prominent rulers of his day. He was an exotic and charismatic figure who regaled his audience with wondrous stories of his sovereign and his independent Jewish kingdom. Reubeni's vivid tales of King Joseph's battles were persuasive or, at the very least, uplifting. He was also a masterful manipulator of the details of the Jewish messianic tradition. His plan seemed both plausible and daring. Reubeni urgently sought an audience with the pope in order to present his mysterious, quasi-political mission. He proposed that the Christian powers equip an army of Jews and Marranos to join with the Christians in wresting Palestine from the Muslim Turks. The Ottomans had recently captured Jerusalem, and their campaign of further conquests seemed unstoppable. The menace of Ottoman expansion into Europe was all too real. Reubeni claims in his diary that he hoped to secure the backing of Rome to cement diplomatic ties between the Holy Roman Emperor Charles V and the king of France.[14]

Possibly Reubeni planned to link up with Jewish tribes in Arabia, perhaps to conquer Mecca, and he simply sought the pope's intercession to obtain a letter of introduction to the king of Portugal to gain maritime assistance. This alternative suggestion is consistent with both the militant messianism of that time and the messianic portents that some observers read into the Muslim–Christian campaigns of the sixteenth century.[15] Whatever his actual plan may have been, Reubeni succeeded in gaining the pope's attention and was dispatched to Portugal, armed with the letter of introduction.

The pope was apparently intrigued by Reubeni's military designs as well as his flamboyant personality. The idiosyncrasies and personal interests of the pope played a role in advancing Reubeni's mission. Pope Clement VII was known to harbour a personal interest in kabbalistic writings and served as the sponsor of a collection of kabbalistic works by the leading Christian humanist of his day, Egidio de Viterbo. Other Italian Christian scholars also nurtured a keen interest in kabbalah. Additionally, the Christian kabbalist Francesco Giorgi dedicated his *De harmonia mundi* to the pontiff.

---

[13] See Dinaburg, foreword (Heb.) to Reubeni, *Sipur david reuveni*, pp. v–xii; on linguistic and geographical data in Reubeni's diary, see Aescoly, notes (Heb.) to Reubeni, *Sipur david reuveni*, 195–238; on Reubeni's probable origins in the Land of Israel, see Benmelech, 'History, Politics, and Messianism', 42–6, 56–7; on Reubeni as a Sephardi Jew, see Yehuda, 'David Reuveni' (Heb.).

[14] Reubeni, *Diary*, in *Jewish Travellers*, 251, 270, 272, 292.

[15] See Benmelech, 'History, Politics, and Messianism', 42–8.

Reubeni's self-promoting diary depicts both the outpouring of honour and excitement that his presence elicited and his dramatic meeting with the pope and the Vatican hierarchy. It contains a carefully scripted scenario, staged to simulate details of the messianic tradition:

I, David, the son of King Solomon . . . entered the gate of the city of Rome on the 15th day of Adar, 1524. . . . I went to the Pope's palace, riding on horseback, and my servant before me . . . and all the Cardinals and Princes came to see me . . . and I spoke to the Cardinal [Egidio of Viterbo, a noted Christian Hebraist] . . . and he promised to bring the matter before the Pope tomorrow. . . . And I fasted on that Sabbath day. All day long men and women, Jews and Gentiles came to visit me until the evening. Cardinal Egidio sent for Rabbi Joseph Ashkenazi to tell me that the Pope was very pleased, and wished to see me on Sunday before 11. And so in the morning, before prayers, they gave me a horse. . . . At eight o'clock I went to the house of the Pope and entered Cardinal Egidio's room, and with me were about twelve old and honored Jews. As soon as the Cardinal saw me he rose from his chair and we went, I and he, to the apartment of the Pope, and I spoke with him, and he received me graciously, and said, 'The matter is from the Lord.' . . . if thou needest help, the King of Portugal will assist thee, and I will write to him and he will do all. . . . When I left Viterbo, Jews on ten horses accompanied me and we stayed at Bolsena over Sabbath . . . and they showed us great honour.[16]

As Reubeni and his entourage travelled through Italy, the pomp of their retinue and the 'messiah-like' details of his passage excited communities along the route. Christians and Jews, particularly Sephardim, showered him with gifts and heralded him as a redeemer:

The household of R. Jechiel gave us all kinds of food and spices and flowers and apple water, and served me with all the delicacies of the world, and did all kindness and truth with me and sent me great presents and silk robes . . . and on the great fast, they came to me with honour in the house of R. Jechiel. His wife, called Diamante, the daughter of R. Asher Meshullam of Venice, and the mother of R. Jechiel, Signora Laura, and her mother, Signora Sarah, and other young women used to dance in the room where I was and the wife of R. Jechiel played the harp. . . . The Gentiles of Pisa came to me to R. Jechiel's house and blew trumpets.[17]

When Reubeni arrived in Lisbon, he bore a banner emblazoned with the Ten Commandments in Hebrew script, a gesture that conformed to details of the messianic tradition in Jewish aggadah. The banner was supplied by Benvenida Abravanel, an aristocratic scion of the Abravanel family, who had served as a tutor to the wife of the duke of Tuscany. The Conversos of Europe, especially the Marranos of Portugal, were

---

[16] Reubeni, *Diary*, in *Jewish Travellers*, 270–1. Some of the chronological confusion surrounding Reubeni's initial mission stems from his apparent reworking of the sequence of events in his diary after his lack of success in Lisbon. For a discussion and reconstruction of events, see Benmelech, 'History, Politics, and Messianism'; on the broader phenomenon of interest in kabbalah, see Idel, 'Spanish Kabbalah after the Expulsion'.   [17] Reubeni, *Diary*, in *Jewish Travellers*, 281–2.

astonished by Reubeni and mesmerized by the wildly hopeful message he delivered to King João III. During his audience, Reubeni requested ships and arms, or craftsmen who could produce them, for King Joseph of Habor. When he conveyed the details of his plan of joint Portuguese–Jewish military action against the Turks, he piqued the interest and excitement of his audience. His plan, to lead the Conversos of Portugal in a great battle that would hasten redemption, was especially stirring to the Conversos. One Marrano courtier in attendance at Reubeni's royal reception, Diego Pires, heeded Reubeni's call, circumcised himself, and changed his name to Solomon Molkho. With this drastic action, a fateful partnership between the two men began. Molkho's career, even more than Reubeni's, highlights the messianic sensibilities of the Sephardim and the struggling Conversos.

Solomon Molkho was born in Portugal in 1500 or 1501, only four years after the forced conversion of the Portuguese Jews. He received a classical Latin education but probably also received secret instruction from his parents in Hebrew, the Bible, and perhaps also Jewish mysticism. Scrutiny of the activities of Conversos in Portugal was notoriously lax in the early years after their forced conversion. Molkho entered the Portuguese judiciary and rose in its ranks to serve as a secretary in the court in Lisbon. About the year 1524, after Reubeni's tumultuous reception in Portugal and his own circumcision, Molkho declared himself the anticipated messiah who was destined, according to some calculations, to appear in either 1524 or 1530. In need of further instruction and fearful of the consequences of his circumcision, a capital offence for Conversos, according to Christian doctrine, Molkho fled Portugal for Salonica, where he was drawn into a circle of charismatic mystics. At the time Salonica was a magnet for Jews interested in the study of mysticism.

Contemporary historian Joseph Hakohen corroborates the sequence of events and the trajectory of Reubeni's career presented in the latter's diary. Of his impact on Molkho, Hakohen recounts:

Now there came out of Portugal a noble whose name was Solomon Molcho. He was of those who had fled there in the days of the Inquisition. While he was still a youth, he served as one of the secretaries of the king. . . . But when he saw David Reubeni, the Lord touched his heart and he returned to the Lord, the God of our ancestors, and he was circumcised.

At that time he knew nothing of the Law or of the Scriptures. After he was circumcised, the Lord endowed him with wisdom. Soon he became the wisest of men, arousing much wonder. He went to Italy, and with great daring spoke of the Divine Law in the presence of Kings. Then he went to Turkey, and later returned to Rome. He spoke with Pope Clement who, against the desire of his intimates, extended every kindness to him. The Pope gave him a letter of safe conduct, signed with his own hand, permitting him to live as he pleased, and without delay Solomon lived openly as a Jew.

Now Solomon became learned in the wisdom of the Kabbalah. From his lips came words of grace. . . . He preached to large audiences in Bologna and in other places. Many followed him both to hear his wisdom and to test him with riddles, but Solomon answered all their questions. . . . He united himself with David Reubeni; in those days they were as one.[18]

Molkho's flight to Salonica reveals the wide geographical dispersion of Jewish mystics. Salonica, where ascetic pietists had gathered from many corners of the Sephardi diaspora, was emerging as a centre of kabbalistic study. With the messianic era theoretically at hand, mystics were convinced that the secrets of the Torah were accessible, if 'properly' studied. Molkho joined a group under the leadership of Rabbi Joseph Taitatzak, an exiled Spanish kabbalist, and began to engage in fasts and vigils, experiencing visions and spreading his messianic doctrine among like-minded penitents. He also visited Safed and Jerusalem during this period of spiritual transformation. As discussed below, exiles from Spain and Portugal were eagerly congregating in Palestine. By the early decades of the sixteenth century the town of Safed in the Galilee was home to an expanding circle of Sephardi exiles drawn to its atmosphere of holiness and mystical enthusiasm.

In 1530, having returned to Europe, Molkho attracted crowds of eager Sephardim to hear his messianic preaching in Ancona. Contemporary accounts suggest that his esoteric teachings included messianic interpretations of dreams and some magical practices. The initial success of Reubeni at the Vatican and the subsequent excitement generated by the two men in Italy may have been due in no small measure to the great interest in magic and the occult in both Jewish and Christian circles in Italy. Meanwhile, rumours that 1530 was indeed the time of the arrival of the messiah were gaining credence among the Jews. Christian observers, caught up in their own messianic speculations about the year 1530, were also fascinated by Reubeni's extravagant descriptions of the fabled kingdom in Arabia. Although Reubeni did not claim a messianic role for himself, his previous acquaintance with Molkho, together with the ostensible 'realism' of his political project, proved compelling. But eventually the novelty of Reubeni and Molkho wore thin. Word of Molkho's adoption of Judaism brought the full weight of the Inquisition upon him. Much to the dismay of the pope, the Conversos of Europe were becoming agitated by Molkho's message. With the uneventful passing of the year 1530, more sober minds began to reconsider the promised redemption and its imminence.

Joseph Hakohen dispassionately described the tragic denouement of events as Molkho and Reubeni proceeded to Ratisbonne, where Charles V was staying. The powerful king of Spain and Holy Roman Emperor had been one of the potentates whom Reubeni hoped to recruit for his mission against the Turks. Instead of persuading the emperor to participate in their fantastic scheme, however, the two men were imprisoned and handed over to the Inquisition for trial. According to Hakohen:

---

[18] Joseph Hakohen, *Sefer emek habakhah*, in *Memoirs of My People*, 62–3.

Now Solomon was accustomed to discuss the beliefs and faith with the Emperor.... When the Emperor was in Ratisbonne [in 1532], he went there and talked with him. But the Emperor was unresponsive and, because of his ill temper, he would not listen to him. The Emperor commanded that he be clapped in prison, he and his friend Prince David and their followers. And they remained there several days.

After the Turks were repulsed there was a period of respite and the Emperor left Ratisbonne. He returned to Italy and he took all the prisoners with him, bound in fetters, in wagons, setting a special guard over them.... They found Solomon guilty and condemned him to death.[19]

In the course of his trial Molkho was offered the choice of penitence and monetary reward if he returned to Christianity or death at the stake. Molkho rejected the earthly riches and clemency. He longed for a martyr's death, yearning to become 'a burnt offering of sweet savour unto the Lord',[20] and daringly declared that if he had anything to repent, it was that he had been a Christian in his youth. Molkho's wish for martyrdom was fulfilled. He was burned at the stake in Mantua in 1532. Reubeni remained imprisoned, disappearing from public view to languish in obscurity until his death in 1538.

In the aftermath of Molkho's martyrdom, many of his Jewish followers in Italy refused to accept that he was dead. It was rumoured that he had disappeared from the pyre, had been sequestered in his home for eight days after the auto-da-fé, and had never been seen again. Fantastic stories continued to circulate recounting his miraculous deeds and magical attire (he was reported to have donned a colourful *talit* with the mystical names of God embroidered on it, in conformity with magical practices mentioned in medieval Hebrew mystical works). Details of Molkho's tragic demise were embellished and recounted beyond Italy after his death. Some of these stories were later linked to the notorious messianic pretender Shabetai Tsevi.[21] Joseph Hakohen, unsure of how to interpret the words and deeds of Molkho, commented at the conclusion of his account: 'Almighty God alone knows the truth. Would to God I could write down with certainty whether his words were true or false.'[22]

Fanciful accounts of exotic Jewish kingdoms and lost tribes continued to circulate during this age of exploration and discovery. The allure of such accounts remained irresistible. Pretence, dissimulation, and false identity were commonplace during the early modern period. Even sober Protestant theologians in London and Amsterdam were intrigued by what purported to be first-hand accounts of the Jewish identity of South American Indians and other native peoples in newly discovered 'lost kingdoms'. The pragmatic Jewish leader of Amsterdam, Manasseh ben Israel, was stirred by

---

[19] Ibid. 66–7.   [20] Ibid. 66.
[21] On the Shabatean links, see Idel, 'Solomon Molkho as Magician' (Heb.); Eliav-Feldon, 'Invented Identities'.
[22] Joseph Hakohen, *Sefer emek habakhah*, in *Memoirs of My People*, 67; see Idel, 'Solomon Molkho as Magician' (Heb.); 'David Reubeni and Solomon Molko', in *The Jew in the Medieval World*, 187.

reports that the Lost Tribes of Israel had been encountered in South America. His correspondence with millenarian Protestant theologians on messianic concerns, and his petition to Oliver Cromwell to readmit the Jews to England in 1655, would strike a chord in ordinarily staid Protestant and Jewish circles more than a century after the events in Italy.[23]

But there were other ways to decipher the mysteries of the universe and to hasten the advent of the messiah, ones more consonant with normative Judaism. Study of the esoteric portions of the Torah was one traditional mode of discerning the End of Days. Organized repentance and prayer were also traditionally considered effective means of hastening redemption. The tradition of pilgrimages to the graves of the ancient rabbis buried in the Land of Israel constituted a time-honoured expression of piety that might serve as a means of drawing closer to the divine. As the migration eastward of the refugees from Spain accelerated, the Land of Israel was once more humming with Jewish life. The genius of the mystics who began to congregate in the Galilean town of Safed after the Expulsion soon infused ancient forms of Jewish devotion with new mystical meanings. Under their inspiration, Safed provided new dimensions of mystical significance to Sephardi history that have suffused the practice of Judaism until today. This small and modest town has remained one of the most creative sites in Jewish history.

The Foundation of Safed and the Sixteenth-Century Spiritual Revolution

Most centres of Sephardi creativity were in places with some economic or political conditions that facilitated their development. This was not the case with Safed, whose sudden and brief efflorescence was determined entirely by the spiritual energy of a generation of charismatic mystics and penitents cast out of Spain and Portugal who sought personal renewal and salvation in the town. Under the influence of the personal religious charisma of a few exceptional leaders, Safed's remarkable population of immigrants endowed it with a sacred character that facilitated human access to the realm of the divine. The ancient aura of the town and its lore added to its mystical potential.

Safed sits on the slope of a mountain and commands a majestic view of the surrounding countryside. In ancient times, when the Temple in Jerusalem was still standing, beacons on the mountain would announce the sighting of the new moon, informing surrounding Jewish settlements of the beginning of festivals. In the valley below lies an ancient cemetery where mystics and rabbis of the talmudic period are buried. Safed's chief attraction throughout the centuries was its proximity to these

---

[23] On Manasseh ben Israel's mission to Oliver Cromwell, see Chapter 6 below.

graves and the cave at nearby Mount Meron where, according to popular tradition, the second-century rabbi Shimon bar Yohai had composed the Zohar while hiding from the Romans for twelve years. Visits to these sites formed part of a traditional Jewish pilgrimage.

After the seventh-century Arab conquest of Palestine, the Jewish population of Galilee dwindled as a result of local maladministration. Damascus, the seat of the Umayyad caliphate, was the focal point of Jewish settlement in the area. Only a trickle of Jews, particularly Middle Eastern Jews, continued to visit and settle in Safed. When the Jews returned to Jerusalem (from which they had been ousted by the Byzantines), the yeshiva in Jerusalem resumed a commanding presence among the Jewish diaspora, even as the actual Jewish population of the province declined. An informal but practical spiritual division was accepted among Jews in the medieval Muslim world: the leading Jewish legal authorities of the diaspora presided in the academies of talmudic learning in Baghdad, while the rabbinic leadership in Palestine retained only a few of its ancient religious prerogatives, such as setting the calendar and declaring the sighting of the new moon, although a few Palestinian intellectual figures occasionally rivalled those of Baghdad in learning and prestige. By the tenth century, regional religious authorities in Spain, North Africa, and Ashkenazi Europe had replaced the former hegemony of Palestine and Babylonia.

Pilgrims came to visit the Land of Israel, the pious among them determined to spend their final days in the Holy Land, but there was little inclination on the part of the majority of the Jews in the diaspora to inhabit this neglected backwater of the Muslim empire. Palestine's roads were abandoned to brigands and Bedouin, and the routes became too dangerous to travel. Proof of the danger of passage to Palestine could be found in the decision of the rabbis of Morocco that wives were no longer required to accompany their husbands should they desire to settle in the Land of Israel.[24] Circles of 'mourners of Zion' and an influx of Karaites kept Jewish settlement alive in medieval Palestine.

Pilgrimages to the Land of Israel, especially by North African and Italian Jews, resumed in the fifteenth century, leading to an increased circulation of Hebrew travel literature. Travellers' accounts emphasized the desolation of the land, but some also included practical travel advice. Many contained suggestions about how to fulfil Jewish observance while on the road or at sea and also offered specific advice on lodgings available in Jewish communities along the pilgrimage routes. Such accounts, along with visitors, multiplied after the Ottoman conquest of Palestine in 1516. The Italian pilgrim Moses Basola, writing in the 1520s, advised Jewish passengers at sea to bribe the deck officer as protection against hostile passengers and recommended special payments to the ship's cook and 'water captain'.[25] In 1563 Elijah of Pesaro set out from

---

[24] On the vicissitudes of Moroccan Jewish emigration to the Land of Israel, see Gerber, 'The Links between Morocco and Palestine'.   [25] Basola, *In Zion and Jerusalem*, 115–16.

Italy for the Middle East on business, writing home to his brother with similar advice on the precautions that a Jewish merchant should take upon undertaking a sea voyage to Ottoman lands:

> Make sure to get on good terms with the ship's cook. Promise him some money if he leaves you a small space on his stove, and if he will prevent other passengers from pushing you aside. Be very tactful with him to avoid any possible dispute, and keep back part of the money for the last day of the voyage.[26]

Not all the chroniclers were pious pilgrims or practical merchants. Some chroniclers were adventurers, more interested in local curiosities and colourful details of nature than in sacred sites. Most travellers, regardless of their faith, were eager to record the natural or man-made wonders that they encountered. The circulation of this travel literature supplemented the generally widespread knowledge of rudimentary facts about the Land of Israel gleaned from the Bible. By the sixteenth century the Hebrew diaries of the medieval Spanish voyagers Benjamin of Tudela (c.1167) and Judah al-Harizi (1216) were also circulating widely, supplementing the growing number of up-to-date travel accounts by Italian Jewish and Christian pilgrims. The cumulative effect of this literature is difficult to measure. Undoubtedly, it played a role in keeping alive a vivid image of the Land of Israel as a concrete place, thereby encouraging the increasing stream of pilgrims through suggesting the land's accessibility and inherent sanctity. One destination for the new cohort of pilgrims was the Galilee, with its ancient lore and graves of the pious.

Safed was designated as the administrative seat of the province of Safed under the Muslim Mameluke regime (1250–1517), a title that belies the fact that it remained little more than the sleepy centre of an unimportant province. During the fifteenth century, however, as conditions deteriorated in Spain, emigration from Spain to Jerusalem increased. European travellers visiting Jerusalem noted with some surprise that Spanish was the tongue most frequently heard in its streets. Letters dispatched from Palestine to Europe reassuringly described the relative safety of the Land of Israel and emphasized the sanctity of the graves of the patriarchs.[27]

The most popular route to Palestine from Europe was via Italy, especially Venice, through Greece to Alexandria, and from Alexandria by sea or overland by caravan to Palestine. The journey usually took several weeks and was often indefinitely interrupted by pirates lurking off Malta. One characteristic traveller's account informed the Italian Jewish reader that 'the terrible news has reached us of the capture by the Knights of Malta of some 102 of our brethren. May God protect and preserve them, our co-religionists who were on board ship bound to settle permanently in Eretz Yisrael.

---

[26] 'Elijah of Pesaro Sets Out for the Holy Land', in *Letters of Jews through the Ages*, ii. 351; see *Letters from the Land of Israel* (Heb.), 165–96. On Elijah, see J. Shatzmiller, 'Travelling in the Mediterranean in 1563'.

[27] See *Letters from the Land of Israel* (Heb.), 178–93; *Jewish Travellers*, 209–34.

Like a gazelle or deer they rushed about, fleeing the great evils that have befallen them and us.'[28]

The pious pilgrims persisted in their journey despite the hazards at sea, finding a sense of tranquillity and holiness in Safed. One traveller from Italy noted in 1495 the special piety of Safed's Jews, and linked the local messianic expectations to the expulsion of the Jews from Spain:

Safed is built on the slopes of a mountain and is a great city. The houses are small and modest, and when the rain falls it is impossible to walk about town on account of the dirt. . . . It is also difficult to go out in the markets and the streets even during the summer, for you must always be climbing up or down. . . . However, the land is good and health giving and the waters are quite good. . . . The holy congregation numbers about three hundred householders, and most of the Jews have shops of spices, cheese, oil, and sundry pulses and fruits. . . . Around Safed there are many caves. . . . I also saw the synagogue of R. Simeon, son of Yohai, and the wall of a big building that had been destroyed. There is a tradition among the people of Safed that when this wall collapses, the coming of the messiah will be at hand. They told me that lightning struck the wall during the expulsion of the Jews from Spain so that it began to collapse.[29]

Because of its remote location, 30 miles inland from the Mediterranean, and the unsuitability of its hilly terrain for agricultural production, it remained of little official interest until the Ottoman conquest of Egypt and Palestine in 1516/17. After the conquest, travel conditions improved considerably in the eastern Mediterranean. The rabbis of Morocco reiterated the traditional Jewish ruling that wives, formerly exempt from following their husbands to Palestine because of the obstacles and dangers to travel, were once again required to accompany them should they decide to emigrate to Palestine.[30] According to the Talmud, 'if [the husband] desires to go up [to the Land of Israel] and the wife refuses to go up, she is to be compelled to go up; and if she still does not consent, she may be divorced without payment of the *ketubah* [the marriage contract]. Conversely, if she desires to go up to the Land of Israel and the husband refuses to go up, he may be compelled to go up, and if he does not consent, he is forced to divorce and pay the *ketubah*' (BT *Ket.* 110b).[31] A Maghrebi influx to the Land of Israel ensued. A group of mystics from southern Morocco migrated to Safed in 1577, joining other Moroccan rabbis who were studying in the circles of Rabbi Isaac Luria (1534–72).[32]

---

[28] Jews of Cori, letter to Don Joseph Nasi, cited in A. David, *To Come to the Land*, 19; see 'The Persecuted Jews of Cori Decide to Follow Joseph Nasi's Call to Rebuild Tiberias, and Appeal for Assistance to Their Countrymen', in *Letters of Jews through the Ages*, ii. 360.   [29] See *Letters from the Land of Israel* (Heb.), 144.

[30] See Gerber, 'The Links Between Morocco and Palestine'; ead., *Jewish Society in Fez*, 73–6.

[31] In general, Sephardi tradition has maintained that residence in the Land of Israel is a continuous obligation. During periods of instability in the Mediterranean, Moroccan rabbis were divided on the compulsory nature of a spouse's emigration to the Land of Israel. While the Talmud enjoined that a wife join her husband if he should decide to go to the Land of Israel, later rabbinic authorities recognized that there were practical limitations (see Toledano, *The Sephardic Legacy*, 191–203).

[32] Ibid. 20; see also Bashan, 'The Attitude of Eighteenth- and Nineteenth-Century Moroccan Rabbis to the Duty of Settling in the Land of Israel' (Heb.).

Despite the improvement in travel conditions, Jews still needed to exercise caution and to travel in groups. Census records reveal that the elderly, widows, and bachelors tended to emigrate to Palestine in disproportionate numbers. Most of them lived off the charitable donations sent by foreign Jewish communities. Local conditions, especially in Jerusalem, remained problematic. The Jewish population in Jerusalem was deeply divided and less than welcoming to newcomers. Intercommunal bickering over tax allocations was aggravated by the extortionate fiscal demands of the Muslim governor. In addition, the city was constantly threatened by Bedouin marauders. Periodic plagues and locust infestations also militated against settlement. Nevertheless, Sephardi immigration increased, spurred on by a new spirit of messianic anticipation.

The new Ottoman administration, in contrast to its predecessors, showed keen interest in the development of Jerusalem and Safed. It realized that Safed, possessing a fresh-water supply, could support a more dynamic and developed economy. Safed's economic transformation thus began in the sixteenth century. It owed much to the vision and statecraft of Sultan Suleiman the Magnificent (1494–1566) and his Jewish advisers, the physician Moses Hamon and the business tycoons and diplomats Doña Gracia Mendes Nasi (1510–69) and her son-in-law Don Joseph Nasi (1524–79). Sultan Suleiman began several ambitious construction and development projects. As part of his imperial policy of consolidating the conquests of his predecessor Sultan Selim I, Suleiman constructed defensive walls around the city of Jerusalem to block Bedouin incursions from the south. Most important for the economy of Safed, the town received preferential tax treatment to support the introduction of a textile industry for the manufacture of silk and wool.

With the encouragement of Sultan Suleiman, an influx of Sephardi refugees, familiar with advanced European industrial skills, introduced textile manufacture to a region that had been primarily agricultural.[33] It is estimated that fully one-third of the local Sephardi population earned a living from the manufacture of wool, with weaving ranking first among the Spanish Jewish crafts. An Italian Jewish visitor to Palestine in 1535 noted the abundance of goods in Safed: 'All articles of commerce are available.... Fibres, spun and unspun, are exported from Safed in great quantities, also oil, honey and small quantities of silk.' The same correspondent extolled the healthy atmosphere of Safed: 'For the water and the air are unusually good. Few illnesses occur here.... Sick people eat big or small cucumbers, gourds, and many kinds of fruit.'[34]

In 1489 Rabbi Obadiah of Bertinoro reported that Safed enjoyed an atmosphere of harmony and tranquillity.[35] Later travellers also noted the calm and sense of well-being pervading the town, one of them singling out the piety and humility of its Jewish residents, remarking: 'none among them is ashamed to go to the well to draw water

---

[33] See Chapter 5 below.
[34] 'A Jewish Merchant Reports on Life in Palestine', in *Letters of Jews through the Ages*, ii. 339.
[35] See *Jewish Travellers*, 209–50.

and carry home the pitcher on his shoulders, and to go to the market and buy bread, oil, and vegetables. All the work in the house is done by themselves.'[36]

With official encouragement and the sizeable Jewish immigration, Safed entered a period of rapid development. The expansion of its Jewish community is captured in the excited letter that a visiting Italian merchant dispatched to his family in 1535:

> What shall I tell you about this country, as so many people before me have reported its character and greatness in writing and orally? In general, I should like to tell you that, just as in Italy, improvements are being made and new settlements founded, while the population is increasing daily. Such is the case here too. He who saw Safed ten years ago, and observes it now, has the impression of a miracle. For more Jews are arriving here continually, and the tailoring trade grows daily. I have been told that more than 15,000 suits have been manufactured in Safed during this year, besides fancy suits. Every man and every woman who works woolen fabric earns an abundant living.[37]

In 1549 Suleiman erected a perimeter wall around the town. A few years later, in 1557, a fort was erected containing warehouses and protected living quarters for many Jews. According to Joseph Karo (1488–1575), the Jews were initially divided in their support of the building, but they eventually banded together to pay the required fees:

> Beforetimes it occurred to several notables to send to our master the King . . . a request that he build a khan for them near the summit. They drew up a detailed reckoning of each one's participation in the construction, wrote letters and had them witnessed. They then forwarded this request to the court of the Sublime Porte, to a certain individual there who could promote this project, who requested a thousand florins as his fee. Upon receiving this reply the notables withdrew from the project and canceled their intentions . . . and each went his own way. Several years later a pasha [district ruler] arrived from Damascus who wished to build a khan in Safed . . . in order to collect its rents. The kehalim banded together and appointed R. Moses Bibas, may God preserve him, to buy up the fields near the summit, regardless of whether they contained olive trees. All were purchased and presented to the said pasha as a gift, so that he would build a khan on the aforementioned fields. The matter was settled and it came to pass that he built the khan.[38]

However, there were limits to the economic capacity of the town to absorb large numbers of immigrants. Basola cautioned his readers about migrating to Safed, injecting a note of practicality into their enthusiastic decision-making by pointing out that it was necessary to possess a means of livelihood and some specific skill in order to succeed in Safed, and that pious sentiments alone would not suffice.

> Generally speaking, there is much more trade in this land than in Italy, for the Muslims purchase more willingly from Jews than from others. But he who has no capital to invest in trade must be a craftsman. . . . One cannot expect to hire himself out as a teacher or as a house servant or shop

---

[36] Schechter, 'Safed in the Sixteenth Century', 262.

[37] 'An Italian Jew Describes the Revival of Safed under the Ottomans', in Stillman, *The Jews of Arab Lands*, 290.   [38] Joseph Karo, *She'elot uteshuvot avkat rokhel*, cited in A. David, *To Come to the Land*, 96.

assistant. Nor can one live at public expense, for the poor are many. Therefore, he who possesses neither craft nor funds should not leave Italy, lest he regret his actions and return, and a word to the wise is sufficient.[39]

Between 1500 and 1600 Safed's Jewish population grew from around 1,200 to approximately 10,000. Immigrants filled its narrow lanes and winding alleyways. Its vast graveyard contained the graves of countless scholars. By the end of the sixteenth century the town contained at least eighteen synagogues, each possessing a school or a centre for talmudic study. Some housed more than one study group. There was also a school for 400 indigent children, supported by the Jewish community of Istanbul. Torah study was ubiquitous: the study circles of the mystics and the learned were replicated by the town's weavers and simple householders, all of whom attended daily study sessions in the synagogues. One visitor reported that during his visit to Safed he found some 14,000 people studying Jewish law, day and night:

> Following prayers, the entire congregation studies regularly. They sit before the rabbis and are divided into about six classes in each synagogue. Each class studies before leaving the synagogue. One class studies *Ein Ya'aqov*, another the laws of blessings, another studies Maimonides, another studies *Mishnah*, another studies the Talmud with Rashi and Tosafot, another studies the *Zohar*, and another studies the Bible. Consequently, no individual leaves for work or business in the morning without regularly devoting time to the Torah, and in the evenings after prayers, they study at greater length.[40]

Safed's Jewish population was divided into three main groups: Sephardim from Iberia, the Arabic-speaking Jews of the Near East known as Mustaribim, and the Maghrebi or Moroccan Jews (many of whom were originally from Spain). Each group was further divided. Smaller numbers of Jews hailing from Hungary, Provence, Italy, Egypt, and Salonica also gravitated to Safed. By the 1530s Spanish Jews were the most numerous in the town. As elsewhere in the Ottoman empire, and in keeping with their particularistic ways, the Sephardi residents were organized into separate congregations (*kehalim*; sing. *kahal*) based on their geographical origin in Iberia: Aragon, Castile, Catalonia, Seville, Cordoba, Evora. Many of the Spanish Jews arrived in Safed after spending some time in Italy or Egypt, bringing with them multiple identities and liturgical traditions. The Portuguese Jews, most of whom were former Conversos, were separately organized and tended to worship apart from the other Sephardim. The leading *kehalim* maintained their own houses of study. The Ashkenazim and the Portuguese each maintained their own courts as well. A 'council of sages' consisting of ten to twenty members drawn from the congregational courts served as an adjudicating body. In addition, a high court was established, chaired by the scholars of the town.

Table 3.1 shows the breakdown of the population of Safed, as reconstructed by

[39] Basola, *In Zion and Jerusalem*, 61.
[40] Zechariah al-Dahiri, *Sefer hamusar*, cited in A. David, *To Come to the Land*, 121.

Table 3.1 The population of Safed, 1525–96

	1525/6	1555/6	1567/8	1596
Muslims				
Householders	693	1,093	986	1,179
Bachelors	40	222	306	386
Religious officials	26	63	42	53
Disabled	9	9	5	
Jews				
Householders	233	719	945	904
Bachelors		63	12	93
Religious officials				8
Disabled				64

Abraham David from the incomplete Ottoman census records of 1525/6, 1555/6, 1567/8, and 1596/7. It illustrates the population trends among Safed's Jewish and Muslim population during the sixteenth century. David further refines his breakdown of the Jewish population according to geographical origin or congregational membership (Table 3.2).[41] Although the figures are incomplete, they illustrate the closing gap between the Muslim and Jewish populations in Safed and the subsequent decline in the number of Jewish inhabitants after 1570. By the 1570s most of Safed's sages had relocated elsewhere.

The harmony reported in travellers' accounts and by enthusiastic followers of kabbalah in the community should not be exaggerated or romanticized. Relations among the heterogeneous Jewish communities were plagued by tensions. The hardships that most immigrants had endured were only one of many factors in their inability to get along with one another. Differences in religious customs and traditions, even the most minuscule, could attain disproportionate significance. For centuries Jewish identities in Spain had been primarily local or regional, and the autonomous Jewish community in each city was long accustomed to acting independently. In Safed, as in Salonica, Istanbul, and elsewhere in the Ottoman empire, each *kahal* zealously guarded its independence and customs and maintained its own institutions. However, the entire community was represented before the government by one organization, the

---

[41] A. David, *To Come to the Land*, table 3 (p. 99). The data were culled from A. Cohen and Lewis, *Population and Revenue in the Towns of Palestine in the Sixteenth Century*, 161. The tax rolls of the Ottoman authorities customarily listed bachelors separately. The presence of such a large number of bachelors and widows reflects the fact that many single men migrated to Palestine, as did many of the elderly in order to be buried there. As discussed below, geographical origin and congregational membership did not always overlap.

Table 3.2 *Kehalim* of Safed, 1525–68

Kahal	1525/6 Households	1555/6 Households	1555/6 Bachelors	1567/8 Households	1567/8 Bachelors
Mustarab	131	98	10	70	
Provençal	48				
Maghrebi	33	38	7	52	3
Portuguese (Converso)	21	143	18	200	
Castilian		181	11	200	
Sevillian		67	4	160	
Aragonese and Catalonian		51	3	72	
Cordoban		35	7	53	2
Italian		29		35	
Calabrian		24		20	
Ashkenazi		20	1	43	7
Apulian		21	1	25	
Hungarian		12		15	

kolel, which was also responsible for dispatching emissaries throughout the diaspora to collect charitable funds for the *kehalim*, schools, and indigents of Safed.[42]

One major area of disagreement among the Jews of Safed was how to determine the proper affiliation of newcomers.[43] This could be quite complicated, since new arrivals had often lived in so many places during their wanderings that their backgrounds were obscured and their ritual practices blurred. Which *kahal* an individual belonged to was important, since it had a bearing on taxation. As in other parts of the Ottoman empire, Safed's Jews were taxed in one lump sum. It was up to the Jews to apportion the tax burden among themselves as they saw fit. The smaller the *kahal*, the less power it possessed in negotiating its share of the community's fiscal obligations. Complaints of disproportionate taxation by smaller *kehalim* frequently led to litigation. In 1562 Rabbi Moses Trani legislated that newcomers should belong to the *kahal* of their father's birthplace:

The congregations in a certain city made an agreement [*haskamah*] that whoever came to the city [Safed] if both he and his father were born in Italy, even though his [father's] father came from Portugal or Castile or Aragon or some other kingdom, he should belong to the Italian congregation. And if his father was born in one of the aforementioned kingdoms, though he was born in Italy he should belong to his father's kingdom, and the same principle applied to all the nations.

---

[42] The institution of the *shadar*, or travelling fundraiser, grew ever more organized and institutionalized in the course of the eighteenth century. On emissaries from Palestine, see Lehmann, *Emissaries from the Holy Land*.

[43] See Chapter 5 below.

Upon this haskamah's renewal, the Aragonese congregation raised objections, saying that it was not right that someone who is [really] Aragonese . . . should be considered Italian simply because he and his father were born in Italy. They argued further that one of the congregations had reached a compromise with the Italian congregation even prior to the haskamah, that if individuals come from Italy who had themselves been born in Italy as were their fathers, they would not be forced to abide by this agreement. Because of this compromise they did not join in the haskamah. They accepted the agreement on a provisional basis only, for if they had protested, the upholding of the agreement between the representatives of the different congregations . . . would have been impossible.[44]

In practice, these were not simply questions of patriotism or ethnicity but also reflected the ongoing competition between the Italian and the Aragonese *kehalim*. With the passage of time, there were fewer new arrivals from Aragon, and the survival and standing of the *kahal* were threatened. Insisting that a Jew whose father was from Aragon was Aragonese solved the problem for a while, but even that became problematic.

Trani adds an interesting coda, stating that if a person's ancestors were from Aragon, 'by virtue of the Aragonese language, he shall belong to the Aragonese congregation according to the established practice that each person is assigned to the congregation to which he belongs according to linguistic criteria'.[45] Linguistic criteria for determining congregational affiliation were no longer used by the end of the sixteenth century. It is not clear whether this was the result of the widespread supremacy of Ladino or whether it stemmed from local or personality factors.

Isaac Luria was more poetic in his approach to the maintenance of prior affiliations and loyalties, justifying the retention of the customs of one's forefathers in the following manner:

Concerning the many differences in the prayers . . . between *minhag* Sepharad [Sephardi customs], *minhag* Catalonia, *minhag* Ashkenaz, and so on. . . . In heaven there are twelve windows corresponding to the twelve tribes, and that the prayers of each tribe ascend through a different gate that is special to that tribe. . . .

Therefore it is proper that each person hold fast to the order of the prayers according to the customs of his forefathers, for although no one living today knows who is descended from one tribe or another, it may be, since his forefathers held fast to those customs, that he is descended from that tribe . . . and that his prayers will not ascend unless they are said in that way.[46]

The divisions in Safed were reinforced by the power of the *kehalim* over their members. Each *kahal* handled its own affairs, chose its own leadership, and assessed its members to meet its share of the community's tax burden. Each *kahal* also had its own confraternities and charity chests. Scholars would preach to different *kehalim* on different sabbaths. Despite the economic quickening of the textile industry in Safed, the

---

[44] Moses Trani, *Responsa*, cited in A. David, *To Come to the Land*, 113. [45] Ibid.
[46] Isaac Luria, *Sefer hakavanot uma'aseh nisim*, cited in Zimmels, *Ashkenazim and Sephardim*, 116 n. 6; see J. David, 'The Reception of the *Shulhan Aruch* and the Formation of Ashkenazic Identity'.

upkeep of the community remained dependent upon charitable contributions from abroad. Contributions to Safed were among the most faithfully remitted because of the special affection that the diaspora held for Safed and its mystical associations. The special charity chests for Safed, clearly labelled collection boxes or slots in the walls and vestibules of synagogues, can still be seen in the now deserted synagogues in many parts of Europe, especially Italy and Croatia. The names of the donors, even the most modest, were recorded in notebooks or ledgers that the emissaries kept, constituting an important source of information on the size and affluence of Jewish communities during the seventeenth and eighteenth centuries. In some instances, more than one emissary was dispatched to the same locale, thereby complicating how poverty-stricken communities allocated their modest donations. Competition among the emissaries from Safed was compounded by the fact that special emissaries were also dispatched from Jerusalem, Hebron, and Tiberias. As a result, in 1623 the Jews of Safed agreed to send one envoy to each locality rather than having the envoys from the Italian, the Maghrebi, and the Sephardi Jews compete with one another. Local communities abroad also strove to work out methods of charitable donation that would relieve their financial burdens. It was customary for Jews in Morocco and elsewhere to earmark special donations to various Palestinian charities on specific occasions such as a wedding, the circumcision of a son, the first day of the month of Adar, or Purim. A special treasurer was appointed in the local synagogues for each collection.[47] The arrival of an emissary from Palestine occasioned great rejoicing. He was treated with deference bordering on veneration; if he died while on his mission, his grave would frequently become the site of annual pilgrimages. Records reveal the excitement of the impoverished communities of the Atlas mountains and the Saharan regions of Morocco at the arrival of an emissary from Safed, and their extraordinary efforts to contribute from their meagre means to each of the emissaries who arrived, one on the heels of the other.[48]

Safed as a Centre of Kabbalah and Spiritual Fervour

Sixteenth-century Safed was noteworthy for the spiritual fervour of its inhabitants. Spiritual considerations had initially guided many of the new residents to Safed. Their quest for purification and spiritual healing lent a special aura to the town. Some, particularly former Conversos, arrived seeking expiation for what they perceived as their sin. Migration to Safed represented an ascent towards collective redemption for many, a place where the act of waiting for the messiah took on new meaning. Perhaps the

---

[47] Details of special charitable arrangements for the cities of Jerusalem, Safed, and Hebron are spelled out in the communal ordinances of Fez (see Ibn Zur, *Leshon limudim*; id., *Mishpat utsedakah beya'akob*, i. 28, 44a). On charitable donations to Palestine, see Gerber, *Jewish Society in Fez*, 68–77; on the organization of donations in the eighteenth century, see Lehmann, *Emissaries from the Holy Land*.

[48] Gerber, 'The Links Between Morocco and Palestine'.

waiting could be shortened, some suggested, through proper collective and individual actions. Under these exceptional conditions, a kabbalistic renaissance soon unfolded in the city's narrow confines.

The mystical circle of the devout in Safed was gripped by a collective sense of the possibility of imminent redemption. Both urgency and certitude in deliverance ring out in the exhortation of one of the city's luminaries, Solomon Alkabetz (c.1505–c.1576). In 1534, just prior to his departure from Salonica or soon after his arrival in Safed, Alkabetz urged his followers to go to Israel in a stirring exhortation:

> Go up to the Land of Israel, for not all times are opportune. There is no hindrance to salvation, be it much or little. Let not your eyes have pity on your worldly goods for you eat of the goodness of the higher land. . . . Make haste, therefore, to go up to the land for I sustain you here and I shall sustain you there.[49]

In Safed, Alkabetz joined a group of like-minded penitents and kabbalists, including his brother-in-law and disciple, the great mystic Moses Cordovero (1522–70). Like Alkabetz, many of Safed's mystics had led a peripatetic existence before settling down in Palestine. They shared a mystical lore they had acquired in Spain or among older Spanish exiles, deepened by their membership in kabbalistic circles in North Africa or the Balkans. Study of the Zohar and other Iberian mystical texts dominated their intellectual life. Some of them also shared unusual states of consciousness, techniques of communion with departed spirits, including the souls of the ancient sages who had authored particular mishnaic teachings.

The biography of Jacob Berab (1474–1541) encapsulates some of the expectations and mindset of the thinkers and mystics congregating in Palestine. Berab was born in Maqueda in Spain and studied at the renowned yeshiva of Rabbi Isaac Aboab in Guadalajara. Soon after 1492 he was in Fez, where, at the age of just 18, he briefly headed a yeshiva. By 1493 he had left Fez and was temporarily in Tlemcen in Algeria. When the Spanish invaded North Africa in 1510, Berab fled to Egypt and became involved in a circle of mystics there. He then moved to Jerusalem, where he headed another yeshiva until 1519. From 1524 until his death he moved back and forth between Damascus and Safed, finally heading a yeshiva in Safed. Such mobility and its attendant sense of rootlessness was characteristic of many of the Spanish exiles of 1492.

While Berab was noted for his erudition, his fame rests upon his introduction of the rite of rabbinic ordination, a rite that had ceased in antiquity. Through this revolutionary act, Berab hoped to transform Jewish life and hasten the course of history to its messianic fulfilment. He began the process by ordaining his star students, believing that they could then serve as judges in a revived Sanhedrin, the ancient Jewish supreme court. His reason for this controversial action was simple, despite its revolutionary

---

[49] Solomon Alkabetz, introduction to Joseph Karo, *Magid mesharim*, in *Jewish Mystical Testimonies*, 101; see Fine, *Physician of the Soul, Healer of the Cosmos*, 50, 378 n. 24.

nature. It was clear to him that his generation was desperately in need of repentance and redemption. The messiah could not usher in redemption until the sins of the Jews, particularly those of the Conversos, had been expiated, but, according to biblical and talmudic tradition, some sins could only be expiated through the administration of punishments, such as flogging, that only the Sanhedrin could impose. Unfortunately, the Sanhedrin had not convened in more than a millennium, and it required seventy ordained scholars. Berab resolved to reintroduce the ancient rite of ordination, beginning with his own in 1538. This controversial measure was immediately opposed by the leading scholar of Jerusalem, Rabbi Levi ibn Habib. The messianic overtones of Berab's act were not lost on the more spiritually oriented of his students, such as Joseph Karo. Indeed, Berab's actions had an electrifying effect, especially on former Conversos. Venerable authorities could be cited for Berab's audacious attempt to restore the ancient ceremony of rabbinic ordination. None other than Maimonides had indicated that at the time of redemption 'the great scholars of the generation gathering in the Land of Israel can elect one of their members and he can ordain others'.[50] As news spread of Berab's attempt to reconstitute the Sanhedrin, messianic excitement mounted, only to subside temporarily with his death.

From Berab's ordination in 1538 to Alkabetz's death in 1576, mystics, including most prominently Moses Cordovero, Solomon Alkabetz, Joseph Karo, and Isaac Luria, continued to seek wholeness and redemption in Safed. Their activities and writings would revolutionize the ways in which later generations of Jews worshipped and thought about the relationship of God to the Jewish people. As one modern scholar noted, 'no place in Jewish history could point to so brilliant a gathering of men, so great in their respective branches, so diversified in the objects of their study, and so united by the dominant thought of religion, as were attracted to Safed during the greater part of the sixteenth century'.[51]

It is significant that the greatest legal mind of the generation, Joseph Karo, was also a kabbalist, combining in one person a towering legal scholar and fervent pietist. Karo was born in Spain or Portugal, and his early years remain largely unknown. At points in his wanderings after the Expulsion he lived in Egypt, Adrianople, Salonica, and Istanbul —all centres of mounting Sephardi spirituality. Karo encountered Molkho in Salonica and was profoundly influenced by his life and death, repeatedly referring to him in *Magid mesharim*. He may also have briefly been a student of Berab's in Egypt; he was certainly one in Safed. He referred to Berab as his master and was one of those whom Berab ordained.[52] Karo played many roles in Safed: administrator, patron of academies, head of the Jewish court, and member of the kabbalistic circle of Alkabetz and Cordovero.

---

[50] Maimonides on Mishnah *San.* 1: 3; see also Dimitrovsky, 'New Documents Regarding the "Semicha" Controversy in Safed' (Heb.).

[51] Schechter, 'Safed in the Sixteenth Century', 278.　　　　[52] Werblowsky, *Joseph Caro*.

Karo began work on *Beit yosef*, his vast commentary on the *Arba'ah turim* of Jacob ben Asher, while he was still in Greece. He laboured on it from 1522 to 1555, completing it in Safed. It was intended as a comprehensive legal guide and to provide a degree of religious uniformity to a generation that had undergone catastrophic upheaval and dislocation. In the work he compiled a vast corpus of Sephardi legal traditions. Ironically, it was the abridgement of this work, known as the *Shulḥan arukh*, which Karo composed as an afterthought, that became the definitive code of Jewish law. When Rabbi Moses Isserles added glosses to Karo's work, the book achieved universal Jewish usefulness and approbation.

In Safed, Karo was soon recognized as a visionary and mystic, even though he is usually remembered today for his law code. His revelations on the law were communicated through his *magid*, a heavenly voice that spoke in Aramaic, which Karo identified as the manifestation of the Mishnah. His contemporaries confirm that when he communicated with his *magid*, he spoke Aramaic in a voice that was different from his usual tone.[53] Xenoglossia, or speaking in a foreign tongue, is a common symptom of spirit possession. Karo recorded all the utterances of his *magid* in his mystical diary, *Magid mesharim*, and claimed that the *magid* inspired him in his performance of personal acts of asceticism and piety. It first manifested itself to him on the night of Shavuot (the festival commemorating the giving of the Torah to the Jewish people) while he was still in Greece, possibly when he was in the circle of mystics of Rabbi Taitatzak.

The eve of the Sabbath, 29th of Iyyar, portion *Be-Midbar Sinai*, I ate but little and drank the same and I studied the Mishnah at the beginning of the night. I then slept until daybreak so that when I awoke the sun was shining. I was very upset, saying to myself: 'Why did I not arise during the night so that the word should come to me as beforetimes?' Nevertheless I began to rehearse the Mishnah and I studied five chapters. As I was reading the Mishnah the voice of my beloved knocked in my mouth and the lyre sang of itself.[54]

The appearance of a *magid* during Torah study was an accepted phenomenon among mystics. Karo's possession by the spirit of the Mishnah did not remain restricted to his circle of fellow mystics, but was soon known throughout the Jewish world. Other mystics in Karo's circle, such as Cordovero, appear to have experienced magidic possession as well. The phenomenon is movingly and dramatically described by Alkabetz:

No sooner had we studied two tractates of the Mishnah than our Creator smote us so that we heard a voice speaking out of the mouth of the saint [Karo]. It was a loud voice with letters clearly enunciated. All the companions heard the voice, but were unable to understand what was said. It was an exceedingly pleasant voice, becoming increasingly strong. We all fell upon our faces and

---

[53] Solomon Alkabetz, introduction to Joseph Karo, *Magid mesharim*, in *Jewish Mystical Testimonies*, 101–3; see also Fine, 'Benevolent Spirit Possession in Sixteenth-Century Safed', 108.

[54] Joseph Karo, *Magid mesharim*, in *Jewish Mystical Testimonies*, 111; see also Fine, 'Benevolent Spirit Possession in Sixteenth-Century Safed', 105.

none of us had any spirit left in him because of our great dread and awe. The voice began to address us, saying: 'Friends, choicest of the choice, peace be to you beloved companions. Happy are you and happy are those who bore you. Happy are you in this world and happy in the next that you resolved to adorn Me on this night. . . . Behold, I am the Mishnah, the mother who chastises her children and I have come to converse with you . . . .' All these things did we hear with our own ears and much more of a like nature. . . . We all broke into tears at the great joy we had experienced and when we heard of the anguish of the Shekhinah because of our sins, her voice like that of an invalid in her entreaties.[55]

Special spiritual preparation was required to enter into this contemplative state. Hayim Vital (1542–1620) used to seclude himself alone in his house so that he would not be distracted, and concentrated on his soul to the extent that he was no longer aware of the presence of his body or any other matter.[56]

Karo and his followers would take long walks on the sabbath to the tombs of ancient teachers in the Galilee, holding special vigils at their graves. There they performed practices such as prostration, prayer, incantation of divine names, fasting, and self-mortification in order to achieve altered states of consciousness, which they believed drew the presence of God (the Shekhinah) to them, gave them new insights into the Torah, and removed their sins, thereby facilitating redemption and the advent of the messiah. Union with the souls of other mystics of prior ages might also occur during such experiences. The sabbath was the most propitious time for such excursions since it was believed that during the sabbath Jews take on an additional soul and God dwells among his people. The excursions were not simply 'returns to nature' but were embedded in a more profound theory of the exile of the Shekhinah and humanity's union with God.[57] When carried to an extreme, some of their techniques were contrary to normative rabbinic teaching.

Solomon Alkabetz is best remembered for his poem 'Lekhah dodi' ('Come, My Beloved'), which has been incorporated into the synagogue service on Friday evening to usher in the sabbath in all branches of Judaism. The mystics' intoxication with the sabbath generated several other mystical hymns, although 'Lekhah dodi' remains the most famous. Rabbi Eliezer Azikri (1533–1600) composed a hymn still widely sung on Friday evenings, 'Yedid nefesh' ('Friend of my Soul'), and Rabbi Israel Najara (c.1555–1628) composed 'Yah ribon olam' ('Master of the Universe').

Alkabetz's 'Lekhah dodi' conveys some of the intensity of the mystical atmosphere of Lurianic kabbalistic circles, and hints at the mystical dimensions that they injected into their sabbath celebrations and daily worship. While the images of the sabbath as a bride and a queen are rooted in rabbinic thought, they were infused by Alkabetz with new mystical fervour:

[55] Solomon Alkabetz, introduction to Joseph Karo, *Magid mesharim*, in *Jewish Mystical Testimonies*, 100.
[56] See Fine, 'Benevolent Spirit Possession in Sixteenth-Century Safed', 106.
[57] Benayahu, 'Devotional Practices of the Kabbalists of Safed in Meron' (Heb.).

Come, my friend, to meet the bride, the Sabbath let us welcome
'Observe' and 'Remember' in a single commandment
God the only one gave us to hear
The Lord is one, and one His name,
For fame, for glory, and for praise
Come, my beloved, to meet the bride, the Sabbath let us welcome

To greet the Sabbath let us go,
For it is ever a fount of blessing
Poured forth of old, at the very beginning,
Last act in creation, first in God's plan
Come my beloved, to meet the bride, the Sabbath let us welcome

Thou shrine of the King, thou royal city,
Arise, come forth from amidst thy ruins.
Too long has thou dwelt in the valley of weeping:
Now will God have compassion upon thee.
Come, my beloved, to meet the bride, the Sabbath let us welcome

Shake off thy dust now and arise,
Shake thee in raiment of beauty, my people;
God has made with thee a covenant of peace;
So pray: Be Thou nigh in my soul; redeem it
Come, my beloved, to meet the bride, the Sabbath let us welcome

Bestir thyself! Bestir thyself!
For thy light has come, arise and shine.
Awake! Awake! And sing thy song,
For the glory of God in thee is revealed.
Come, my beloved, to meet the bride, the Sabbath let us welcome

Be not ashamed! Be not ashamed!
Why be downcast? Why be sad?
My afflicted people in thee will take shelter,
In the city rebuilt on its ancient site.
Come, my beloved, to meet the bride, the Sabbath let us welcome

Despoiled be all that would despoil thee,
And banished all that would destroy thee;
Thy God will take delight in thee
As a bridegroom rejoicing in his bride,
Come, my beloved, to meet the bride, the Sabbath let us welcome

Thou wilt spread abroad to right and left,
And in gratitude adore thy God,
Delighting ever in His salvation;
Then will we rejoice and be glad.
Come, my beloved, to meet the bride, the Sabbath let us welcome

> O come in peace, thy husband's crown,
> Come in joy and exultation,
> Amidst the faithful of God's treasured people,
> Come, Sabbath bride! Come, Sabbath bride!
> Come, my beloved, to meet the bride, the Sabbath let us welcome.[58]

The kabbalists of Safed would leave the town on Friday evening to greet the sabbath in the fields, re-enacting a practice described in the Talmud: 'Rabbi Hanina robed himself and stood at sunset of the sabbath eve and exclaimed, "Come and let us go forth to welcome Queen Sabbath!" Rabbi Yannai donned his robes on the sabbath eve and exclaimed, "Come, O Bride, Come, O Bride!"' (BT *Shab.* 119a). Today, this practice has been condensed into the recitation of the hymn in the synagogue at the beginning of the Friday evening service: at the final verse of the hymn, the congregation customarily rises, turns towards the west and bows. According to Hayim Vital, these events and rituals were carefully orchestrated by Isaac Luria:

> Go out into an open field and recite: 'Come and let us go into the field of holy apple trees in order to welcome the Sabbath queen . . . .' Stand in a certain place in the field: it is preferable if you are able to do so on an elevated spot, one that is clean in front of you, as well as behind you, for a distance of four cubits. Turn your face towards the west, where the sun sets, and at the very moment that it sets, close your eyes and place your left hand upon your chest and your right hand upon your left. Direct your concentration, while in a state of awe and trembling as one who stands in the presence of the King, so as to receive the extra Sabbath holiness. . . . Begin by reciting the psalm 'Give to the Lord, O heavenly beings' [Ps. 29], singing it entirely in a sweet voice. Following this, recite three times: 'Come, O Bride, Come O Bride, O Sabbath Queen.' Next recite 'A psalm, a song for the Sabbath day' [Ps. 92] in its entirety, followed by 'The Lord is King; He is robed in majesty' until 'For all time' [Ps. 93]. Then open your eyes and return home.[59]

The mystical practices of Karo and Alkabetz reached their apogee in the greatest of the Safed mystics, Isaac Luria. Luria was born in Jerusalem in 1534 to an Ashkenazi father and a Sephardi mother. Orphaned at an early age, he was reared by an uncle in Egypt, where he studied kabbalah while also engaging in commerce, travelling throughout the country on business. This combination of mysticism, mundane economic activities, and social interchanges was common for the mystics of his generation. It was later considered as paradigmatic for Sephardim. The Sephardi mystics were not ascetic recluses removed from society but married people, actively engaged in commerce or crafts. By the time that Luria moved to Safed in 1569, the city's dual reputation as a centre of talmudic scholarship and a gathering place of the pious was widespread. He had already developed a set of esoteric doctrines compatible with the

---

[58] Solomon Alkabets, 'Lekhah dodi', in *Sabbath and Festival Prayer Book*, 11–12. Reproduced with the permission of the Rabbinical Assembly.

[59] Hayim Vital, *Sha'ar hakavanot*, cited in Fine, *Physician of the Soul, Healer of the Cosmos*, 249.

mindset and aspirations of his Safed contemporaries, and seemed tailor-made for the society in which he immediately immersed himself.

At the time of Luria's arrival, Safed was awash with messianic expectation, mystical exercises, and fervent study. His charismatic personality was instantly recognized. It was said that he could understand the language of animals, especially birds, and the conversation of trees, and that he knew the healing properties of plants. One hagiographical account of Luria's life, written by a follower, Shelomoh Dresnitz, in 1607, illustrates the enormous personal impact he had upon his contemporaries and disciples:

> First, I would like to say something about the loftiness of the ARI, Rabbi Isaac—of blessed memory—although what I say amounts to only a drop in the bucket. . . . At his birth Elijah—of blessed memory—appeared to his father . . . and said to him: 'Take heed, now, on the day of the circumcision, not to circumcise this child until you see me standing beside you in the synagogue'. . . . After the child had been circumcised, Elijah returned the child to his father, saying: 'Here is your child, Take good care of him for a great light shall shine forth from him upon all the world.'[60]

The figure of Elijah is, of course, intimately connected with the Jewish messianic tradition. Dresnitz provides numerous examples of Luria's miraculous gifts:

> Luria knew all the deeds of men and even their thoughts. He could read faces, look into the souls of men, and recognize souls that migrated from body to body. He could tell you about the souls of the wicked that had entered into trees and stones and animals and birds; he could tell you what commandments a man had fulfilled and what sins he had committed since his youth; he knew wherein a sinful man had been punished by God and would prescribe 'improvements' to remove a moral blemish, and he knew just when such a moral defect had been corrected. He understood the chirping of the birds, and through their flight he divined strange things, as is referred to in the verse: 'For a bird of the air shall carry the voice, and that which hath wings shall tell the matter.' All of this he acquired because of the piety, asceticism, purity, and holiness that he had exercised since his youth.[61]

Luria and his circle engaged in a variety of techniques and practices familiar to other mystical traditions to enhance their spiritual experience. Some of their practices, such as the repetition of key words or verses of Scripture, were accepted modes of study and meditation among Jews. Other techniques included writing words in certain combinations, concentrating intensely and exercising self-hypnosis, and undergoing long periods of solitary meditation. Although these activities were not necessarily antithetical to normative Judaism, they had generally been carefully controlled and limited to small circles of devotees. It is therefore not unusual that Luria was reluctant

---

[60] Shelomoh Dresnitz, 'A Short Biography of the "Lion"', in *The Jew in the Medieval World*, 289. On Luria as a messianic figure, see Fine, *Physician of the Soul, Healer of the Cosmos*, 322–6; on the place of Elijah in Safed circles, see Werblowsky, *Joseph Caro*, 40–1, 269–70.

[61] Shelomoh Dresnitz, 'A Short Biography of the "Lion"', in *The Jew in the Medieval World*, 289–90.

to teach large numbers of disciples, focusing instead on a small group of followers whose souls he sought to mend and to relieve of their 'burden of sin'. He emphasized ethical behaviour and disciplined fulfilment of the commandments in order to repair the broken world and the cosmic order. It is noteworthy that, although Luria's techniques were radical, the kabbalists nevertheless remained within the confines of Jewish law, never deviating from halakhah. Their radicalism was more theoretical than practical.

Luria's kabbalistic teachings contained a radical and dynamic philosophy of Jewish history. Instead of contemplating the End of Days and redemption, Luria and his disciples strove to understand the beginning of the universe. Luria's elaborate theory of redemption was based upon his original notions of creation. In his theoretical formulations and visions, Luria provided new twists to the traditional kabbalistic notion that human action can influence the divine realm, daringly suggesting to his fellow mystics that the exile of the Jews was not the result of divine punishment. Rather, the divine was also, as it were, in exile. Indeed, the dispersion of the people Israel mirrored the divine state. In this context, Luria worked out an elaborate theory of creation that did not ignore history, as philosophers were wont to do, but instead placed the fate of the Jews at its very core: the history of the people of Israel mirrored the events of the cosmos. Divine sparks, he explained, had been scattered everywhere and entrapped during the original act of creation and needed to be liberated and reconstituted. The task of reconstituting the divine and restoring those sparks to wholeness was a Herculean one, but one that the exiled Jews of his generation were in a unique position to perform. His doctrine of *tikun olam* (repair of the world) embodied a complex theory of creation and the role of the Jews in the universe. Luria posited that the healing of the cosmos was dependent upon the virtuous behaviour and self-purification of the Jews. While the idea that performance of the commandments ensured interaction with the divine and maintained harmony and unity in the cosmos was not original to the mystics of Safed, it was developed by them in new and daring ways. According to Luria, the sufferings of his generation were neither a sign of God's abandonment of his people nor a punishment for their sins. On the contrary, the Jews' suffering served a cosmic purpose. Through their dispersion and their correct performance of the commandments, they could gather the divine sparks dispersed or entrapped among the nations and become partners with God in his self-liberation. Moreover, Luria assured his disciples, the process of cosmic restoration was not merely in progress, but was practically complete. Through the efforts of his generation, including the performance of new mystical rites and the recitation of esoteric texts of the Bible and the Mishnah, the last and most difficult steps to redeem God and the world might be completed. Thus, the kabbalists of Safed endowed the practice of Judaism with the loftiest of possible achievements, participation in the inner mysteries of the divine. They also provided an ingenious rationale for the sufferings and dislocations of their generation.

Luria felt himself to be in contact with the souls of pious teachers of the past, especially the second-century sage Shimon bar Yohai, the putative author of the Zohar. He would spend many hours in prayer and meditation at Bar Yohai's grave. He developed a full-blown doctrine of metempsychosis, or transmigration of souls. The new religious practices introduced by Luria included the exorcism of evil spirits that were believed to have entered a living soul in past lives. His followers reportedly beheld apparitions of the dead: the experience of being 'possessed' by the dead entered the lore of Safed and was carefully recorded by some mystics.[62]

Some of the beliefs of the Safed mystics were later adopted and reinterpreted by the Shabateans and were ultimately repudiated after the failure of the Shabatean movement. Other Safed practices, however, entered into the mainstream of Jewish worship and remain part of contemporary Jewish observance. Thus, for instance, the fasting of the first-born male on the day before Passover and the night vigil of study and intense prayer before Shavuot and Hoshanah Rabbah originated among the mystics of Safed. So, too, the main mystical text of Safed mysticism, the Zohar, found a place in the libraries of many Jews, particularly Sephardim. Luria's unusual personal activities, such as his graveside prostrations and communion with the souls of ancient teachers, would become the source of mystical study and exegesis alongside his teachings. His memory remained especially vivid among Jews in Muslim lands.

Luria's stay in Safed was brief but productive—indeed, revolutionary. In less than three years, he captured the imagination of his generation with his charismatic personality and daring doctrines. He injected new life and structure into Jewish mysticism, infusing many prior practices with messianic meaning. His premature death at the age of 38 did not spell the end of his movement. A vivid hagiographical literature soon arose. His immediate followers, after initially withholding information on his life and teachings from the public, eventually began publishing and publicizing his sayings and deeds. Hayim Vital added his own rites and rituals to those of his master. Vital's habit of reciting the Mishnah in seclusion drew upon Safed practice and added a new emphasis on the notion of personal exile that created a permanent connection between Sephardim, spiritual devotion, and the town. In the generation following Luria's death, his mystical genius was slowly accepted in kabbalistic circles abroad as hagiographical biographies multiplied and the teachings of Safed were disseminated through its printing press and the printing establishments in Italy.

'From Tiberias, the Redemption will Begin'[63]

Sephardi settlement in Palestine involved both pragmatic and spiritual considerations. While the mystics flocked to Safed, more sober-minded Sephardi statesmen in Istanbul

---

[62] Fine, 'Benevolent Spirit Possession in Sixteenth-Century Safed', 106–23.
[63] BT *RH* 31b; see also Maimonides, *Mishneh torah*, 'Laws of the Sanhedrin', 14: 12: 'According to tradition,

attended to the mundane details of the process. With the encouragement of his trusted advisers Doña Gracia and Don Joseph, Sultan Suleiman turned his attention to bolstering the economy of other points in the Galilee. The city of Tiberias on the shores of the Sea of Galilee was the focus of much of the attention of Doña Gracia and Don Joseph. Unlike Safed, whose importance was based on the ancient sages who were buried there, Tiberias had been the historic seat of Jewish scholarship and jurisprudence since the destruction of the Second Temple. It was where the compilers of the Palestinian Talmud and the redactors of the text of the Bible known as the Masoretes had worked. Tiberias had also been the seat of the Jewish patriarchate, the last vestige of Jewish autonomy in Palestine, until the institution was extinguished by the Byzantine authorities in the fifth century. Its hot springs and a scattering of ancient tombs of rabbinic leaders ensured a small but continual flow of visitors throughout the centuries.

When the Ottomans conquered Palestine in 1516, Tiberias and its surroundings were barren and neglected, its terrain of black basalt rocks rendering agricultural cultivation almost impossible. Only a handful of Jews lived uncomfortably among its ruins. But Don Joseph and Doña Gracia had ambitious plans for Tiberias. They dreamed of establishing a textile industry there, much like Salonica's, and of creating a self-supporting economy. They probably also envisioned the creation of a refuge for the Sephardi outcasts of Europe, much in the vein of the later Zionist movement. Doña Gracia, already well on in years, hoped to spend her last years in retirement in Tiberias, and she commissioned a grand villa to be erected there. In 1560 the sultan granted her the concession to Tiberias and its surrounding villages, including permission for Jews to settle there and the right to build a wall around the town in return for an annual fee of 1,000 gold pieces, which he confirmed in 1566.[64] Doña Gracia died in Istanbul in 1569 before she could retire to the shores of the Sea of Galilee, and no traces of her retirement villa have been found.[65] However, the news that she was coming to settle there electrified the local Jews, who were facing many adverse conditions.

In 1563 Don Joseph obtained a charter from Sultan Suleiman to collect the taxes of Tiberias and seven surrounding villages. In the light of the domination of Safed by mystics, Tiberias seemed to Don Joseph to possess better prospects for economic development. To this end, he ordered the planting of mulberry trees and sugarcane,

---

Israel is destined to return first to Tiberias and proceed thence to the Temple'. The idea that the redemption will begin in Tiberias when the wall there is rebuilt appears in Zeph. 1: 11; BT *Shab.* 31b (see Vilnay, *Legends of Galilee, Jordan and Sinai*, 157). Rabbinic legend also states that the messiah's staff of almond wood is concealed in Tiberias (Ps. 110: 2; Vilnay, *Legends of Galilee, Jordan and Sinai*, 162, 391 n. 162).

[64] Baron, *A Social and Religious History of the Jews*, xviii. 110–18.

[65] On Doña Gracia's activities in Venice and Istanbul, see Chapters 4 and 5 below. A Dona Gracia Hotel opened in Tiberias in the 1990s. Its lobby contains a small museum that houses a series of life-sized exhibitions of various dramatic moments in her career. Seminars dedicated to the study of Jewish women are often held at the hotel.

and introduced the cultivation of silkworms and the necessary infrastructure for the manufacture of soap. A wall was erected around the town and a new aqueduct, flour mills, and olive presses were constructed. In addition, the governor of Damascus ordered a contingent of janissaries to guard the fledgling Jewish community at night, and the sultan ordered that regular market days should be held there. Don Joseph began to import Spanish wool and merino sheep with the intention of starting a textile industry. For a brief moment, it appeared as if Tiberias might become a major manufacturing centre, possibly even succeeding in cutting into the Spanish and Venetian monopoly on the manufacture of wool and textiles. In the minds of Doña Gracia and Don Joseph, a rebuilt Tiberias would serve as the vanguard for Sephardi settlement in a renewed Land of Israel.

The sudden development of the area around the Sea of Galilee could not help but ignite Jewish hopes that a Jewish principality was in the making. One echo of this excitement is preserved in a letter from Italy mentioning the planned departure for Tiberias of an entire community of Jews from the small town of Cori, near Rome. Economically crushed by the introduction of a ghetto in Cori as elsewhere in the Papal States in the aftermath of the promulgation of the papal bull *Cum nimis absurdum* in 1555, the Jewish residents decided to emigrate. According to their account of the events, word had reached them that Don Joseph had 'lavished money from his purse and arranged in many places, such as Venice and Ancona, ships and help, in order to put an end to the groaning of the captives'.[66] Most of the Jews of Cori never reached Palestine. Many were unable to reach the ports where Don Joseph's ships were waiting; most of the rest were captured and enslaved by the Knights of St John of Malta. After lamenting their fate, the writer remarks:

> We have indeed learned that many have already set out and crossed the seas, with the assistance of the communities and the aforementioned Prince [Don Joseph Nasi]. It has been told us, moreover, that he seeks especially Jews who are craftsmen, so that they may settle and establish the land on a proper basis. Hearing all this, we became stirred with a single heart and went as one man to the synagogue.[67]

In 1569 700 Italian Jews congregated in Pesaro and Senigaglia awaiting passage to Palestine. Their ultimate fate is unknown.

Don Joseph's ambitious plans for the development of Tiberias eventually failed. The local Muslim and Christian clergy opposed the plan and aroused the surrounding Arab population to resist the efforts. A rumour was spread by one of the local sheikhs that Islam would fall when Tiberias was rebuilt by the Jews, and Muslim masons refused

---

[66] 'The Persecuted Jews of Cori Decide to Follow Joseph Nasi's Call to Rebuild Tiberias, and Appeal for Assistance to Their Countrymen', in *Letters of the Jews through the Ages*, ii. 362; see also C. Roth, *The House of Nasi*, 126–7.

[67] 'The Persecuted Jews of Cori Decide to Follow Joseph Nasi's Call', ii. 362; see also Baron, *A Social and Religious History of the Jews*, xviii. 115.

to continue working on the project.⁶⁸ Bonifacio di Ragusa, head of the Franciscan order in Palestine, stirred up the native Christian population with another rumour that the Jews intended to take over a local church and convert it into a synagogue, although it was actually an ancient synagogue on the shore of the lake that had been reopened. At the same time the Turkish guards sent to keep out marauders were negligent in their duties.⁶⁹ Eventually local Muslim and Christian opposition, coupled with the death of Selim II (1574) and his vizier, Mehmet Sokollu (1579), put an end to the project. Don Joseph's interest in Tiberias had waned and his energies were diverted by the Ottoman–Venetian War over Cyprus and his plans to develop his dukedom on the island of Naxos, recently bestowed on him by Selim II. However, the significance of the abortive project should not be underestimated. It reveals the enterprising mentality of sixteenth-century Sephardim and the proactive behaviour of Sephardi courtiers in Istanbul.

There were many causes for the decline of the Jewish community in Safed. Plagues and earthquakes devastated the indigent province, but the political policies and corruption of the Ottoman provincial administration proved to be the greatest deterrents to continuing immigration and development. In the wake of the Ottoman conquest of Cyprus in 1571, Selim II attempted to forcibly deport the most productive segment of Safed's Jewish community, in keeping with the traditional Ottoman policy of *sürgün* (forced population transfers) that was routinely applied to consolidate Ottoman rule in newly conquered regions. The order was suspended on 23 May 1578, but Jewish emigration from Safed in anticipation of the deportations had already begun.⁷⁰ Only months after the order was rescinded, the Jewish inhabitants of Safed petitioned the authorities again, protesting at their continual harassment, the exorbitant taxes and bribes they were forced to pay to corrupt officials, and the havoc wrought by unruly janissary troops. The following decree vividly conveys the growing dysfunction of the once smoothly operating Ottoman administration:

The Jews of Safed have now presented a petition . . . and have complained of wrong doing to them. They have stated: Although according to their customs Jews do not do any work on Saturdays, the Sanjaq-Beg troubles us at present saying, 'Most certainly you shall work.' He also demands excessive amounts of money. As we are not in a position to pay the money he makes us transport dung on that day. Moreover, robbers raid the house of a Jew. In the ensuing fight the Jew is wounded and after two or three days, he dies. Alleging that we have killed him, the Beg detains us for three days. . . . When we want to come before the Qadi and complain, he gives us permission, but says 'Be careful [in what you are going to state].' The next day, the Sanjaq-Beg imprisons the Jews, gives each of them one hundred strokes with the *capraz* [a metal whip] and demands five hundred gold pieces. Moreover, the Beg's soldiers break into houses at night. The next day, he

---

⁶⁸ Joseph Hakohen, *Sefer emek habakhah*, in Stillman, *The Jews of Arab Lands*, 293.
⁶⁹ Heyd, 'Turkish Documents Concerning the Reconstruction of Tiberias in the Sixteenth Century' (Heb.).   ⁷⁰ See Chapter 5 below.

imprisons some Jews saying 'In the Jewish quarter houses were broken into. Find the thief!' He gives them seventy or eighty strokes with the *kirbac* [a leather whip] and extracts from them a high fine.[71]

A census of Jews aimed at increasing tax receipts was ordered in Safed in 1577. In 1584 the sultan agreed to investigate Muslim complaints that the thirty-two Jewish synagogues in Safed owned too much property.[72] Furthermore, it was suggested, these synagogues might be newly established and hence illegal. In a similar spirit the government ordered the closure of the Nahmanides Synagogue in Jerusalem, arguing that the Muslim residents of the quarter found the sound of the Jewish prayers intolerable. The tide had turned for Jewish settlement in Palestine, and migration from Safed accelerated. At the same time, the town's textile industry declined as a result of growing competition from Europe.

Despite the decline of the Safed community, emissaries from Safed continued to be dispatched to collect funds for the dwindling group of mystics and the growing number of paupers. Safed remained one of the designated 'holy cities' of the Land of Israel, deserving of support from all over the diaspora. Its pleas for assistance were generally honoured in deference to its pious past and the reputation of its great mystics. Ashkenazim and Sephardim as far away as Prague, Morocco, and even the Caribbean and American colonies continued to welcome the emissaries of Safed. The religious vitality generated in sixteenth-century Safed was not spent after the first and second generation of kabbalists had passed from the stage: the dilemma of how to attain spirituality and end the suffering of the Jewish people was by no means resolved. The teachings of Safed were spread rapidly and widely by the new Hebrew printing presses in Italy and Poland.

Safed lost its most illustrious and charismatic leader with the death of Luria in 1572. He left no written works, and he instructed that his doctrines should remain hidden after his death. But his disciples continued to expand upon his practices and soon began to collect and preserve his teachings. Hayim Vital initially refused to divulge his master's secrets, but his biography of Luria included many anecdotes about his behaviour. Soon, however, manuscripts of Luria's doctrines, some modified by other pupils, began to circulate. By the 1590s the highly recondite teaching that became known as Lurianic kabbalah appeared in print in Venice and quickly spread among Christian and Jewish kabbalistic circles in Europe. The warm reception accorded the writings of Cordovero and Alkabetz in Italy was matched in Turkey and North Africa. Stories of the magidic phenomenon also spread rapidly. The central Lurianic doctrines, that humanity played a critical role in influencing the historical process and that the sins of the generation could be exorcised through prayer characterized by special piety and

---

[71] 'The Jews of Safed Seek Redress from the Ottoman Sultan for Persecution by Local Officials', in Stillman, *The Jews of Arab Lands*, 298–9.   [72] Baron, *A Social and Religious History of the Jews*, xviii. 110–18.

intentionality combined with inwardness and spontaneity, were ultimately embraced by many Jews, Ashkenazi as well as Sephardi. Although the Safed mystics were consumed by a sense of the imminence of the fulfilment of history, for all their daring mythic theological notions and innovative practices they nevertheless managed to stay within the fold of normative Judaism and never wavered in the practice of the commandments that Judaism had prescribed. After Luria, the feeling that redemption was close at hand did not subside, but, on the contrary, grew stronger. Safed had set the messianic tools in place, leaving a mantle of leadership for others to assume. While Sephardi spirituality remained closely associated with the Land of Israel, and especially with the city of Safed, its repercussions soon reverberated throughout the Jewish world. The doctrines of Lurianic kabbalah, when manipulated by the false messiah Shabetai Tsevi in the mid-seventeenth century, threatened to temporarily overwhelm the entire Sephardi diaspora.

CHAPTER FOUR

THE JEWS OF VENICE: BETWEEN TOLERATION AND EXPULSION 1516–1648

> The Jews must all live together in the Corte de Case, which are in the ghetto near San Girolamo, and in order to prevent their roaming around at night: Let there be built two gates, on the side of the old ghetto where there is a little bridge, and likewise on the other side of the Bridge . . . closed at night by four Christian guards appointed and paid by the Jews at the rate deemed suitable by Our cabinet.
>
> VENETIAN SENATE, decree establishing the ghetto

> There is no doubt that among all the states and places in the world, the Jewish people is pleased by the very gentle government of the Most Serene Republic, because its government is stable and not variable on account of the changeability of the thoughts of one sole ruler and the instigations of counsellors.
>
> SIMONE LUZZATTO, *Discorso circa il stato de gl'Hebrei*

IN 1516, after several ballots and some sharp exchanges, the Jews finally won the right to live in Venice.[1] They would be part of, yet live separately from, the vibrant commercial republic on the Adriatic Sea. But their right of residence was not automatic: it would require periodic renewal of specific charters of limited duration. The German and Italian Jews were granted a five-year charter. The charter for Spanish Jews, promulgated in 1541 and expanded in 1589 to include the Portuguese, would be valid for a period of ten years. These legal arrangements and designations reflect the heterogeneity of Venetian Jewry and the separate role each group played in the economy and in the minds of Venice's rulers and citizenry. As the expiry of each charter approached, the right to continue living in Venice hung in the balance. Renewal and ratification of the charters were never certain, but persuasive arguments and 'donations', coupled with the pragmatism of the Venetian Board of Trade, outweighed the calls from ecclesiastical quarters to exclude the Jews.

But the God-fearing Christians of Venice would not countenance the dispersion of the Jews throughout the city. The decree establishing the ghetto solemnly declared in

---

[1] On the various stages of the formulation of the conditions of residence, see Ravid, 'The Religious, Economic, and Social Background and Context of the Establishment of the Ghetti of Venice', 215–21; Calimani, *The Ghetto of Venice*, 28–40.

no uncertain terms that from 29 March 1516 the Jews would be confined to a separate island in the northern part of the city, far from the commercial centre, surrounded by walls and water. The decaying area housed an abandoned foundry (*getto*) formerly used for the manufacture of bronze and copper for artillery and was hence known as the Ghetto Nuovo district. The area was enlarged twice by the addition of small enclaves, the Ghetto Vecchio (1541) and the Ghetto Nuovissimo (1633). The two earlier sections of the ghetto were associated with foundries, while the Ghetto Nuovissimo derived its name purely from its association with the other two. The salient features of compulsory segregation, economic restrictions, overcrowding, and poverty that distinguished the Venetian district designated for Jews would serve as a model for the subsequent segregated quarters of Jews elsewhere in Italy, and they became known as 'ghettos'. By the seventeenth century, after a century of forced enclosure of Jews in limited areas throughout Italy, the word 'ghetto' had acquired the meaning of a compulsory, walled-in Jewish quarter.

Dwelling in Venice on 'sufferance and not as of right' and in a legal arrangement that required periodic renewal, the Jews in Venice were suspended between acceptance and rejection.[2] But once the ghetto principle was implemented, Venice emerged as the site of an unusually diverse community of Jews who hailed from other parts of Italy, Spain and Portugal, Germany, Greece, North Africa, and the Ottoman empire. Tension between religiously motivated antagonism and economically motivated toleration frequently made Jewish life unpredictable: more than once expulsion was imminent or partially implemented. While the Jews were physically marginalized, the cultural and economic borders between the ghetto and the rest of Venice were porous. As a result of this unique physical and legal arrangement, Jewish Venice emerged as the site of a highly organized Jewish communal structure that boasted an extremely rich culture. Sephardi migrants, only recently expelled or forcibly converted on the Iberian peninsula, found refuge and renewal behind its walls. When the morning bells in St Mark's Square chimed, the Jews could leave the confines of the ghetto walls until the evening curfew. They drew inspiration from the dynamic civilization beyond the ghetto walls, locked in, yet not totally cut off. These contradictory realities provided the stimulus for the creation of an unusual synergy of multiple Jewish cultures and Renaissance Italy.

Venice was at her most magnificent in the sixteenth century. Signs of wealth were ubiquitous: sumptuous palaces with marble facades and frescoed interiors were springing up along the city's canals; dazzling churches, decorated by famous artists and

---

[2] On the successive charters granting Jews the right to live in the ghetto, see Ravid, 'The Socioeconomic Background of the Expulsion and Readmission of the Venetian Jews'; id., 'The Religious, Economic and Social Background and Context of the Establishment of the Ghetti in Venice'; id., 'New Light on the Ghetti in Venice'; id., 'The Venetian Government and the Jews'; id., 'Between the Myth of Venice and the Lachrymose Conception of Jewish History'; id., '"On Sufferance and Not As of Right"'; id., 'The Third Charter of the Jewish Merchants of Venice'.

sculptors, were multiplying; local and foreign artists captured the light of the Venetian sky reflected on her sparkling waterways on huge canvases that adorned both palaces and churches. The city's mythical accomplishments were enhanced by her location. Her claim to the mantle of Christian imperial power embodied in Byzantium was at its strongest. St Mark's Basilica housed ancient relics that were the objects of Christian devotion. Her unique governmental structure was the envy of the inhabitants of many kingdoms. Her ample fleet proudly exited her harbour, defiantly confronting an ascendant and mighty Ottoman presence in the Mediterranean. Throughout much of the sixteenth century Venice dominated the trade in wheat, pepper, spices, and textiles to points north and east. Yet, as early as the 1540s, cracks in her imperial might were already apparent. By the seventeenth century Venetian commercial supremacy had been outstripped as a result of several factors. Her patrician class had retreated from commerce to their country estates, fearful to venture out against Muslim corsairs in the Mediterranean; trans-Balkan trade routes were in Ottoman hands; the expanding Ottoman ports of Salonica and Istanbul were undercutting Venetian maritime supremacy; and the Venetian empire was contracting as a result of protracted warfare in the eastern Mediterranean.

Domestic challenges to Venetian commerce were mounting as well. In the Italian port of Ancona, Portuguese and indigenous Jewish merchants provided fierce competition for trade with the Levant. By the end of the seventeenth century Venice also confronted formidable commercial competition from the free port of Livorno on the western coast of Italy. Livorno's location was especially advantageous once global commerce shifted from the Mediterranean to the Atlantic. Although the efflorescence of Venice and its Jews was relatively brief, the city deserves special consideration in Sephardi annals.

The ghetto of Venice played many roles in shaping Sephardi history. Despite its inconvenient location and fetid alleyways, the ghetto provided an indispensable asylum for Iberian Jews and Conversos precisely when most of western Europe was barred to them. Its numerous and elaborate networks of charitable organizations would ransom Jews captured by Mediterranean pirates while also rehabilitating the stream of escapees from the Iberian peninsula. For some, Venice served simply as a transit point on the hazardous journey to the Ottoman empire. For many, however, the ghetto provided much more than a temporary shelter. New ideas, such as the mysticism of Safed, flowed through its gates. These ideas found printers and a reading public in Venice, whence they were disseminated to the Jews of central Europe. The communal institutions of the ghetto provided a model for new Sephardi settlements in western Europe and the New World. The Venetian ghetto provided precedents for the organization of nascent Jewish communities and modes of governing a heterogeneous Jewry. The ghetto's charitable organizations were emulated elsewhere, as new Jewish enclaves began to take their first tentative steps towards establishing Jewish life in the west.

Conversos from the Iberian peninsula embarking upon the uncharted journey to Jewish life sought and found rabbis, teachers, Judaica, and legal guidance in the ghetto of Venice.

Venice was the most important centre for the production of Hebrew books of quality and beauty during the sixteenth century, attracting scholars from all corners of the Mediterranean. The exiled scholars of Spain might publish their private manuscripts and find a reading public; former Conversos could explore the complexities of their forgotten faith; and curious Christians become acquainted with Jewish traditions and ideas. In response to Venetian Jewish insecurity, Rabbi Simone (Simha) Luzzatto (1583–1648), one of the most talented thinkers of the Venetian ghetto, put forward the first arguments for the right of Jews to live in Europe, and new synagogue music and forms of worship were defended by Rabbi León de Modena (1571–1648), the most famous Venetian rabbi. These several accomplishments emanated from the meeting of Sephardi, Italian, and Ashkenazi Jews in one confined space at a critical moment in Jewish history.

Ghetto Boundaries, Residents, and Restrictions

In preparation for the transfer of the Jews to their confinement in the ghetto, high walls were constructed around the island, and outward-facing windows were blocked up. The Christian residents of the area were evicted, and the transplanted Jews were compelled to compensate the landlords at a rate one-third higher than the previous one. There were two gateways to control entry and exit. The gates were locked one hour after sunset in summer and two hours after sunset in winter and guarded at night by four guards, paid for by the Jewish community. Additionally, the Jews were required to provide two boats to patrol the surrounding waters. All Jews were expected to be within the ghetto when the gates were locked or incur a fine. Repeat offenders were punished by imprisonment. Some exceptions to the curfew and the compulsory distinctive Jewish clothing and headgear required of its inhabitants were granted to Jewish doctors treating Christian patients, merchants who represented the Jewish community to the government, and dancers and singers performing in the city at carnival time.

However, for many Jews, the right to remain in Venice outweighed the humiliating restrictions. Although living space in the ghetto was limited and would become more so with the passage of time, they enjoyed daily access to the main part of the city. The resulting status of the Venetian Jews was paradoxical. Although an integral part of the city, they were strictly excluded from it; while they were locked into a confined area where they engaged in a constant struggle for space, they were free to move anywhere within it. The ghetto of Venice lasted from 1516 until the entry of Napoleon's armies in 1797. When the ghetto gates were demolished by the French forces, cries of 'Liberty' erupted, and the assembled ghetto population, men alongside women, burst into 'democratic dancing'.

The establishment of the ghetto was not the first time that Venice had placed restrictions on Jews. During the Middle Ages, they were barred from trading in the city, with the occasional exception of moneylenders and pawnbrokers who were either local Jews of German background (such as the famous Luzzatto family, originally from Lausnitz in Austria) or Jews from other regions in Italy. These two ethnic groups constituted the original ghetto inhabitants and were collectively known as Tedeschi (Germans). Many of the Italians among the Tedeschi had made their way northward from various points in Italy during the fourteenth and fifteenth centuries. Others were descendants of earlier migrants from Germany who resided for generations in the nearby cities of Padua, Verona, Mestre, and Brescia. When the Veneto was overrun by the armies of the League of Cambrai in 1509, the fleeing Jewish population of the mainland joined the wave of Christian refugees who sought temporary shelter in Venice. The Jews were admitted with severe restrictions, including having their occupations limited to pawnbrokerage, moneylending, and trade in second-hand goods. These occupations remained the economic mainstay of the Tedeschi after the ghetto was established and were repeatedly denounced by the ecclesiastical authorities, subjecting the Jews to further humiliation. Yet the value of Jews as a source of cheap credit for the poor was also repeatedly acknowledged.

The Sephardim, typically merchants of Iberian origin actively engaged in commerce with or in the Ottoman empire, were treated differently. They were known in Venice as Levantini, Levantine Jews, and were widely recognized as a special population in the ghetto. The Levantini were appreciated by pragmatic Venetians as a positive addition to the city because of their prominence in the trans-Balkan trade and their far-flung trading networks. Many of the Sephardim were not actually permanent residents of Venice but merchants from the Ottoman empire who spent considerable amounts of time in the city and eventually brought their families to stay with them. Their residential status did not differ markedly from that of other merchant groups such as Greeks or Turks. Around the time of the establishment of the Inquisition in Portugal in 1536, another strain of Sephardim began to seek shelter in Venice, Conversos, arriving either directly from Portugal or via an intermediate stopover in Antwerp, Ferrara, or Mantua, all towns with small, dynamic Portuguese Jewish merchant enclaves. Not all the Portuguese Conversos chose to live as Jews in the ghetto. Some preferred to continue their trade with the Iberian peninsula as Christians, enjoying the greater safety and mobility that their Christian identity gave them as they moved back and forth across western Europe. Conversos who remained Christian and were consequently able to live outside the ghetto often had commercial and religious ties with the ghetto inhabitants. Others simply blended into the Christian population in Venice and disappeared from Jewish annals. The Portuguese Conversos who became ghetto residents and adopted Judaism were known as western or Ponentine Jews. The Venetian authorities preferred to regard the Ponentine Jews as Ottoman subjects rather than as transgressing Christians who had fled Portugal and returned to Judaism immediately upon their arrival in Venice, since it muted ecclesiastical opposition to their presence. They recognized the considerable commercial talents of the Levantine and Ponentine Jews and were willing to overlook the dubious religious identity of the latter. The status and charters granted to Levantini and Ponentini, for example, were more favourable than those granted to Tedeschi. Levantini and Ponentini were permitted to deal in commerce; the Tedeschi, despite their repeated petitions, were not granted similar permission until 1641. The charter for the Levantini was valid for a period of ten years. In addition they were excused from many of the frequently humiliating or onerous obligations that were imposed upon the Tedeschi. In this fashion, Sephardim of various stripes were lumped together and their separation from the Ashkenazim was solidified through legal instruments and separate rights and disabilities.

The number of Jews in the ghetto rose throughout the sixteenth and early seventeenth centuries. Refugees fleeing the Protestant upheavals in the north and Jews expelled from various Italian cities and kingdoms and from Provence all swelled the ranks of the Tedeschi. Sephardim also arrived from various parts of Europe and the Middle East. Some Sephardim arrived after encountering great hardships and a difficult and alien environment in North Africa; others came from the Ottoman empire following initial attempts to re-establish themselves there after 1492. Conversos came from the Iberian peninsula, and Marranos from Habsburg Antwerp. The diversity was expressed and to some degree institutionalized in the separate synagogues and rituals that each group maintained in the ghetto.

The ghetto area never provided adequate living space. Its occupants tended to live wherever they could find a roof over their heads. They did not own their own apartments, but, since the right to live in a particular apartment was bequeathed in wills, housing tended to stay within the same family for generations, thereby preserving traces of the original topographical ethnic divides. According to the 1659 testimony of a Venetian patrician, Loredan, before the Venetian senate: 'Where twenty Jews live, there would not live more than four to eight Christians.'[3] By 1633 several Jewish subcultures coexisted under one communal umbrella, each retaining its separate set of communal institutions but generally united vis-à-vis the outside world and the Venetian authorities. Most of the legal distinctions between the groups were blurred by this point, although some separate traditions were maintained in the synagogues. The Sephardim and Tedeschi were not officially recognized as a single legal entity under one unitary charter until 1728, since the authorities wanted the Tedeschi to continue serving as moneylenders, especially to the urban poor. At the same time the Sephardim were

---

[3] Loredan, speech before the Venetian senate, cited in Pullan, *The Jews of Europe and the Inquisition of Venice*, 158.

eager to formalize their few privileges (such as the right to engage in commerce) in legal instruments and resisted being lumped together with the Tedeschi. The divisions between the Sephardim and the Ashkenazim that characterized the few other European cities where Jews were permitted to live were reinforced in Venice by the separate charters.

Residence in Venice carried some stigmas to which Jews from elsewhere were not necessarily accustomed. As early as the fourteenth century Jews in the Veneto were ordered to wear a yellow circle on their outer garment. In 1497 this was changed to a yellow head-covering in order that they might be more easily recognized from afar. The colour of the discriminatory headgear varied over the centuries, often reflecting the specific origins of the Jews. At one time Tedeschi were required to wear yellow caps, while Sephardim had to wear red ones. These differences were not accidental: yellow was the identifying colour for prostitutes; red was associated with nobility. Clothing distinctions were generally strictly enforced. Any Jew caught outside the ghetto without the distinctive headgear would be fined fifty ducats. The rationale for the regulations was that Jewish men should be identifiable at all times, lest they engage in sexual relations with Christian women. Presumably, Jewish males would otherwise have been indistinguishable from the Christian majority.

Contemporary travellers did not fail to comment on the physical differences and distinctive clothing and headgear of the ghetto residents. The English traveller Thomas Coryate (1577–1617) recorded the Jews' sartorial diversity in the notes of his visit in 1608:

I was in a place where the whole fraternity of the Jewes dwelleth together, Which is called the Ghetto, being an Iland: for it is inclosed round about with Water. It is thought there are of them in all betwixt five and six thousand. They are distinguished from the Christians by their habits on their heads: for some of them doe weare hats and those redde, onely those Jewes that are borne in the Westerne parts of the world, as in Italy, etc, but the easterne Jewes being othersie called the Levantine Jewes, which are borne in Hieruslaem, Alexandria, Constantinope, etc. weare turbents upon their heads as the Turkes do: but the difference is this: the Turkes weare white, the Jewes yellow.[4]

Limiting Jewish residence to certain areas was not a new phenomenon. There had been separate Jewish quarters or cordoned-off streets in various parts of Europe and the Muslim world. Probably the most famous were in Prague (established in 1262) and Frankfurt am Main (established in the 1460s). In the fifteenth century the forcible separation of the Jews from the surrounding Christian population was widely imposed in many Spanish cities. The first compulsory Jewish quarter in North Africa was founded in Fez in 1438. Contemporary Jews did not view the Venetian ghetto entirely negatively. Although they were segregated, their specific economic role as providers of

---

[4] Coryate, *Crudities*, i. 370; see Yardeni, *Anti-Jewish Mentalities in Early Modern Europe*, 75, 86 n. 28. Coryate's diary contains perhaps the first occurrence of the word 'ghetto' in English. See also Strachan, *The Life and Adventures of Thomas Coryate*.

small loans brought them into daily contact with all classes of the Christian population. Moreover, the presence of international Sephardi merchants endowed the ghetto with a cosmopolitan dimension not present in many medieval or early modern ghettos. Christian visitors often entered the ghetto seeking diversions, whether legal or otherwise.

The establishment of the ghetto averted the immediate threat of expulsion in the early sixteenth century. The ghetto also provided a modicum of protection from the unruly mobs that often threatened the Jews with violence, especially during Holy Week, but it was never able to assure total physical security. No resident of the ghetto, especially a Sephardi one, could ignore the fact that the Inquisition in Venice met every Tuesday, Thursday, and Saturday and was eager to catch local Jews who had practised Judaism while professing Christianity elsewhere and planned to return to open Judaism in Venice. The secret observance of Jewish practices by Christians, reversion to Judaism, and adoption of Judaism by descendants of Conversos were tantamount to heresy. Only a small percentage of the victims of the Venetian Inquisition were Jewish, but a Jew, especially one of Spanish or Portuguese origin, could never breathe easily in a city where an inquisitorial tribunal functioned. They could never know when they might be unmasked or falsely denounced and condemned to the galleys, confined in the House of Catechumens, banished for life, or burned at the stake. Such sentences could also be meted out for circumcising a newly arrived Converso or for publishing a Hebrew or Spanish book without the censor's licence.

Allegations of blasphemy and Judaizing were frequent. Thus, for instance, a young Christian sailor, Giorgio Moretto, was sentenced to three years in the galleys in 1589 for frequenting the ghetto in romantic pursuit of a Jewish woman named Rachel. In his defence, Moretto claimed that he was trying to convert her so that they could marry. But the Inquisition was unimpressed, since he was known to have participated in Jewish holiday celebrations and had reportedly been seen wearing a yellow hat. Clearly, Moretto was a secret Jew or a Christian cavorting with a Jew. In either event, he deserved to be prosecuted in the eyes of the Inquisition. In 1585 a Jewish dance master called Giuseppe was threatened with three years' service in the galleys for flirting with the mothers of his Christian students.[5]

Despite the long arm of the Inquisition, Venice continued to be a favoured destination for Portuguese Conversos during the sixteenth century. The city's civil authorities were aware that they were not always firm in their Christian faith, but they usually chose to turn a blind eye. Many of the newcomers were determined to find their way back into the Jewish fold after living in limbo for decades as wavering Christians. They hoped that they might slip into the ghetto and inconspicuously return to the faith of their parents. One of the attractions of Venice was precisely that it offered

---

[5] Melammed, *A Question of Identity*, 118–29; Pullan, *The Jews of Europe and the Inquisition of Venice*, 61–2, 77, 96–7, 103, 164–5; Zoratinni, 'The Inquisition and the Jews in Sixteenth Century Venice'.

Conversos the chance to live as Jews and still maintain contact with relatives who were leading a clandestine Jewish existence elsewhere. For some Converso merchants, a brief stay in the Venetian ghetto provided temporary spiritual sustenance before they returned to their disguises and secret lives. Countless others chose not to join the Jewish community, mixing freely with Christian merchants and nobles outside the ghetto and pursuing their trade without interference. They met with little opprobrium from the Venetian Jews for doing so, a response that differed greatly from those of Amsterdam, Bayonne, or Bordeaux.[6] For those Portuguese Conversos who were unsure of what religious identity they wanted to adopt, it was possible to move back and forth between religious identities in Venice, behaving as Jews in the ghetto and as Christians outside it. Many of them had different Jewish and Christian names, and were described by the Inquisition as resembling 'a ship with two rudders'.[7]

Venice was one of the few European cities where the mask of Christianity could be discarded more or less safely during the sixteenth century. Ferrara and Mantua also encouraged the settlement of Sephardim of various stripes. Both the Estensis in Ferrara and the Gonzagas in Mantua were tolerant of the Jewish presence in their towns. Ancona's arrangements with Conversos were more precarious. The Ottoman empire was clearly the safest place for Conversos to return to Judaism; nevertheless, many Portuguese Jews chose to live in Venice, where they could remain within a European cultural environment, despite the uncertainties at the time of each charter renewal.

Development of the Ghetto

The island site on which the first Jews were confined in 1516 quickly proved to be inadequate. It soon became so cramped that it could scarcely accommodate the original 700 Jews, their descendants, and the growing number of Sephardi merchants arriving in the city to pursue commerce with the Ottoman empire. The inhabitants of the ghetto tended to reside on the upper floors of buildings, their workshops, stores, or warehouses located on the ground floor. Since there was never enough space, it was not uncommon for inhabitants to divide apartments horizontally as well as vertically. As a result, an apartment might contain ceilings that were lower than 6 feet. Some apartments lacked windows entirely. Through such desperate measures, the buildings could accommodate more families in separate units. The irregularly placed windows, still visible today, on the facades of ghetto buildings attest to their unusual internal subdivisions. More than once, houses collapsed as one floor was built on top of

---

[6] For the communal ordinances against travel to the 'lands of idolatry' and the conversion of Portuguese Conversos to Judaism, see Chapter 6 below; see also Y. Kaplan, 'The Struggle Against Travellers to Spain and Portugal in the Western Sephardi Diaspora' (Heb.); id., 'The Travels of Portuguese Jews from Amsterdam to the "Lands of Idolatry"'.

[7] See Pullan, '"A Ship with Two Rudders"'; id., 'The Inquisition and the Jews of Venice'.

another. Such tragedies were especially common when a wedding or circumcision ceremony filled the already overcrowded structures. The buildings were also firetraps and breeding grounds for disease.

An additional area of Jewish residence was added to the ghetto in 1541. Known as the Ghetto Vecchio, it was theoretically restricted to Sephardi merchants. The Ghetto Vecchio was laid out along an avenue that led outside the original ghetto and initially contained open spaces, some gardens, a few small squares, and courtyards. A wall was built around the two ghetto areas, joining them together while cutting them off from the outside world. By the seventeenth century every inch of the Ghetto Vecchio was occupied, its empty spaces filled in, and its apartments subdivided into minuscule flats within a maze of passageways in order to accommodate ever-increasing numbers of people. This newer ghetto area was described by visitors as 'old, ruined, and in a bad state'.[8] This extension temporarily relieved the extraordinary overcrowding of the ghetto and provided what seemed, at the time, to be sufficient living space. At its peak, immediately prior to the plague of 1629–31, according to some estimates the 6-acre site held a population of 5,000 to 6,000.[9] The Ghetto Nuovissimo, consisting of twenty mostly small and decrepit multi-storey buildings, was added in 1633.[10]

The charter issued to the Levantine Jews in 1541 was a reaction to an invitation from Pope Paul III in 1535 to Sephardim to settle in the rival port of Ancona. The terms of the Ancona invitation were particularly enticing: Jews would not be harassed during Holy Week, their disputes would be judged by the Levantine consul, they would not be required to wear distinctive clothing, there would be no restrictions on the goods they could trade in, they would be exempt from major customs duties, and they could bring their families and would not be restricted residentially. These rights were reaffirmed by Pope Julius III in 1553. Conditions of Jewish settlement were equally attractive in Ferrara. In 1538 the duke of Ferrara, Ercole II, extended a general safe-conduct to 'Spaniards and Portuguese, Levantines, Slavs, Dalmatians, Greeks, Turks and (men) of every other nation, whether Christian or infidel, who may come to live and trade within our territories, cities or in whatsoever place of our state and domain'.[11] Ferrara's invitation undoubtedly influenced the Venetians in their deliberations about

---

[8] On the establishment of the Ghetto Vecchio, see Ravid, 'The Establishment of the Ghetto Vecchio of Venice'; id., *Economics and Toleration in Seventeenth-Century Venice*, 29–33; on complaints by Levantine Jews about its ruinous condition in 1576, see Pullan, *The Jews of Europe and the Inquisition of Venice*, 157.

[9] Pullan, *The Jews of Europe and the Inquisition of Venice*, 156–7. Pullan cites a rise from 1,694 in 1586 to 2,671 in 1642, an increase of 60 per cent despite the heavy losses in the plague. Pullan also includes the testimony of Loredan that the Jewish population numbered 4,860 in 1660. The higher number of 5,000 to 6,000 is provided by Calimani (*The Ghetto of Venice*, 148); according to Luzzatto, the Jewish population had reached almost 6,000 by 1638 (see Baron, *A Social and Religious History of the Jews*, xiv. 101–2).

[10] Pullan, *The Jews of Europe and the Inquisition of Venice*, 157.

[11] For a discussion of the policies of Ercole II, see Cooperman, 'Venetian Policy towards the Levantine Jews', 65 ff.

admitting the Sephardim. The less attractive conditions that they offered might reflect Venetian views that their city was sufficiently attractive to Sephardi merchants without having to match the exact terms of their economic rivals.

The two sections of the ghetto differed in tempo and commercial character as well as in the ethnic background of their residents. The streets of the Ghetto Nuovo, housing the Ashkenazi and Italian old-clothes dealers and their pawnshops, were crowded during the day, bustling with Christian customers from outside the ghetto. In contrast, the Ghetto Vecchio was more tranquil. Many of its inhabitants worked at the port and in the main business section of the city and were therefore absent from the ghetto during the day. Its shops generally provided for the people living in the quarter. Conditions in the Ghetto Vecchio were hardly idyllic, however: it was described by the residents in 1576 as a 'den of thieves and harlots, troubled by rows, clashes of weapons, and threats', and in 1581 they complained of the 'many bold creatures who give shelter in the Ghetto Vecchio to vagabond Jews, who have no business or occupation, but merely dwell in the Ghetto, committing many violent acts, and troubling the merchants of the Ghetto'.[12]

In theory, the Levantine Jews assigned to the Ghetto Vecchio were bachelors on business trips and only temporarily residents of Venice. Their status was thus the same as that of visiting Greeks, Armenians, and Turks, all of whom were housed in special inns, separated from the rest of the Venetian population: they were not allowed to bring their families into the ghetto, could only engage in commerce, and could not stay there for more than four months.[13]

However, some of them had already brought their families to Venice, and it is unclear how many of them were actually residents of the Ottoman empire and how many were Conversos. Few questions were raised about their precise origins or faith, as long as they stayed out of trouble and obeyed the various trade and other restrictions imposed on resident Jews. The newcomers were assured that they would not be investigated or punished for apostasy or heresy as long as they met their fiscal obligations and were unostentatious in their religious practices. These official assurances constituted a clear signal to all Conversos that it was safe to settle in Venice, despite the presence of an inquisitorial tribunal.

It was not only pragmatic politicians who saw a use for Jews in the city. The religious rationale for allowing them to remain in Venice was that they would prevent Christians from lending at interest in violation of both church and civil laws.[14] There were many other advantages accruing to the state from the Jews: they paid special taxes; they were willing to underwrite or finance clearly unprofitable lending banks; they could be forced to make extraordinary payments, such as special levies in times of

---

[12] See Pullan, *The Jews of Europe and the Inquisition of Venice*, 157.

[13] See Ravid, 'The Legal Status of the Jewish Merchants of Venice', 515; on the discriminatory clothing, see id., 'From Yellow to Red'.

[14] See Pullan, *Rich and Poor in Renaissance Venice*, 521.

war; and they invariably met all the other special provisions and services that were demanded of them, such as providing the decorations for the doge's palace during public banquets or furnishing the official lodgings for high-ranking visitors to the city. The authorities were also aware that most Jews, particularly the German and Italian ones who were required to act as bankers and pawnbrokers, unobtrusively discharged the many fiscal burdens and unpopular tasks assigned to them at almost no profit. The Sephardi merchants were more problematic. Their diverse origins, religious ambiguity, assimilated attitudes, and the fact that many of them did not move into the ghetto raised altogether different challenges for Venetian clerics and politicians.

Mediterranean geopolitics also influenced how the Sephardim were treated in Venice. As the periodic charter renewal approached in 1550, internal debates sharpened about the desirability of retaining Sephardim who were suspected of being loyal to the Ottoman sultan. These suspicions led to increasing demands that they be expelled. It is unclear whether the expulsion was implemented, but new threats to the Sephardim loomed. During the protracted wars between the Venetians and the Ottomans in the 1560s Venetian merchants were arrested in Istanbul, their ships detained in Ottoman ports, and their merchandise confiscated. In reprisal, Jewish and Muslim merchants in Venice who had Ottoman papers were detained and accused of pro-Turkish loyalties. When Cyprus fell to the Turks on 1 August 1570, Venetian panic reached a peak. Although there is no evidence that the Jews of Venice were assisting the Turks, Jewish loyalties were, nevertheless, suspect. Only two years before, in 1568, the Jews had been accused of setting fire to the Venetian arsenal. The prominent advisory role played by Don Joseph Nasi in the sultan's palace in Istanbul was well known. In this context the periodic charter negotiations became more difficult, and expulsion loomed once again.

Portentous events unfolded on the international scene during the 1570s. The Ottoman defeat at Lepanto in 1573 marked a turning point in European diplomacy, halting the Venetian reverses. After decades of mutual hostility, Venice and Turkey suddenly found themselves unexpectedly thrown together to confront a formidable new alliance between Spain, Austria, and the papacy. The appearance of French, Dutch, and English fleets in the Mediterranean posed new commercial challenges to the Italian ports. If the Jews had appeared to Venice to be expendable in 1570, a new calculus was at work after Lepanto. Voices were now raised in favour of Jewish merchants whose family networks extended from the ports of the west to deep in the Ottoman empire. In response to the evolving international situation, Venice decided that Sephardim should be encouraged to settle in the republic, subject to only limited restrictions.

Daniel Rodriga's Plan

In October 1573 an intriguing proposal to boost Venetian commerce in the Adriatic was suggested. It was the brainchild of a remarkable Portuguese Jewish merchant,

Daniel Rodriga. Rodriga had been trading in the Mediterranean for decades and was thoroughly familiar with the local conditions in the Adriatic Sea, including the growing commercial threat to Venetian trade from Ancona and the Republic of Ragusa (Dubrovnik). He was also familiar with the movements of the Uskok pirates in the Adriatic, who preyed on Venetian shipping. Rodriga had an additional asset: he was personally acquainted with both Ottoman and Venetian officials and understood the advantages that could accrue to both the Ottomans and Venetians if the Ancona–Ragusa trade link could be challenged and trade diverted from the pirate-infested region of the Adriatic. Rodriga proposed to develop a trading facility, including a customs house, storage warehouses, and quarantine facilities, in the port of Spalato (Split) north of Ragusa that would avoid the pirates, undercut Ragusa, and divert trade to Venice. Rodriga submitted his proposals to the Venetian senate, accompanied by a specific request for trading and settlement rights for a group of Sephardi merchants. The promises of his expanded 1577 proposal were grandiose:

I can confidently promise not only to increase trade in this glorious city, but to ensure the safety of the gulf and remove many hindrances which, owing to the Uskoks [pirates] trouble your serenity. . . . I offer to erect in your territory of Spalato a vast, rich port, taking upon myself the burden of working all about, fixing the roads, building inns, preparing houses and setting up commerce by establishing an important channel in this city. . . . Through this very important port of call much merchandise will come to this city. . . . With traffic diverted from the port of Ragusa, the port of Spalato will be of great help in transporting the riches of the Levant all entire into our city.[15]

Rodriga suggested that fifty Jewish merchants, each of whom would be willing to pay 100 ducats annually to Venice, be admitted to Spalato to upgrade the port. The economic potential of his plan was promising. Although official talks went nowhere, Rodriga persisted in his scheme, building the projected roads and other infrastructure around Spalato at his own expense. He also sent personal gifts to Ottoman officials to help further the project.

Opposition to the Sephardim was growing in Venice: each charter renewal was passed by a narrower and narrower margin. At the same time, the Jewish need to find a secure refuge was also mounting. Arguments about the 'utility' of the Jews suddenly assumed new urgency with the union of Spain and Portugal in 1580. The ease with which Conversos or those of Converso descent could leave the Iberian peninsula had varied during the course of the sixteenth and seventeenth centuries depending upon local politics and the degree of vigilance or zealotry of the local Inquisition. Exit from Portugal had been temporarily permitted after the anti-Converso pogrom in Lisbon in 1506, but the prohibition was reinstated in the 1520s. Emigration accelerated in the 1530s when exit was briefly possible, but was again prohibited after the Portuguese Inquisi-

---

[15] Daniel Rodriga, proposal to the Venetian senate, in Ravid, 'An Autobiographical Memorandum by Daniel Rodriga'; see also id., 'Daniel Rodriga and the First Decade of the Jewish Merchants of Venice'. A plaque honouring Daniel Rodriga is affixed to a building in contemporary Split in Croatia.

tion consolidated its power. With the union of Spain and Portugal, Conversos from Portugal found it possible to escape the Iberian peninsula if they first migrated to Spain. However, the Jews of Venice knew that the borders of Iberia might close again at any moment, and the possibility of emigration might evaporate. Renewal of the Venetian charter was imperative, if only for temporary asylum.

Rodriga's petitions for the inclusion of Portuguese Conversos in his scheme were deliberately vague. He called them Ponentini, or western merchants, avoiding any mention of their religious background or provenance. As a result of his petitions and evasions, Portuguese Converso merchants managed to renew their charter with Venice. Their settlement in Spalato was also approved. The terms of the new charter allowed the Ponentine merchants to stay in Venice with their families, to engage in wholesale trade in goods, and to practise Judaism in the ghetto. This explicit guarantee of religious freedom went beyond anything the Conversos had been offered in Venice before. When the terms of the charter were challenged by the papal authorities, they were defended by Fra Paolo Sarpi on the grounds that Converso settlement in Venice was good not only for Venice but for Christendom as a whole. Without it, the prelate warned, Conversos would settle in the Ottoman empire. Moreover, he argued, could Venice, in good conscience, offer less than what the pope himself had granted to the Conversos in Ancona in 1552?[16]

Conversos leaving the Iberian peninsula were not the only ones seeking admission to Venice. Hundreds of Jews, most of them former Conversos, were expelled from Ferrara in 1581 and permitted to enter Venice. The simultaneous decision by the Venetian authorities to permit the resumption of the publication of Jewish books in Spanish after a thirty-year ban was construed as a sign that their presence in the city was welcome. Conversos coming directly from Iberia were slipping into the ghetto without further ado and quietly reclaiming their Jewish identity. Those who opted to remain Christian were settling in the main part of Venice and acquiring some of its grandest palaces. Regardless of religious identification, the Portuguese Conversos tended to be affluent, highly assimilated into European, specifically Hispanic, high culture, and well connected commercially, forming a trading nation that stretched across the globe. In recognition of this, the 1589 Venetian charter to the Sephardim regularized the status of the Portuguese Conversos and extended their residency rights. Both Levantine and Ponentine Jews would be permitted to reside in the ghetto and engage in trade. The charter was passed by a vote of 110 for and 11 against with 13 abstentions. In no small measure, this was a result of Daniel Rodriga's tenacity. The charter declared:

The merchants descending from Jewish families, of whatsoever Nation, be allowed to practise their religion, without inquisition by any office or magistrate, either ecclesiastical or secular, although

---

[16] Ravid, 'Venice, Rome, and the Reversion of Conversos to Judaism'; id., 'A Tale of Three Cities and their Raison d'Etat'.

they may have lived in another place, under another guise or religion, but that after coming to this state, they be allowed to live freely as Jews.[17]

Although they were still barred from entering the Venetian guilds and restricted in living space, the Portuguese Conversos were finally officially permitted to openly revert to Judaism and remain in Venice. This charter has been described as a 'defiant *raison d'état*': the interests of the Venetian state were formally recognized as taking precedence over theological concerns about the 'heretical' implications of Converso adoption of Judaism.[18]

Shortly afterwards, in 1591, the Medicis extended broad rights of settlement in Livorno to Muslims, Jews, and other merchants, including more freedoms and fewer restrictions than those offered anywhere else in western Europe. Duke Ferdinand I hoped to convert Livorno into the major port on the western coast of Italy. To this end, he offered the Jews a twenty-five-year charter, renewable automatically for another twenty-five years, with notice of cancellation to be given five years before its expiry. Jews were not required to wear any distinguishing marks or to live in a ghetto. At the same time, Portuguese Jews were readmitted to Ancona.[19]

Historic Synagogues of Venice

The Venetian ghetto is a popular tourist attraction for contemporary visitors to Venice, and in some respects the entire ghetto area constitutes one large museum. The ghetto has attracted the interest of foreigners since as early as the seventeenth century, when Thomas Coryate visited it. His remarks display a combination of some of the more common prejudices and anti-Jewish stereotypes of his day and a new appreciation of Jews. Coryate noted some of the 'curiosities' of the Jewish religious services:

They have divers Synagogues in their Ghetto, at the least seven, where all of them, both men, women and children doe meete together upon their Sabbath, which is Saturday, to the end to doe their devotion, and serve God in their kinde, each company having a several Synagogue .... In the midst of the Synagogue they have a round seat made of Wainscoat, having eight open spaces therein, at two whereof which are at the sides, they enter into the seate as by dores.[20]

Coryate was struck by the red cape worn by the rabbi and the red hats of the congre-

[17] Venetian senate, charter with the Sephardim, in Ravid, 'The First Charter of the Jewish Merchants of Venice', 205–6.

[18] Israel, *European Jewry in the Age of Mercantilism*, 47. On the simultaneous deliberations concerning the admission of the Jews in Livorno, see Cooperman, 'Trade and Settlement'.

[19] Cooperman, 'Venetian Policy towards the Levantine Jews'. It is noteworthy that the first Portuguese Jews also appeared in London and Amsterdam in the 1590s. On the origins of the Jewish community of Amsterdam, see Chapter 6 below.

[20] Coryate, *Crudities*, i. 371; see Yardeni, *Anti-Jewish Mentalities in Early Modern Europe*, 75, 87 n. 29. On the reactions to the Jews on the part of Protestant visitors to the synagogues in Amsterdam and the comments of Samuel Pepys on the 'lack of decorum' in the Bevis Marks Synagogue in London, see Chapter 6 below.

gants in the Spanish synagogue, providing eyewitness testimony to the colour that distinguished Sephardi Jewish clothing in the early seventeenth century. He was dismayed at the seemingly chaotic nature of the service (he apparently visited during Simhat Torah) and denounced the 'exceeding loud, undecent roaring' and 'beastly bellowing':

> One custom I observed amongst them very irreverent and prophane, that none of them, eyther when they enter the Synagogue, or when they sit downe in their places, or when they go forth againe, do any reverence or obeisance, answerable to such a place of the worship of God, eyther by uncovering their heads, kneeling, or any other externall gesture, but boldly dash into the roome with their Hebrew bookes in their handes, and presently sit in their places, without any more adoe.[21]

Coryate approvingly noted, however, that the Jews possessed no images in their synagogue and praised their strict observance of the sabbath, ruefully remarking: 'I would to God our Christians would imitate these Jewes herein.' While criticizing their mode of worship, Coryate noted the diversity of the Jews and specifically praised the Sephardim for their elegance in dress and demeanour:

> I observed some fewe of those Jewes, especially some of the Levantines to bee such goodly and proper men, that then I said to my selfe our English proverbe: To looke like a Jewe (whereby is meant sometimes a weather beaten warp-faced fello, sometimes a phreneticke and lunaticke person, sometimes one discontented) is not true. For indeed I noted some of them to be most elegant and sweet featured persons, which gave me occasion the more to lament their religion. For if they were Christians, then could I better apply unto them that excellent verse of the Poet, then I can now: 'Gratior est pulchro veniens e corpore virtus'.[22]

Coryate compared the Sephardi women in the women's gallery favourably with aristocratic women in England:

> Many of the Jewish women, whereof some are as beautiful as ever I saw, and so gorgeous in their apparel, chaines of gold, and rings adorned with precious stones, that some of our English countesses do scarce exceede them, having marvaiolous long traines like Princesses that are borne up by waiting women serving for the same purpose. An argument to prove that many of the Jewes are very rich.[23]

The three oldest synagogues in the ghetto belonged to the Tedeschi: the Scuola Grande Tedesca, the Scuola Canton (1532), and the smaller Scuola Italiana (1571). Access to the Scuola Grande Tedesca and the Scuola Canton is by a narrow staircase to the second floor in which they are housed: they are indistinguishable as synagogues from the street. Only the five windows, symbolizing the five books of Moses, on the top floor betray the fact that it houses the Scuola Italiana. The three synagogues were connected within the block that houses them, probably for reasons of security. Although the

---

[21] Coryate, *Crudities*, i. 371.
[22] Ibid. The Latin means: 'ability is more pleasing in a beautiful body' (Virgil, *Aeneid*, 5: 344).
[23] Coryate, *Crudities*, i. 372–3; see Pullan, *The Jews of Europe and the Inquisition of Venice*, 159 n. 66.

worshippers were officially lumped together and designated as Tedeschi, the separate structures indicate the desire of the Ashkenazi and Italian Jews to preserve their distinctive rituals. León de Modena delivered eloquent sabbath sermons in several of the synagogues. He defended the diversity of Jewish customs that flourished in the ghetto's worship and daily life, pointing approvingly to the habit of the Italian Jews to go bareheaded except during prayer services, in contrast to the practices of the German and Levantine Jews:

> Most of this community, and most Italian Jews, do not customarily [cover their heads], and I felt it important to tell them that this was permissible, I would do the same thing concerning several other matters about which Italian Jews are attacked and concerning which the great scholars among us should either rule that they are permitted or [at least] should explain [the Italian custom] and not concede to the Levantines and the Ashkenazim that we are heretics and they are pious Jews. The Lord spoke to us as well, and we and our children accept and love his written and oral law for all time.[24]

The name of the Scuola Canton probably derives from the Venetian dialect word *canton*, meaning 'corner', since the synagogue is located in a corner of the square.[25] The ark and *bimah* are at opposite ends of the room facing each other, strongly resembling the historic synagogues of Carpentras and Cavaillon in France. The unusual design may have been transported to Venice by refugees from Provence following their expulsion in 1498. Several smaller prayer halls bearing Italian family names (including that of the Luzzatto family) also existed.

In contrast to the inconspicuous Tedeschi synagogues, the two synagogues of the Sephardi Jews, the Scuola Levantina (1538; Plates 11, 12) and the Scuola Grande Spagnola (1584; Plate 13) are large, free-standing structures that closely resemble some of the opulent palaces of the nobility that line the Grand Canal. They were built in the sixteenth century, renovated and enlarged to their present size in the seventeenth and eighteenth centuries, and have since undergone considerable restoration. The two edifices face each other on a small square in the Ghetto Vecchio known as the Campiello delle Scuole (the Little Square of the Synagogues). Their grandeur and elegance attest to the affluence of their mercantile Sephardi founders and suggest a sense of security and self-confidence. The Scuola Grande Spagnola is the most impressive structure in the ghetto, reflecting the status and size of the ghetto's Sephardi population, and hosted most community events, the ghetto's self-governing bodies, and many of its charitable institutions.

Both Sephardi synagogues were planned and executed by highly respected Renaissance and Baroque artists and architects, including Baldassare Longhena, who built

---

[24] Modena, *She'elot uteshuvot ziknei yehudah*, 21: 36.

[25] Curiel and Cooperman, *The Venetian Ghetto*, 57. 'Canton' is not, according to Curiel and Cooperman, the name of a German Jewish family, as suggested by Rachel Wischnitzer (*The Architecture of the European Synagogue*, 64).

many of Venice's churches. The Sephardi synagogues tended to be the ones that Christians frequented when they visited the ghetto, curious to learn more about the 'exotic' Jews and to hear the eloquent Italian sermons of Rabbis León de Modena and Azariah da Fano. Modena's colourful autobiography immodestly depicts how friars, priests, nobles, and other dignitaries crowded in to listen to his rhetorical talents:

> The first time I preached in the great synagogue was on the Sabbath following the Ninth of Ab. There were so many people, including scholars, that the synagogue could not hold all of them. It was printed in my book of sermons, *Midbar Yehudah*. God helped me make a favorable impression upon all who heard me. In the month of Iyar, 5354 [1594], the wealthy gentleman Kalonymous Belgrado established an academy in his gardens. I was the main preacher, and I have continued so for twenty-five years to this day, establishing a reputation throughout the land for my preaching, as is well-known. For more than twenty years I have taught Bible and rabbinic literature each weekday evening and morning, and preached on the Sabbath in three or four different places, yet this congregation has never grown weary of hearing my sermons. Indeed, each time listeners find them totally new. Friars and priests, nobles and dignitaries also come to hear me . . . they extol me and give me praise.[26]

In a separate entry Modena proudly recalls the visit of French royalty:

> I preached in the synagogue of the Sephardim. . . . In attendance were the brother of the King of France, who was accompanied by some French noblemen and by five of the most important Christian preachers who gave sermons that Pentecost. God put such learned words into my mouth that all were very pleased, including many of the Christians who were present. All the congregations gave great praise and thanks.[27]

A man of exceptional and varied talents, Modena sought to explain the rites of the Jews to a Christian audience. In his famous apologetic work *Historia de' riti hebraici* (written in 1616 and first published in 1637), Modena sought to prove to Christian detractors that Judaism was a rational faith grounded in the Bible; he may also have been responding to critiques of the rabbinic tradition by Conversos, perhaps hoping to persuade them to return to Judaism.

En Route to the Ottoman Empire: Doña Gracia Mendes Nasi

The arrival of a female Converso in sixteenth-century Venice, a city bustling with commercial activity, would not usually attract much attention. The ghetto of Venice offered hospitality to many wayfarers and was a convenient stop for numerous Jews leaving Europe. But the arrival of this particular Converso, Doña Gracia Mendes Nasi, still known at this point as Beatrice de Luna, could scarcely go unnoticed. Her fame and fortune had preceded her. She was reputedly one of the wealthiest and most powerful women in Europe. Among the several fortunes she controlled was a dowry of 250,000 ducats for her 8-year-old niece. No doubt the other large sums of money she controlled

---

[26] Modena, *The Autobiography of a Seventeenth-Century Venetian Rabbi*, 96. [27] Ibid. 131.

also impressed the authorities. The government of Venice issued a safe-conduct to her and her entourage of thirty without any time limits when she arrived in the city in 1546. She had fled Antwerp and moved around western Europe engaging in business and associating with various monarchs. She was already supporting many of the Sephardi rabbis and scholars who were wandering penniless around Europe seeking an outlet for their talents. As one of the major players in the international spice and gem trade, Doña Gracia understood the role that Venice could play as a base for her commercial operations while she retrieved the fortune that had been confiscated in her escape from Antwerp. In addition, Venice provided a suitable way station en route to the Ottoman empire. Funds could be transferred from Venice to another port in the east, and final preparations to leave Christendom could be made.

The arrival of Doña Gracia undoubtedly occasioned some excitement in the ghetto. Her exploits were already known in Jewish circles. Born in Portugal in 1510 into a family that had been forcibly converted to Christianity in the mass conversions of 1497, she was married at an early age to the banker Francisco Mendes, a member of the prominent Spanish Jewish family of Benveniste. Her husband owned a bank in Lisbon with his brother Diogo, and the two men regularly travelled back and forth between Lisbon and Antwerp trading in gems and spices. Their investors included members of several European royal families, including King João III of Portugal, Charles V, Holy Roman Emperor and king of Spain, and King François I of France. Francisco Mendes was the largest depositor of silver at the Lisbon mint between 1517 and 1534, and the family owned the concession to the entire pepper and spice supply of Portugal from 1525. Despite the close business dealings between the Portuguese Crown and the Mendes family, their interests were not always congruent. The Mendes family were among the most active opponents of the establishment of the Inquisition in Portugal; however, King João III finally agreed to it in 1531.[28]

Doña Gracia became adept in banking and trade early in her marriage, assisting her husband and brother-in-law. She probably also became skilled in the subterfuges and surreptitious practices that were required of Marranos in post-Expulsion Portugal. Her brother-in-law and business partner lived under a cloud of suspicion. In 1532 Hebrew books were seized from Diogo's Antwerp home and dispatched to the theologians at the University of Louvain for examination.[29] Such measures were often a prelude to more severe inquisitorial activities. A royal edict promulgated in 1497 had decreed that the possession of Hebrew books by Conversos, with the sole exception of medical texts, was a criminal offence.[30] Once he had been called in for questioning, it was only a

[28] On Doña Gracia's marriage and the family's business links with the Portuguese Crown, see Salomon and Di Leone Leoni, 'Mendes, Benveniste, de Luna, Micas, Nasci'.

[29] Di Leone Leoni, *The Hebrew Portuguese Nations in Antwerp and London*, 89–96.

[30] See Kayserling, *Geschichte der Juden in Portugal*, 136, 141; Usque, *Consolations for the Tribulations of Israel*, 13; M. A. Cohen, notes to Usque, *Consolations for the Tribulations of Israel*, 292 n. 7.

matter of time before she, too, would be suspected of practising Judaism in secret. When Francisco died in 1535 she continued the family business, while secretly planning her flight. Within a year she had left Portugal for Antwerp with her young daughter, Reyna, and probably her sister, Brianda, as well as several nephews and attendants, including her young nephew, João, later known as Don Joseph, who would become her closest aide and confidant. Precipitous flight was to prove to be the pattern of her life for more than a decade.

The years that Doña Gracia spent in Antwerp were active ones as she immersed herself in the expanding family business with Diogo. The Mendes holdings steadily grew, along with their business and social relationships with European royalty. Doña Gracia's friendship with Maria of Hungary, sister of Charles V and queen regent of the Netherlands, led to marriage proposals for her daughter and niece. She rejected the offers, perhaps assuming they were an attempt to acquire her wealth or, in all likelihood, in order to safeguard the Jewish identity of her daughter and niece. This seemed to confirm the suspicions circulating in official circles that Doña Gracia was a secret Jew.

Doña Gracia's secret Jewish activities increased in Antwerp:[31] the family met for prayers in Diogo's home; there is some evidence that they observed *kashrut* (they travelled with their own cook and ate within their enclosed compound with their relatives);[32] they fasted on Yom Kippur and prepared unleavened bread on Passover. It was not unusual for a wealthy Marrano to accommodate dozens of relatives and business associates in their home where prayer services might more safely be held. Living within an extended family provided cover for clandestine religious activities, but potential informers always posed a danger. Curious or venal household employees or vindictive relatives and associates might notify the Inquisition of forbidden Jewish practices, especially as most Converso families were a complex mix of Jewish, new Christian, and old Christian members. It was especially difficult for a prominent businesswoman like Doña Gracia to conceal her Jewish activities. Charles V was willing to tolerate some questionable practices in the name of commerce but was fiercely opposed to the use of Antwerp as a migration route, and instructed the imperial police and officials at court to monitor the small but highly visible Portuguese business enclave. At the same time that he promoted their participation in commerce, he was not averse to employing accusations of heresy as a pretext for imprisoning wealthy merchants in order to collect a handsome ransom for their release. Secrecy and subterfuge were essential.

Suspicions about the religious identity of the Mendes family and their associates in

---

[31] Aron de Leone Leoni provides interesting data on Marrano activities in Antwerp culled from the Antwerp archives. The sixty-seven documents in French, Italian, and Portuguese that he reproduces suggest the types of material sought and confiscated by the authorities ('Documentary Appendix', in Di Leone Leoni, *The Hebrew Portuguese Nations in Antwerp and London*, 129–238).

[32] See Di Leone Leoni, *The Hebrew Portuguese Nations in Antwerp and London*, 89–91.

Antwerp mounted in the 1540s and escape became essential again. Movement between the Low Countries and the Ottoman empire via Italy was quite common, and Portuguese Conversos had ready access to Antwerp, since both Spain and the Low Countries were under the Habsburg Crown. Nevertheless, escape routes had to be carefully charted.

A remarkable document in the Royal Archives in Brussels, probably dating from 1544, reveals the subterranean and perilous world of the Conversos. It contains instructions to Marranos on their hazardous journey out of Habsburg territory. It may even shed light on the clandestine activities of Doña Gracia, perhaps filling in some of the gaps in her biography during the 1530s and 1540s:

In the first place, you will leave here in a carriage, which will take you to Cologne. The carriage costs around twelve ducats. Carriage and carter are pre-paid and you must not pay anything. The carter will take you to the inn called Vier Escara in Cologne. He will also hire on your behalf a boat that will take you to Mainz. The boat will cost six ducats. . . . In Cologne there is a man called Pero Tonnellero who speaks good Spanish. He will accompany you at his own expense. You need to take him along in case there might be guards inspecting the boats along the river. Do not be afraid of them. It is normal that they come to inspect the ships to see if they carry merchandise. Do not give them anything. When you leave Cologne and board the boat early in the morning, it shall be in a secret manner as discretion and honesty are appropriate everywhere. You will rent the boat on condition that you may sleep on board, so you will have fewer expenses. During the journey, the stronger ones among you will go with Pedro Antonello to buy food and other provisions that you might need. And, under any circumstance you will behave as decent people avoiding all quarrels and arguments that may occur among people. And you will share all expenses. . . . Two eleven- or twelve-year old boys will pay as one adult. Older boys will be counted as one man. Babies will not pay anything. . . .

After you leave Cologne (early in the morning) you will proceed to the city [of Mainz] where you will stay at the inn with the sign of a fish; you will send [one of your company] with Pedro Antonello for Comrade . . . . He is a very decent person who speaks good Spanish. He will lead you to the place where you will hire wagons. You must state that you want to go to Ferrara along the old route, i.e. the route of Altdorf and along the lake, as far as Pavia. So, in Mainz, you are to rent wagons that will take you fifty or sixty miles. . . . By these wagons, you will travel as far as the lake and after the lake you will rent horses in order to cross the German Alps. Those who are in better shape can go on foot in order to save some money. It shall be wise to buy some food as you will be traveling in foreign countries and you will not find anybody who will help you. By horseback, you will go until the place where you will rent that boat that will take you to Ferrara . . . always behave as decent people and God will help you. Once in Ferrara those who wish to live in Ancona will be told how to proceed further. In each of the abovementioned ports you will get information about the way ahead. The less you talk, the better.

May God lead you. Amen.[33]

---

[33] 'Instructions for Those Who Set Out, with God's Help, on the Journey from Antwerp to Ferrara', ibid. 187. Reproduced by permission of the American Sephardi Federation, Sephardic House.

In 1543 Charles V attempted to confiscate the Mendes family holdings. It is not clear whether this was caused by personal pique at Doña Gracia's rejection of the suggested royal match for her daughter or was simply the emperor's method of cancelling his debts to the Mendes' bank. With the help of Don Joseph, Doña Gracia salvaged part of her fortune and purchased a safe-conduct to Venice. She was still officially a Christian when she arrived in Venice, and therefore not obliged to settle in the ghetto. She ensconced herself in a palace on the Grand Canal. However, it was not long before friction with her sister-in-law surfaced, either from jealousy over Doña Gracia's control of the family fortune, the division of expenses incurred in acquiring safe-conduct to Venice, or religious differences. The lives of Sephardi refugees were frequently caught up in webs of intrigue involving business, divergent faiths, and dysfunctional family relations. Doña Gracia was denounced to the authorities and accused of planning to escape to the Ottoman empire in order to return to Judaism. At the same time, secret conversations between Doña Gracia, Don Joseph, and the Ottoman sultan were under way to arrange for ships to take the entire family to Ottoman territory. The complicated family imbroglio collided with powerful political and religious factions in Venice who were fed up with Marranos and were seriously contemplating the expulsion of all Conversos. They decided to arrest Doña Gracia and impound her property. It was precisely at this juncture that the charter of the Levantine Jews expired, and Venice refused to renew it.

In 1550 several Marranos were expelled from Venice, and Doña Gracia sought temporary refuge in Ferrara where she openly acknowledged her Jewish identity and increased her philanthropic activities on behalf of Marranos.[34] She is described as 'la muy magnifica Señora Dona Gracia Naci' ('the most magnificent Lady Dona Gracia Naci') in the dedication of *Consolation for the Tribulations of Israel* by the Portuguese Jewish author Samuel Usque. Usque's dedication acknowledges her financial support in publishing the book and lauds her activities on behalf of Portuguese Conversos, calling her 'a pillar of strength' and 'an eagle's outstretched wings' and stating that she has 'inherited [Moses' sister] Miriam's innate compassion', 'governed like the prophetess Deborah', and possesses Esther's 'boundless virtue and surpassing piety in rescuing her people'.[35]

Her inspiration greatly encouraged your needy children in Portugal, who were too poor and weak to leave the fire, and to undertake a lengthy journey. She generously provided money and other needs and comforts to the refugees who arrived destitute, sea-sick and stuporous in Flanders and elsewhere. She helped them overcome the rigors of the craggy Alps in Germany and other lands, and she hastened to alleviate the miseries caused by the hardships and hazards of their long journey. . . . She sent boats laden with bread and provisions and revived the starving people from

---

[34] On the problems of Doña Gracia's stay in Ferrara, see Salomon and Di Leone Leoni, 'Mendes, Benveniste, de Luna, Micas, Nasci'; Cohen, notes to Usque, *Consolations for the Tribulations of Israel*, 295 n. 40.

[35] Usque, *Consolations for the Tribulations of Israel*, 37, 230.

the grave which famine had prepared for them on Italian shores. Thus with her golden hand and angelic purpose, she lifted the majority of our people from the abyss in Europe. . . . She continued to guide them until they were in safe lands, and until she had returned them to the obedience and precepts of their ancient God.[36]

Doña Gracia supported the publication of several other important books in Hebrew, Spanish, and Portuguese, including the famous translation of the Bible that would assist Conversos in their return to Judaism. In Ferrara, her business contacts expanded and her financial position improved. But her personal relations with the leading Spanish Jewish family in the city, the Abravanels, appear to have been tense. The divisions between the Spanish and Portuguese refugees have yet to receive the attention they deserve in studies of the Sephardi diaspora. The Jews of Spain who left the Iberian peninsula in 1492 lost everything and endured much suffering while remaining constant to their faith; the Jews who went to Portugal were forcibly converted in 1497 and entered Portuguese society and assimilated into its culture but kept their wealth. When the two groups encountered each other again, it was as strangers. The Spanish Jews who had remained Jewish often feared that the presence of Marranos in their midst would endanger their relationship with the Christian authorities.[37] This fear was not unfounded in Ancona, Pesaro, and elsewhere.

When plague broke out in Ferrara in 1551 'the people fancied that the Hebrews had spread [it]', according to Usque,[38] and the frightened and superstitious inhabitants of the city induced the generally tolerant Duke of the House of Este to expel both Spanish Jews and Portuguese Conversos. Doña Gracia returned to Venice and began her final preparations for flight to the Ottoman empire. Brianda agreed, for the moment, to drop all charges against her, and the Venetian government made a galley available to take her to Istanbul (after confiscating much of her fortune[39]). After further family altercations, in which even the papal nuncio got involved, the Mendes family finally escaped.[40] Many details of Doña Gracia's exploits in Italy still remain buried in the archives. Her experiences underscore how the misadventures of individual Marranos could easily engulf local Jewish communities, even those that were officially tolerated.

City of Hebrew Books

Cultural considerations have frequently played a major role in Jewish choices of where to settle. One attraction of Venice was its pre-eminence as the Jewish publishing centre

---

[36] Usque, *Consolations for the Tribulations of Israel*, 230.
[37] Segre, 'Sephardi Settlements in Sixteenth-Century Italy'.
[38] Usque, *Consolations for the Tribulations of Israel*, 213.
[39] Intercession by Moses Hamon, the sultan's Sephardi physician, probably ensured her departure from Venice, safe passage to Istanbul, and the retention of a portion of her fortune (see Chapter 5 below).
[40] On the complex fiscal and political ramifications of the many claims against Doña Gracia, see Salomon and Di Leone Leoni, 'Mendes, Benveniste, de Luna, Micas, Nasci'.

of sixteenth-century Europe. Many wandering scholars from North Africa and the Levant were attracted to Venice in order to publish their manuscripts. Some found employment as well as a publishing outlet. Portuguese Conversos could acquire knowledge of their suppressed heritage; those who simply loved books could assemble a fine library of Judaica.

The invention of movable type in the fifteenth century marked a revolution in human culture. As the tedious process of copying manuscripts by hand was replaced by the new technology of printing, affordable books became available in large numbers, thereby democratizing knowledge. The Jews enthusiastically adopted movable type after its introduction to Germany in 1470, and the art of printing spread rapidly from Germany to Spain, Portugal, and Italy. Sephardi women and men, Jews and Conversos, were all involved in the earliest Hebrew printing endeavours.[41] Almost one-quarter of all known books printed prior to 1500 were in Hebrew, a remarkable figure considering that the Jews constituted less than 1 per cent of the population of Europe, and even more so in light of the number of book burnings by the Inquisition and the losses occasioned by the expulsions from Spain, Provence, Naples, and elsewhere.

When the Sephardi exiles arrived in Italy several Hebrew printing presses were already functioning, among them that of Gershom Soncino, whose family, of German Jewish origin, had settled in Soncino in the fifteenth century. Italian presses had supplied books to the Spanish Jewish market prior to the Expulsion, and many Spanish printers had learned their trade at them. Until the Jews were expelled from the Kingdom of Naples in 1506 and 1541, Hebrew printing was actively pursued in the south of Italy. Most of the presses moved north, to Mantua, Venice, Rome, Trino, Bologna, and Ferrara. Manuscripts written in the Ottoman empire were brought to Italy for printing and distributed from there to the Ottoman provinces and other parts of Europe. Hebrew publishing had enjoyed a brief infancy in Fez, only to have its supplies of paper from Spain cut off by the Inquisition, leading many refugee scholars from Morocco to seek printers for their works in Venice. Manuscripts that might otherwise never have reached beyond the study group of a confraternity were brought to a wider audience through the work of Venetian printing houses. Italian Hebrew books even found their way into the libraries of Christians. Venetian printing was key to the introduction of works of Lurianic kabbalah into Europe. Mystical thought had previously been

---

[41] The Judaizing and printing of Hebrew books by Juan de Lucena, the son of Marranos, and his daughters is revealed in Inquisition records. The testimonies of witnesses and former employees vividly describe the secret Jewish practices in their home. Trials against Juan's daughters continued into the 1530s. One daughter, Theresa de Lucena, was condemned to life imprisonment in 1531 for assisting her father in the printing of Hebrew books as far back as the 1480s. Early Hebrew printers tended to seek inconspicuous towns in Italy in order to evade the scrutiny of the ecclesiastical authorities, and Spanish Hebrew printers appear to have followed the same procedure (see Bloch, 'Early Hebrew Printing in Spain and Portugal'). It is noteworthy that the first important Venetian publishing venture in Hebrew was by a Christian, not a Jew or a Converso.

confined to elite circles, mostly by design. Once it appeared in print, its impact was felt in Christian and Jewish circles throughout Europe.

No other city was as important as Venice in the production of Hebrew books in the decades following the Expulsion. Venice gained its reputation as 'the city of Hebrew books' thanks to the skills of its printers and the quality of its paper.[42] Venetian printing attained a level of excellence unmatched in other Hebrew printing centres of the time. The earliest Hebrew books from Venice are considered to be among the finest specimens of Hebrew printing in the world. One of the most striking features of the Venetian Hebrew printing industry was the role played by Christians. Despite the large number of Jews gravitating to Venice, including many scholars, licences to print books, including Hebrew books, were usually reserved by the authorities for Christians, especially members of patrician houses. Although the Venetian printers' guilds were closed to Jews, Jews and Conversos were employed by Christian publishing houses as editors, typesetters, and proofreaders, as they usually had the best knowledge of Hebrew.

Daniel Bomberg (1483–1553), 'the prince of all printers', stands out among the pioneers of Venetian printing.[43] The son of a rich Christian burgher from Antwerp, Bomberg arrived in Venice at the beginning of the sixteenth century with skills in typography. In 1515, armed with a printing permit from the pope, Bomberg established the first Christian-owned establishment for printing in Hebrew. He sought permission from the local authorities to employ Jews to oversee this aspect of his business, requesting that they be exempted from the discriminatory clothing regulations so that they could reach his workshop unmolested. In 1516, the same year as the establishment of the ghetto, the first Hebrew book rolled off the Bomberg press. While other Hebrew presses would be established in Venice in the course of the century, some Jewish-owned and others Christian-owned, Bomberg's remained by far the most important. His team of Hebrew-speaking editors and proofreaders consisted of a number of learned men, including Elijah Levita, the teacher of many distinguished Christian humanists.[44] Bomberg's practice of employing Jewish and Christian typesetters and proof-readers who worked co-operatively provided an arena for Jewish–Christian intellectual exchange, and his printing house has been described as 'an intimate space of non-belligerent encounter between Jews and Christians'.[45] It was one that would bear important intellectual fruit.

Bomberg conscientiously sought out the most accurate manuscripts, paying handsomely to ensure the quality of his work. He was also forced to petition the Venetian

---

[42] See C. Roth, *History of the Jews of Venice*, 245.

[43] Rosenfeld, 'The Development of Hebrew Printing in the Sixteenth and Seventeenth Centuries', 92; see also Bloch, 'Venetian Printers of Hebrew Books'. [44] Nielson, 'Daniel van Bombergen'.

[45] Ruderman, 'The Hebrew Book in a Christian World', 106; id., *Early Modern Jewry*, 111–19; see also Putnam, *Books and Their Makers during the Middle Ages*, i. 365. On the relationship of the early printed page to the Hebrew manuscript, see Ruderman, *Early Modern Jewry*, ch. 3.

senate repeatedly for copyrights at great personal expense, and was often reproached for having squandered his patrimony on Hebrew printing. Nevertheless, he doggedly persisted in his endeavours. The printing process that he employed was original: a specially skilled worker would plan the layout of the page, based on several manuscript copies of a text; other experts would then proofread the text, and still other specialists would cut the type moulds and set the typeface. Joseph Hacohen described Bomberg's workshop in 1554: 'There went in and out of his house many learned men and he never withdrew his hand from giving unto all in accordance with his demands and to the extent of the means which God had endowed him.'[46] Bomberg's discriminating taste and business acumen also extended to the acquisition of fine Flemish paintings and tapestries. His involvement with Conversos in Flanders appears to have gone beyond mere business. It is possible that he received Iberian manuscripts from Marrano circles in Antwerp. His complicated and far-flung trading network brought him into contact with the Francisco and Diogo Mendes brothers' bank: possibly he also dealt with Doña Gracia.

Bomberg was responsible for publishing 200 Hebrew titles. His first major work, an edition of *Mikraot gedolot* (1516–17), contains the complete Bible with several rabbinic commentaries. His enduring place in Jewish history, however, lies in his printing of the entire Babylonian Talmud (1519–23) as well as the Jerusalem Talmud. Following Soncino, Bomberg designed what is now the standard layout of the Talmud with the text in block letters in the middle of the page accompanied by the Targums and commentaries by the Tosafists, the medieval Ashkenazi scholar Solomon ben Isaac (Rashi), and others in a cursive script that is now known as Rashi script (although it was not actually used by Rashi) (Plate 14). The importance of Bomberg's innovation transcended his typographical originality. By placing multiple commentaries from many eras around the text of the Talmud, he brought the full range of Sephardi scholarship to the attention of a much broader Jewish audience. Ashkenazim and Sephardim were brought into dialogue with one another through the printed Hebrew word.

Bomberg's printing house brought Sephardi commentaries, Italian sermons, medieval philosophical traditions, and even the scientific studies of Padua's famed medical faculty to a new and wider audience. Yeshiva students in Kraków, Christian burghers in Amsterdam, and Jewish scholars in Constantinople were, for the first time, exposed to some of the same Jewish voices. As David Ruderman has convincingly argued, this print revolution shattered the localized Jewish traditions of medieval times, making Jews of all backgrounds, not just those in rabbinic circles, more aware of one another.[47]

Christian and Jewish collectors turned to Bomberg with specific orders for fine Hebrew books to include in their personal libraries. The new German universities also sought Hebrew books from him. Some of his books printed for specifically Christian

---

[46] Joseph Hakohen, 'History of the Kings of France and the Ottoman Empire', cited in Nielsen, 'Daniel van Bombergen', 58.   [47] Ruderman, *Early Modern Jewry*, 99–132.

audiences featured Hebrew and Latin pages facing each other. Jewish communities from as far away as Aleppo and the Crimea commissioned Bomberg to print their prayer books. His books were reportedly even shipped to Ethiopia, the Indies, and Egypt.[48] He printed material for specific rites, such as the Romaniote prayer book. Other important works included Isaac Alfasi's code of Jewish law, *Sefer hahalakhot*, and the responsa of the prolific Spanish scholar and communal leader Solomon ibn Adret. Joseph Karo's *Shulḥan arukh* was printed by the Bomberg press in 1565 soon after its arrival in Italy. Its republication with the glosses of the Ashkenazi scholar Moses Isserles in 1578–80 in Kraków marked a turning point in Jewish learning and the beginning of a cultural fusion of the Ashkenazi and Sephardi intellectual worlds.[49] The Hebrew presses of Venice and subsequently of Amsterdam and Livorno played a major part in the formation of an interconnected early modern Jewish culture, as both Sephardi and Ashkenazi works became more widely available.[50]

The Venetian Hebrew book industry proved to be a magnet for Jewish scholars because it enjoyed relative freedom, and for the quality and variety of its printings. Of the 3,986 Hebrew titles printed in Europe before 1650, 1,284 were printed in Venice. Most of these were traditional: almost 300 were prayer books, 460 were talmudic and midrashic, 47 were Hebrew grammars or lexicons, 37 were books of Jewish thought and philosophy, 35 were kabbalistic, and 10 were books of Jewish history.[51] The texts Bomberg selected for the Spanish-speaking market were often quite basic: there was a Spanish version of the *Shulḥan arukh* and a Spanish–Hebrew digest of the laws of *sheḥitah* (ritual slaughter). These primers of Jewish living were essential for Jews arriving from the Iberian peninsula and retrieving their Jewish heritage.

Censorship and the Counter-Reformation

Conditions in Italy deteriorated rapidly for Jews in the middle of the sixteenth century. Frightened by the advances of the Reformation and incorrectly ascribing the Protestant movement to Jewish incitement and collaboration, the Catholic Church decided to promulgate far-reaching legislation separating Christians from Jews in order to thwart new 'heretical' movements. Among its targets were Hebrew books. In November 1548, without waiting for directives from Rome, the Venetian authorities directed that all Hebrew books be expurgated of anything that might be a danger to Catholicism. Bomberg objected to the censorship, arguing that changes could not be made to ancient manuscripts. Papal policy took a harsher turn. The Talmud, for centuries the target of physical or verbal assaults, was burned on papal orders on the Campo de' Fiori in Rome on 9 September 1553. Soon afterwards, on 21 October 1553, thousands of talmudic

---

[48] Nielsen, 'Daniel van Bombergen', 71, 247 n. 106.
[49] On the internal transformations of Ashkenazi learning resulting from the printing presses in Venice and elsewhere, see Ruderman, *Early Modern Jewry*, 99–125. [50] Ibid. 102. [51] Bonfil, 'A Cultural Profile'.

tractates and other Hebrew books were publicly burned in St Mark's Square in Venice. During the following months, the Talmud was also burned on the Venetian-held island of Crete. Hundreds of thousands of Hebrew books were confiscated and consigned to the flames all across Italy. In 1554 Pope Paul IV ordered the Jews of the Papal States to be confined to a ghetto. Enforced ghettoizations followed in Florence and Siena (1571), Verona (1600), Padua (1603), Mantua (1612), Rovigo (1613), Ferrara (1624), and Modena (1638).

On 29 May and 18 December 1554, in response to repeated Jewish petitions, the incoming pope, Julius III, consented to allow Jews to possess censored Hebrew texts. Taking their cue from the discriminatory tone and intent of the papal bull *Cum nimis absurdum*, the Italian rabbinical authorities convened in emergency session in Ferrara, where they decided that Hebrew authors should subject their books to pre-censorship, modifying or eliminating those passages that might be deemed by the papal authorities to contain heresy or false and radical views. The assembled Jewish leadership decreed that no book was to be printed by Jews in Italy without the prior approval of three rabbis and the heads of the local Jewish community, who would attest, after careful examination of the book, that it contained no expressions offensive to Christianity or to Judaism. As a result of these censorship boards, subsequently published Hebrew books were filled with emendations and lacunae.[52]

The attack on Hebrew printing did not cease after the introduction of pre-censorship. When Hebrew publishing resumed in Venice in 1559, the publication of the Talmud and its commentaries was prohibited. Despite Jewish precautions, Hebrew books became the target of renewed attacks by the Inquisition. In September 1568 thousands of recently printed books were destroyed and their printers heavily fined. These measures may have been connected with rumours that the Jews were Turkish agents and that the Hebrew presses constituted a danger to the security of Venice.[53] The witch hunt against Hebrew publishers persisted, especially against the patrician Giustiniani's publishing house. In 1571 the Venetian senate prohibited the employment of Jews in any part of the printing industry. Hebrew books were now subjected to censorship by expurgators who were either apostates or ignorant of Hebrew. As a result, Venetian Hebrew books entered into rapid decline in both accuracy and presentation. At the same time, the quality of paper, which had distinguished the earlier books, deteriorated. By the mid-seventeenth century the golden age of Hebrew publishing in Venice was over. Although Hebrew printing continued, multiple obstacles were imposed upon the presses. León de Modena, who worked as a proofreader and typesetter in order to pay his gambling debts, described some of these obstacles in his autobiography:

---

[52] Shulvass, *The Jews in the World of the Renaissance*, 267. On Jewish self-censorship, see Hacker, 'Sixteenth-Century Jewish Internal Censorship of Hebrew Books'.

[53] See Grendler, 'The Destruction of Hebrew Books in Venice'.

In Adar 5394 I began to have [*Beit yehudah*] printed. Many impediments intertwined concerning it, however... before that, in Elul 5394 [August–September 1634] some of the scoundrels from among our own people had informed the Cattaver [magistrate's office] about the printing, and it closed down the print shop. It remained tightly sealed off for about six months. Then it was opened and they (the printers) returned to their work and to printing my aforementioned book, which was almost entirely done by my grandson, Isaac min Haleviim . . . on Wednesday the 28th of Iyyar [16 May 1635] police suddenly entered the shop and arrested my grandson Isaac along with two of his young friends; they put them in prison, in darkness, and sealed off the print shop once again. I was very distressed when, despite great efforts at intercession, I was unable to conclude the matter and set him free. With difficulty, after fifteen days, they allowed him to leave the darkness for the light though still in prison, and he remained there for a total of sixty-six days.[54]

By the 1630s, the leadership in Hebrew printing had passed permanently from Venice to Prague, Kraków, Livorno, and, especially, Amsterdam, where deluxe editions of the Bible and prayer books with picturesque title pages produced on copper plates commanded a growing and increasingly discerning market of European readers and collectors.

One major consequence of Hebrew printing in Venice was the gradual change in the perception of Jewish culture. A new class of Jewish reader emerged alongside the old intellectual rabbinic elite. Perhaps as, if not more, important was the new Christian interest in Jews. León de Modena was keenly aware of the power of the printed word and eager to reshape the image of Judaism when he had his *Historia de' riti hebraici* published. The Christian who read his book was introduced to the world of Jewish culture, even if this did not necessarily translate into greater toleration of Jews.

Culture and Acculturation: The Illuminated *Ketubah*

Despite the new restrictions on Jewish residency introduced by Pope Paul IV in the middle of the sixteenth century, Jews continued to engage in dialogue with their Christian neighbours, and Jewish cultural expression continued to flourish in the ghettos of Venice and other Italian cities. The new art of printing did not totally eliminate the production of illuminated Hebrew manuscripts. One expression of Sephardi creativity is the richly decorated marriage contracts, or *ketubot*, which began to appear in northern Italy at approximately the same time as Hebrew printing emerged. The decorated and illuminated *ketubot* were privately commissioned to satisfy the demand and the tastes of a particular clientele. Their production reached its artistic zenith in sixteenth- and seventeenth-century Italy when Venice, in particular, became a site of rich Sephardi and Italian artistic interchange.

According to Shalom Sabar, the appearance of the illuminated *ketubot* in Venice is directly related to the influx of Portuguese merchants.[55] Until the fifteenth or sixteenth

[54] Modena, *The Autobiography of a Seventeenth-Century Rabbi*, 141; see Ravid, 'The Prohibition against Jewish Printing and Publishing in Venice', 141–2 n. 28. [55] Sabar, 'The Beginnings of *Ketubbah* Decoration in Italy'.

century the Jewish marriage tradition consisted of two distinct ceremonies, the betrothal and the nuptials. The two ceremonies were separated from each other by a set interval of time that was prescribed in the talmudic tractate *Ketubot*. At the first of the two ceremonies, the marital obligations between the contracting parties, including monetary arrangements, were spelled out. Although no cohabitation between the betrothed couple followed this ceremony, they were considered to be legally married: if they chose to nullify their agreement, full divorce procedures were applied. The betrothal tended to be a private affair, akin to the closing of a business arrangement. Only later, at the actual wedding ceremony, did the bride receive her *ketubah*. The contents of the *ketubah* had already been agreed by the two families and were now publicly announced, but its stipulations were obviously widely known, given the time that had elapsed between the betrothal and wedding ceremonies.

As long as the *ketubah* remained a private document, even though its contents might be generally known, there was apparently no particular incentive to decorate it or to display it publicly. A plain contract, carefully and properly executed by a scribe, was officially transferred to the bride under the marriage canopy in a rolled-up scroll. At some point in the Middle Ages, earlier in the Ashkenazi diaspora than in Spain, probably for socioeconomic reasons or perhaps in consonance with changes in Christian marital customs, the two ceremonies of betrothal and marriage were joined. Once the two ceremonies were merged, it became customary to read the *ketubah* aloud under the marriage canopy. This reading was probably accompanied by a public display of the document. In order to avoid the social pressure that might arise from the public announcement of the actual amount of money involved in the transaction, Ashkenazi Jews introduced a standardized monetary formula. As a result of this innovation, perhaps also to preserve the pride or modesty of the families or in response to the greater Jewish pietism in German lands, Ashkenazi *ketubot* were not generally decorated, and their physical appearance remained relatively unimportant. Public display of the *ketubah* was not felt to be necessary, although it was always publicly read and witnessed. The names of the betrothed and the location of the wedding may have been inserted into a standard contractual document. In contrast, Sephardi marriage customs—at least among members of a certain affluent class—included the commissioning of richly decorative *ketubot*. By the fifteenth century the Sephardi wedding ceremony included the reading aloud of the *ketubah* with much flourish, and the richly decorated *ketubah* was proudly displayed to the assembled crowd.

The *ketubah* that Abraham, son of Solomon Abrabanel, gave to the daughter of Aaron de Paz, in 1614 (Plate 15) displays the horseshoe arches characteristic of Jewish manuscript art in Spain. The right-hand arch contains the marriage contract; the articles of the dowry are listed in the left-hand one. The dowry of 5,500 ducats, augmented by 2,750 ducats, is similar to those of many affluent Venetian families. The Hebrew quotation that forms the frame is from Ruth 4: 11–12 and refers to the birth of Perez, one of the ancestors of King David. The Abrabanels thus proudly alluded to their Davidic descent in their decorative marriage contract.

Significantly, most of the Venetian illuminated *ketubot* date from between 1597 and 1624, soon after the Portuguese merchants arrived and gained official recognition as a separate Jewish group in the ghetto. Many *ketubot* of Italian provenance are also quite decorative, and those originating in the Sephardi community include Mudéjar motifs. These were probably inspired by earlier *ketubot* executed in Spain and Portugal. Wherever the Sephardim settled, including in the Italian ghettos, they transported their Iberian aesthetic tastes with them.[56] Although it is highly unlikely that the Jews who came from Portugal would have produced decorative *ketubot* when they lived precariously as Marranos, *ketubot* were vital documents that were carefully preserved as heirlooms in most families. Many Converso newcomers to Venice were eager to enter into Jewish marriages now that they could openly embrace Judaism. The presence in the ghetto of a large and successful Portuguese Jewish merchant class who had patronized the arts of Iberia contributed an additional layer to the richly textured Jewish culture in the difficult ghetto surroundings. It is noteworthy that the *ketubot* of Venice, like those of Mantua and other Italian cities, also contained Italian motifs, such as *putti* and monumental pedestals or columns symbolizing the architecture of the Temple of Jerusalem. The combination of Iberian and Italian artistic motifs is consonant with Sephardi tastes and traditions of cultural accommodation.

The acquisition of fine printed Hebrew books and the commissioning of richly decorated *ketubot* were only two manifestations of the broad cultural horizons and artistic tastes of some of the Sephardi and Italian ghetto residents. The Jews of Venice were often profoundly Italianized and eager to partake of aspects of the extraordinary culture beyond the ghetto walls where musical and literary expressions flourished. While the Jewish gaze looked outwards, Christian noblemen and literati, ever eager for novelty and entertainment, were drawn to the ghetto for their own recreation. Literary salons, especially that of the Jewish poet Sara Copia Sulam, were attractive to some of the nobility and clergy. Jewish dance masters and musicians from the ghetto were also in high demand among their Christian neighbours.

Cultural Exchanges: Permitted and Prohibited

Fraternization of Christians and Jews was a daily occurrence despite the segregation imposed by the ghetto walls, but both the Jewish and the Christian authorities, for different reasons, found it troubling. Special laws were promulgated in both communities to limit informal social encounters. Italian Jewish leaders, always concerned that displays of Jewish affluence would stoke the envy and hostility of their non-Jewish neighbours, addressed issues of the socialization of Jews and Christians. Mentions of

---

[56] On the Hispanicity of the Portuguese Jewish merchants in Amsterdam, see Chapter 6 below.

romantic liaisons between Christians and Jews in rabbinic responsa attest to a social reality that included many informal contacts: Jewish legislation was usually silent on the daily relations between the two groups unless some problematic or grey area arose. The Jewish authorities in Venice were particularly concerned about the widespread practices of gambling and duelling in the ghetto. Gambling periodically brought its colourful and versatile rabbi León de Modena to the brink of bankruptcy.[57] His son, Zevulun, was ambushed and murdered by some members of a gang to which he belonged. Modena witnessed the murder, but was unable to save him.[58] Modena's remarkable autobiography recreates the many areas of Jewish engagement in the broader Venetian culture of the upper and lower classes.

In the atmosphere of violence, insecurity, and licentiousness pervading early modern Venice, Jewish leaders also felt compelled to address issues of female attire and modesty. In 1616 Venetian Jewish women were prohibited from wearing silk or velvet dresses, clothing interwoven with silver or gold thread, or fancy headdresses in public. Women's necklines were to be modest; high heels and the dyeing of hair were proscribed. Jewish women were counselled to wear opaque head coverings rather than elaborate wigs or diaphanous veils. Husbands were held responsible for any infractions committed by their wives. In neighbouring Padua, the Jewish community attempted to limit the appearance of women in public altogether (in 1599 and 1630) on pain of a fine and excommunication. The rigour of this legislation should be understood in light of the relative laxity of the Sephardi, especially Portuguese, immigrants. The many strictures of rabbinic Judaism, and its emphasis on female modesty in particular, ran counter to the somewhat flamboyant tastes of the Portuguese Jewish commercial elite. Their affluent lifestyle contrasted sharply with the general condition of poverty in the ghetto.

Not all Jewish women in Italy accepted the rabbis' standards of modesty and chastity. Jewish women, like Italian women in general, were assuming an increasingly prominent public profile in late sixteenth-century Venice. They served as witnesses in public records, initiated litigation, and engaged in a variety of commercial activities. They also played a role in the ghetto economy. Their handiwork was essential in transforming the old clothes given to them as pledges and unredeemed into new articles of clothing for sale. Italian Jewish women also acted as financial agents for their husbands and served as moneylenders, brokers, medical practitioners, and healers. Women from Venice even travelled as far as Leipzig to attend its great fair. Some Jewish women learnt Hebrew and could read Italian written in Hebrew characters. They also led other women in prayer during the sabbath and holiday services.[59] Their self-confidence may be inferred from their recitation of a daily prayer of thanksgiving to God for having

---

[57] See Modena, *The Autobiography of a Seventeenth-Century Venetian Rabbi*.   [58] Ibid. 119–21.
[59] Stow and Debenedetti Stow, 'Donne ebree a Roma nell'eta del ghetto affetto, dependenz, autonomia', 81. On the occupations of women in Italy, see Adelman, 'Italian Jewish Women'; id., 'Rabbis and Reality'.

created them female, a mirror image of the traditional male prayer. Jewish women, although not counted in the *minyan*, participated in daily prayer, some of them even wearing *tefilin*.[60] Reportedly, they were accustomed to interrupting the service to air their grievances against their husbands.[61]

The life of Sara Copia Sulam (1592–1641) reveals the degree of cultural freedom that an educated Jewish woman could enjoy in the ghetto and suggests that the boundaries of permissible cultural exchange between Jews and Christians were quite flexible, despite the ghetto walls. She was trained in rhetoric, classical languages, and secular literature, as were other women of her class. While the Jewish community may have lagged behind Italian society in this respect, it too was re-evaluating women's capacities and their nature under the influence of Italian humanism.

Copia Sulam was reportedly a woman of unusual beauty. She was reared in the home of a prominent Italian Jewish family, where she acquired a broad literary knowledge. After her marriage to a businessman from the Venetian Jewish community she conducted a literary salon in her home, where she recited her poetry, accompanying herself on a guitar or lute. While still a young bride, she initiated a correspondence with a nobleman from Genoa, Ansaldo Cebà, after discovering his epic poem 'La Reina Ester'.[62] A four-year correspondence between the talented Jewish woman and the ageing count ensued. In her letters to Cebà, Copia Sulam expressed her boundless admiration for his poetic talents. Cebà responded happily to her flattering literary overtures, confessing that he hoped to ultimately convert her to the 'truth of Christianity'.[63] Their communication progressed from the exchange of letters and original sonnets to an exchange of portraits. Cebà's frustration grew at his inability to convert Sara. In one sonnet he exclaimed:

> What are you thinking, Jewess, and what are you doing?
> Do you not bathe your golden hair yet in the holy fount?
> Are you shutting your charming, blue eyes
> At the sight of the Sun that blazes upon the mount of Calvary?
> The Sun I show your rebellious thoughts
> Is not just one that falls or sets,
> Rather it is a beam that shines amidst scourges
> And a light that appears amidst disgraces.
> Ah, what an infernal cloud obstructs you
> If you are not able to see the pearls and the ornaments
> That the holy wood offers your eyes!
> The cross that you decline and disdain
> Outshines gems and crowns
> By flashing, in glory, before kings.[64]

---

[60] Adelman, 'Italian Jewish Women', 154 n. 4.   [61] Ibid. 80.   [62] *Sarra Copia Sulam*, 117.
[63] Ansaldo Cebà, letters to Sara Copia Sulam, in *Sarra Copia Sulam*, 35–7, 43–5, 115–267. On his wish to convert her, see ibid. 208, 210.
[64] Ansaldo Cebà, 'Che pensi, Hebre, che fai? Nel sacro fonte', in *Sarra Copia Sulam*, 208–9.

The two never met, however. Copia Sulam's steadfast adherence to Judaism ultimately convinced Cebà that he had to break off the correspondence. As they parted, Cebà exclaimed in frustration: 'If you do not mean to convert, lay down your pen; for without this, I cannot use my own.'[65] The thwarted suitor ultimately confessed his proselytizing intentions in verse:

> When to the limit of my long life
> Already my foot draws nigh.
> A woman, who does not believe,
> Attempts to make me sigh and moan for love.
>
> Fresh is her grace, and her beauty supreme,
> Wherewith she kindles and calls forth my desires,
> But she harbors neither piety nor Faith
> Wherefore I fear not the bonds of her dominion.
>
> Still in the darkness of Hebraic rites
> She sees no Latin torch nor Greek,
> That might discover to her eyes what it reveals to mine.
>
> But were it not that Heaven shields me,
> Vainly would I combat the arrows
> Shot by a little boy for a blind woman.[66]

Copia Sulam's correspondence with Cebà was not her only foray into religiously questionable territory. In 1621, while recovering from a miscarriage, she began a literary exchange with another Christian intellectual who frequented her salon, the archdeacon and later bishop of Treviso, Baldassare Bonifaccio. Their conversations on poetry soon shifted to matters of theology. Before long, Bonifaccio became a fierce critic of Copia Sulam, accusing her of denying the doctrine of the immortality of the soul. The accusation exposed her to the possibility of disciplinary reproof or worse in both the Jewish and Christian communities. But she held her ground, refuting Bonifaccio's charges in an Italian work entitled *The Manifesto of Sarra Copia Sulam, a Jewish Woman, in which She Refutes and Disavows the Opinion Denying the Immortality of the Soul, Falsely Attributed to Her by Signor Baldassare Bonifaccio*.[67] She was probably assisted in her response by Rabbi León de Modena. Modena held Copia Sulam in high esteem. He dedicated his Italian adaptation of Samuel Usque's play *Ester* to her in 1619, praising her 'frank, yet delightful conversation; her singular manners; and her sundry virtues and talents, among them her skills in, and understanding of, Italian poetry'.[68]

---

[65] Ansaldo Cebà, letter to Sara Copia Sulam, in *Sarra Copia Sulam*, 118; 'The Poet Ansaldo Ceba Tries to Convert Sara', in *Letters of Jews through the Ages*, ii. 436–40.

[66] Ansaldo Cebà, letter to Sara Copia Sulam, in *Sarra Copia Sulam*, 256.   [67] *Sarra Copia Sulam*, 311–31.

[68] León de Modena, dedication to the 'Very Illustrious Signora and My Most Respected Patroness', in *Sarra Copia Sulam*, 511–14; see also Harrán, notes to *Sarra Copia Sulam*, 55 n. 352; Adelman, 'Jewish Women and Family Life', 147; id., 'Success and Failure in the Seventeenth Century Ghetto of Venice'.

Copia Sulam's theological boldness was matched by her naivety. Her faulty judgement of the character of her bohemian and aristocratic visitors eventually proved to be her undoing. She surrounded herself with sycophants, both Jewish and Christian, lavishing gifts on them as well as her dazzling conversation. Ultimately, she fell victim to a confidence scheme involving magic and witchcraft hatched by a penniless painter, a French friar, and a group of charlatans, among whom were her personal servants. Much of her property was stolen in their scheme.

Copia Sulam died in 1641 at the age of 49. The epitaph on her tombstone in the Jewish cemetery on the Lido, like many of the other epitaphs in the historic cemetery, was composed by León de Modena. It reads:

> The tombstone of the virtuous Signora Sarra Copia,
> Wife of the honourable Signor Jacob Sullam
> (may his Rock protect and preserve him).
>
> The oppressive angel
> shot his arrow
> And a foremost lady of fine discernment
> Was destroyed and killed.
>
> Wise was she among women
> A jewel for the miserable,
> And of every poor soul
> A friend and companion
>
> If she, today,
> Has been irreparably deposited
> As solace for worms,
> Moths, and spiders.
>
> On the day the Redeemer comes,
> God will say:
> 'Return, return.
> O Sulamite.'
>
> She died on the eve of the sixth day, 5 Adar 5401.
> May her soul dwell at ease![69]

Sara Copia Sulam was not an isolated figure in the artistic life of the ghetto. In a study of wills drawn up by Venetian notaries, Carla Boccato notes that most of the Jewish women who possessed significant assets were from the Ghetto Vecchio or the Ghetto Nuovissimo, the sections of the ghetto where the Ponentine and Levantine merchants resided. The act of registering a will with a Venetian notary was in itself a statement of some degree of acculturation: neither the Venetian nor the rabbinic authorities required it. The wills have common traits: men tended to bequeath books, while women bequeathed jewels and brocades. Although outright Jewish ownership of

---

[69] *Sarra Copia Sulam*, 521–2.

real estate in the ghetto was prohibited, Jewish women owned residential rights to their dwellings, which they passed on to their heirs. These bequests did not necessarily follow strict rabbinic lines of inheritance but tended to follow the inclinations and affections of the female decedents—another sign of the acculturation of Sephardi women.[70]

Music and Art in the Ghetto

The city of Venice was awash with music. Proficiency in music was esteemed by the Jews as well as the Christians. Jewish soloists and musical ensembles performed before mixed audiences within the confines of the ghetto. Copia Sulam was admired for her talents in musical performance as well as poetry. Jewish dancers and musicians were exempted from wearing the distinguishing clothing and were permitted outside the ghetto after curfew, especially during carnival time. One musician, a certain Ioseppo, was permitted to enter the houses of noblemen at night with two fellow lute players. Another musician was given licence to enter the houses of eleven noblemen and five others 'to teach their children to sing, dance, and play musical instruments freely and without restraint'. In 1590 a group of fourteen musicians was granted special permission to leave the ghetto at night in order to perform an opera. In 1613 a Jewish singer, Rachel, was permitted to traverse the city after dusk in a gondola while entertaining with song.[71] These allusions suggest that music played a conspicuous role in the life of the ghetto dwellers. It certainly played a large role in the life of León de Modena.[72] Among the twenty-six occupations that Modena claims to have practised during his lifetime, several relate to music: he was the director of a music academy, served for several decades as a cantor, was employed as a music editor and teacher, and acted as a choir conductor and composer of songs. He became maestro di capella of the music academy in the ghetto, the Academia degl'Impedita, in 1628. In this capacity, he led rehearsals for a choir that performed at synagogue celebrations during festivals and the inauguration of a Torah scroll, in private homes at weddings and circumcisions, and at the conclusion of group study of a talmudic tractate (the *siyum*). It is not clear whether women sang in the choir at the synagogue, although Modena was familiar with women singing. When speaking of his son's death, Modena wrote, 'my soul refuses to be comforted and I will no longer hear the voice of male and female singers'.[73] His musical compositions, a cross between traditional cantorial music and art music with counterpoint, were 'a new thing in the land'.[74] Members of Modena's family also engaged in music: his son sang in the Scuola Grande Spagnola in 1622 at a *siyum* not long before his death; his son-in-law Jacob Halevi was employed as a dance master and music teacher.

---

[70] Boccato, 'Aspetti della condizione femminile nel ghetto di Venezia'; Adelman, 'Jewish Women and Family Life', 151.   [71] Harrán, 'Jewish Musical Culture', 213, 218.
[72] Ibid.; Harrán, *Salomone Rossi*.   [73] Modena, *The Autobiography of a Seventeenth-Century Venetian Rabbi*.
[74] See Harrán, 'Was Rabbi León Modena a Composer?'

In his autobiography, Modena described the course of study he received in his youth as 'a little instruction in playing an instrument, in singing, in dancing, in writing, and in Latin'.[75] It is not entirely clear where his rabbinic studies fit into this Renaissance curriculum. While still a young rabbi, Modena was called upon to render a talmudic opinion on the permissibility of innovation in synagogue music.[76] He wrote at least two responsa on the question in the course of his career. In 1605, in response to a conflict regarding the introduction of part-singing in the synagogue of Ferrara, he justified the introduction of polyphonic music in synagogue services in Italy. In 1622 he wrote another responsum in connection with a controversy in Senigallia over the repetition of God's name in music.[77] His early responsum defending the legitimacy of part-singing and art music was included in his preface to Salomone Rossi's 'Songs of Solomon', the most important polyphonic work written by a Jewish composer until modern times. Modena played a major role in the inception, composition, publication, and introduction of the work. In his responsum defending art music in general, Modena included a condemnation of the traditional cantorial music of the synagogue.[78] He contrasted the polyphonic music of Rossi favourably with traditional cantorial music, which he derisively described as 'braying like asses' and 'an embarrassment to the nations'.[79] In his defence of the new synagogue music, Modena claimed that polyphony was not introduced by Jews in emulation of Christian services; rather, it was the music that had been performed in the Temple in Jerusalem, but it had disappeared from Jewish worship as a result of the destruction of the Temple in 70 CE and the subsequent perpetual mourning of the Jews. In fact, Modena daringly suggested, the music of the Church constituted a replication of ancient Jewish music. He called for a restoration of similar music in the synagogue.

Modena's relationship with Salomone Rossi marked a major advance in the history of synagogue music. Modena, along with Sara Copia Sulam, encouraged Rossi to write his 'Songs of Solomon'. They may even have been Modena's idea. Modena helped in the selection of the Hebrew texts, checked them before their submission to the publisher, and provided a solution to the problem of notating a Hebrew text for Western music. The difficulty was that Hebrew reads from right to left, whereas Western music reads from left to right. Modena wrote the Hebrew words in reverse order, confident that the singers would know the words of the psalms by heart and could sing them while reading the unfamiliar contrapuntal music. He was thus a guiding light in adapting Hebrew lyrics to Western musical modes. In his preface to 'Songs of Solomon',

---

[75] Modena, *The Autobiography of a Seventeenth-Century Venetian Rabbi*, 86.

[76] Modena, *She'elot utshuvot ziknei yehuda*, 15–20. On the 1605 responsum and the legitimacy of art music in the synagogue, see Harrán, *Salamone Rossi*, 201–18.

[77] See Adler, *La Pratique musicale savante dans quelques communautés juives en Europe*, 70–9, 262.

[78] On Modena's prefatory remarks to the published edition of the 'Songs of Solomon', see Harrán, *Salamone Rossi*, 16, 19, 35, 39, 201–18.   [79] Modena, *She'elot uteshuvot ziknei yehudah*, 15.

Modena compared Rossi to King David.[80] His claims that the 'Songs of Solomon' were not novel notwithstanding, they represented a radical intrusion of Western art music and counterpoint into synagogue music.

The ghetto was divided on this musical innovation, with many opposing changes in the name of tradition and many defending Rossi's music. Modena's defence of a type of music identified with the secular and sacred music of non-Jews was quite controversial. His attempt to get the Venetian rabbis to concede that the Jewish people were not required to lament the destruction of their Temple in their synagogue music for ever, and his dream of introducing contrapuntal choral music into the synagogue, were short-lived.

Modena dared to ask: If the voice of one cantor is pleasant to hear, how much more so if it sounded as many? 'One should praise God with whatever talents he has bestowed upon one, and surely', he argued, 'it is meritorious in one with a sweet voice to raise it up in song to him. And if such a person were joined by several others with equally good voices surely this would bring about even more devoted prayer to God.' How could anyone deprecate Salomone Rossi, Modena asked rhetorically, since the great composer only sought to restore music 'to its ancient estate as in the days of the Levites on their dais in the Temple'?[81] The new songs would, moreover, serve to glorify God, a time-honoured notion of the purpose of music in the synagogue. Like Rossi, Modena rebelled against traditional chant, and probably perceived music as a way to bring the ghetto Jews into the wider world and to earn the appreciation of any Christian who heard it in the synagogue. In his defence of Western music and his advocacy of musical innovation, Modena anticipated the musical developments introduced by the Reform movement in Germany by several centuries.

Venice served as a transit point for Converso musicians as well as merchants. Beginning in the 1520s, several musical families from Italy joined the Tudor court in England as performers, instrument makers, or composers. They were Portuguese or Spanish in origin, outwardly Christian but, in all likelihood, Jewish. Perhaps they felt relatively safe in England, since Henry VIII's split with Rome guaranteed that an Inquisition would not be introduced there. Or perhaps they fled northern Italy when invading Spanish armies raised fears among Marranos of increased Inquisition activity in the region. It is not known whether Henry recruited any of his court musicians in 1531 when he sent representatives to the ghetto of Venice to enquire about the biblical law of levirate marriage in order to justify his divorce from the childless Catherine of Aragon; however, he was passionately devoted to music and sought the best musicians from Europe for his court, and Venetians soon formed the backbone of the Tudor musical establishment.[82] He probably suspected that some of them were Jews,

---

[80] See Harrán, *Salamone Rossi*, 209; 'Leone da Modena to the Jewish Public', in *Letters of Jews through the Ages*, ii. 416–19.   [81] 'Leone da Modena to the Jewish Public', in *Letters of Jews through the Ages*, ii. 419.

[82] See Adelman, 'Custom, Law, and Gender', 113–14; Lasocki, 'The Bassanos', 174.

appreciated their talents, and did not ask too many questions. The Bassano family, serving as musicians in the English court, were probably connected with the Italian town of Bassano del Grappa near Venice. The name was well known in northern Italy in the fifteenth and sixteenth centuries. In the early sixteenth century Jews were excluded from the town, and the Bassanos began to spread through northern Italy: Jeronimo Bassano appeared in Venice. Four of the Bassanos became court musicians and instrument makers in England in 1531. They not only were performers but played an important role in introducing new forms of wind instrument to Venice before moving on to London.

Another Italian family of Jewish background was already active in the musical scene at Henry's court: six viol players, the Lupo brothers, were Marranos. They arrived at the English court in around 1520. For more than one hundred years, the extended Bassano and Lupo families played a central role in the musical life of the English court, performing at several coronations and composing many pieces for the viol. In the years after 1520 more crypto-Jewish musicians left Italy for England. In 1540 Henry sent to Italy for additional musicians, and from then on the majority of the foreign musicians at his court were Jews. Their garbled names, a mixture of Italian, Hebrew, and Portuguese, hint at the largely concealed footprints of an odyssey that brought many Marrano musicians and their innovations to the courts of Europe.[83] While there is nothing Jewish about their music, they probably incorporated Spanish and Portuguese elements. Only briefly, in 1541, when Henry sought to ingratiate himself with Charles V, did the king turn against his musicians, imprisoning them, perhaps as a way of proving himself to be a true Catholic. The emperor's sister, Mary dowager queen of Hungary, interceded on their behalf, as did the king and queen of Portugal.

Moneylending and the 'Utility of the Jews'

The plague reaped its grim harvest in 1630 and 1631, spreading panic in Venice and spurring Jewish emigration. Forty-six thousand people from a population of 140,000, or roughly one-third, died in the pestilence. The stark inscription '1631' carved into a small tombstone marks a mass grave that can still be seen in the old Jewish cemetery on the Lido of Venice. As Modena lamented in his autobiography: 'Above and below me and on all sides, left and right, people have taken ill and died.'[84] When the plague finally abated, prayers of thanksgiving were instituted in the ghetto synagogues. To commemorate their deliverance, attributed by the Venetians to the presence in the city of a precious Byzantine icon (the Nicopeia) and the relics of Venice's first patriarch, Lorenzo Giustinian, the Venetians declared a festival. As part of the thanksgiving fes-

[83] Prior, 'Jewish Musicians at the Tudor Court'.
[84] Modena, *The Autobiography of a Seventeenth-Century Venetian Rabbi*, 134.

tivities, Modena noted, the doge donated a gold lamp to the shrine of the Madonna's house at Loreto, while the Venetian senate ordered the construction of the Church of Santa Maria della Salute in gratitude to the Virgin.[85]

The ghetto population had scarcely recovered from the devastating effects of the plague when the 'Bergonzi affair' rocked the city. On 20 March 1636 three Jews were discovered to be hiding goods that had been stolen by a group of Christian smugglers from a Christian merchant named Bergonzi. This led to calls for the expulsion of all the Jews from Venice. According to León de Modena:

> On Purim of 6396 [31 March 1636] the entire community turned from joy to mourning when trouble began for the community as a whole, for some individuals in particular, and for myself. . . . It was because the crime of Grassin, Scaramella, and Sabbadin Catelano was discovered. They had received goods and cash—silk, silk clothing, and gold—worth seventy thousand ducats, stolen by some Christians in the Merceria from the merchant Bergonzi, and had put them in a room in one of the houses in the ghetto. A worthless scoundrel named Isaac son of Jacob Senigo . . . had informed against them and disclosed the affair. The government agents came and arrested Sabbadin, who showed them where the money was, but Grassin escaped. Menahem d'Angelo and Isaac Scaramella were involved with them through the accusation, even though they were innocent. On Purim the ghetto compound was closed off in order to conduct a house-to-house search for them. The outcry against and contempt for all Jews on the part of everyone in the city —nobles, citizens, and commoners—increased as usual. For when one individual committed a crime, they would grow angry at the entire community.[86]

Modena's son-in-law was caught up in the reprisals and fled to Ferrara.

The charters permitting Jewish residence in the ghetto were invariably premised on the benefits that accrued to the Christian residents of the city from Jewish moneylending. Even after the Sephardim succeeded in expanding the original ghetto area and winning official recognition of their contribution to the commercial life of the city in 1541, Jewish involvement in pawnbrokerage and moneylending remained the primary reason that the religious authorities allowed the renewal of the Tedeschi charters. As a result of the hysteria generated by the plague and the Bergonzi affair, fingers now pointed at the Jews as the source of all the city's problems. If plague had carried off one-third of the city's inhabitants, surely it was God's punishment for the presence of Jewish moneylenders. Now that the plague had passed, some counselled, an appropriate thanksgiving to God ought to include the expulsion of the Jews.

The problems associated with moneylending were well known to the Jews. But their choice of occupation was usually out of their hands. While moneylending made them tolerable and at times indispensable to Venice's Christians, it exposed them to constant ecclesiastical opprobrium, popular abuse, and manipulation. Both Jews and Christians were prohibited from lending money to their co-religionists at interest, on the basis of the biblical prohibition of usury: 'Thou shalt not lend upon interest to thy

---

[85] Modena, *The Autobiography of a Seventeenth-Century Venetian Rabbi*, 250. [86] Ibid. 143–4.

brother; interest of money, interest of victuals, interest of anything that is lent upon interest. Unto a foreigner thou mayest lend upon interest, but unto thy brother thou shalt not lend upon interest' (Deut. 23: 20–1). But all societies require a source of credit, preferably a source that can be controlled. Thus Christian rulers turned to the Jews to provide credit for Christians.

Jews were never the sole nor even the main source of credit in medieval times, but they were the most conspicuous and the most vulnerable. They were often the only source of loans for poor members of society who were not deemed creditworthy. Thus a vicious circle developed: Jews would be invited into a city or province and their presence tolerated as a source of credit. They would then be expelled, sometimes in order for the rulers to confiscate their wealth, sometimes so that the rulers could wipe out their own debts, and sometimes to deflect the anti-regime sentiments of a poverty-stricken populace. Expulsions of Jews often occurred during times of plague or famine, when they provided a convenient scapegoat. However, the expulsion of the Jews provided only temporary relief for the indebted classes and, given the lack of other creditors, the masses often clamoured for their return, and the vicious cycle would start again.

The secular authorities of Europe generally favoured and protected Jewish money-lenders. Christian moneylenders were less malleable, charged higher rates of interest, and would reject the less creditworthy, as they were often able to operate without any official restraints. However, secular authorities also wanted to keep the number of Jews to the bare minimum. Italian Jewish settlement was based upon this economic and religious calculus. Italian Jewish enclaves often consisted of one moneylender, his household, and the few helpers he could persuade the authorities to admit to assist him. Usually, the communities did not even have sufficient numbers to form a prayer quorum of ten males.

One solution proposed to alleviate the credit shortage without recourse to Jewish lenders conceived and popularized by the Franciscans was to establish quasi-charitable loan banks known as *monti di pietà*. The introduction of a *monte di pietà* in a given location was accompanied by much fanfare, frequently including inflammatory sermons, riots, and expulsion of the Jews. However, these new banks did not solve the credit problems. If they were to function as charities rather than as banks that collected interest and offered incentives to depositors, they were clearly not going to be profitable. In order to be profitable, they had to either charge interest or reject the uncreditworthy. Additionally, few controls against embezzlement were written into their charters, and fiscal improprieties were soon rampant. At the Council of Trent in 1475 the *monti di pietà* were transformed into commercial banks, thereby enabling them to charge interest. At the same time the pretence was maintained that they were charitable institutions. As the failings of the Franciscan banks grew more obvious, demands for the admission of Jewish moneylenders mounted in various parts of Italy.

The possibility of a *monte de pietà* being established in Venice had influenced the original decision to admit the Jews in 1516. Venetian secular authorities adamantly opposed such a development several times, turning to the Jews instead, not out of any concern for the well-being of the poor, but because the *monti di pietà* had become uncontrollable in many Italian cities.[87] The clergy tended consistently to oppose admitting Jews. When the final vote was passed in 1516, it was clear that the Jews represented a preferable alternative to the *monti di pietà*. Nevertheless, many Venetians remained convinced that it was preferable to have Christians perform moneylending functions and to keep the Jews out entirely. Segregation would at least provide a partial solution to their unwanted presence. A constant oscillation ensued between the forces advocating renewal of charters to Jewish moneylenders and hostility towards the continued presence of the Jews.

In 1638, in the aftermath of the Bergonzi affair, a small but influential text of Jewish apologetics and polemics entitled *Discorso circa il stato de gl'Hebrei et in particolar dimoranti nell'inclita Città di Venetia* ('A Discourse on the State of the Jews, Particularly those Dwelling in the Illustrious City of Venice') appeared, written by Simone Luzzatto.[88] Luzzatto wrote in defence of the economic utility of the Jews, while also setting forth an explanation of their religion and mores and refuting some of the antisemitic canards that had persisted from antiquity.

Simone Luzzatto was born in Venice in 1583. He was a man of enormous abilities, and was highly respected in the Venetian ghetto and beyond for his rabbinic learning, his eloquence, and his knowledge of mathematics. His treatise provides both a historical overview of the economic history of Jews in Venice and a reasoned plea for the toleration of their presence. In *Discorso circa il stato de gl'Hebrei*, Luzzatto reminds his readers that Jews were allowed to live in Venice expressly for the purpose of providing loans whose rate of interest was set by charter. Each time the charter came up for renewal, the Jews demonstrated that their expenses exceeded their profits and that all the ghetto residents had therefore to subsidize the loans they made. This caused tensions and rancour between Ashkenazi residents, who were legally compelled to engage in usury, and Sephardi residents, who, as wealthy merchants, found themselves saddled with underwriting the bulk of the subsidy that the Ashkenazim required in order to remain in Venice.[89] Instead of accusing the Jews of exploitative and usurious activities, Luzzatto argued, their economic role in Venice should be appreciated by the populace. Furthermore, he pointed out, since the Jews were the weakest and least respected inhabitants of Venice, poor Venetians would not hesitate to complain about

---

[87] Ravid, 'Moneylending in Seventeenth Century Jewish Vernacular Apologetica', 262; id., *Economics and Toleration in Seventeenth-Century Venice*.

[88] See Ravid, *Economics and Toleration in Seventeenth-Century Venice*, 16; Shulvass, 'A Story of the Misfortunes which Afflicted the Jews in Italy' (Heb.).

[89] Poliakov, *Jewish Bankers and the Holy See*, 94, 211–18; Pullan, *Rich and Poor in Renaissance Venice*, 443–578.

any Jewish infraction of the terms of their loans. Other types of loan arrangements, Luzzatto hinted, such as the introduction of the *monti de pietà*, would be much more burdensome for the Venetian populace. Additionally, he explained, the Jewish merchants' presence benefited the city, since their lively trade added customs revenue to the Venetian coffers. Jewish merchants also provided raw materials, such as wool and silk, for the use of Venetian craftsmen, and their commerce facilitated the sale of Venetian processed and manufactured goods. Finally, Luzzatto asserted, the Jews made good 'citizens', unlike 'foreigners', who drained a city by sending their funds to their home country. Luzzatto pointed out that the Jews were different since, 'having no country of their own to which they aspire to transfer the property they amass, nor do they have the faculty or the ability to acquire real estate . . . once accepted in a city, they firmly resolve not to leave'.[90] Of all the trading nations, he concluded, the Jews were the best, precisely because they were stateless and defenceless. Luzzatto's pleas for toleration of the Jews in Venice on the grounds of their economic utility and his refutation of classical antisemitic charges did not fall on deaf ears. The charter of the Jews of Venice was renewed, and the immediate threat of expulsion averted.

Discorso circa il stato de gl'Hebrei was a response to an immediate crisis, but its defence of the Jews eventually reached beyond Venice to a much larger audience. Although Luzzatto couched his arguments in the language of prevailing political thought and addressed specific Venetian conditions, they proved cogent in other contexts. His was the first systematic defence of the Jewish right to live in Europe on the basis of *raisons d'état*. His suggestion that the Jews' firm adherence to Jewish law was not a destabilizing force in the state was novel. On the contrary, he argued, Jewish law enjoined its adherents to honour and obey their temporal rulers. Many of Luzzatto's arguments were subsequently taken up by other thinkers. Manasseh ben Israel quoted him directly in his famous petition to Oliver Cromwell for the readmission of the Jews to England. He was cited verbatim by John Toland in his advocacy of the naturalization of the Jews in England in 1714. Toland's work, in turn, formed an integral part of the new thinking on religious toleration that emerged on both sides of the Atlantic in the eighteenth century.[91] Although Luzzatto is not cited by name in the constitution of South Carolina, the document carries his invisible signature. Luzzatto concluded *Discorso circa il stato de gl'Hebrei* with the observation that cities, particularly port cities with foreign populations, were ideal places for Jews to live.

---

[90] Simone Luzzatto, *Discorso circa il stato de gl'Hebrei*, cited in Ravid, *Economics and Toleration in Seventeenth-Century Venice*, 63.

[91] See Barzilay, 'John Toland's Borrowings from Simone Luzzatto'; M. R. Cohen, 'Leone da Modena's Riti'; Toland, *Reasons for Naturalizing the Jews in Great Britain and Ireland On the Same Footing with all other Nations*. For Manasseh ben Israel's petition, see Chapter 6 below.

Venice as a Sephardi Community Model

Early in the seventeenth century Venice was the principal link between Europe's Jews and the Jewries of the Land of Israel and the Levant. Donations from Europe in support of the Jews of Palestine would be collected and dispatched from Venice. In addition, the model of Venetian Jewish life served as an example for other Jewish centres struggling to establish themselves. One characteristic of all communities where Sephardi Jews settled was their internal diversity. Sharp conflicts between indigenous Jews and newcomers were commonplace across North Africa, Ottoman Turkey, Palestine, and elsewhere. In Morocco, for instance, parallel institutions for indigenous Jews and Sephardi newcomers split the community in two, with each group fiercely intent upon defending its ancestral customs through separate schools, courts, butchers, and other vital services. The deep divide between indigenous Jews and Jews of Portuguese origin persisted in Tunis until the twentieth century. The fractionalization of Ottoman Jewry was even more pronounced. Rifts between Ashkenazim and Sephardim splintered the Jews of Amsterdam and Hamburg.[92]

Venice was the first important city in which Ashkenazim, Italian Jews, Sephardim from the Levant, and former Conversos from Portugal were organized in separate units but lived in one ghetto and acted as one community. The Venetian model of Jewish self-governance was instructive to other communities. In a confined space, the Jews hammered out a viable working community, generally acting as one body in vital matters, such as apportioning tax contributions and ransoming captives, following a system of proportional representation within their governing council. Jewish Venice also served as a model for other communities in re-Judaizing Conversos.

The Venetian ghetto also furnished teachers and rabbis to the nascent community of Portuguese Jews during Amsterdam's golden age. One of Amsterdam's founding Jewish leaders, Jacob Tirado, had a brother living in Venice who could act as guide and conveyor of communal advice, and Amsterdam's foremost rabbi in the seventeenth century, Saul Morteira, was trained in Venice. When the Amsterdam congregations were unable to resolve theological problems in the early years of their formation, they turned to Venetian rabbis for guidance. Even Venetian terms entered Amsterdam usage: the word *tudesco* or *todesco*, used to refer to Ashkenazim in Amsterdam, is derived from the Venetian word for Germans, initially employed by the Italian government in its designation of Ashkenazim.[93] Portuguese Conversos in Amsterdam received their first teachers from the Venetian ghetto; they framed their synagogue by-laws, the rules and regulations for their governing council, and their communal ordinances (*ascamot*) according to the precedents of the Venetian ghetto; and they developed their unusual

---

[92] On Fez, see Gerber, *Jewish Society in Fez*; on Rome, see Stow, 'Ethnic Rivalry or Melting Pot?'; on Amsterdam, see Chapter 6 below; see also Malkiel (ed.), *'The Lion Shall Roar'*.

[93] Bodian, *Hebrews of the Portuguese Nation*, 59.

ballot system and internal taxation 'segindo ho estilo de Veneza' ('following the style of Venice').[94] The Venetian example was invoked anew when the first Portuguese congregation, Kahal Kadosh Sha'ar Hashamayim, was established in London in 1665. Its *ascamot* (in Portuguese) also acknowledged 'the Usage of Venice' as its model.[95] The dowry society of the Portuguese Jews of Amsterdam, founded in 1615, was modelled on the Venetian Jewish dowry society.[96] Amsterdam, in turn, exported rabbis and students to England and across the Atlantic to Curaçao, Jamaica, Suriname, and Recife as these communities were founded. Thus the Venetian ghetto can be considered a 'mother of Israel' alongside the great contemporary eastern Sephardi diaspora in Salonica and Istanbul.

Despite its many crises and threatened expulsions, the Venetian ghetto represented an oasis of relative stability during the tumultuous sixteenth century, providing refuge to Sephardim in the west. In Venice, the Portuguese and Spanish Conversos could openly return to Judaism. It also was uniquely suited to serve as a crucible of a new Hispanic Judaism as the eastern and western Sephardim crossed paths and came together. It is difficult to assess how much of the intellectual liveliness of the ghetto of Venice was the product of its heterogeneity and how much derived from its exciting encounter with the broader Italian culture. Openness to change was characteristic of Jewish life in Italy, best expressed by León de Modena:

I have heard that on Sunday or Wednesday next week... there will be staged a great festival on the water of a kind which has not been seen for a long time; they have received money, indeed rather a lot of money, for this purpose from the Jews too, because the latter will also enjoy the splendid sight. Although I regret that such a performance is taking place in these days [of mourning], between the 17th of Tammuz and the 9th of Ab [the traditional three weeks prior to the destruction of the Temple of Jerusalem], when it is our duty to mourn and be afflicted because of the destruction of our Sanctuary, I beg your excellency to let me know when the festival will take place, and to provide me a stall in order that I too can come there and be among the onlookers, *because one is desirous of everything that is new*.[97]

The Venetian ghetto occupies a prominent place as a *lieu de mémoire* in a European continent filled with Jewish graveyards.[98] Crossing a narrow wooden bridge and traversing a passageway through a building, the visitor to the Venetian ghetto enters what used to be its main square, the Campo del Ghetto Nuovo, the sole open space in the original ghetto. The *campo* contained the ghetto's shops and banks and its wells, and

---

[94] Bodian, 'Amsterdam, Venice and the Marrano Diaspora'.

[95] *El Libro de los Acuerdos*, 3; Bodian, 'The Escamot of the Spanish-Portuguese Jewish Community in London'.

[96] Bodian, 'The "Portuguese" Dowry Societies in Venice and Amsterdam'; ead., *Hebrews of the Portuguese Nation*.

[97] 'Leone da Modena Wishes to see a Regatta', in *Letters of Jews through the Ages*, ii. 413 (italics added).

[98] *Lieu de mémoire* ('site of memory') is a term coined by the French historian Pierre Nora to describe places and objects which are significant in the collective memory of a group (see Nora (ed.), *Realms of Memory*).

was therefore its busiest thoroughfare. What was once the watchman's cubicle at the entryway is now a barred-up window, but traces of its wooden gates are still visible. Multi-storey buildings line the narrow streets that once overflowed with people. Silence prevails where a cacophony of languages—Spanish, Portuguese, Yiddish, Ladino, Arabic, and Italian—could be heard among its jostling crowds of residents and visitors. The bitterness of daily ghetto life was sweetened by a host of organizations and confraternities dedicated to study, sociability, and the performance of various charitable works: funds for poor widows, dowries for unmarried women, visiting the sick, clothing the indigent, preparing the deceased for ritually proper burials, and ransoming captives. The names of some of these societies are carved in stone collection boxes still embedded in the walls of the deserted synagogue antechambers. Organized prayer groups of especially pious individuals would meet before dawn for daily worship.[99] One such group, originally founded by Italian Jews and known as the Shomrim Laboker, had counterparts among the other ethnic groups in the ghetto. Multiplication of charitable organizations was commonplace, based on their Ashkenazi, Italian, Levantine, or Ponentine origins.

Silence fills the once bustling ghetto area today. The formerly crowded streets are virtually empty, except at the height of the tourist season. Documents alone, such as the following ordinance in the *Libro grande* from 1604, recall the rhythm of Jewish life:

Having seen the great usefulness resulting to all inhabitants of the Ghetto from the trumpet that every Sabbath eve toward sundown sounds to warn all Israel and especially to advise the women that they should prepare everything to honor the Sabbath, kindling the Sabbath lamp to differentiate the working days from the feast day, and it being necessary to pay the aforementioned trumpeter, let a faithful man go about once a week with an alms-box through the two ghettos and collect from the blessed among the people, who will each put in the aforesaid box however much he pleases to help pay the aforesaid player.[100]

The former complexity of the ghetto site has been transformed by alterations that began when the walls were demolished in 1795. The Jewish Museum of Venice now adjoins the Grande Scuola Tedesca and a kosher restaurant run by Chabad, and several art galleries and souvenir shops cater to the visitor from abroad. A memorial plaque for the fallen ghetto residents of the First World War is affixed to one wall of the Grande Scuola Tedesca, and a plaque inscribed with the names of the Venetian victims of the Holocaust is mounted on a wall of the *campo*. The house of Rabbi Ottolenghi, murdered in Auschwitz, is identified by a plaque on a building joining the old and new ghettos.

More than providing an exit from Europe, important as that was, the Venetian ghetto provided a place to renew Sephardi life in the sixteenth century. The substantial

---

[99] Horowitz, 'Processions, Piety and Jewish Confraternities'; id., 'Speaking of the Dead'.
[100] *Libro grande*, cited in Calimani, *The Ghetto of Venice*, 147.

restrictions written into the terms of Jewish residency in Venice, coupled with the temporary nature of the residential charters, should have made life intolerable. But by instituting a ghetto and locking the Jews inside, Venice inadvertently provided a refuge where the Sephardim could retrieve their Jewish identity while facing the perennial challenge of balancing Jewish cultural needs and the allure of the surrounding culture. In the process, the Sephardim shared some exciting cultural innovations with their Italian neighbours and co-religionists. In the final analysis, the Venetian ghetto recalls the promise of refuge reluctantly granted to Sephardi wanderers in the sixteenth century, and owes its existence, in large measure, to the Venetian understanding of what they could gain from the lively commercial and cosmopolitan presence of the Spanish and Portuguese Jews.

CHAPTER FIVE

RECONSTRUCTING SEPHARAD IN ISTANBUL AND SALONICA 1492–1600

> Deshame entrar yo me hare lugar
> [Let me enter, I will make a place for myself]
>
> Ande vamos, bendigamos
> [Let us move, let us bless]
>
> LADINO PROVERBS

IN THE SAFETY of the expanding Ottoman empire, especially in its two largest cities, Istanbul and Salonica, the reconstruction of Sephardi intellectual and communal life began soon after the Expulsion. Salonica's impact on Sephardi reconstruction was primarily cultural and economic, while Istanbul's was political and demographic. The two cities sheltered the largest concentrations of Sephardim in the sixteenth century and provided conditions for the emergence of a new transnational people. The process of constructing a new Sephardi entity was gradual, with the 1492 cataclysm serving as a watershed. Prior to 1492 Spain was not a unified kingdom, and the identities of Iberian Jews, like Iberian Christians, were usually local in nature. After the Expulsion their association with specific cities or provinces in Spain and Portugal persisted, only gradually blurring over time. The majority of the Iberian refugees settled in the Ottoman empire in the sixteenth century and ultimately melded into one Ladino-speaking Sephardi diaspora. The small number of Iberian refugees, primarily from among the Conversos of Portugal, who found refuge in the West followed a different trajectory entirely.

Salonica, as the closest Ottoman port to Europe, received the first groups of sea-borne refugees in the summer of 1492. It continued to be a favourite destination for Sephardim for approximately a century. Since the city had been stripped of most of its native population after the Ottoman conquest in 1430, the new arrivals from Spain and Italy were able to assume commercial leadership and soon became the majority ethnic group in the city. They were concentrated in the city's central and port area and dominated its trade and textile industry. Before long, Salonica housed a galaxy of Sephardi rabbis who had been trained in the Iberian peninsula as well as locally. They painstakingly strove to adjust the traditions of Iberia to the unfamiliar Ottoman conditions while adjudicating some of the thorny issues raised by the forced conversions that the Jews had recently experienced in Iberia. The rabbis of Salonica produced an outpouring of responsa, while its *talmud torah*, founded at the beginning of the sixteenth century, trained countless Jews from Salonica and from many other towns across the empire. A majority of Salonica's Jews earned their living from the production of textile and woollen goods, employing the advanced manufacturing techniques they had acquired in Spain and southern Italy.

The Iberian immigrants to Istanbul joined a long-established and diverse Romaniote population (Greek Jews from the former Byzantine empire), Karaites (a Jewish sect originating in Baghdad in the Middle Ages), and Jews from many corners of Anatolia, the Balkans, and Europe. The Jews of Istanbul constituted one of many minorities in a cosmopolitan setting that included Greeks, Armenians, Muslims of several ethnicities (including a large and vocal group of Morisco refugees from Spain), Slavs of various nationalities, and resident Europeans. Since Istanbul was the seat of a dynamic empire with a swelling administrative apparatus, Sephardi newcomers could continue to engage in the long-familiar activities of statecraft and diplomacy. Most of the Jews, however, were neither courtiers nor statesmen: they were involved in commerce or crafts. Some Sephardim also resumed their former involvement in medicine and banking. The Ottoman authorities recognized that the multilingual Sephardi refugees could repopulate their newly conquered cities, bolster the ranks of their depleted commercial class, and provide the empire with some of the latest European technical knowledge and skills. The Sephardim were also attractive as a potentially loyal population, whose enmity towards Spain might usefully be harnessed in the ongoing Ottoman military confrontations with Europe.

In both Ottoman cities the Jewish exiles regrouped and formed new communal associations. Within a century of their arrival the diverse and differentiated groups of Sephardi outcasts bore all the markings of a new civilization that preserved many linguistic and literary traditions of medieval Castilian, combined with elements of the local cultures they encountered and their Hispano-Judaic heritage. By the mid-seventeenth century the long process of reconstructing Sepharad was well advanced, and a formerly splintered Jewry had become the Sephardi diaspora of the Mediterranean.

In the Footsteps of Doña Gracia Mendes Nasi

The journey from Iberia to Istanbul was arduous in the mid-sixteenth century. Pirates and brigands threatened both the sea and land routes. But it was undoubtedly eased for refugees from Europe like Doña Gracia Mendes Nasi by the legendary hospitality of new Sephardi enclaves that dotted the routes of commerce throughout the Balkans and south-eastern Europe. Crossing the Adriatic from Venice in the middle of the sixteenth century, the intrepid businesswoman arrived within a few days at the port of Ragusa, where a small but successful maritime and commercial centre of Sephardim had recently been established. Doña Gracia lingered in the city after her escape from Venice, contacting her commercial agents who were already active and expanding the network she would soon draw upon for her future trading endeavours between the Ottoman empire and Italy. As was already manifest in her European activities, Doña Gracia was an astute businesswoman. She managed to arrange with the senate of Ragusa for the storage of wool, linen, wine, and spices being shipped from Italy to the Ottoman empire at special rates and to bid successfully for tax-farming concessions.

Ragusa, by dint of its location on the eastern shore of the Adriatic, functioned as a transit point for overland and sea routes between Europe and the eastern Mediterranean.[1] It ranked third, after Venice and Ancona, of the ports on the Adriatic. Ragusa also served as a centre of espionage where information on the formation and movement of Turkish, Spanish, and Venetian fleets was exchanged. On 25 February 1546 the senate of Ragusa decreed that the Jews reside in a ghetto consisting of one alleyway adjoining the palace complex. The establishment of a ghetto represented a compromise between several opposing forces: on the one hand, the local Inquisition sought to curb the influence of Portuguese Conversos, and Venetian merchants wanted to minimize economic competition in Ragusa; on the other, the Venetian senate felt that the settlement of Sephardim in Ragusa would advance Venice's interests, particularly in financial services, such as maritime insurance, letters of exchange, and tax collection. The Sephardim were also welcomed as commercial agents or *fattori*. Despite the establishment of a ghetto in Ragusa, the Jews enjoyed a degree of relative economic freedom and a modicum of physical security. By 1572 thirty of the city's *fattori* were Jews.

Doña Gracia appears not to have been in a hurry to leave Ragusa, solidifying her business connections with Jews further inland and probably also ensuring that her funds from Italy would be transferred to the Ottoman empire. After making preparations for the final leg of her journey to Istanbul, arranging for the future storage of merchandise, especially fabrics, in Ragusa's warehouses, and depositing a hefty sum in escrow against future tax payments and other expenses, she wound up her stay and continued eastward. She later recalled the warm reception she had received in Ragusa during which visit her business agents were apparently permitted to live outside the ghetto.[2]

Visitors approaching Istanbul by ship through the Dardanelles and proceeding up

---

[1] Wimmer, 'Jewish Merchants in Ragusa' (Heb.); Burdelez, 'The Role of Ragusan Jews in the History of the Mediterranean Countries'; Arbel, 'Venice and the Jewish Merchants of Istanbul'. On the brief sojourn of Doña Gracia in Ragusa, see Orfali, 'Dona Gracia Mendes and the Ragusan Republic'.

[2] Orfali, 'Dona Gracia Mendes and the Ragusan Republic', 187–8.

the strategic waterway of the Bosphorus in the sixteenth century would be struck by the majesty of its shoreline and the ever-multiplying minarets and mosques perched on the city's several hilltops. The harbour of the Golden Horn was arguably one of the finest anchorages in the world. Its natural defences had enabled the city, as the Byzantine imperial capital Constantinople, to withstand over seven centuries of Muslim attacks until its fall on 29 May 1453. Under the able rule of a series of energetic and forceful sultans, especially Suleiman the Magnificent (r. 1520–66), the city's architectural and public-works projects multiplied and its vital water-distribution system was established. The sultans of the sixteenth century promoted the economic revival of Istanbul, building a great indoor market and forcibly relocating Christians and Jews to repopulate the city. The city's chief architect, Sinan, enjoyed a generous purse to embellish the imperial capital with beautifully tiled mosques and mausoleums. The royal Topkapı and other palaces employed an army of engineers, architects, accountants, calligraphers, book-binders, masons, physicians, goldsmiths, jewellers, and metal workers. During Suleiman's long reign Ottoman Turkish was consolidated as a literary language. The sultan, also a poet, personally played an active cultural role as patron of poets and scholars. The public-works programmes that he inaugurated buttressed his position as supreme ruler, lawmaker, and benefactor of his people. Suleiman's military victories in Europe and Asia brought far-flung Jewish communities under one imperial umbrella. The fruitful decades of Suleiman's rule coincided with the peak of Sephardi migration to Ottoman lands. On the battlefield, in the palace chambers, or aboard the Ottoman commercial fleets, Sephardim could be found serving the bellicose but pragmatic Ottomans.

Doña Gracia's arrival in Istanbul in 1553 did not go unnoticed. Her grand entry and impressive entourage were recorded by more than one observer. A Spanish prisoner of war, Andres Laguna, noted her regal arrival 'with forty horses and four triumphal chariots full of ladies and Spanish servants'.[3] Another observer, Hans Dernschwam, representative of the German banking house of Fugger, remarked in his diary on her dramatic arrival and impressive entourage, adding that the local Jews were extremely proud of her, and called her La Seniora or Hageveret, an appellation akin to Her Royal Highness.[4] She settled in the Galata section of Istanbul, a verdant quarter inhabited primarily by foreign envoys and merchants 'in luxury and extravagance with many servants, maids also, among them two from the Netherlands'.[5] Almost immediately, she discarded her Christian name of Beatrice, adopting the name Gracia Mendes Nasi,

[3] Andres Laguna, *Viaje de Turquia*, cited in Lewis, *The Jews of Islam*, 231 n. 19.

[4] See Ben-Naeh and Saban, 'Three German Travellers on Istanbul Jews'; Rozen, *A History of the Jewish Community in Istanbul*, 210.

[5] Hans Dernschwam, *Tagebuch*, cited in Ben-Naeh and Saban, 'Three German Travellers on Istanbul Jews', 39; see also *The Jew in the Medieval World*, 474. On the European ambience of Galata, see Matran, 'Foreign Merchants and the Minorities in Istanbul', esp. 131–2 n. 18.

and plunged into the affairs of Sephardi community-building and Ottoman commerce and diplomacy.

Few Sephardi refugees possessed the means to travel as comfortably and transplant themselves as smoothly as Doña Gracia. For most, the journey was fraught with uncertainty and obstacles. Even after the refugees finally found shelter in the Ottoman empire, their interrupted lives could not be restored to what they had been. Few Jews reached the shores of the Golden Horn with either their family or their fortune intact.[6] Above all, psychological problems abounded as a result of the forced conversions. Physical resettlement was only the prelude to a prolonged period of communal and cultural reconstruction.

Ottoman Conquest and Settlement Policies

The prolonged siege of Constantinople in 1453 precipitated the flight of the city's foreign merchants and was followed by the deliberate Ottoman deportation of the remaining indigenous Christian population.[7] In general, populations that refused to surrender to the Turkish conquerors were severely punished and forcibly relocated in a policy known as *sürgün*. In contrast to Ottoman policies elsewhere, which usually included the forced deportation of indigenous Jews, the ethnically mixed Jewish population of Constantinople was permitted to remain in the city and was augmented by Jewish deportees from elsewhere in the empire.[8]

After the fall of Constantinople, the Muslim troops were allowed to pillage for several days before the triumphant Sultan Mehmet II the Conqueror (r. 1444–6, 1451–81) and his generals restored order and began to repopulate the city. Mehmet forcibly transferred Jewish communities from the Balkans and Anatolia to Istanbul. This is confirmed by census figures from 1455 and the names of the new synagogues established in the wake of the conquests, such as Achrida or Yambol.[9] As late as the seventeenth century Ottoman tax registers still divided the Jews of Istanbul into two groups based on their origin, forcibly settled residents called *sürgünlis* and refugees from Europe called *kendi gelen* (lit. 'those who came of their own free will'). Hungarian Jews were

---

[6] On the first arrivals in the summer of 1492, see Rozanes, *History of the Jews in the Ottoman Empire* (Heb.), i. 60–2; on the vicissitudes of the exiles, see Ibn Verga, *Shevet yehudah*, 120–5; Rozen, 'Collective Memories and Group Boundaries'; see also Bornstein-Makovetsky, 'The Jewish Community in Istanbul in the Mid-Sixteenth Century' (Heb.).

[7] See Inalcik, *The Ottoman Empire*, 23–6; Lewis, *Istanbul and the Civilization of the Ottoman Empire*, 25–7; Kefadar, *Between Two Worlds*; Eldem, 'Istanbul', 150–6.

[8] On the Istanbul Jewish community, see Rozen, *A History of the Jewish Community in Istanbul*, 55–61.

[9] See Inalcik, 'Foundations of Ottoman–Jewish Cooperation', 5. On Istanbul's Jewish demography, see Heyd, 'The Jewish Communities of Istanbul in the Seventeenth Century'; on Salonica, see Vryonis, 'The Ottoman Conquest of Thessaloniki'; see also Benbassa and Rodrigue, *The Jews of the Balkans*, 10; Hacker, 'The Ottoman Policy towards the Jews and Jewish Attitudes towards the Ottomans', 124.

included among the *kendi gelen* even though they had been forcibly removed to Istanbul in the sixteenth century at the time of the Ottoman victories.

Mehmet the Conqueror's policy of offering asylum to Sephardim and resettlement for indigenous Jews was continued by his son, Bayezid II (r. 1481–1512). Allowing Jewish immigrants from Europe to settle in the city at will, forcibly settling Jews from other parts of the empire there, and retaining the existing Jewish population created a dynamic but fractious Jewry. Exactly what Mehmet and Bayezid sought to achieve by their treatment of the Jews is uncertain and has been obscured by much myth, ahistorical commentary, and romance. The contemporary Jewish chronicler Eliyahu Capsali, in his *Seder eliyahu zuta*, compared Bayezid's policies to those of the ancient Persian king Cyrus. He described the Ottoman resettlement policy in quasi-biblical terms, linking the Jewish population movements and the persecutions of 1492 to a broader divine plan:

Pass through the gateways of this book, turn to the ways of God, study its tales, read and see that God, in his wisdom and understanding, rendered this Turkish nation great. . . . The Turk is the rod of His wrath, the staff of His anger, and by means of him He takes vengeance of the gentile nations and tongues and states whose time has come.[10]

Capsali hyperbolically described Mehmet as possessing a 'soul steeped in goodness; not only didn't he drive the Jews out from before him, he even gathered them together from the distant towns and brought them to the capital city of the Kingdom'.[11] The magnanimity of the sultans was one manifestation, in Capsali's mind, of God's intervention in history:

Just as Sultan Mehmet gathered the Jews living in other communities and brought them to live with him in Constantinople and said: Come and shelter in my shade as we have written, similarly his son, this Sultan Bayezid treated the seed of Abraham, servants of God, well . . . and did not cast them out from before him as some of the Gentile Kings did to us. . . . Were it not for this, the remnant of Judah and traces of Israel, exiled from Spain and Aragon and Portugal and Sicily by the unsheathed sword of the wicked king of Spain would have been lost.[12]

However, Bayezid was hardly a benevolent ruler. He is recorded to have refused permission for the erection of new synagogues and strove to convert the Jews to Islam. Despite the harsh policies that all the subject minorities experienced at his hands, the image of a benevolent and open-hearted Ottoman dynasty was fostered by nineteenth-century Ottoman reformers and their Jewish subjects, perhaps to cultivate patriotism or to inculcate a sense of gratitude among the restive minorities of their day. The resulting reconstruction of Ottoman history has tended to ignore much of the violence

---

[10] Capsali, *Seder eliyahu zuta*, i. 10. On the ingathering of the Sephardi refugees in the Ottoman empire as a portent of the messianic era, see ibid. 367; on the comparison with the edict of Cyrus, see ibid. 240; on the treatment of the Jews of Istanbul at the time of the conquest, see Baron, *A Social and Religious History of the Jews*, xviii. 22–3, 31, 51–3, 450–1, 463–4.   [11] Capsali, *Seder eliyahu zuta*, i. 42, 51.   [12] Ibid. 141–2.

and cruelty that accompanied the spread of Turkish rule. This ahistorical account also obscures the prominence of the indigenous Greek and Karaite Jewish population in Istanbul at the time of the conquest.[13]

The Ottoman policy of *sürgün* was designed to control and develop the empire. Both Jewish and Christian populations were relocated: Christians in order to remove their potentially disloyal presence from newly conquered cities and vulnerable borders, and Jews usually in order to introduce an urban element in areas from which Christians had fled or been forcibly deported. Local populations were removed from recently conquered areas so that they could not rebel, and presumed loyal populations from other parts of the empire were moved in to develop the vacated areas. Uprooting Greek-speaking Jewish communities from the Balkans and Anatolia undermined their vitality before the Sephardim arrived, in no small measure accounting for their eventual absorption by the Sephardim in most places. The deportations, naturally, evoked terror in the hearts of the uprooted subjects, who had no right of appeal. After resettlement, moreover, it was forbidden for the deportees to leave their new place of residence without express permission from the chief of police, permission that was granted very sparingly and only on payment of enormous bribes. Even the *sürgünli*'s descendants were not permitted to leave their place of enforced settlement or to change their occupation. The status of a *sürgünli* was somewhat akin to that of a vassal in medieval Europe. A responsum of Rabbi Eliyahu Mizrahi alludes to the dilemma that arose when a 'free' Jew discovered that his betrothed was descended from deportees. The prospective groom asked the rabbi to cancel his marriage, fearing that his future wife's status would perpetually tie them to her place of residence.[14]

The forced population transfers were lamented by their victims. Eliyahu Capsali, whose information was based on eyewitness accounts, mentions the deportations of Greek Jews in an otherwise laudatory account of the freedoms accorded to the Jews by the Turks: 'From that day on, whenever the king conquered a place where there were Jews, he would immediately shake them up and drive them away from there—and dispatch them to Constantinople.'[15]

Ottoman colonization policies were more oppressive to Christians than they were to Jews, entailing the abduction of Christian boys and their forced conversion to Islam and induction into the janissary corps or court service (the *devshirme* system). While

---

[13] On rewriting the Ottoman past, see J. P. Cohen, *Becoming Ottoman*, 48–9, 160 n. 22; Naar, 'Fashioning the "Mother of Israel"'; on philo-Islamic Jews who went to great lengths to praise the Ottoman empire, see Kramer (ed.), *The Jewish Discovery of Islam*; Lewis, *Islam in History*, 123–37. The Ottoman open-door policy towards Jewish settlement has been repeatedly lauded, most recently in the many celebratory events connected with the quincentennial of the Expulsion from Spain.

[14] Eliyahu Mizrahi, *Mayim amukim*, cited in Rozen, *A History of the Jewish Community in Istanbul*, 327.

[15] Capsali, *Seder eliyahu zuta*, ii. 218; see also Baron, *A Social and Religious History of the Jews*, xviii. 22–3, 31, 51–3.

these measures were opportunities for advancement, there is little doubt that the victims did not see the removal of their children in such a positive light. One Jewish author, Abraham of Ankara, details the human dimensions of the *devshirme* system in his lament on the fate of Jewish and Christian families in the wake of the Turkish victories:

> He also issued a stern order
> Causing anguish to all who heard it
> To all the cities of Rum
> Which were under his dominion.
> He said to remove men with their families,
> To bring and settle them in this city;
> This brought great grief to the Turkish nation,
> Who are lamenting with bitter tears.
> For they separated fathers from sons,
> They separated daughters from mothers,
> They separated brothers from one another
> They deprived many of their ancestral homes.[16]

The *sürgün* policy continued for several generations. When Sultan Selim I (r. 1512–20) conquered Egypt in 1516 he forcibly transferred 600 prominent families, including many Jewish craftsmen and merchants, from Alexandria to Cairo in order to augment the middle class in the capital of Egypt. Although his successor, Suleiman the Magnificent, permitted Egyptian Jewish *sürgünlis* to return home as one of his first acts as head of state, his reign was noted for other arbitrary and oppressive policies. When he conquered Rhodes in 1523, he ordered 150 wealthy Jews transferred from the island to Salonica. During the Hungarian campaign, the Jews of Buda were gathered in boats after the battle of Mohács in 1526 and forcibly removed. They continued to appear as a separate community in the census lists of 1568 and 1603 in Edirne (Adrianople) and Istanbul, identified by their ancestors' Hungarian origins.

In the wake of the Ottoman conquest of Cyprus in 1571, Sultan Selim II issued an order to the Jews of Safed: 'I command that as soon as this order arrives, without delay. . . . You register one thousand rich and prosperous Jews and send them, with their property and their effects and with their families, under an appropriate escort to the said city [Famagusta].'[17] After much pleading and the customary bribes, the number of deportees was reduced to 500. Finally, the sultan rescinded the decree altogether. Jewish arguments that the deportations would spell economic ruin for Safed were convincing. Although the text of the Jewish petition is no longer extant, its argument can

---

[16] Abraham of Ankara, lament over the fate of the Armenians, cited in Hacker, 'Ottoman Policy towards the Jews and Jewish Attitudes towards the Ottomans', see also Hacker, 'The Sürgün System and Jewish Society in the Ottoman Empire', 45 n. 28.

[17] Sultan Selim II, 'Order to the Sanjaq Bey of Safed and to the Qāḍī of Safed', in *Notes and Documents from the Turkish Archives*, 33.

be reconstructed from the Ottoman response:

> You have sent a letter and have reported that representatives of the Jews residing in the town of Safed have come to the law court complaining that orders have been given to deport them from this holy land to Cyprus. From the time this news spread, those who are traders have not attended to trade and other business, but have abstained from it completely. Until now, whenever their poll tax, amounting to a fixed sum of 1,500 florins and the extraordinary levies fell due, they were paid in full to the imperial treasury. . . . If it is decided to deport them to Cyprus, the Public Revenue will lose the above-mentioned amount of money and the town of Safed will be on the verge of ruin. The treasury of Damascus will suffer a great loss since the collection of the poll tax, the imposition on their houses liable to pay extraordinary levies, customs duties, stamp duty on broadcloth, customs on felt, and the tax farming of the dye houses will all be discontinued. Their houses will also remain deserted; no buyer will be found for them. Their landed property will go for nothing. . . . If, on the other hand, they stay, the Treasury will derive great benefit in every respect. Hence you have suggested that they shall be excused from being deported to Cyprus.
>
> I have therefore commanded that when this firman arrives you shall desist from deporting the Jews to Cyprus.[18]

The deportation from Safed was suspended by imperial order of 23 May 1578. Ultimately a much smaller group of 100 Jewish pilgrims aboard ship in the port of Famagusta on their way to Palestine was forced to settle in Cyprus in their stead.

Another aspect of the *sürgün* policy was particularly important in undermining the Romaniote Jews. Deportees were liable for taxes in their former place of residence as well as in their new location. Rabbis were adamantly opposed to such double taxation, but they could not prevent it, and it eventually sapped the strength of the Romaniote community. Although their separate synagogues persisted in name, their communities dwindled in numbers and their cultural distinctiveness waned in the course of the sixteenth century. Ironically, it was preferable to be a Jewish refugee from a foreign land than a long-time Jewish resident of Greek origin in sixteenth-century Turkey.

Jews, regardless of origin, were regarded as *dhimmis*, a 'protected' but inferior status assigned to non-Muslims in the early centuries of Islam. On the one hand, *dhimmis* were permitted to practise their religion; on the other, they were subjected to various social, personal, and economic restrictions. They were required to pay a discriminatory poll tax, the *jizya*, and were subjected to a host of special levies and sumptuary restrictions, which varied from place to place and were not consistently implemented. They were not allowed to live next to a mosque, and their synagogues or churches were required to be modest. No synagogues or churches were to be repaired without permission, and no new ones were to be erected. *Dhimmis* were considered to be socially inferior to Muslims, and thus were required to show deference to Muslims at all times and could not hold positions of authority over them. The theory underlying many of these restrictions was to display the superiority of Muslims and, by

---

[18] 'The Sultan Rescinds the Order of Deportation', in Stillman, *The Jews of Arab Lands*, 296; see also Heyd, *Ottoman Documents on Palestine*, 121, 164, 167–8.

implication, of their religion. Distinctive clothing was an essential marker in a society possessing elaborate rules of status: Muslims generally wore bright clothing, especially green, with white turbans; Jews were required to wear dark or black fabric with wide sleeves over a plain or striped gown and a distinctive head covering (for Jewish men, a cylindrical turban, for women, a wide shawl); Christians were also distinguished in the colour of their clothing. Even the shape and colour of the shoes worn by Christians and Jews were different from those of Muslims. In practice, the Ottoman state, especially in its heyday, often ignored many of its restrictive anti-*dhimmi* measures, and the Jews benefited from the official guarantees of freedom to practise their religion, provided it did not offend Muslims. The Sephardim wore distinctively European clothing and built new synagogues in their new areas of settlement despite the Islamic prohibitions against erecting new Jewish houses of worship or repairing ones that had fallen into disrepair.

In the long run the *sürgün* policy created new Jewish urban centres that were strategically placed at trade junctions and ideally suited to Sephardi commercial traditions. Thus, for instance, Sarajevo's Jewish quarter originated as a result of *sürgün*. Soon after Belgrade was captured by the Ottomans in 1521, a small Sephardi community was established there. Similarly, the transfer of sixty Jewish families to Sofia created the nucleus of a new Sephardi settlement in Bulgaria. Older settlements, such as Edirne and Bursa, enjoyed a new lease of life with the infusion of new Jewish populations, including some indigenous Greek Jews.

The bellicose fifteenth- and sixteenth-century sultans were filled with religious zeal by their heady conquests. Yet they were also pragmatic rulers intent upon the restoration of economic life after their devastating campaigns. The population of Salonica, decimated during the last two decades of Byzantine rule, was overwhelmed by the Ottoman army in 1430, and everything in the city was taken away or destroyed, after which the city languished for several decades. Both Greek Christians and Greek Jews suffered various deportations. A series of droughts and plagues also undermined the city. The Ottoman census of Salonica in 1478 reveals a small population consisting of a majority of Greek Orthodox, a small number of Catholic Christians, some Muslims, but no Jews. When the Sephardim began to arrive in the 1490s, few people remained in the city. As a result, the choicest districts of Salonica were vacant. The refugees took up residence in the abandoned districts and soon formed a majority of the city's inhabitants. Though there were fewer Sephardim in Salonica than in Istanbul, Sephardi and Italian Jewish immigrants in Salonica had a greater impact on their adopted city.

According to a survey in 1510, Salonica contained 681 Jewish households. The number had jumped to 2,645 by 1520, constituting the majority of the city's 4,863 households.[19] According to another estimate, Salonica contained 2,509 Jewish households

---

[19] Lewis, *The Jews of Islam*, 118; Heyd, 'The Jewish Communities of Istanbul in the Seventeenth Century';

(approximately 17,563 people) in 1530, and by 1589 there were 23,942 Jews in Salonica.[20] Jewish immigration continued, although at a reduced pace, during the seventeenth century. Nevertheless, the Jews were the largest group in the city until the twentieth century. While the Jewish population in Istanbul was larger in absolute numerical terms, Jews formed only a small percentage of the total population of the imperial capital.

Composition of the Jewish Population

The Jews who came to the Ottoman empire in the sixteenth century had diverse origins. The first waves of Sephardim arrived in the summer of 1492 as the deadline for departure from Spain loomed, including thousands from Spanish-controlled Sicily. Boatload after boatload followed after a series of expulsions in Europe. There was a partial expulsion of Jews from the city of Naples in 1496, many of whom were refugees from Spain and Sicily, followed by another temporary expulsion from the Kingdom of Naples under Charles VIII in 1510, and a final expulsion in 1540. There were expulsions from Portugal in 1496, from Apulia in 1497, from Calabria in 1502, and from the Papal States in 1569. The Calabrians formed their own synagogue, augmented soon after by exiles from Otranto. The threat of expulsion from Venice in 1571 brought more Jews of Italian origin to the Ottoman empire. Italian Jews tenaciously maintained their rituals and customs for some time: the Sicilian Jews only reluctantly discarded their separate ritual and adopted the closely related Sephardi ritual in 1585; some Jews from Syracuse held on to a few unique customs and rituals for much longer. Loyalty to the customs and rituals of their country of origin, often coupled with distrust of Portuguese Conversos, led to friction between the various groups and added a special edge of rancour to the constant pressures they all faced.

The fourfold division of Istanbul's Jewish community into Romaniotes, Karaites, Ashkenazim, and Sephardim masks the great diversity that prevailed in the city. According to Bernard Lewis, the Jewish population of Istanbul contained 1,647 households out of a total population of 16,326 households or approximately 10 per cent of the total population of the city between 1520 and 1530. Only a few years later, in 1535, the number of Jewish households had jumped to 8,000, or approximately 50,000 people, with Sephardim constituting a clear majority.[21] Hans Dernschwam noted the heterogeneity of Ottoman Jewry (his blatant anti-Jewish prejudices notwithstanding):

Rozen, *A History of the Jewish Community in Istanbul*, 50–5; see also Lowry, 'When Did the Sephardim Arrive in Salonica?', 203–13.

[20] Shaw, *The Jews of the Ottoman Empire and the Turkish Republic*, 38. It is not clear what constituted a 'household' (the taxable unit). In addition, communities generally under-reported numbers in order to reduce their tax burdens.

[21] Lewis, *The Jews of Islam*, 118. Another estimate offers the figure of 56,490 Jews dwelling in 8,070

In Turkey, you will find in every town innumerable Jews of all countries and languages. And every Jewish group sticks together in accordance with its language. Wherever Jews have been expelled in any land they come together in Turkey, as thick as vermin; speak German, Italian, Spanish, Portuguese, French, Czechish, Polish, Greek, Turkish, Syriac, Chaldean, and other languages.... As is their custom, every one wears clothes in accordance with the language he speaks.... In Constantinople, the Jews are as thick as ants.... The Jews are despised in Turkey as they are anywhere else; possess no estates, although many own their own homes.... There is no spot in the world which hasn't some of its Jews in Constantinople and there are no wares which the Jews do not carry about and trade in.[22]

The Romaniotes were also extremely diverse internally. Many had been brought to Istanbul from the Balkans and Anatolia as deportees. Their many origins are reflected in the names of their *kehalim*: Istip (Štip), Manastir (Bitola), and Ohrid from Macedonia; Niğbolu (Nikopol) and Yanbol from Bulgaria; Izdin (Lamia), Kesriye (Kastoria), Dimetoka (Didymóteicho), Great Selanik (Salonica), and Little Selanik from Greece; Budun from Hungary; Antalya and Sinop from Anatolia. Their separate prayer books incorporating their unique rites were among the earliest printed books in Istanbul and Venice. Many Romaniotes joined Sephardi *kehalim* during the sixteenth and seventeenth centuries, sometimes as a result of marriages between the two groups, more often as a result of the economic and cultural dominance of the Sephardim. The Karaites also retained their own separate *kahal* and observed their distinctive rites and customs. They did not recognize the authority of the Talmud and consequently drew further and further away from the religious practices of rabbinic Judaism, and their relations with other Jews were often strained. They guarded their own customs, worshipped separately, and generally married among themselves. They remained Greek-speaking after the arrival of the Sephardim and only gradually integrated into the Romaniote and Sephardi communities.[23]

The exiles from Spain had wandered, in some instances, for years and had endured repeated sufferings before reaching the Ottoman empire. They had lost their homes, their wealth, their libraries, and their livelihoods. In many cases families were torn apart: some members converted and remained in Iberia; others stayed Jewish and departed; children and grandparents died on the way. One chronicler describes how former ties among them were strained and frequently broken:

Men arrived without their wives, and women, without their husbands. They were beset by poverty and travail, want and famine and loneliness, and their cares broke their strength. And when they

---

households, with Muslims constituting 46,635 households and Christians 25,292 households (Shaw, *The Jews of the Ottoman Empire and the Turkish Republic*, 37).

[22] Hans Dernschwam, *Tagebuch*, cited in Ben-Naeh and Saban, 'Three German Travellers on Istanbul Jews', 39.

[23] For Eliyahu Mizrahi's prohibition on teaching Karaites either secular or Judaic subjects in a Romaniote synagogue, see Rozen, *A History of the Jewish Community in Istanbul*, 339–55.

PLATE 1. 'How a Jewess was near death in childbirth and called on Holy Mary and was delivered at that moment', *Cantigas de Santa Maria*, no. 89 (Spain, *c*.1280)

Royal Monastery of El Escorial Library, Madrid, MS T.I.1, fo. 131ʳ. © Patrimonio Nacional

PLATE 2. Jews and Muslims playing dice, *Libro de ajedrez, dados y tablas* (Toledo, 1283)

Royal Monastery of El Escorial Library, Madrid, MS T.I.6, fo.71ᵛ © *Patrimonio Nacional*

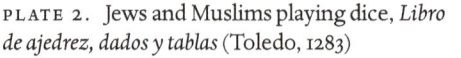

blanco en la tercera casa del Rey blan
co. E si los blancos entren de tir xaque
ca aules al Rey prieto. es el Rey blanco
mate en esta iuega. dar la xaque cō los
dos roques prietos. qual se quiere. en la
casa del Rey blanco. o del cauallo blāco.
⁊ si se encubriere cō ell alffil blanco. to
mar lo con este mismo roque. ⁊ dar la
xaq̄ ⁊ encobrir sa el Rey blanco cō so al
fferza blanca. ⁊ dar la xaque ⁊ mate cō
el roque prieto en la segunda casa del ro
que blanco e guarda del alfil prieto. et
es el departimiento deste iuego. ⁊ es
ta es la figura del entablamiento:

Este es otro iuego departido en que ha
ueynte ⁊ dos trebeios que an a seer enta
blados assi como estan en la figura del
entablamiento. ⁊ an se de iogar assi.
Los prietos iuegan pri
mero ⁊ an mate al Rey
blanco en cinco uezes
delos sus iuegos mis

mos en la casa o esta entablado. El
primero iuego dar la xaque con el
roq̄ prieto tomando el cauallo blā
co que esta en la casa dell alffil blā
co. ⁊ tomar lo a el Rey blanco. con so
alffil blanco. El segundo iuego
dar la xaque con ell otro roque pri
eto en casa dell alfferza blanca. ⁊ to

PLATE 3. A Jew and a Christian playing chess, *Libro de ajedrez, dados y tablas* (Toledo, 1283)

Royal Monastery of El Escorial Library, Madrid, MS T.I.6, fo. 2.0. © Patrimonio Nacional

PLATE 4. Micrography: carpet page in Mudéjar style, Damascus Keter, Burgos, 1260

National Library of Israel, Jerusalem, Heb. 4°790, fo. 310ᵛ

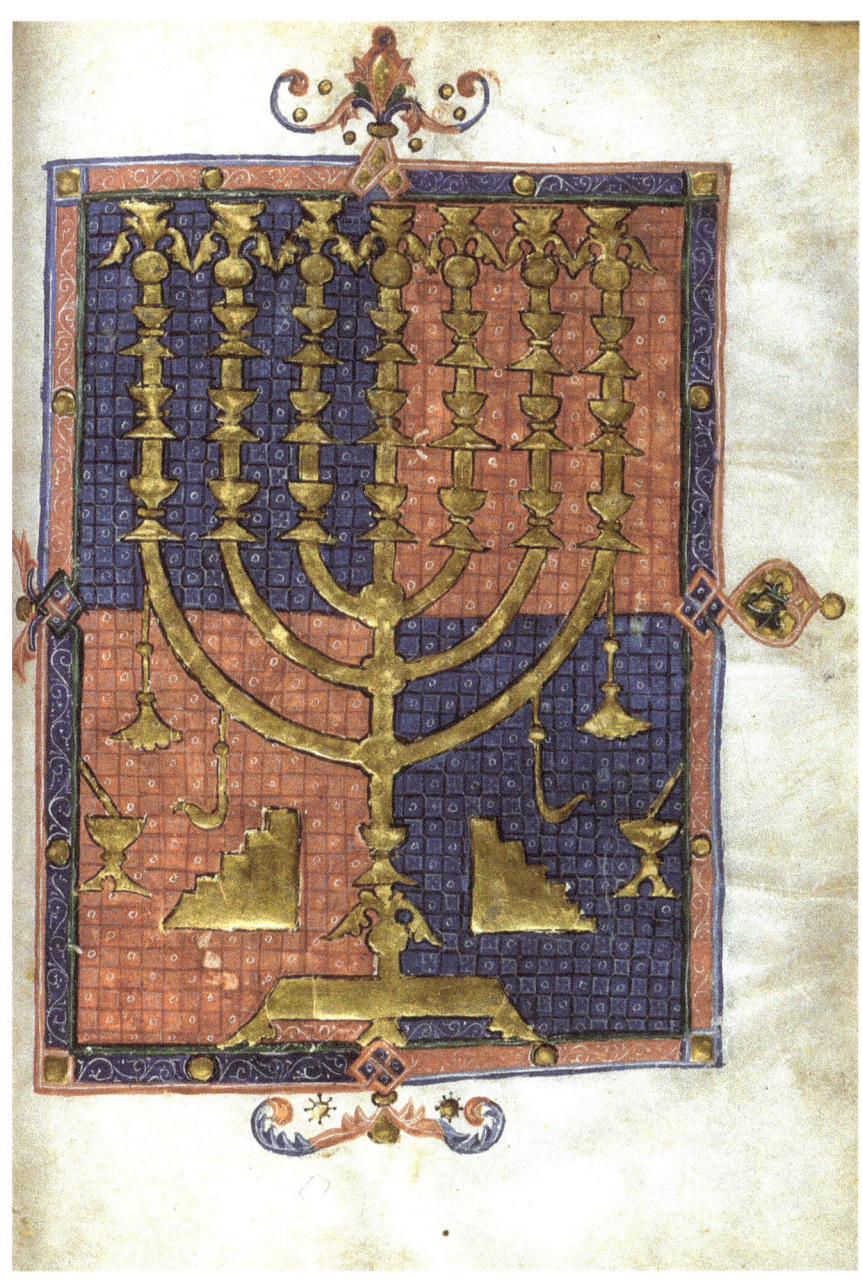

PLATE 5. Temple implements depicted in the Duke of Sussex's Catalan Bible, Catalonia, fourteenth century

BL MS Add. 15250, fo. 3ᵛ. © The British Library

PLATE 6. *Matsah*: Kaufmann Haggadah, Catalonia, fourteenth century

Library of the Hungarian Academy of Sciences, Budapest, MS Kaufmann A422, fo. 39ʳ. Reproduced by permission of the Library of the Hungarian Academy of Sciences, Budapest

PLATE 7. Stucco decoration, Alhambra palace, Granada

Javier Carro. Reproduced under the terms of the Creative Commons Attribution Licence, CC-BY-SA-3.0 (http://creativecommons.org/licenses/by-sa/3.0/), from Wikimedia Commons

PLATE 8. Stucco decoration, Alcazar of Seville

Alberto Bravo, 2013. CC-BY-SA 4.0 (https://creativecommons.org/licenses/by-sa/4.0), from Wikimedia Commons

PLATE 9. Stucco decoration, El Tránsito Synagogue, Toledo

By Olivier Lévy (collection personnelle).
CC-BY-SA-3.0 (http://creativecommons.org/licenses/by-sa/3.0/), from Wikimedia Commons

PLATE 10. Hebrew inscriptions and decorative Mudéjar stucco ornamentation, El Tránsito Synagogue, Toledo

Mordechai Omer et al., La Sinagoga de Samuel ha-Levi ('El Tránsito') Toledo, España, exhib. cat. (Genia Schreiber University Gallery, Tel Aviv University, (1992)), half-title page. Photo: Avraham Hay

PLATE 11. Scuola Levantina, Venice

Roberta Curiel and Bernard Cooperman, The Venetian Ghetto (New York, 1989), 124.
© Graziano Arici. Reproduced with permission

PLATE 12. Detail of *bimah*, Scuola Levantina, Venice

Roberta Curiel and Bernard Cooperman, The Venetian Ghetto (New York, 1989), 134.
© *Graziano Arici. Reproduced with permission*

PLATE 13. Scuola Grande Spagnola, Venice

Roberta Curiel and Bernard Cooperman, The Venetian Ghetto (New York, 1989), 102.
© Graziano Arici. Reproduced with permission

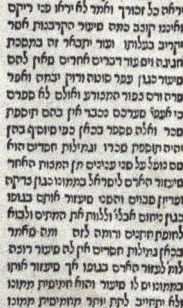

PLATE 14. Bomberg Babylonian Talmud, *Pe'ah* 1a, Venice, 1519–23

Jewish Theological Seminary Library, New York.
The Dorot Jewish Division, New York Public Library, Astor, Lenox and Tilden Foundations. © NYPL

PLATE 15. *Ketubah*: Abraham, son of Abrabanel, to Dona Gracia, daughter of Aaron de Paz, Venice, 1614

Jewish Museum, New York, JM68-60 © 2018. The Jewish Museum/Art Resource/Scala, Florence.
© Photo Scala, Florence

PLATE 16. Emanuel de Witte, *Interior of the Portuguese Synagogue Amsterdam* (1680)

Rijksmuseum, Amsterdam

PLATE 17. Romeyn de Hooghe, *Dedication of the Portuguese Synagogue in Amsterdam* (1675)

Rijksmuseum, Amsterdam

PLATE 18. Romeyn de Hooghe, *Herengracht with the Baron Belmonte House* (c.1700)

Rijksmuseum, Amsterdam

PLATE 19. Jacob van Ruisdael, *The Jewish Cemetery* (1655)

Detroit Institute of Arts, USA / Bridgeman Images

PLATE 20. Romeyn de Hooghe, *Funeral at the Portuguese Jewish Cemetery in Ouderkerk aan de Amstel* (1680)

Collection Jewish Historical Museum, Amsterdam

PLATE 21. Salom Italia, portrait of Manasseh ben Israel (1642)

Rijksmuseum, Amsterdam

PLATE 22. Rembrandt van Rijn, portrait of Manasseh ben Israel (1636)

Rijksmuseum, Amsterdam

recalled the destruction of their homes, they became despondent. But as each one found himself alone, he sought a helpmate, and they found a way to obtain what they needed. And as they assembled, men and women courted without respect for the lineage and social standing.[24]

The subsequent leadership structure that emerged reveals that the former hierarchy quickly reasserted itself, especially in Salonica.[25]

The names of the Sephardi *kehalim* reflect their great diversity and their continuing identification with their Iberian past: Spanish cities, such as Cordoba, Saragossa, Badajoz, and Seville, or regions, such as León, Catalonia, and Aragon. Cities and regions of southern Italy also lent their names to synagogues. When the Jews of southern Italy and Sicily were expelled, many of them also moved to the eastern Mediterranean and formed separate *kehalim* in the Ottoman empire that reflected their prior affiliations and origins, such as Otranto, Calabria, Syracuse, Apulia, or Sicily. The Italian *kehalim* were especially prone to divisions and splits: the Sicilian *kahal* split in 1505, and the Apulian *kahal* formed five separate congregations in 1550.[26]

Portuguese Jews also exhibited considerable diversity. Their cultural identities depended a great deal upon how long they had been in Portugal, when they left the country, and whether they had lived for any length of time as Conversos. At the time of the Expulsion in 1496 some Jews hastily departed. Most, however, remained until the date of departure only to be forcibly converted in 1497 and forbidden to leave. Thereafter opportunities for Conversos to leave the Iberian peninsula arose sporadically as a result of changing and unpredictable official emigration policies. The later Portuguese immigrants, unlike those who left in 1496, tended to be totally immersed in Lusitanian and Christian culture. They tended to settle in districts near other European merchants, such as the Galata district in Istanbul. A trickle of Conversos continued to leave after the Inquisition was established in 1536. Possibilities for flight improved considerably with the union of Spain and Portugal in 1580. Even then, however, escape often required elaborate planning and ample funding. Some took several years to get out. Few of the Portuguese Jewish fugitives arrived in the Ottoman empire with their wealth and trade connections intact. These fortunate few continued to maintain strong commercial and emotional ties with their kin in Spain or Portugal. Their ethnic solidarity with other Portuguese Jews was strong, but many were estranged from and indifferent to traditional Judaism. Others were particularly passionate in their faith after the suffering and stigmatization that they had endured as Conversos in Portugal.

The Sephardim in Europe were aware that the Ottomans had little interest in the previous or current religious practices of former Conversos and that reversion to Judaism in the Ottoman empire posed no dangers. Perhaps the Ottomans also recognized

---

[24] Moses ben Baruch Almosnino, *Crónica de los reyes otomanos*, cited in Ray, *After Expulsion*, 83.

[25] Levy, *The Sephardim in the Ottoman Empire*, 126.

[26] Shaw, *The Jews of the Ottoman Empire and the Turkish Republic*, 47–8; on tensions in the Italian congregations, see Rozen, *A History of the Jewish Community in Istanbul*, 78, 203.

that the Sephardim's familiarity with European commerce and languages could be useful to the economy and statecraft of the growing empire.

Residential Patterns and Community Organization

For administrative purposes, each individual in the Ottoman empire was a member of a particular tax-paying religious collectivity recognized by the state. The Jews, like the Greeks and the Armenians, were recognized as a *dhimmi* community. Their status bore no resemblance to the theoretical parity of different groups or respect for the 'Other' that ideally animates modern pluralist societies. Despite the plurality of religious groups and peoples in the Ottoman empire, Muslims had rights and privileges guaranteed by the full might of the state.[27] Assertions of Ottoman tolerance have been repeated so often since the nineteenth century that they have taken on a life of their own, but they are not borne out by the evidence of disdain for non-Muslims that permeated Ottoman society.

Observers have frequently assumed that the many internal divisions of the Sephardim are symptomatic of their fractious nature. According to Joseph Hacker, the splintered organizational framework that crystallized in the sixteenth century was already an established reality during the fifteenth century, and the precedent of the compulsory transfer of the various Romaniote communities as units provided the model for the communal organization of the Sephardim when they arrived, not their temperament or their particularist tendencies. Hacker contests the usual explanation that the Sephardim lacked a 'national' past in the Iberian peninsula and were hence unable to form one community. Rather, Iberian Jews may have found the established pattern of organization along geographical divisions particularly suitable to their own needs as refugees.[28]

As in Safed,[29] Jews from the same place of origin tended to form their own *kehalim*. This was not a uniquely Ottoman phenomenon: sixteenth-century Roman Jewry was also organized along geographical lines, with Jews from Sicily, Provence, Catalonia and Aragon, Castile, and northern Europe all maintaining their own synagogues. Most Ottoman *kehalim* were distinct in language, customs, culinary practices, and, frequently, dress. From the point of view of the rabbinic leadership, each *kahal* was considered a separate unit within the city. From the point of view of the government, the Jews of each city were regarded as one tax-paying unit. Their ethnic subdivisions were of little interest to the authorities. Unlike the Christians, who retained their patriarch and the hierarchical structure of the Byzantine period, the Jews did not possess a chief rabbi to represent the entire community until the Ottoman reforms of the nineteenth

---

[27] Rodrigue, 'Difference and Tolerance in the Ottoman Empire'.

[28] Hacker, 'The Sürgün System and Jewish Society in the Ottoman Empire', 35; id., 'The Sephardim of the Ottoman Empire in the Sixteenth Century'.   [29] See Chapter 3.

century, when the *millet* system was established. Though the Jews had an elected body for inter-Jewish affairs, they relied upon a few grandees with court connections (almost always Sephardim) when they required special intercession or representation.

The Jews of each city were required to pay their tax in one lump sum, and the *kehalim* had to decide collectively how much each individual *kahal*'s share would be. Each *kahal* then had to decide on each individual Jew's contribution to its share. The apportionment of the tax burden was influenced in large measure by the size, prestige, and influence of the particular *kahal*. How each congregant was appraised was determined by a combination of self-assessment and assessment by appointees of the *kahal*. The names of individual Jewish tax-payers are listed by households in the tax registers, ranked according to official categories of wealth: upper-class, middle-class, and poor. These were determined by internal tax assessors, who were either elected by the members of the *kahal* or appointed by its leaders. The size and affluence of a particular *kahal* thus was not simply a matter of prestige but had many practical ramifications. The larger *kehalim* had more influence over how the tax burden was spread, could provide more services, and were more likely to survive as the levies against the Jews grew more extortionate in the course of the seventeenth century. Furthermore, if an individual or family chose to leave their *kahal*, their departure would impose additional tax burdens on those who remained, and this would compound the financial burden of membership in a small *kahal*. The decision to leave a *kahal* was not taken as lightly as modern religious affiliation, since all social life and much economic life occurred on the congregational level. Nevertheless, movement from neighbourhood to neighbourhood occurred repeatedly in Istanbul, often driven by economic forces. As people moved to new neighbourhoods, they joined *kehalim* on the basis of their proximity to their homes and businesses, discarding affiliations based on ancestry or geographical origin. Again, there were advantages to joining a larger *kahal*. The original names of the *kehalim* based on the 'old country' persisted, but the actual membership had ceased to mirror the origins of its founders by the end of the sixteenth century. In addition, it was frequently difficult to ascertain which *kahal* a newcomer should join since their wanderings made it hard to determine their place of origin.

Each *kahal* provided for almost all of the social needs of its members. They had their own schools, charity chests, and sometimes their own burial grounds, courts of law, and libraries. They elected their own officeholders, with wealthier members generally exercising a controlling influence, as they paid for most of the social services and met the bulk of the tax burden.[30] Some officials, such as the rabbi and his assistants, were exempt from contributing to the tax. All the *kehalim* in a city were loosely joined in a representative body that dealt with issues that concerned the whole Jewish

---

[30] See Bornstein-Makovetsky, 'Structure, Organization, and Spiritual Life of the Sephardi Jews in the Ottoman Empire'; see also M. Molcho, 'The "Communities" (Synagogues) in Salonica' (Heb.); on Istanbul, see Rozen, *A History of the Jewish Community in Istanbul*.

community, such as meeting emergency government levies and fines, responding to demands for textiles or other goods for the janissary corps, ransoming Jewish captives, or appointing delegations to represent the entire community in cases of blood libel. In Salonica, as in the rest of the Balkan peninsula, each *kahal* was autonomous, and the representative body only met on an ad hoc basis; in Istanbul, as in the Jewish communities of the Levant, the representative body met regularly and the will of the majority of congregations prevailed. According to Rabbi Joseph ibn Leb:

In Salonica, every [Jewish] man speaks his own native tongue. When the exiles arrived each vernacular group founded an independent congregation, there being mobility from congregation to congregation. Each congregation maintains its poor; each congregation is entirely separate in the Crown register. Thus each congregation appears to be an independent city.[31]

Among the Romaniotes of Istanbul alone, forty-seven different *kehalim* were counted in the 1540 census.[32] By 1555 the Sephardim were divided into ten congregations.[33] These figures underscore the Jews' heterogeneity but also hint at the many forces at play in the community. The increasing number of *kehalim* was not only the product of constant immigration but also a result of congregational splits. Ottoman taxation policies put a severe strain on the Jewish community and may, ironically, have reinforced the Jews' propensity towards a multiplication of institutions and services, as people opposed to their tax assessment quarrelled with one another and went their separate ways. Some of the new *kehalim* were also precipitated by communities being forced to move as a result of fires and the declining economic status of members. Varying customs were only one potential cause of defections and congregational splits.

Jews, Christians, and Muslims lived together in most quarters of Ottoman cities—people with the same occupation often lived near their specific bazaar—but their lives were nonetheless quite separate.[34] Since Jews had to live within walking distance of a synagogue because of the sabbath restrictions, Jews from the same *kahal* tended to live in the same area, and as Jews from the same *kahal* tended to be of the same ethnic origin, parts of cities tended to be populated by Jews of the same ethnic origin, further accentuating the cultural differences among the Jews. Much of the life of the Jewish male revolved around the synagogue. Women were not required to attend synagogue, did not vote in communal affairs, and enjoyed less mobility than men in Muslim cities. Much of their social life took place in the courtyards of their multi-family dwellings. Those who engaged in crafts also performed them in the courtyards in the company of other women and children. Most of the textile production of Salonica took place in this manner. However, Ottoman Jewish women engaged in prayers in their own women's *minyanim* and enjoyed a rich subculture in their Judaeo-Spanish dialect.

---

[31] Joseph ibn Leb, *Responsa*, cited in Bornstein-Makovetsky, 'Structure, Organization, and Spiritual Life of the Sephardi Jews in the Ottoman Empire', 316.
[32] Rozen, *A History of the Jewish Community in Istanbul*, 64.   [33] Ibid. 81.   [34] Ibid. 62.

There were also wealthy and poor areas of cities, and a wealthy Jew might live next to a wealthy Muslim or Christian, while a poor Jew inhabited the same neighbourhood as poor Muslims and Christians. In short, several factors, not simply ethnic origin or religious affiliation, determined the breakdown of a particular quarter. Istanbul's Jews lived in over thirty neighbourhoods in the city in the sixteenth century. They were often on the move, primarily as a result of the devastating fires that constantly engulfed the crowded city but also as their socioeconomic conditions changed.

From the outset Salonica's Jewish community was more homogeneous than Istanbul's. There are no Jews recorded in the 1478 Ottoman tax register. This situation changed rapidly after 1492. The 1519 tax register lists twenty-four *kehalim*, with Jews comprising more than half the total population. By 1539 Salonica housed 2,509 Jewish households (totalling 17,563 people). By 1589 their number had risen to 23,942 people. In 1613 there were twenty-five *kehalim* composed of 2,933 households and 2,230 bachelors, making up 68 per cent of the city's population. In the 1589 tax register, the Aragonese *kahal* had the largest number of tax-paying households with 257, followed by the Lisbon *kahal* with 231, and the Évora *kahal* with 231. The general category 'Ashkenazi' contained 239. The community also boasted several hundred households from various parts of southern Italy, including Sicily, Otranto, Apulia, and Calabria.[35]

However, deep changes leading to Sephardi dominance were occurring just beneath the surface heterogeneity. The eventual Sephardicization of Ottoman Jewry and the decline of its Greek-speaking population had more than one cause. Membership of Sephardi *kehalim* often proved attractive to Romaniote Jews: the *kehalim* were generally larger and more affluent and therefore more capable of meeting the needs of their members, and their rites were considered more orderly and pleasing. Yet many Romaniotes found the self-confidence and self-esteem of the Sephardim personally offensive. Some Romaniotes joined Sephardi *kehalim* as a result of marriage, others were motivated by tax considerations. Changing synagogue membership might, in some cases, be the only recourse available to someone who found the tax imposed upon him by the assessors in his *kahal* unbearable. Instances of shifting congregational affiliation appear repeatedly in the responsa literature. In one instance, a man who had donated ritual objects to a synagogue asked Rabbi Aharon Halevi whether he could take them with him as he was going to join another synagogue. His request was denied.[36] In another instance, some Romaniotes justified their departure from their *kahal* for a Catalan one on the grounds that they preferred the music and order of prayer. In the Lisbon *kahal*, differences between those who had continued to practise Judaism in secret after their forced conversion and those who had not caused a split into Old Lisbon and New Lisbon in 1536. Portuguese Jews who reached the Ottoman empire

---

[35] Lewis, *The Jews of Islam*, 123; see also M. A. Epstein, *The Ottoman Jewish Communities and Their Role in the Fifteenth and Sixteenth Centuries*; Shaw, *The Jews in the Ottoman Empire and the Turkish Republic*, 38.

[36] Aharon Halevi, *Zekan aharon*, cited in Rozen, *A History of the Jewish Community in Istanbul*, 329–32.

early in the sixteenth century generally had some familiarity with Jewish tradition and memories of a shared communal life. They were frequently at odds with Portuguese immigrants who arrived later and had spent their entire lives either as Marranos or Catholics. Some of the later immigrants brought considerable fortunes from Europe, identified with the background of the European Christian merchants living in the Europeanized sections of Galata and Pera in Istanbul, and shared feelings of solidarity with other Portuguese Jews, wherever they resided. Congregational arguments were sometimes so bitter among the Portuguese that the local police were called on to intervene. In one instance, it was the rabbi who summoned the police to restore order.[37] Inner divisions were not limited to the Portuguese. In 1510 the Catalan *kahal* of Salonica split into the Old Catalan and the New Catalan. Their division centred around the appointee to head their *talmud torah*. Rabbi Samuel de Medina succeeded in reconciling the two groups in 1540, but the union was only temporary, and it split once again. The Sicilian *kahal* divided in two in 1505, maintaining separate institutions under one roof until 1562. Despite pleas for unity on the part of the rabbinic leadership, Jewish community life followed a turbulent course. When an Ashkenazi *kahal* became divided between those who opposed the adoption of Sephardi customs and those who favoured it, its members asked for the opinion of De Medina:

Question: A congregation, the members of which followed the order of service of their forefathers, settled in Turkey. In the course of years almost all of the diverse immigrant Jewish communities in Turkey abandoned their own order of services and adopted that of the Sephardic Jews, because the latter constituted a majority of Turkish Jewry and because the language of Sephardic prayers is clear and pleasant. This change to the Sephardic rite became the general trend in the city of Salonica, where congregations Calabria, Provence, Sicily, and Apulia adopted the Sephardic rite. There remained but one German congregation that persisted in its adherence to its own order of services. Recently the majority of this German congregation, too, chose to follow the Sephardic rite. There is, however, a minority of worshippers who insist upon the continuation of the German ritual and vigorously oppose the change. The majority of the members, on the other hand insist upon the use of the Sephardic rite, giving as their reason that they have become accustomed to it and that they are no longer familiar with the German ritual. . . . They therefore inquire as to whether they are justified in continuing the Sephardic order of services.[38]

In his response, De Medina acknowledged certain principles that transcended the details of the case. He upheld the right of a majority of Jews to abandon their established customary order of prayers in favour of another, describing the Sephardi rite as simple, reliable, and clear, and therefore suitable for both the learned and the ignorant. He concluded: 'I therefore regard it as your religious duty to continue using the Sephardic rite since it is beneficial to those who follow it. Besides, it has become the

[37] See Goodblatt, *Jewish Life in Turkey in the XVIth Century*, 14.
[38] De Medina, *She'elot uteshuvot meharashdam*, vol. i, no. 35; see also 'Short Biographies of the Hakhamim', in Goldish, *Jewish Questions*, pp. lvii–lxiii.

general practice among all the Jews of Turkey.'[39] Among the thousands of responsa that have been preserved from the Ottoman empire, a large number concern questions of competing customs and loyalty to the traditions of the past.

Textile Production in Salonica

Although the Jews did not constitute more than 3 per cent of the Ottoman population during the empire's golden age, the Sephardim played a conspicuous role in some branches of the economy. They could be found in all strata of society, from bankers and diplomats to artisans and craftsmen. The Romaniotes tended to be concentrated in more modest sectors of the economy.

Migrant groups often play a key role in the diffusion of new technologies.[40] In the case of the Sephardim, their skills in medicine, commerce, and the manufacture of cloth injected a new dynamism into the Ottoman economy in general and the port of Salonica in particular. Their concentration in textile production, particularly in the manufacture of woollen broadcloth, constituted the mainstay of the community for generations. Salonica possessed a number of features that made it ideal for the production of textiles: an agricultural hinterland, providing pasture for sheep; streams to drive the fulling mills; and excellent port facilities. Furthermore, it had access to Balkan land routes and Mediterranean sea routes, enabling the Sephardim to maintain commercial contact with family members in Italy, Spain, Portugal, the Low Countries, and North Africa. Other natural advantages included proximity to mineral resources and raw materials essential for the dyes that were needed by the textile industry.

Salonica was probably a textile-producing centre in Byzantine times. The arrival of the Sephardim transformed the traditional textile industry through the introduction of a particular new technology, the mechanical fulling mill. Fulling involved washing and beating the cloth to give it a closer, denser weave. The new technology saved time and money and produced a stronger fabric that was thicker and heavier.[41] The same technology was also introduced to Safed by the Spanish exiles. By the middle of the sixteenth century both the workforce and the terminology employed in the manufacturing process were Spanish. The various steps of the woollen industry in Salonica appear in an important responsum of Samuel de Medina.

After the cloth has been woven it is give to the fuller [*batañero*] who fulls it. Then it is given to the comber [*perharo*] who performs the task of combing [*bettildar*]. Then it is given to shearing [*tundir*]. After this task is done they see if the cloth is pure and clean of oil. If it is not clean as it should be it is given to another man to degrease and this task is called bleaching [*desteñir*]. Nitre and water are

---

[39] De Medina, *She'elot uteshuvot meharashdam*, vol. i, no. 35.
[40] Glick, 'Moriscos and Marranos as Agents of Technological Diffusion', 20–39.
[41] Braude, 'The Rise and Fall of Salonica Woollens', 224, 225 n. 22.

placed upon the cloth. After it has been degreased the comber takes it to comb [*perhar*] a second time.[42]

Textile production using the fulling mill became the economic mainstay of the Jewish community of Salonica: it is described in a 1540 document as 'the sole support' of most of the population of the city.[43] Even the *talmud torah* of Salonica operated its own textile factory.[44] Most of the textiles were produced in the home, with men, women, and children working on various stages of the process, although some men worked in factories. Women of more modest backgrounds were sometimes forced to sell embroidery or cloth in the markets or bazaars. The textiles were exported to Venice, Istanbul, and cities in the Balkans, North Africa, and the Low Countries. Venice is mentioned more frequently than any other foreign city in Samuel de Medina's responsa. Given the close commercial relations between the Sephardi merchants in Venice and the textile industry in Salonica, it is not surprising that the fluctuating political relations between the two empires played a major role in the vicissitudes of the Jews of Salonica in the sixteenth and seventeenth centuries. When commercial relations between the Ottomans and Venice were suspended between 1571 and 1573 as a result of the battle of Lepanto and the conquest of Cyprus, Jewish consignments were seized at sea, Turkish Jews residing in Venice were imprisoned, and Jews in Salonica suffered hardship and were unable to meet their tax assessments.

Salonica's textile industry produced approximately 40,000 pieces of woollen cloth a year by the middle of the sixteenth century, making it one of the main producers of cloth in the world. The single most important customer of the Salonica textile industry by the mid-sixteenth century was the Ottoman government. The improved cloth from Salonica was particularly suited to the requirements of the Turkish army. As Ottoman armies pushed further into the colder climes of central Europe, the demand for warmer uniforms increased. At first the government paid outright for the cloth, which was marketed by entrepreneurs in the Jewish community who dealt directly with the manufacturers or producers. In 1545 the Jewish cloth-dealers of Salonica formed a cartel to deal with the Ottoman government and employed a military officer to supervise it. They soon held a monopoly on the supply of broadcloth to the Turkish army. At its peak, the Jewish textile industry of Salonica was delivering 180,000 metres of woven broadcloth to the Ottoman authorities and remitting part of the *jizya* in bolts of cloth for the janissary corps.

However, the cloth manufacturers of Salonica experienced challenges on several fronts. The Italian textile industry competed for the supply of raw wool from the

---

[42] De Medina, *She'elot uteshuvot meharashdam*, vol. iv, no. 45.

[43] *Yosef da'at*, cited in Braude, 'The Rise and Fall of Salonica Woollens', 220 n. 5; see also Avitsur, 'The Woollen Textile Industry in Salonica' (Heb.), 159.

[44] Goodblatt, *Jewish Life in Turkey in the XVIth Century*, 54–6.

Balkans, leading to a steady rise in costs. In the 1580s the newly formed British Levant Company began to flood the market with British cloth. In addition, recurrent natural disasters took a heavy toll on the industry, particularly on those who transported the wool and wove it into thread. Plagues occurred with increasing frequency and virulence during the sixteenth century, and Salonica and its textile workers were especially hard hit since the city was located at the intersection of several major trade routes and boasted an extremely active port. Like all cities of the time, it lacked proper hygiene, with refuse allowed to pile up in narrow streets, and its dense neighbourhoods were a breeding ground for contagion. The process of cloth production, moreover, was conducive to infection, as woollen cloth can host plague carriers such as parasites for extended periods of time. Wool-carriers and weavers in particular were exposed to infected wool.[45] Outbreaks of plague in Salonica are reported in 1530, 1532, 1534, 1545, 1546, 1548, 1550, 1552, 1554, 1556, 1561, 1564, 1568, 1572, 1577, 1581, 1586, 1591, 1592, 1594, 1596, and 1598.[46] The one in 1548 reportedly killed 7,000 Jews, a figure that may be inflated but which reflects contemporary perceptions of its severity.[47]

Demand for woollen broadcloth kept increasing, and towards the middle of the sixteenth century the Ottoman government began to set quotas on cloth from Salonica and to hold Jews as surety that the quotas would be met. However, at the outbreak of plague, those who could afford to would flee to neighbouring villages, leaving the burden of fulfilling the quotas on those too poor to escape. Some workers even had looms stored in the villages to meet such emergencies. Muslims and Christians also fled the towns when plague struck, although in the case of Muslims the first response advocated in plague manuals was not flight but the recitation of prayers and the preparation of amulets and talismans.[48] In 1568 Jews were prohibited from leaving the city despite the plague. During the 1570s the Jews who remained in the city were overwhelmed with the tasks of burying the victims and caring for the orphaned and were unable to meet the quotas. Jewish leaders would send delegations to Istanbul for a postponement of delivery or a reduction in the amount required.

In 1577 a twelvefold increase in the price of wool occurred. Nevertheless, the government insisted that the quotas be filled and the cloth supplied at the old price. In the 1580s alone the cloth requirements of the Ottoman army doubled, and demand for raw wool tripled. In 1637 official demands for cloth reached a peak, and the Jews dispatched yet another delegation to Istanbul to defend the broadcloth producers after the quality of their cloth was declared unacceptable. Following months of arguments, Rabbi Judah Covo, the leader of the delegation, was beheaded on the grounds that he had delivered adulterated cloth. By this point, the textile industry of Salonica was already in terminal decline.

---

[45] Varlik, 'Plague, Conflict and Negotiation', 273; Braude, 'The Rise and Fall of Salonica Woollens'.
[46] Varlik, 'Plague, Conflict and Negotiation', 265 n. 15.
[47] Ibid. 270.   [48] Ayalon, *Natural Disasters in the Ottoman Empire*, 135–71.

An earlier delegation to the Ottoman court to object to excessive government demands in 1566 had included Rabbi Moses ben Baruch Almosnino, whose career throws light on the continuity of Sephardi diplomatic activities despite the totally new conditions of life in the Balkans.

Moses ben Baruch Almosnino

Rabbi Moses ben Baruch Almosnino (c.1510–c.1580) combined the traditional roles of scholar, courtier, and diplomat that had appeared frequently on the Iberian peninsula. He was born in Salonica into a scholarly family, several members of which had been martyred by the Inquisition in Aragon.[49] His father, Baruch, settled in Salonica soon after 1492, where he built up a successful business and became a patron of learning with his newly acquired wealth. Almosnino was encouraged to become a scholar. His literary output reflects the breadth and versatility of the Sephardi intellectual tradition and the continuity of its activism and public role. He wrote biblical commentaries, super-commentaries on Rashi's and Ibn Ezra's biblical commentaries, and commentaries on Aristotle's *Ethics* and *Physics* and al-Ghazali's *Intentions of the Philosophers* as well as an important work on Jewish liturgy. He wrote on topics as diverse as the interpretation of dreams, astronomy, free will, and the education of children. He even claimed to have written a book on astronomy in Castilian from memory while away from home without access to his books.[50] Almosnino was a popular preacher and delivered sermons on special holidays and community occasions in at least seven synagogues and the *talmud torah* of Salonica, as well as eulogies for important members of the community, including one to mark the thirty-day mourning period following Doña Gracia Mendes Nasi's death. He mentions a collection of 'sermons on women' which is, unfortunately, no longer extant. His most famous work, *Extremos y grandezas de Constantinopla*, an account of the city of Istanbul, was written in Ladino during one of his diplomatic missions to the capital and published in Latin characters in Madrid in 1567.

By no means a cloistered scholar, Almosnino exhibited all the worldliness of the Iberian Jewish leadership. In the spring of 1566, just prior to Suleiman the Magnificent's departure for his final and fatal military campaign in Hungary, Almosnino joined a delegation of five Jews, including court physician Joseph Hamon and courtier Don Joseph Nasi, to the Ottoman court. In addition to an audience with Sultan Suleiman, the delegation met with the grand vizier, the imperial treasurer, and Piale Pasha, Suleiman's son-in-law and admiral of the Turkish fleet. They succeeded in getting several especially onerous levies and tithes rescinded, such as the obligation to supply workers

---

[49] I. Molcho, 'Rabbi Moses Almosnino' (Heb.), 246; see also Saperstein, *Jewish Preaching*, 217–39; Ben-Menahem, 'The Works of Rabbi Moses Almosnino' (Heb.); Benayahu, *Moses Almosnino of Salonica* (Heb.). Almosnino's *Crónica de los reyes otomanos* reveals a keen observer of the Ottoman administration, the city of Istanbul, and Jewish society.

[50] Markova, 'El Tratado de astrolabio de Mosé Almosnino en un manuscrito de Leningrado'.

for the silver mines in Macedonia and large numbers of sheep for the authorities. Possibly, it was at this time that, despite some opposition within the Jewish community, the delegation reached an agreement that the Jews of Salonica would provide a set amount of broadcloth to outfit the janissary corps as payment in kind for the *jizya*. Five of Almosnino's six lobbying efforts in Istanbul were unsuccessful, but, with the help of other courtiers in the palace plus a large bribe, he was finally successful in having some of the privileges of the Salonica community renewed and some of the more oppressive levies modified.

While in Istanbul, Almosnino had much free time on his hands. He used it to advantage, chronicling his trip and composing his history of the Ottoman sultans, *Crónica de los reyes otomanos*.[51] In it, Almosnino describes the inner workings of the Ottoman state, including its institutions, its demography, the make-up of the Ottoman armies and navy, details on court plots, and insights into Ottoman intellectual life. He presents a rare contemporaneous account of Suleiman's death and Selim's accession and coronation parade on 5 December 1566.[52] His comments on Ottoman life reveal an astute observer alert to the nuances of life around him. Almosnino's erudition in such a broad array of subjects was part of a long Sephardi scholastic tradition. Prestige in the community, however, was no longer measured by scholarly attainments but by wealth and connections.[53]

Fires in Istanbul and the Decline of the Romaniotes

Plague was not the only disaster to strike the Jews of the Ottoman empire. Istanbul, in particular, was prone to fires. The fires eventually transformed the topography of Jewish settlement in the city as well as the fortunes of its Jewish population. Most of Istanbul's Jews lived in densely occupied multi-family dwellings set around courtyards that they rented from Muslims. Moses Almosnino provides an especially vivid portrait of one Jewish residential neighbourhood:

Not a single empty plot of land was available for construction in the quarter; the only way to add dwelling space was to build additional floors on existing buildings. The result was an area of very narrow streets, with wooden houses rising upward on both sides. The best apartments were on the top floors, because their windows were open to the southwest breeze. On the other hand, the one-storey houses and the first floors of high buildings were very hot in the summer and very cold in the winter. Since there was no sewage system, the residents of the upper floors threw their garbage and their excrement onto the lower floors . . . . The upper floors were occupied by the rich; the lower floors, by the poor. This was more than a matter of convenience or status; it also meant that to be poor was to be dirty, to smell, and to be more exposed to maladies.[54]

[51] Benayahu, *Moses Almosnino of Salonica* (Heb.), 150 n. 4.
[52] Almosnino, *Extremos y grandezas de Constantinopla*, 57–8.
[53] Rozen, *A History of the Jewish Community in Istanbul*, 263.
[54] Moses ben Baruch Almosnino, *Crónica de los reyes otomanos*, cited in Rozen, 'Public Space and Private Space among the Jews of Istanbul', 338.

Fires would sweep through the densely packed multi-storey wooden houses in the congested residential quarters and would rapidly devour entire neighbourhoods. They were particularly devastating in poorer neighbourhoods, such as those where the Romaniotes were concentrated. Forced repeatedly to evacuate their homes, many Romaniotes could not afford to rebuild their synagogues and eventually joined Sephardi *kehalim* in their new neighbourhoods. As a result, they abandoned Greek for Ladino, something they had long resisted. In 1569 a major part of Istanbul's commercial district, an area densely inhabited by Jews, was destroyed. Fifteen synagogues and the mansion of the court doctor Moses Hamon were consumed. The Jews were not permitted to rebuild their homes in their old neighbourhoods and sought shelter, with great difficulty, in other parts of the city. The feelings of personal loss and dispossession were expressed by Isaac ben Abraham Akrish in the introduction to his commentaries on the Song of Songs:

Istanbul and everything in it was burnt. Its palaces were burnt, and so were its beautiful villas and the objects of art in them. And the fire was enormous, ravaging days and nights, and no one was able to extinguish it. And I am at the heart of the fire . . . and I ran away like a bird from the trap, leaving my house and all my beloved books to burn . . . and I was lying stranded on the seashore for five days and five nights, as did many others, and there is no rescue. . . . After a month I returned to Istanbul, to a place to which havoc did not get, a place of very few people of Romaniot origin called Kastoria, and I stayed with them for four years in great poverty.[55]

Between 1606 and 1698 twenty-six major fires destroyed large parts of Istanbul. Jews were forced to move from quarter to quarter in 1618, 1633, 1640, and 1660. The most catastrophic conflagration occurred in July 1660. The fire ripped through every neighbourhood in Istanbul, burning out of control for almost fifty hours. It is estimated that 280,000 houses were reduced to rubble and perhaps as many as 40,000 people lost their lives. Thousands of additional deaths occurred in the plague that followed. By the end of the summer two-thirds of Istanbul had been destroyed. After the fire, the remaining Karaites and Romaniotes were no longer able to rebuild their communal institutions, and most were finally absorbed into the Iberian *kehalim*. As a result of official policies and repeated dispersals the connection between a family's ethnic origins and its place of residence was definitively broken. They had already abandoned many of their distinctive customs and rituals as well as their language.[56]

Discriminatory housing policies by government and religious authorities added to the Jews' misery. After the great fire of 1660 the mother of the new sultan, together with the grand vizier and the sultan's preacher, forbade the Jews to return to their old neighbourhood. The Islamization of Istanbul by ousting both Jews and Christians was an attempt to demonstrate the piety and legitimacy of a regime made increasingly

---

[55] Isaac ben Abraham Akrish, *Three Commentaries on Canticum Canticorum*, cited in Rozen, 'Public Space and Private Space among the Jews of Istanbul', 335 n. 20.

[56] See M. D. Baer, 'The Great Fire of 1660 and the Islamization of Christian and Jewish Space in Istanbul'.

unpopular by the economic problems caused by its military defeats. By this time the Jews had lost their political power in the court to the Greek Christians and could no longer defend themselves effectively. Fully two-thirds of Istanbul's Jews lived in a neighbourhood now declared off-limits.[57] They were sent across the Golden Horn to Haskoy, far from the commercial hub of the city.[58] The old Jewish neighbourhoods were destroyed, and with these changes the formerly very specific Iberian and Italian Jewish identities weakened. The poll tax registers of 1691 confirm the widespread economic decline of Istanbul's Jews as well, with only 4 per cent of the Jewish households of Haskoy described as wealthy.

Sephardi Group Identity

It is difficult to define the Sephardim of the Ottoman empire in the sixteenth century. Individual identity was often fluid. The Converso background of Portuguese Jews further complicated matters. Many Sephardim had lived in several countries, spoke more than one language, and had followed more than one rite. As a result, place of origin, mother tongue, and ritual preference were not necessarily accurate measures of identity. Furthermore, old loyalties became blurred as the immigrant generation passed away.

Newcomers were initially assigned to a particular *kahal* on the basis of where they came from, although the community attempted to spread the burden of integrating the refugees equitably and to ensure that no *kahal* expanded at the expense of the others. However, as more refugees arrived, with experience of worshipping in several countries or with no Jewish experience at all, it became vital to find a means of determining how a person should integrate into the community. The *kehalim*, after all, provided much more than a place of worship. They assisted the poor and the sick, provided burials and cemeteries, adjudicated in their courts on all matters of personal status, and some even had rudimentary economic guilds. In order to keep the peace and a sense of equity, the community of Salonica made anyone immigrating to the city whose father was Italian join the Italian *kahal*, even if his grandfather had been born in Iberia. However, if his father had been born in Portugal, Castille, Aragon, or any other Iberian kingdom, he joined that *kahal*. The Jews of Aragon protested, fearful that their *kahal* would not be sustainable since no one of Jewish origin remained in Aragon after 1492.

It is still not clear precisely why the original fragmentation of Ottoman Jewry along ethnic lines persisted as long as it did. Possibly the *sürgün* policy played a role in the case of the Romaniotes, since the status of *sürgünli* was passed down from an individual to his descendants. Moreover, the precedent of the transplantation of the

---

[57] M. D. Baer, 'The Great Fire of 1660', 170, 172.

[58] On the shifting boundaries and disappearance of formerly Jewish neighbourhoods, see ibid. 168–9; Heyd, 'The Jewish Communities of Istanbul in the Seventeenth Century', 300–5.

entire population of a village as a unit provided a viable official model of resettlement of Christians and Muslims that antedated the arrival of the Sephardim. Possibly the tenacious identification with particular towns or provinces in Spain or Portugal reflected other pre-1492 conditions, such as a local 'patriotism' that may have mirrored extended family ties. The Ottoman experience of separatism based on geographical origin was not unique. Sephardi exiles in Rome initially joined to form one community but soon separated: Catalan and Aragonese Jews worshipped together but separately from Castilian and Provençal Jews. Iberian Jews in Rome maintained three separate congregations based on their origins in Aragon, Castile, or Catalonia in order to maintain the uses and customs of their forefathers. Similarly, in Fez, Jews from Seville retained their separate identity until as late as 1526, distinguishing themselves from the three Castilian congregations in the city in a heated controversy concerning *kashrut*.[59] The newcomers also held themselves aloof from the indigenous Jews. Some of the most bitter controversies between them revolved around questions of the continuing validity of *minhag*, or communal custom, rather than law, especially concerning the preparation of food. Both Sephardi immigrants and indigenous Jews manifested deep pride in their *minhagim*, hallowed by the practices of parents and grandparents. Some also probably held on to them out of respect for communities that had been destroyed. Possibly the persistence of Jewish social fragmentation was furthered by the unofficial policies of the rabbinic authorities, who hoped that community identity would encourage greater religious loyalty. This is suggested by one of Egypt's great sixteenth-century Sephardi rabbis, David ibn Abi Zimra:

With the breaking away of groups from their fellow-townsmen and their common language, there is also a corresponding breaking up of devout hearts; nor are their prayers of praise to God united. But if they are of one city of origin and of one language, then will peace dwell among them, for each will feel at home and know his status.[60]

The multiplicity of *kehalim* also served the needs of the large number of scholars pouring into the empire, each often possessing his own loyal following and personal ambitions.

The Sephardi population of the Ottoman empire retained many of the features of its Iberian past. Honour remained an extremely important social value, particularly the honour of the patriarch of the family, as did the chastity of women.[61] Initially, the old elite lost some of its status, but with the passage of time it regained its standing. Having experienced a precipitous decline in status in their last years in Spain, the Sephardim were especially sensitive to questions of dignity. However, they also acknowledged the

---

[59] On Rome, see Ray, *After Expulsion*, 84; on Fez, see Gerber, *Jewish Society in Fez*, 52, 55.

[60] David ibn Abi Zimra, *She'elot uteshuvot haradbaz*, cited in Goldman, *The Life and Times of Rabbi David ibn Abi Zimra*, 84–5.   [61] Ben-Naeh, 'Honor and Its Meaning among Ottoman Jews'.

ignominy of their expulsion from Iberia. Each fresh outrage against Jews or Conversos in Europe sent waves of empathy through Sephardi communities everywhere. A new genre of historical literature appeared, including Joseph Hakohen's *Emek habakhah*, Solomon ibn Verga's *Shevet yehudah*, and Eliyahu Capsali's *Seder eliyahu zuta*. Their lachrymose accounts of ancient and modern expulsions and persecutions leavened with hopes of redemption enjoyed instant success.[62]

Questions of identity were complicated by the forced conversion many immigrants had been subjected to. Ottoman rabbis were forced to wrestle repeatedly with complex issues of the status of Conversos and their relationship with Conversos who were still Catholics in Portugal. At first, the Ottoman rabbis tended towards leniency and accepted the Conversos as Jews. It was widely understood that the victims of forced conversion in 1492 and 1497 had no choice in their abandonment of Judaism. The succeeding generations who remained Catholic, whether out of ignorance or fear, however, raised more problematic questions. How should they and their descendants be regarded in matters of marriage and divorce? What was the status of their relatives who were still in Iberia? Were levirate marriages required? The rabbis of the Ottoman empire, like their counterparts in North Africa and Europe, were loath to declare the Conversos who remained practising Catholics in the Iberian peninsula non-Jews, as they hoped that they would eventually leave Iberia and rejoin the Jewish people.[63]

Scholarship in Salonica

As thousands of Jews streamed into the cities and towns of the Ottoman empire, Jewish intellectual life quickened. Even though scholarship had not died out among the Jews of Constantinople, the arrival of European Jews after 1492 led to an extraordinary concentration of new intellectual energy that quickly overwhelmed the old Romaniote community. Given the number of scholars among the immigrants, fierce competition for communal positions arose. Well-known and less well-known scholars, heads of academies in Spain, teachers, and printers, as well as a broad class of educated lay people, energized the main Jewish centres of Salonica, Istanbul, Bursa, and Edirne. With qualified personnel abounding, even small Sephardi *kehalim* could boast of competent teachers and some talmudic learning. This was not the case among the Romaniotes. In Salonica the prominent scholars were either refugees themselves, such as Joseph Taitatzak from Lisbon and Levi ibn Habib and Joseph Karo from Toledo, or had been born in Salonica of Spanish refugee parents, such as Samuel de Medina. The quality of their erudition and their sheer numbers guaranteed a general Sephardization

---

[62] On Jewish historiography in the sixteenth century, see Yerushalmi, *Zachor*, ch. 3.

[63] Tam ibn Yahya, *She'elot uteshuvot ohalei tam*, cited in Goldish, *Jewish Questions*, 99–101. For useful older treatments of Ottoman responsa, see Goodblatt, *Jewish Life in Turkey in the XVIth Century*; Shmuelevitz, *The Jews of the Ottoman Empire*.

of Jewish culture. Salonica attracted the largest number of Iberian scholars. Many studied in the city for years before moving on to other Jewish communities in the Near East. As fortunes were recouped, wealthy families, such as the Hamon and Mendes families, financed the study of the Torah. The homes of some, such as the Alatun family, were transformed into centres of study, creating a broad stratum of educated males taught by refugee scholars.[64] Scholars lectured regularly in the synagogues and compiled their commentaries and sermons for publication.

European culture continued to be appreciated in Salonica throughout the sixteenth century. In 1570 a literary society was founded in the home of Guedalia Yahya. Its programme was similar to those of the salons of Iberia, where poetry, musical compositions, and liturgical works were shared. Salonica, like Istanbul, also housed groups of scholars engaged in philosophical study. Taitatzak headed a school of philosophers, while Almosnino explored Arabic philosophy.[65] Undoubtedly the most famous Jewish cultural institution in Salonica was the *talmud torah*,[66] which educated children from the most elementary to the most advanced level. It was a unique, community school that taught close attention to the linguistic and logical form of the talmudic text according to the method of Rabbi Isaac Campanton, one of the great teachers of Spanish Jewry. His yeshiva in Zamora was among the last bastions of Jewish learning in pre-Expulsion Spain. Its curriculum also included secular subjects. The *talmud torah* served all of the *kehalim* of Salonica under the leadership of a community-wide board of directors. It also housed students from other parts of the Ottoman empire and Ashkenazi Europe. It was supported through charitable endowments, rent from landed property, the income from shops that had been donated to it, and the proceeds from textile manufacturing. Social pressure to support the institution was strong. Doña Gracia Mendes Nasi and Don Joseph Nasi were among its patrons. The *talmud torah* evolved into much more than just a school: its premises were used for community gatherings and its services included a hospital, a mental asylum, a hostel, and, later, in the eighteenth century, a printing press. It had a charitable fund for the poor, and at Hanukkah its students received free clothing.

The Jewish community of Salonica also sponsored a school of science, medicine, and astronomy,[67] and study groups abounded. Scholars reportedly opened their private libraries to the public, and educated philanthropists shared their personal collections of books and manuscripts.[68] Jacob ibn Habib and Samuel de Medina gratefully acknowledged their use of the books and manuscripts of the Benveniste family, whose library is

---

[64] Hacker, 'The Intellectual Activity of the Jews of the Ottoman Empire', 109.   [65] Ibid. 117–19.
[66] Levy, *The Sephardim in the Ottoman Empire*, 38; Hacker, 'The Intellectual Activity of the Jews in the Ottoman Empire'; see also Bentov, 'Methods of Study of Talmud in the Yeshivahs of Salonica and Turkey' (Heb.); Ben-Naeh, 'The City of Torah and Learning' (Heb.).
[67] Schmelzer, 'Hebrew Manuscripts and Printed Books among the Sephardim', 265.   [68] Ibid. 384 n. 50.

listed among the cultural institutions destroyed in a major fire in 1545.[69] The city was compared to Jerusalem by contemporaries, and later praised with a biblical paraphrase: 'From Salonica shall go forth Torah.'[70] Samuel de Medina patriotically declared that no other city in the diaspora could compare to Salonica in learning, and averred that settlement there constituted an act of piety.[71] Most of the great Sephardi rabbis of the early sixteenth century studied in Salonica, and the legal decisions in responsa that emanated from there number in the thousands. The city was also home to an important circle of mystics, part of the international Jewish fraternity of students of the esoteric traditions. Salonica did not become an important centre of kabbalistic study until the last twenty years of the sixteenth century, and even then mystical studies were limited to a closed group of devotees. Contrary to conventional wisdom, kabbalah did not thrive in broad Sephardi circles at this time, in contrast to the widespread popularity of science and philosophy.[72] The erudition of sixteenth-century Salonica became part of the Sephardi mystique disseminated by nineteenth-century scholars in the east as they, sometimes apologetically, contemplated the scholarly achievements of the Ashkenazim in Europe and decried the 'cultural backwardness' of their own community.[73] The total destruction of the Jewish community of Salonica during the Second World War further contributed to its mystique.

Printing and the Triumph of Ladino

Perhaps no single institution was more important in promoting the Jewish cultural renaissance or the reconstruction of Sephardi culture than the Ottoman Hebrew printing industry. Printing played a major role in the triumph of Ladino over all the other languages the Jews of the empire spoke. The first Hebrew printers in the Ottoman empire, the brothers David and Samuel ibn Nahmias, arrived in Istanbul and set up a press in 1493. Their first publication, Jacob ben Asher's *Arba'ah turim*, followed almost immediately. Soon afterwards the Bible, with commentaries by Abraham ibn Ezra, Rashi, and David Kimhi, was published (1505–6), as well as Maimonides' *Mishneh torah* (1509), and Isaac Alfasi's *Sefer hahalakhot* (1509). A printing press was established in Salonica, perhaps as early as 1503 and definitely by 1510, which printed the Torah and *Midrash rabah* (1512). In Istanbul David ibn Nahmias was succeeded by the Gedaliahs, a Jewish family from Portugal, who arrived in 1512. Other printing presses were introduced in

---

[69] See Amarillio, 'The Great Talmud Torah of Salonica' (Heb.); Recanati (ed.), *Salonica* (Heb.); Emmanuel, *Histoire des Israélites de Salonique*, i. 104–12; see also M. Molcho, 'The Talmud Torah School' (Heb.).

[70] See Naar, 'Fashioning the "Mother of Israel"', 3.

[71] See ibid. [72] Hacker, 'Intellectual Activity of the Jews of the Ottoman Empire', 122 n. 61.

[73] On Ottoman Jewish views of Salonica, see Naar, 'Fashioning the "Mother of Israel"'; J. P. Cohen, *Becoming Ottoman*; on European Jewish idealizations of the Sephardim, see Efron, *German Jewry and the Allure of the Sephardic*; Schorsch, 'The Myth of Sephardic Supremacy'; on perceptions of Ottoman Jewish backwardness by the Alliance Israélite Universelle, see Rodrigue, *French Jews, Turkish Jews*.

Edirne (1554), Cairo (1557), and Safed (1578). Gershom Soncino transferred his pioneering printing house from Italy, establishing a press in Salonica in 1527 and in Istanbul in 1530. He printed over a hundred titles in Hebrew, Greek, Latin, and Italian. He was succeeded by his son, Eliezer. His grandson established a press in Egypt in 1557.

Books in Spanish were in high demand among the first generation of Sephardim to settle in the Ottoman empire. The first book printed in Ladino was on the ritual slaughter of animals, *Dinim de shehita y bedika* (1510). The Torah was published in a Ladino translation in Hebrew letters by Eliezer Soncino's press in Istanbul in 1547 and in Latin characters in Ferrara in 1553. Its word-for-word translation from Hebrew into Spanish set the standard for Ladino production. Translations of the Sephardi prayer book followed. A continuous flow of printed kabbalistic works emanated from Safed in the latter part of the sixteenth century and spread to other centres of mystical study. Most *kehalim* printed their own prayer books, which contributed to the preservation of their distinctive rites and rituals.[74]

One of the great accomplishments of the Ottoman printing industry was its preservation of the works of the last generation of rabbis in Spain that were, sometimes serendipitously, saved by refugee scholars and brought to the Ottoman empire. Abraham Saba, one of the last of the prominent Jewish scholars in Iberia, brought some of his manuscripts with him. Manuscripts were also sought by printers among Sephardi refugees in western Europe and North Africa. The intellectual and material losses of 1492 loomed large in the consciousness of scholars and printers. In the introduction to Rashi's *Commentary on the Torah, Haftorah and Five Megillot*, printed in Istanbul in 1506, the printer laments the great loss of books, acknowledging the connection between those losses and the popular support for the newly established presses:

Since that day when God confused the languages of the earth by the sudden and bitter expulsion from Spain . . . books were also abandoned in the trauma of destruction and the confusion of sudden change, for the constant afflictions have left us as an empty shell . . . and because of troubles of the times and the lack of books, people have neglected the education of their children. So that even if they have the Chumash they lack the Targum and if they find that, then they lack the commentaries. May their hearts inspire them to spread the knowledge of the Torah in Israel . . . and to replace some of the numerous works which have been destroyed.[75]

A similar lament appears in the colophon of a copy of the *Mishneh torah* from 1509.

Publishers had to search far and wide for a complete text of any work they wanted to print. Gershom Soncino describes how he sought out works to publish on the title page of the last book that he printed in Istanbul in 1534: 'I sought out and found books that had been blocked off and sealed up for an age, and I brought them forth to the eye of the sun. . . . I went as far as France and Chambery and Genevre, to the rooms where

---

[74] Ya'ari, *Hebrew Printing in the Middle East* (Heb.).

[75] Introduction to Rashi, *Commentary on the Torah, Haftorah and Five Megillot* (Istanbul, 1506), cited in Schmelzer, 'Hebrew Manuscripts and Printed Books among the Sephardim', 264.

they were born, to benefit the multitude with them, for in Spain and in Italy and in all the lands they were unheard.'[76]

The Muslim authorities were extremely suspicious of the printing press, and allowed the Jews to establish their own printing establishments on condition that they use only Hebrew and Latin typefaces, not Arabic. When the Christians introduced their own printing presses more than a century after the Jews, they turned to the Jews for technical advice and assistance. The Muslim printing press would not appear for another century.

The timing of the establishment of printing among the Jews in the Ottoman empire was fortuitous. As in the west, the Sephardim in the east were traumatized by the loss of their libraries and material culture. Their respect for their ancestral heritage did not diminish, even as their knowledge waned. Aware of the fact that their culture was now endangered, they hoped to preserve and renew it through books, schools, sermons, and popular study. Many of their offspring needed guidance and instruction in Judaism. The titles produced in Salonica and Istanbul reflect the varied interests and requirements of this diverse Jewish population. On the one hand, there was a felt need for 'how-to' books for Conversos who were returning to Judaism; on the other, there was a large demand for collections of responsa and sermons of famous scholars. The classic texts of Judaism were also in demand to rebuild lost libraries. Titles of a secular nature, such as scientific literature, works of poetry and drama, travel literature, and history, all rolled off the new presses to quench the thirst for secular texts among many acculturated Iberian immigrants. Menahem Schmelzer speculates that the first collections of midrashim printed in Salonica and Istanbul were produced in response to popular demand, given the amount of midrashic material in Ottoman rabbinic sermons, especially sermons that offered consolation and guidance to a generation in need of both.[77]

The printing houses of Salonica and Istanbul were also instrumental in preserving the language of fifteenth-century Castile that the refugees brought with them and which became known as Ladino, Djudezmo, or Judaeo-Espagnol. It was printed in Rashi script and standardized through being printed. It developed its unique flavour through the addition of words from Turkish, Greek, Arabic, and the other languages of the Ottoman empire. At the same time, it preserved words and expressions that fell into disuse in Spain after 1492 when the Sephardim were cut off from ongoing linguistic developments there. Ladino also preserved the oral traditions of medieval Iberia. Many Sephardi women were illiterate, but they transmitted a rich culture of Ladino proverbs, stories, legends, and songs that formed the identity of their children and celebrated their Jewishness. Ladino drew the Jews of Spain closer together and, paradoxically,

---

[76] Gershom Soncino, title page of David Kimhi, *Mikhlol* (Constantinople, 1534), cited in Glatzer, 'Early Hebrew Printing', 90.

[77] Schmelzer, 'Hebrew Manuscripts and Printed Books among the Sephardim', 264.

further from their past, and played a major role in melding the Sephardi diaspora of Ottoman lands into a people with a common culture.

Beginning with the publication of the first volume of *Me'am loaz* in 1730 (an encyclopedic Ladino work of biblical stories, folk tales, and popular wisdom), the soul of the Sephardim of the Ottoman lands found its greatest cultural expression. The motto 'Favla de djidyo a djidyo' ('Speak to me as one Jew to another [that is, in Ladino]') embodies this affectionate blending of the Hispanic and the Judaic that characterized the Sephardi diaspora in the Ottoman empire.[78]

Prototypes of Secular Leadership: Sephardi Doctors and a 'Woman of Valour'

One area in which Jews were particularly prominent during the sixteenth century was medicine. In spite of papal efforts to restrict their activities, doctors of Converso background held positions in the palaces of the queen of England, the tsar of Russia, the stadholder of the Netherlands, the kings of France and Denmark, and the pope. The Ottoman sultans had no inhibitions when it came to employing Jewish and Converso doctors. They turned to Sephardi physicians almost immediately upon their arrival and even recruited their services in Europe.

The success of Sephardi doctors in Christian and Muslim kingdoms in the sixteenth century was based on several factors. With many branches of the economy closed to Conversos in the Iberian peninsula, a disproportionate number of them turned to the faculties of medicine and theology in post-Expulsion Spain and Portugal. The Iberian universities in Évora, Salamanca, Valladolid, and Alcala were among the most respected in Europe as centres of advanced scientific instruction. Why so many Conversos entered medical faculties is unknown: perhaps the *numerus clausus* was not as stringently applied to medicine;[79] or, since medicine was a traditional Jewish calling that was passed down from father to son, they simply remained in the occupation of their fathers; or a medical career may have demanded less Christian conformity on the part of the practitioner.[80] Whatever the reasons for the prominence of Conversos in medicine, the phenomenon was so obvious during the early years of the reign of Philip IV that it led a group seeking to reform the blood purity laws to enquire somewhat rhetorically: 'Why is a swordmaker automatically considered *limpio* [pure of blood], while a physician is invariably held to be a Jew?'[81] Their popularity and recognized expertise continued in their many lands of dispersion.

The appeal of Jewish physicians to the sultans is undeniable. Unlike their Muslim or

---

[78] On the development of Ladino, see Bunis, 'Distinctive Characteristics of Jewish Ibero-Romance'; id. 'The Language of the Spanish Jews' (Heb.). [79] See Sicroff, *Les Controverses des statuts de 'pureté de sang'*, 211.

[80] On the medical training of Isaac Cardoso and the university ambience in Iberia, see Yerushalmi, *From Spanish Court to Italian Ghetto*, 70–3   [81] See Yerushalmi, *From Spanish Court to Italian Ghetto*, 70–3. 70.

Christian counterparts, whose training was text-based, the Sephardi doctors were products of the new medical curriculum of Europe, including the use of clinical observation as a diagnostic tool. When Mehmet II and his son Bayezid II each founded a medical college in Istanbul, they recruited staff from Europe and actively sought out Sephardi doctors. Between the Expulsion and the seventeenth century, the number of Sephardi doctors in Ottoman court circles increased dramatically. A Turkish government register of court physicians lists four Jews serving alongside fourteen or fifteen Muslim colleagues in 1536/7. Twelve years later, the number of Jewish palace doctors had increased to thirteen or fourteen, alongside seventeen Muslim physicians: an increase from 25 to 47 per cent. By the beginning of the seventeenth century, Jews filled forty-one of the sixty seats on the physician's council at the palace, or 66 per cent.[82] Jewish doctors formed a separate guild of their own in the Ottoman court alongside the Muslim one.[83] The sultans, always wary of assassination at the hands of contenders to the throne, trusted their Jewish physicians, as they usually lacked any ties with the harem, where conspiracies and intrigues flourished. Naturally, not all of the Jewish physicians were politically neutral, and some even met a violent end. Jacobo (Yakub) Hekim, chief physician to Mehmet II, died under mysterious circumstances at the age of 52, probably as the result of a plot instigated by the sultan's son and successor, Bayezid II. An earlier plot on the sultan's life, initiated by the Venetians, had been intercepted by Hekim. Between 1475 and 1477, a total of fourteen attempts on Mehmet's life were recorded.

The history of the Hamon family reflects the intersection of scientific training, social status, community service, and access to broader political circles that was the hallmark of Sephardi courtiers. Joseph Hamon was born in Spain and rose to medical prominence in the final years of the Muslim kingdom of Granada. At the time of the Expulsion, he moved to the Ottoman empire and entered the palace medical corps in the service of Sultan Bayezid II. He subsequently practised medicine for six years under Sultan Selim I (r. 1512–20). Hamon accompanied the sultan as his physician on several military campaigns, including the victorious campaigns against the Mamelukes in Egypt and Syria in 1516. He died in 1518 under unclear circumstances, possibly assassinated in a conspiracy against the sultan. His son Moses (1490–1554) succeeded him in the palace medical corps.

Moses Hamon served in the courts of Selim I and Suleiman the Magnificent, and eventually became one of the most powerful men in Turkey. His career intersected with the saga of Doña Gracia Mendes Nasi, then the most powerful Jewish woman in Europe. Moses Hamon apparently hoped to betroth his son to Doña Gracia's daughter, although the match did not materialize. However, he was able to facilitate the rescue of Doña Gracia and Don Joseph from the intrigues of the Inquisition in Venice and

---

[82] Baron, *A Social and Religious History of the Jews*, xviii. 74–7.
[83] Rozen, *A History of the Jewish Community in Istanbul*, 208.

managed, with the help of the sultan, to spirit them out of Europe to Istanbul and to salvage some of her fortune.

Moses Hamon also supported several Jewish schools in Istanbul and sponsored the publication of the works of refugee scholars. He founded and supported a yeshiva where Joseph Taitatzak presided, and a Hamon Synagogue is listed among those of sixteenth-century Istanbul. Like many contemporary Iberian aristocrats, Hamon was a discerning book-collector who accumulated an outstanding library. He is also remembered as the author of the first treatise on dentistry written in Turkish. When a blood libel was raised against the Jews of Amasya in 1553, Hamon interceded on their behalf. As a result, Suleiman decreed that all future accusations of blood libel should be brought directly to the sultan himself. Suleiman's response may have been a reiteration of an earlier order issued by Mehmet II.

Despite, or perhaps as a result of, his warm relationship with the sultan, Hamon was accused by Muslim doctors of purposely erring in his treatment of the sultan's gout.[84] He died in 1554, in the wake of the dismissal of his protector, Grand Vizier Rustem Pasha. Despite the dangers of practising medicine in an increasingly politicized court, Moses' son Joseph followed in the footsteps of his father and grandfather, continuing the multiple roles of the traditional Sephardi courtier. He was succeeded in turn by his son Isaac Hamon. For approximately a century, members of the Hamon family served as court doctors.[85] Another famous Sephardi physician, Amatus Lusitanus, arrived during the wave of Portuguese Jewish immigration in the middle of the sixteenth century. His tumultuous life was characterized by professional dedication, multiple identities, and constant wandering. He was born João Rodrigues de Castelo Branco in Portugal in 1511 and grew up in a Marrano household where he acquired some Jewish knowledge and a strong Jewish identity. He received his medical training at the University of Salamanca, and after the completion of his studies, either unable or unwilling to return to Portugal, he left Iberia and began a lifetime of exile. In 1535 he joined the stream of Conversos as they fled before the establishment of the Portuguese Inquisition.

Lusitanus initially settled in Antwerp, where he joined a growing colony of Marranos and became the medical attendant to the Mendes family. He followed Doña Gracia quite suddenly from Antwerp to England and Holland and settled in Italy in 1546. During a brief stay in Venice, he came into contact with the philosopher Jacob Mantino and treated the niece of Pope Julius III, before moving on to the University of

---

[84] Heyd, 'Moses Hamon', 163; see also id., 'Blood Libels in Turkey in the Fifteenth and Sixteenth Centuries' (Heb.); A. Cohen, 'Ritual Murder Accusations against Jews during the Days of Suleiman the Magnificent'; Gross, 'La Famille juive des Hamon'.

[85] See Bornstein-Makovsky, 'The Jewish Community in Istanbul in the Mid-Seventeenth Century'; A. Cohen, 'Ritual Murder Accusations Against Jews during the Days of Suleiman the Magnificent'; Heyd, 'Moses Hamon'; see also Murphey, 'Jewish Contributions to Ottoman Medicine'.

Ferrara in 1546 at the invitation of Duke Ercole II to teach anatomy and medicinal plants. In 1547, while lecturing in Ferrara, he performed a dissection on twelve cadavers, demonstrating the function of venous valves in the circulation of blood. He reportedly stunned the professional medical audience, since his demonstration contradicted the accepted medical wisdom of his day. Among those in attendance was Giambattista Canano, to whom the discovery of valves was later erroneously attributed.[86] Lusitanus also treated Pope Julius III several times during his sojourn in Italy. Rejecting an invitation from the king of Poland to serve in his entourage, he moved to Ancona in 1550, where he was caught in the papal round-up of Portuguese Jews. He succeeded in fleeing, later recalling sadly the loss of several of his medical manuscripts.[87] From Ancona he moved to Pesaro and on to Ragusa, ultimately arriving in Salonica in 1559, where he returned openly to Judaism. His last years were filled with service to Muslims and Christians, medical research, and the training of doctors. He died in 1568 while treating victims of one of Salonica's notorious plagues.[88] Amatus Lusitanus wrote in Latin and his medical publications enjoyed wide fame in Europe's most advanced medical circles, particularly his multi-volume *Curationum medicinalium centuriae septem*, written between 1549 and 1561, in which he presented 700 medical case histories, describing their treatment and results. His works reveal familiarity with classical literature and new scientific methodologies. Although Sephardim remained in medical fields into the eighteenth century their contacts with European scientific advances diminished, and in their political influence they were eventually replaced by Ottoman Christians.

Sephardi Leadership and the Quest for Unity: The Boycott of Ancona

Perhaps the greatest test of the Sephardi community and the efficacy of the diplomatic skills of Doña Gracia was the boycott of Ancona in 1556. The incident began in the port of Ancona in the Papal States, where 100 Portuguese Jewish men and women were arrested and charged with Judaizing in 1555. This charge carried the death sentence. Former Conversos had settled earlier in the city with the express assurance of the city's authorities that they would enjoy the same protections and privileges as other foreigners, it being understood that they would not be prosecuted for their former or current religious persuasions. They were also assured that there would be no ghetto,

---

[86] Friedenwald and Sigerist, 'Biography of Lusitanus'.

[87] Feingold, *Three Jewish Physicians of the Renaissance*; Friedenwald, *The Jews and Medicine*, i. 332–80.

[88] Leibowitz, 'Amatus Lusitanus', 35. Lusitanus's medical oath, composed in 1559, is still administered today at the Albert Einstein Medical College of Yeshiva University in New York. It bears the Hebrew date: 'Thessalonicae datum: Anno Mundi 5319'. He has been belatedly recognized by Portugal: his picture is located above the door of the Medical Faculty at the University of Coimbra, and he appears in a pictorial representation of 'Portuguese medicine' in the Medical Faculty at the University of Lisbon.

that they would not be compelled to wear distinguishing clothing or pay any taxes that were not applicable to all other foreign merchants in the city, and that they would be free to come and go as they pleased. Such rights were enjoyed by the Levantine merchants in a few other cities in Italy and had been confirmed by successive popes. Pope Julius III (r. 1550–5) had even acknowledged that the conversion of the Jews to Christianity in Portugal had been forced upon them and, consequently, lacked legitimacy in the eyes of the Church.

However, the accession of Pope Paul IV (r. 1555–9) marked a new era for Europe and its Jews. A stalwart advocate of Christian orthodoxy, Paul IV is most closely identified with the Counter-Reformation, and perceived himself as the defender of Catholicism against heresy. Refusing to be bound by the promises his predecessors had made, he launched a fierce campaign against Jews of various backgrounds. One of his first acts upon election to the papacy was the revocation of all earlier concessions that had been made to both Marranos and practising Jews. On 14 July 1555 he promulgated the bull *Cum nimis absurdum*, which condemned the Jews of the Papal States to ghettoization, and imposed severe restrictions on Jewish economic activity. Soon thereafter Portuguese Jews in Ancona were rounded up and tortured. One victim committed suicide, and twenty-four others were eventually burned at the stake. Amatus Lusitanus was among those rounded up, but he was later released. As the news of the burning of the twenty-four victims spread, prayers were recited as far away as London. It was not unusual for the fate of a condemned Marrano to reverberate among far-flung Marrano enclaves in Europe.

As the drama of Ancona was unfolding, Duke Ercole II of Ferrara watched the events with keen interest. He contemplated the possible benefit to his realm if he could embrace the hapless victims of Ancona. At the same time Guidobaldo II, duke of Urbino, offered shelter to some of them in his port of Pesaro, only 37 miles from Ancona. He was persuaded by Jewish arguments that Pesaro would benefit from their presence and the trade they would bring. While negotiations were under way to resettle the Portuguese Jews of Ancona, the Jews engaged in their customary response to persecution: bribes, prayers, and quiet diplomacy. The persecution in Italy would provide an unusual test of Ottoman Jewry.

As soon as word of the arrests reached Istanbul, Doña Gracia and the Sephardim were galvanized into action.[89] If former Conversos, who had been promised immunity from the Inquisition by Popes Paul III in 1535 and Julius III in 1553, were not safe in papal Ancona, clearly former Conversos were unsafe anywhere in Christendom. At least two of Doña Gracia's business agents were caught in the round-up, and she turned to Sultan Suleiman to intervene on their behalf. She stressed that the imprisonment of her agents

---

[89] See C. Roth, *The House of Nasi*, 134–75; Saperstein, 'Martyrs, Merchants and Rabbis'; Bonazzolli, 'Ebrei italiani, portoghesi, levantini sulla piazza commerciale di Ancona'; Cooperman, 'Portuguese Conversos in Ancona'.

and other Levantine Jews (and their potential condemnation) would cause grave economic loss to the sultan, and argued that the pope's actions insulted his dignity since they violated the rights of his subjects.[90] Suleiman was the mightiest military figure of his day: his formidable janissaries had recently annexed Hungary, and the siege of Vienna had brought Muslim armies into the heart of Europe. He was receptive to the determined woman's arguments.

Doña Gracia prevailed upon the sultan to send a letter of protest, which she and Don Joseph might well have drafted, on behalf of the Jews of Ancona to the pope:

> When you shall have received my Divine and Imperial Seal, which will be presented to you, you must know that certain persons of the race of the Jews have informed My Elevated and Sublime Porte that, whereas certain subjects and tributaries of Ours have gone to your territories to traffic ... their goods and property have been seized at your command. This seizure has resulted in the loss of Our Treasury of the amount of 400,000 ducats, over and above the amount of damage caused to Our subjects, who have been ruined and cannot meet their obligations to Our said Treasury arising from the customs duties and commerce of Our ports, of which they are in charge. We therefore request Your Holiness, that by virtue of Our universal and illustrious Seal, which will be brought to you by Secretary Cachard, a man of the service of the Most High and Magnanimous King, Prince of Princes of the said generation of the Messiah Jesus, His most Christian Majesty, the king of France, Our very dear friend, you will be pleased to set free Our abovementioned ... subjects, with all the property which they had. ... In this way, they will be able to satisfy their debts, and the above-mentioned customs officials will no longer have an excuse for their failure to pay by virtue of the arrest of said prisoners. By so doing, you will give Us occasion to treat in friendly fashion your subjects and other Christians who traffic in these parts.[91]

Despite the none-too-subtle threats against the sultan's Christian subjects, the note was only partially successful. The pope agreed to release those prisoners who could be considered Levantine subjects by virtue of having resided in the Ottoman empire, including one of Doña Gracia's agents.

After the prisoners who refused to renounce Judaism were burned at the stake, a scheme to boycott Ancona and divert all Ottoman trade to Pesaro began to take shape. The duke of Pesaro welcomed the opportunity to strengthen his city's commerce at Ancona's expense. Each party had much to gain from an effective economic boycott. However, in order to be effective the boycott would require solidarity among the Ottoman Jewish merchants. But co-ordinated action is no simple matter for a widely dispersed and internally divided minority. The proposed boycott highlighted the conflicting national interests of the Jews and the challenges posed by their Converso past. The affluent Portuguese Jews in Italy, with their patrician airs and more acculturated European demeanour, were resented by the poorer Italian and Ashkenazi money-

---

[90] See Baron, *A Social and Religious History of the Jews*, xiv. 35–43, 319 n. 35; Saperstein, 'Martyrs, Merchants and Rabbis'; C. Roth, *The House of Nasi*, 134–74. Several details of the event are confirmed by contemporary historian Joseph Hakohen in his *Sefer emek habakhah*.

[91] Suleiman the Magnificent to Pope Paul VI, cited in Baron, *A Social and Religious History of the Jews*, xiv. 40.

lenders and pedlars, and by the descendants of the Spanish Jews who had lost everything when they fled in 1492.

The Ashkenazi and Italian Jews in Ancona were alarmed at the possible repercussions they might suffer from a boycott, including economic sanctions and even expulsion. Led by their elderly rabbi, Moses Basola, they immediately dispatched their own letters to the Jews of the Levant, warning them of the dangers of papal reprisals should the boycott be successful. They also pointed out that the port of Pesaro was vastly inferior to that of Ancona.[92] The question was also raised as to what would be the fate of the Jews of both Ancona and Pesaro should the boycott fail.

The Jewish merchants of Salonica, many of whom were former Marranos, wholeheartedly agreed to divert their trade to Pesaro, on condition that those of Istanbul, Edirne, and Bursa also did so. The Jews of Salonica may have calculated that a blow to Ancona would further benefit them since Ancona possessed a rival textile industry. The response of the Jews of Istanbul was more hesitant. Rabbi Joshua Soncino, of the prominent family of printers, reported that he openly wept upon hearing of the fate of the Jews of Ancona and would enthusiastically join with the other kehalim of the city in implementing the boycott, but he needed clarification of the conflicting accounts of the events in Italy to determine what were the legal parameters of the case.[93] He agreed to join the boycott for the trial period of eight months—from summer to Passover of 1556—at the end of which the boycott would either become permanent, if all the Ottoman Jews had joined, or expire. However, several pointed practical as well as legal questions were raised: should the port of Pesaro really be rewarded for the crimes of Ancona, since it had only recently indulged in an antisemitic outrage of its own which included the desecration of Torah scrolls? The perpetrators of these acts reportedly included the brother of the duke himself. Moreover, Guidobaldo II had recently served as captain general of the papal armies. Why assist in enriching a man of his ilk? Other factors, Soncino added, also required consideration. How would the duke of Urbino react if the anticipated enrichment of Pesaro did not occur? How would the pope respond to the spectre of a successful boycott? What reprisals might be taken against the Jews still residing in Ancona? And what danger did the boycott pose to the Jews in the Papal States in general?[94]

Perhaps the most revealing objection Soncino raised concerned the equity of boycotts and the wisdom of the Portuguese Jews in settling in the Papal States in the first place. After all, he argued, Italy was not their only option. Had they chosen to come to the Ottoman empire, they would not have endangered their Jewish brethren:

It cannot be said that it is a commandment to ratify this covenant in order to avenge the spilled blood of our brethren. These Jews used to live according to the Gentiles in Portugal, and came to live under the wings of the Holy Presence according to the laws of Moses. . . . They should not have

---

[92] Baron, *A Social and Religious History of the Jews*, xiv. 41.
[93] Soncino, *Naḥalah leyehoshua*, 39b–40a.   [94] Ibid. 46a–b.

made their residence in the lands of the Gentiles, even though they were given all sorts of promises, since it is well known that the Gentiles would take revenge on them because they denied their faith. They brought the damage upon themselves. And lost their lives with their own hands.[95]

Soncino's resentment of the Portuguese Jews was palpable. Clearly, the Portuguese were not entitled to endanger other Jews for the sake of business. The fact that they had lived as Christians and returned to Judaism in, of all places, the Papal States was especially troubling.

The fissures in the Ottoman Jewish community surfaced soon after the boycott commenced. The Jews of Bursa adamantly refused to take part, citing the inferiority of the port of Pesaro; however, there was no Portuguese *kahal* in Bursa and consequently little empathy for and probably few commercial relations with the Portuguese Jews of Ancona.[96] Merchants in other cities seemed no less reluctant to divert their trade to Pesaro. Even before the expiry of the eight-month trial period many had violated the boycott. The Jews of Pesaro, fearing reprisals since the promised prosperity to the city had not materialized, pleaded desperately for Ottoman solidarity and turned personally to Doña Gracia.

Doña Gracia and Don Joseph urged Ottoman rabbis to send letters in support of the boycott. Doña Gracia argued that the lives of the Jews of Pesaro were now at stake, and she threatened to withhold her considerable financial support from recalcitrant Ottoman *kehalim*. Despite this, the Ottoman Jews remained unaccommodating. Many had never experienced the Inquisition personally and felt more sympathy for the vulnerable Italian Jews in Ancona than for the former Conversos. Doña Gracia and Don Joseph decided to bring particular pressure to bear on Joshua Soncino for his refusal to support the boycott. Soncino, although of Italian background, led a Spanish *kahal* in Istanbul. When further prodded, he pointed out that conflicting accounts of the boycott had reached the Ottoman empire and offered to pay for an emissary to be sent to the Jews of Venice and Padua to clarify all the facts of the case and to ascertain what the ramifications of a boycott would be on Jews in both Pesaro and Ancona. He also suggested that the duke of Urbino be informed that implementation of a boycott was impossible since 'there is no king of the Jewish people, it is impossible to achieve uniformity of opinion and to compel the merchants to carry out the condition which the refugees made with them'.[97] It was hoped that this might deflect the duke's anger and protect the local Jews.

Soncino's reservations were only the beginning of the rupture within Istanbul Jewry. Two Sephardi *kehalim*, Kahal Portugal and Kahal Gerush, decided to implement the boycott, as did the two factions of the Ashkenazi *kahal*, although the latter two

---

[95] Soncino, *Naḥalah leyehoshua*, 39b–40a.

[96] On the sequence of the events and responses of other contemporary Ottoman rabbis, see Saperstein, 'Martyrs, Merchants and Rabbis', 225, 227 nn. 36, 37.   [97] Soncino, *Naḥalah leyehoshua*, 45a.

were probably bowing to Don Joseph's threats to withhold financial contributions and to expel their rabbi from his yeshiva. The other Sephardi congregations of Istanbul refused to join. Soncino remarked on the gravity of the divisions among the Sephardim: 'the ten Sephardic congregations here in Constantinople had never been divided among themselves on a matter of such great importance'.[98] When the Romaniote Jews were asked to join the boycott, they replied that they had not been approached throughout the affair and had no commercial relations with Ancona; nevertheless, for the sake of Jewish solidarity, they would join. In the meantime, Doña Gracia's ships were avoiding Ancona, docking instead in Pesaro.

Despite Soncino's insistence that more information was necessary before a boycott could take place, Doña Gracia decided to proclaim the boycott in the name of Istanbul's Sephardi *kehalim*. Those who did not comply, she warned, would face excommunication. Soncino refused to be cowed, asserting that, under Jewish law, agreement elicited under pressure had no validity; no one was permitted to protect themselves at someone else's expense; and a minority was not bound by the opinions of the majority, if the minority had consistently expressed dissent in the matter.[99] Soncino also asserted that it was not clear from the correspondence with Ancona and Pesaro which community was telling the truth, and he feared that implementing the boycott would exacerbate already existing frictions among the Jews in Italy. Agreeing to it without further verification of the facts would impugn his rabbinic integrity.[100]

Doña Gracia next turned to all the Sephardi rabbis, reminding them of the danger to Pesaro's Conversos that was now imminent. Such a danger should take precedence over any financial losses that might be incurred. She received the backing of two leading authorities, Joseph Karo and Moses Trani. However, the boycott of Ancona failed for lack of Jewish solidarity. As many feared, Duke Guidobaldo II succumbed to Vatican pressure and ousted the Ancona refugees from his territory.

Doña Gracia understood the real dangers that the Portuguese Jews faced in Europe, but her campaign was thwarted by the splintered nature and divergent interests of Ottoman Jewry. The various opinions of the Ottoman rabbis reflected different assessments of the situation, different loyalties and economic interests, and ultimately the different backgrounds of their respective communities. Many Ottoman rabbis were probably nonplussed by Doña Gracia's imperious behaviour, compounded by the anomaly of a politically powerful Jewish woman. The entire drama illustrates how deeply divided Ottoman Jewry was in the 1550s. It was a collection of disparate immigrant groups speaking a variety of languages, drawn to different narratives of their past, and experiencing the plight of the Jews in Europe in a variety of ways. The Ashkenazim and the Romaniotes were separate from the Sephardim, although already strongly identified with the Spanish majority. The Portuguese Jews, only recently Conversos, were not easily integrated into the older communities. Their deepest bonds

[98] Ibid. 46b.   [99] See Saperstein, 'Martyrs, Merchants and Rabbis', 225.   [100] Ibid. 223.

were with fellow former Marranos. It was premature to speak of a Sephardi Ottoman Jewish entity in 1556. As is known from the American Jewish attempt to introduce a boycott against the Nazis in the 1930s, it is almost impossible to induce a widely dispersed people like the Jews to implement an effective boycott.

The End of the Ottoman 'Silver Age'

During the sixteenth century the Ottoman empire proved to be not only a refuge but the fertile soil in which a new Sephardi civilization took root. Whereas in the 1560s Joseph ibn Leb could speak of Salonica as a city in which 'every [Jewish] man speaks his own native tongue' and 'each congregation appears to be an independent city',[101] and Eliyahu Mizrahi declared that 'each congregation has the status of a separate city' in regard to customs and ordinances,[102] by the end of the century, the former identities of the Jewish groups were beginning to fade as a new Sephardi entity emerged. That entity was predominantly urban, Ladino-speaking, and the proud possessor of an Iberian Jewish past that it now romanticized and idealized.

The Sephardi civilization that coalesced in the Ottoman empire between 1492 and the end of the sixteenth century combined Jewish scholarship from Spain, mysticism from Safed, and Hispanic customs with music from the Turkish courts and bazaars, and indigenous folk traditions and wisdom rooted in the Mediterranean Muslim world. This new Sephardi community displaced the Greek civilization of the Romaniotes, the Converso leanings of the Portuguese, and the language and rituals of the exiles from southern Italy. It was eventually shared by young and old, the rabbinic elite, the urban middle class of industrious merchants, the thousands of skilled craftsmen and artisans, and the tens of thousands of indigent Jews. Salonica was its intellectual centre: in the words of Samuel Usque, a 'madre de Judesmo', 'a mother of Judaism'. Istanbul was its political centre.

The eastern Sephardi diaspora reached a peak at the end of the sixteenth century, at the same time as the Ottoman empire reached its zenith. However, the smoothly running Ottoman state was beginning to slowly unravel. Signs of decay were manifest. The competence of the sultan was critical to the proper functioning of the Ottoman state, and the early sixteenth-century sultans were aggressive, engaged in leadership battles, and open to innovation. These qualities boded well for the resettlement and development of Ottoman Jewry. After the death of Suleiman the Magnificent in 1566, his successors grew increasingly removed from the conduct of public affairs, secluded in their palaces, subject to the machinations of their viziers and the conspiracies of competing wives and concubines in the harem. Incompetence and mediocrity replaced

---

[101] Joseph ibn Leb, *Responsa*, cited in Bornstein-Makovetsky, 'Structure, Organization, and Spiritual Life of the Sephardi Jews in the Ottoman Empire', 316.

[102] Eliyahu Mizrahi, *Responsa*, cited in Rozen, *A History of the Jewish Community in Istanbul*, 317.

dynamism. Similarly, the office of the grand vizier, with brief and noteworthy interruptions, passed from men of merit to the victors of intrigue and corruption. Abuses of power soon permeated every level of government.

The traditional Ottoman landholding system also began to break down. By the 1590s entire provinces were in revolt against military conscription, excessive taxation, and widespread corruption. Merchants could no longer travel safely in the countryside. The well-disciplined Ottoman armies began to experience military stalemates followed by a chain of decisive setbacks. As the prolonged Ottoman campaigns against the Venetians in the Mediterranean, the Habsburgs in central Europe and the Balkans, and the Persians and the Russians on the eastern borders stalled, the empire began to contract. One of the economic consequences of military defeat and agricultural collapse was the debasement of the Ottoman currency. Each military campaign brought new taxes to compensate for the shrinking state coffers. The minorities were especially vulnerable to abuses of power and the breakdown of public order.

The impact of these events affected Jews of every class. The wealthy grew poorer, and the ranks of the impoverished swelled. The decline of the affluent affected the learning of the community, since they provided most of the support for educational institutions. In addition, the Jews could no longer boast of their personal knowledge of European technologies. Jewish immigration from Europe waned, and, with it, the number of Sephardi diplomats decreased. The Sephardi elite lost their positions of power in the palace: Greek and Armenian Christians now acted as diplomats and translators, sending their sons to Europe to serve as liaisons between Europe and the Ottoman empire. Jewish expertise in crafts and manufacturing also declined. The English, Dutch, and Tuscans competed successfully with the weavers of Salonica in the textile industry. The Ottoman Jews were supplanted economically and politically at home and abroad.

The Jews, like the Muslims of the Ottoman empire, looked back with nostalgia at their history. The Ottomans invoked the virile Turkish warriors of Anatolia and their early victorious sultans to counteract the spectacle of mounting military defeats and territorial losses. The Jews recalled the medieval courtiers of Spain, the rabbis of Castile, and the lineage and honour of their ancestors in a golden age in Spain to compensate for their diminishing fortunes. While the classic Sephardi courtier had provided services in the past, the descendants of the courtiers now possessed mostly hollow pretensions.

Some observers have attributed the decline of Ottoman Jewry in the seventeenth century to the cataclysmic debacle of Shabateanism. True, the Jewish masses in the east and the west were surprisingly receptive to the bizarre messianic claims and antinomian behaviour of Shabetai Tsevi, and greeted his messianic pronouncements in 1665 with almost uniform enthusiasm. The mournful spectacle of Ashkenazi refugees from the pogroms that occurred between 1648 and 1654 streaming into Istanbul seemed to confirm that the end was nigh. Not even Shabetai Tsevi's shocking conversion to Islam in 1666 or his death in 1676 could end the messianic enthusiasm entirely. Confusion and disillusionment soon prevailed among Ottoman Jewry. The Jewish authorities introduced strict censorship and greater rabbinic control in order to blot out all mention of the messianic fiasco. Even uttering Shabetai Tsevi's name was banned as a reminder of the community's embarrassment and disgrace.

The blow to the Ottoman Jewish community caused by Shabetai Tsevi's career fell most heavily on Salonica, where hundreds of Jewish families converted to Islam in imitation of their leader. They formed a separate, influential sect, known as the Dönmeh (from the Turkish word meaning 'to turn') that persisted until the twentieth century.[103] Yet, despite the seriousness of the threat that the Dönmeh posed, it cannot be asserted that the tragic Shabatean movement caused the decline of Ottoman Jewry; rather, it accelerated processes of change already in motion. By the mid-seventeenth century the Jews of Istanbul and Salonica were no longer a fractious group of outcasts from Europe. The diversity of customs that had enlivened the first generations of Sephardi life in the Ottoman empire had slowly evolved into a new Sephardi entity. As the failed boycott of Ancona suggests, they were divided in their views of themselves as a community. Some detached themselves from the Sephardim who remained in Europe; others still viewed them as part of the same people with a common destiny. The melding of the many Jews in Ottoman lands during the sixteenth century is described by Samuel de Medina:

And customs became confused and almost everyone adopted the liturgy of the Sephardim since they are the majority in the empire and their liturgy is pure and sweet to every one, or most people abandoned their ritual and were attracted to the Sephardi rite as it exists today in the great city of Salonica. . . . Almost the only one that has not changed its ritual is the Ashkenazi community.[104]

By 1650 the Sephardi diaspora had many of the hallmarks of a Sephardi people, speaking to each other in Ladino, a language both Hispanic and Ottoman, Jewish and transnational, reflecting the wisdom and lived experience of generations of Jews.

[103] M. D. Baer, *Dönme*.
[104] Samuel de Medina, *Oraḥ ḥayim*, cited in Hacker, 'The Sephardim in the Ottoman Empire', 116.

CHAPTER SIX

JEWISH LIFE IN AMSTERDAM AND THE FORMATION OF THE WESTERN SEPHARDI DIASPORA 1579–1700

> Plainly, God desires them to live somewhere.
> Why, then, not here rather than elsewhere?
> HUGO GROTIUS, *Remonstrance Concerning the Regulations to be Imposed upon the Jews*

> Blessed art thou, O Lord our God, who has shown us your wonderful mercy in the city of Amsterdam, the praiseworthy.
> ZADOK PERELHEIM upon the inauguration of the Talmud Tora Synagogue in Amsterdam

> For they are very particular and do not mingle . . . with the Jews of other nations.
> ISAAC DE PINTO, *Apologie pour la Nation Juive*

Throughout the sixteenth and seventeenth centuries a steady stream of Conversos embarked upon a twofold journey: a physical trek northward to freedom and a spiritual journey to the practice of Judaism. Born in Spain and Portugal several generations after the Expulsion, they had no personal experience of life in a Jewish community. What united them was a sense of shared oppression at the hands of the Inquisition and the collective memory, however faint, of being *portugueses de la nación hebrea*, *homens de nação*, or simply members of the *nação*, the 'Nation'. They formed a distinctive social unit with extraordinarily tight bonds in Seville, Madrid, Lima, and elsewhere, and nurtured close family ties and a sense of kinship with other Portuguese and Spanish Conversos, wherever they were. This background, so different from that of those Sephardim whose ancestors migrated to Italy or the Ottoman empire immediately after the Expulsion and who consequently remained anchored in Jewish life without interruption, produced a new and different historical trajectory. During the course of the seventeenth century the few nascent Portuguese Jewish communities that emerged in the west won the right of residence and worship in countries where Jewish residence had been either non-existent or unknown for hundreds of years. The Amsterdam community outstripped the others in culture and affluence and served as their model and guide. Amsterdam, in turn, drew its models of Jewish community from the Sephardim of Venice.

The city of Amsterdam was on the cusp of its greatest flowering at the time of the arrival of the first Portuguese Jews in the 1580s and 1590s. An ingenious system of canals had been created in the sixteenth century to link the various parts of the city. An enormous new canal belt was initiated in 1613, and newly filled-in land served to house an expanding population. In 1600 the city contained 50,000 inhabitants; by 1650 the number had surpassed 150,000; and by 1750 it had reached 250,000. Immigrants were pouring in by the thousands: Huguenots from France, Mennonites and migrant workers from Germany, Dutch fleeing the wars between the Catholics and Protestants in the Netherlands, and mulattos from Suriname. Its Jewish population grew apace: from the Iberian peninsula, France, Germany, Poland, the Ottoman empire, and Italy. A new political reality, the United Provinces of the Netherlands, was emerging, and with it a new model of Jewish community, the western Sephardi diaspora.

According to the Union of Utrecht, which brought the new political entity into being, 'nobody shall be persecuted or examined for religious reasons'.[1] Although Jews were not specifically mentioned, and the article was intended to bring a measure of peace between warring Catholics and Protestants, it suggested the possibility of Jewish settlement. Popular myth notwithstanding, the United Provinces of the Netherlands did not constitute a haven of religious freedom. While a kaleidoscope of religious groups, including Remonstrants, Mennonites, Socinians, Quakers, Catholics, Lutherans, Calvinists, Arminians, and Jews, dwelt in Amsterdam, the public practice of any religion outside the Calvinist Reformed Church was forbidden: freedom of conscience was guaranteed, provided that non-Protestant worship was conducted privately. Dutch tolerance, mythologized by Sephardi author Daniel Levi de Barrios in his *Triompho de govierno popular, y de la antiguedad holandesa* (1683/4), was in reality in short supply. A paradoxical situation existed: the Dutch republic was religiously pluralistic under an officially intolerant Calvinist Church. Each city in the union retained its autonomy and could decide whether it would admit Jews. In those few Dutch places where Jews were tolerated, it was as a result of Dutch pragmatism rather than principle. Within these limitations, various Christian confessions and a limited number of oppressed Jews from east and west were able to carve out social and political space for themselves.[2]

Amsterdam soon proved to be a magnet for Jews, Conversos, and Marranos. Conversos began to arrive during the last decade of the sixteenth century, and continued to come in small groups or as individuals throughout the seventeenth century. Most arrived via France, where they had lived as Catholics. Sephardi settlers increased steadily in the course of the seventeenth century. From 200 in 1609, the Portuguese

---

[1] Union of Utrecht (1579), Art. 13.
[2] Bodian, 'Liberty of Conscience and the Jews in the Dutch Republic'. Each city retained the right to admit or deny admission to Jews according to the Union of Dordrecht of 1580.

congregation grew to 1,000 in 1630; 2,500 in 1675; and reached approximately 3,000 members in 1700. Some estimates of the Sephardi population are as high as 5,000.[3] Portuguese Conversos did not remain the Jewish majority for very long. Ashkenazi refugees fleeing the devastation of the Thirty Years War (1618–48) in Germany, pogroms in Poland, and the Swedish invasions of Lithuania (1648–52) began to arrive, and outnumbered the Sephardim by the latter part of the seventeenth century. While the Sephardi population in Amsterdam remained steady thereafter at approximately 3,000, the population of Ashkenazim rose to 21,000 by 1795.

Amsterdam was the centre of global commerce in seventeenth-century Europe. In 1631 the philosopher Descartes famously declared: 'In this city there is no one, except me, who is not involved in trade.'[4] It was unlike the handful of other cities where Jews lived in western Europe. It possessed few palaces, and the churches tended to be austere and aniconic. The soul of Amsterdam was trade. Its warehouses overflowed with timber and grain from the Baltic region and tobacco, cacao, and sugar from the western hemisphere for transhipment to other parts of western Europe. Shipbuilding, even including ships for its enemy Spain,[5] and commerce kept much of the city's population employed. With the fall of Antwerp to Philip II of Spain in 1585, the city was subjected to a naval blockade by the Dutch which lasted ten years. As a result, the River Scheldt silted up, and about half the population of Antwerp, including numerous artists, diamond cutters, and a small number of Conversos, left for Amsterdam. According to Jonathan Israel, the rise of the Amsterdam Jewish community was not the result of migration from Antwerp, although some Portuguese Jews were included in the wave of immigrants from there. Rather, it was the extended blockade of Antwerp that acted as the 'midwife of Dutch Sephardic Jewry'. The Dutch ban on maritime trade with Flanders in 1595 compelled the Lisbon traders to send their own agents directly to the main distribution centres of Amsterdam, Rotterdam, Rouen, and Emden.[6] With the cessation of hostilities between Holland and Spain in 1609, Portuguese Jewish merchants found themselves in the ideal position to conduct trade between Holland and the Iberian peninsula. Amsterdam quickly emerged as the main centre for Portuguese merchants and as the centre of the western Sephardi diaspora. The Conversos who appeared at this point in Amsterdam were not relegated to a ghetto but concentrated voluntarily in a few neighbourhoods. They eagerly seized the opportunities which the new society promised, embracing its cosmopolitanism and openness. These qualities

---

[3] On population figures, see Swetschinski, *Reluctant Cosmopolitans*, 67–8. Bloom offers the figure of 2,500 Sephardim in 1674 (*The Economic Activities of the Jews of Amsterdam*, 31 n. 138, 203 n. 4); Jonathan Israel estimates 6,200 Jews in all of Holland, with the Sephardim numbering 3,000 in Amsterdam ('The Republic of the United Netherlands', table 3.1 (p. 100)). The Italian historian Gregorio Leti claimed there were 1,400 Jewish families in the Netherlands in 1690 (see Israel, 'Gregorio Leti', 270).

[4] René Descartes, letter to Guez de Balzac, in Descartes, *Correspondance*, 203.

[5] Israel, 'The Economic Contribution of Dutch Sephardi Jewry to Holland's Golden Age', 513–23.

[6] Israel, *The Dutch Republic*, 508.

would prove challenging to the Jewish newcomers as they sought to regulate their interactions with other groups.

By 1600 a handful of Conversos had settled on the Breestraat, a newer part of Amsterdam, in the Vlooienburg district. The economically and ethnically mixed neighbourhood offered sufficient land for the regents of Amsterdam and wealthier immigrants from Antwerp to build palatial townhouses, but it also included the ateliers of artists and the modest dwellings of craftsmen. It was here that Rembrandt lived side by side with Portuguese Conversos—he could see into the house of the congregation's chief rabbi, Saul Morteira, from his window, and rented out his basement as storage space to Portuguese merchants[7]—finding their mien and way of life a fascinating subject for artistic depiction. Significantly, nobody took special note of this aspect of the popular artist's work: the Portuguese Jewish presence was apparently not considered remarkable or even particularly noteworthy in Amsterdam's cosmopolitan setting.

Newly arrived Conversos were generally eager to begin the difficult process of Judaization immediately. Not having experienced life in an organized Jewish community and finding none in place, they were forced to build their institutions from scratch. In the process, they devised new patterns of identity in which loyalty to the group was fundamental, but what constituted that group was determined equally by their Iberian cultural background, their bonds of kinship, and their idiosyncratic notions of Judaism. Portuguese remained their spoken language; Spanish was, by and large, their language of literary expression; and Hebrew and Spanish were their liturgical languages. The customary institutions of a Jewish community, such as synagogues, charitable funds, and community regulations (*ascamot*), were quickly established. However, the *ascamot* did not apply Jewish law to commerce. This novel separation of spiritual life from day-to-day existence was perhaps inevitable since the Portuguese Conversos had never experienced an all-embracing Jewish life.

At the same time as they were creating a normative Jewish community for themselves, the Portuguese Jews embraced many features of the surrounding Dutch culture, especially its bourgeois and material aspects. According to some historians, this blend of Jewish and secular cultures and the blurring of boundaries between the two spheres renders the Portuguese Jews of Amsterdam the first 'modern' Jews or, at the very least, harbingers of modernity.[8] Such comparisons must be made cautiously, however. Openness to the culture of the host society had always been a trait of the Jews of the Iberian peninsula. The Sephardi Jew in medieval Cordoba who recited poems to music in the Arabic style, or the Jewish courtier in Toledo who commissioned a private synagogue with the template of the Alcazar in Seville and the Alhambra in mind, and the Venetian

---

[7] Nadler, *Rembrandt's Jews*, 1–16; Zumthor, *Daily Life in Rembrandt's Holland*, 1–36.

[8] On Jewish modernity in Amsterdam, see Baron, *A Social and Religious History of the Jews*, vol. xv; Y. Kaplan (ed.), *An Alternative Path to Modernity*; id., 'The Portuguese Community of Amsterdam'; Bodian, '"Men of the Nation"'; see also Yovel, *The Other Within*.

Jew from Spain who worshipped in a synagogue whose exterior matched Renaissance and Baroque churches were also open to the surrounding culture. The experience of the Portuguese Jews of seventeenth-century Amsterdam represents another form of Sephardi accommodation to the broader society, distinct from those of medieval Spanish Jewish courtiers and from those of the modernizing Jews of Germany in the late eighteenth and nineteenth centuries.

As they turned to Judaism, the Conversos of Amsterdam challenged the boundaries between the secular world and traditional society. Some were hard pressed to submit to the norms of rabbinic Judaism. Noting their cosmopolitanism, their level of acculturation, and their high level of religious doubt, some scholars have tended to exaggerate the challenge that they confronted.[9] The dramatic examples of dissidents, such as Spinoza, Juan del Prado, and Uriel da Costa, have tended to colour the views of later historians. Notwithstanding these notable exceptions, most Portuguese Conversos experienced a generally smooth transition to Judaism and participated simultaneously in the wider society and the Jewish community.[10] They did not question the core tenets of Judaism, even if they personally did not practise many of them. Dutch Sephardi radicalism, if one can call it that, was rooted in their Iberian experience and the wider context of Amsterdam's distinctive culture. After generations of separation from Judaism, the Sephardi diaspora in Amsterdam succeeded in rapidly constructing a vibrant Jewish society where none had existed before, which served as the model for new communities emerging in western Europe and the Atlantic world.

Becoming Jewish in the Western Sephardi Diaspora

The Conversos' motives for leaving the Iberian peninsula in the sixteenth and seventeenth centuries varied from individual to individual and even within the same individual at different times. Some yearned to return to Judaism and were willing to undergo whatever hardships were necessary to reach a Jewish community or a land of relative safety. For many, economic reasons were of primary importance. As Conversos, they were barred from lucrative parts of the economy, including the military, guilds, and municipal office. In addition, the 'purity of blood' statutes closed most faculties in the universities to them, their advancement in the Church was limited, and they were intermittently barred from travel abroad and access to the New World colonies. For many Conversos, the threat of investigation by the Inquisition was enough to precipitate flight. Rumours of impending interrogations tended to set extended families, neighbours, and even the mere acquaintances and servants of the suspect in motion.

Most of the Jews who underwent forced conversion in Portugal in 1497 were

---

[9] On the relative ease of adaptation, see Yerushalmi, 'The Re-education of Marranos in the Seventeenth Century'; on their scepticism, see Yovel, *The Other Within*.

[10] Yerushalmi, *From Spanish Court to Italian Ghetto*, 35, 44, 271–301; Melammed, *A Question of Identity*, 75.

refugees from the Expulsion from Spain in 1492. They had chosen to leave Spain rather than convert to Catholicism and were presumably determined to remain Jewish. The fact that they did not leave Portugal in 1497 might indicate that departure was impossible or that they were unwilling to undergo yet another exile. Nevertheless, many were determined to practise and transmit what Judaism they could. They pursued clandestine worship and lobbied collectively in Lisbon and Rome against the introduction of an Inquisition in Portugal. Over the course of time, their Judaism became distorted and partial. Bereft of an open community, teachers, books, and the Hebrew language, their Judaism was one of memory, generally transmitted by the women within the confines of the house. When the Inquisition finally arrived in Portugal in the late 1530s, life became precarious and the impetus to flee increased. The new Portuguese and Spanish colonies across the Atlantic proved attractive to many. The rate of emigration from Spain and Portugal ebbed and flowed as the gates of Iberia alternately opened and shut during the sixteenth and seventeenth centuries.

The union of Spain and Portugal in 1580 brought increased inquisitorial activity in Portugal. According to the purity of blood laws adopted in the sixteenth century and rigorously applied for centuries thereafter, the blood of the Conversos was tainted, and even baptism could not remove the stigma. The mere hint of Jewish ancestry was often enough to raise suspicions of Marranism: a capital offence. But the terms of the union included assurances that Judaizing in Portugal would not be prosecuted in Spain, so many Conversos moved from there to Spain. Although the separate Inquisitions in the two countries did exchange information about suspected secret Jews, Spain decided not to extradite fugitives from the Portuguese Inquisition who came under its jurisdiction. The unanticipated result of the union was the creation anew of a Marrano problem on Spanish soil and the acceleration of Converso flight from the Iberian peninsula. By the seventeenth century the Spanish Inquisition was focused on other groups, such as Protestants, followers of Erasmus, witches, and homosexuals. Many Marranos therefore found it preferable to live in Spain, where they could either share in the general flourishing of the Spanish empire or more easily depart than they could from Portugal. Those who fled to Spain after 1580 were suspected of Marranism, and the label 'Portuguese' became synonymous with 'Jew' or 'Judaizer' wherever the Portuguese New Christians appeared.

Flight from the Iberian peninsula was often an elaborate process, involving property transfers, deception, and subterfuge and requiring capital and family or business connections in other Converso communities. Many Conversos sought refuge in Spanish and Portuguese territories overseas, where Judaism was proscribed but detection more difficult. Flight to the New World also held out the possibility of shedding the last traces of Jewish ancestry. Despite these clear advantages, the Atlantic colonies presented their own dangers. The Inquisition's informers were everywhere, and Converso merchants were never totally safe or at ease, no matter how lucrative the new markets were. Others escaped to neighbouring France, where entry was relatively easy and surveillance of Conversos sporadic. The Ottoman empire was not necessarily seen as a suitable place of refuge, since it was difficult to reach and reputedly culturally alien and backward. The Low Countries, although under Spanish occupation, were the favoured destination. They offered easy access, lively economic opportunities, and fairly lax supervision of Converso behaviour. Moreover, business ties with the Iberian peninsula could be maintained through relatives left behind. Beginning in the early seventeenth century the Low Countries even offered a modicum of religious freedom. Portuguese merchants in Antwerp, although under the Crown of Spain, could secretly engage in Jewish practices and openly enjoy the economic opportunities of living in a major hub of global commerce. These advantages continued until Emperor Charles V ousted the Portuguese merchants. After Holland freed itself from the Spanish yoke and the Protestant north formed a union based on religious tolerance (of Protestants), Amsterdam received its first Marranos. The majority of the Portuguese Jews who registered their marriages in the town registry of Amsterdam in the seventeenth century listed France as their country of origin. The Portuguese quickly became a vital part of Holland's global trade, especially welcome for their commerce in coveted products that were not in competition with those of the Christian merchants.

The Jewish life that emerged in Amsterdam was quite different from that in other places where the Sephardim settled: the practices of a second- or third-generation Iberian Marrano were very different from those of a Jew who departed in 1492 or 1496. The Inquisition's swoops on the Converso communities in Spain in the 1480s were terrifying, but the Expulsion occurred soon after and forced the Jews out of its clutches. The Portuguese Conversos' encounter with persecution was more violent and more sustained. When the Inquisition was introduced in Portugal in 1536, no Converso was safe, especially not if a relative was summoned to appear before it. Marranism was widespread, but more concentrated near the Spanish border, where many refugees from Spain had sought what they thought would be only temporary asylum. Marranos had to learn to live secret lives. Probably most Portuguese Conversos who fled Iberia seeking to live as Jews could scarcely imagine what it would involve. Three or four generations separated them from any open, authentic Jewish life; they had usually received some education in the Church; and they subconsciously imbibed attitudes that were hostile towards rabbinic Judaism or understood Judaism in a Christianized version, with individual salvation as its core doctrine. Other ideas that they transported to their new Judaism in Amsterdam were also related to their specific circumstances. Immortality of the soul, for example, assumed a prominent role, as former Conversos were concerned about the fate of relatives who had remained in Spain and had not been able to leave the Christian faith. What, they wondered, would happen to them in the afterlife? Some Conversos found spiritual sustenance in the wave of mysticism that penetrated Iberian Christian circles in the sixteenth century. Many were sceptical of all organized faith or turned to Protestantism as an 'improved' Christianity. Others were drawn to deism. The vestiges of Judaism that managed to survive among the Marranos, even those with the highest motivation, were those practices that were most easily hidden from view. Thus, knowledge of Hebrew practically disappeared, except for the word *adonai*, 'Lord'. Circumcision was one of the most risky practices, and therefore one of the first to be discarded. A few of the more ascetic practices of Judaism, such as fasting on specific holidays, became more pronounced. Belief in the law of Moses without observing any of its precepts was another unusual crypto-Jewish stance.

Although most of them eventually adopted normative Judaism, many Conversos from Iberia simply disappeared into the surrounding Christian society. In southern France, for instance, considerable pressure was exerted on Conversos who vacillated between Christianity and Judaism. Many chose to remain in the Christian fold rather than convert to a faith still formally proscribed. Some Conversos were reluctant to openly espouse Judaism since they continued to move in and out of Iberia on business or had relatives there whom they might endanger by their adoption of Judaism. Some even returned to live in Iberia for economic or social reasons. Others chose to remain on the margins of the emerging Jewish communities.[11] While the total number of Portuguese Conversos who adopted Judaism in western Europe never exceeded the thousands, their impact went far beyond their numbers. As Conversos who chose to 'return' to Judaism after generations living as Christians, they hold a special place in Sephardi history.

Return to Judaism, however, should not be taken literally, since the Conversos of Amsterdam had never been Jews. They quickly discovered that 'feeling' Jewish as a result of discrimination was different from 'being' Jewish as a result of upbringing. Their return to Judaism was not an organic process of retrieving a heritage passed down from generation to generation, but rather one of willing themselves to accept a tradition that they had never lived and barely understood. Bereft of books, leaders, and schools and deprived of any possibility of open Jewish observance, the descendants of former Jews of Spain and Portugal were only dimly aware of the Judaic content of their heritage. Sometimes they had encountered Jews and Conversos who had come to the Iberian peninsula on business or in a diplomatic capacity furtively bringing some books, but such meetings were random and serendipitous. Systematic instruction in Judaism was lacking, even among those who managed to obtain Spanish translations of

---

[11] Graizbord, *Souls in Dispute*. Graizbord's study of individual Inquisition cases provides rich material on the split identities of the Conversos. On Portuguese Jews from Amsterdam proselytizing among Conversos in Catholic lands, see Y. Kaplan, 'The Travels of Portuguese Jews from Amsterdam to the "Lands of Idolatry"'; on reluctance to adopt Judaism by those who travelled back and forth to the Iberian peninsula on business, see id., 'Amsterdam, the Forbidden Lands and the Dynamics of the Sephardi Diaspora'; id. 'The Travels of Portuguese Jews from Amsterdam to the "Lands of Idolatry"'; for specific examples in London and Bayonne, see id., 'Wayward New Christians and Stubborn New Jews'.

the Bible, the prayer book, and other works printed in Italy or the Ottoman empire. The path to Judaism, therefore, involved many difficult steps. One can only marvel at the process of transformation that was necessary for someone like Isaac Orobio de Castro, who studied medicine and theology in Spain, was arrested and tortured by the Inquisition, and escaped to France where he served as a professor of medicine at the University of Toulouse. He finally ended up in Amsterdam, where he turned openly to Judaism and became an outspoken intellectual and apologist for Judaism.[12]

The return to Judaism in Amsterdam was generally accompanied by the adoption of a Hebrew name, circumcision, and remarriage in the Jewish tradition (frequently with the couple's children also under the wedding canopy). Most converts adopted biblical names while retaining their former Spanish or Portuguese ones for business purposes. As a result, there is a profusion of Abrahams and Isaacs in the registers of the Jews of seventeenth-century Amsterdam. After such largely symbolic acts, re-education as Jews, including systematic instruction, would begin.[13]

The Portuguese Conversos who arrived in Amsterdam in the seventeenth century felt strong ethnic ties with each other. These bonds embraced family, linguistic traditions, customs, and a penchant for commerce. They also drew, whether consciously or subconsciously, on Iberian notions of pure blood. They valorized Jewishness rather than Judaism, which formed one part, and not necessarily the dominant part, of their ethnic identity. The endogamous marriage patterns that had helped them maintain their secret Jewish subculture in Iberia continued in Amsterdam. Ignorant of Hebrew, they used Spanish to read their sacred texts, and Portuguese as their language of commerce and daily life. Portuguese remained the official language of the community throughout the seventeenth century, and the *ascamot* and minutes of the Portuguese congregations in Amsterdam, London, and New York were recorded in Portuguese long after the members ceased speaking the language on a daily basis. This attachment to the languages of Iberia was a sign of their communal conservatism as well as of their devotion to a Hispanic culture which distinguished them from other Jews. Even those who showed no interest in adopting Judaism or in belonging to a Jewish community retained ties with the western Sephardi diaspora. Portuguese Conversos formed a transnational trading network that was ideally suited to the needs and opportunities of the Dutch republic in the seventeenth century. Their dispersed kin and far-flung business partnerships enabled them to cross the borders of empires with ease. Even their cosmopolitanism, so often cited as a sign of modernity, bore only a

---

[12] The complexity of returning to Judaism and the intellectual climate of the Converso diaspora are superbly reconstructed in Kaplan's biography of Orobio de Castro, *From Christianity to Judaism*; see also Yerushalmi, *From Spanish Court to Italian Ghetto*.

[13] Yerushalmi, 'The Re-education of Marranos in the Seventeenth Century'. Yerushalmi argues that the Conversos' adoption of Judaism was not necessarily a traumatic process and questions the commonly held notion that they lacked any exposure to rabbinic traditions prior to their exit from Iberia.

faint resemblance to the later cosmopolitanism of the modernizing Jews of the eighteenth and nineteenth centuries. Rather, it was the cosmopolitanism of a scattered multilingual family that knew no borders.[14]

Founding Myths and Self-Perception

The founding myths of the Jewish community of Amsterdam reveal more about Portuguese Jewish self-perception than about their actual historical antecedents. Founding myths form an essential part of the collective identity of any group. In the case of the Portuguese Jews of Amsterdam, their myths of origin were matched to their tragic past. Printed versions began to circulate at the time of the inauguration of the Esnoga, the great Portuguese synagogue, in 1675, over three generations after the first settlement. According to one, the first settlers were Miguel Lopes and his niece and nephew, Maria Nunes and Manuel Lopes Pereira, Portuguese Marranos who set out from Spain in either 1591 or 1593 in flight from the Inquisition. En route northward, they were intercepted by the English navy and brought to London. Hearing of Maria's beauty, Queen Elizabeth paraded her through the streets of London and tried to entice her to marry one of her dukes. Maria obstinately refused to relinquish her Jewish faith and eventually reached Amsterdam in 1598, where she married her cousin, living out the rest of her life as a Jew.[15]

Another account recalls the arrival of a group of Spanish Conversos in Emden in 1603/4. They approached the Ashkenazi rabbi Moses Uri Halevi and his son, Aron, the only Jews in the Lutheran town, confiding that they sought to become Jews and asking to be circumcised. Halevi advised them to go to Amsterdam, assuring them that he would soon follow. Not long afterwards, Halevi joined them, circumcised them, and worshipped with them in a rented room. But they were denounced and arrested, whereupon Moses and Aron immediately praised the city of Amsterdam, asserting that they could have easily gone elsewhere, but chose instead to come to Amsterdam, assuring the city elders that if they saw fit to allow the Jews to live there, within a year over fifty families of Spanish and Portuguese Jews with huge capital resources would come to Amsterdam and make it the leading commercial centre of Europe.[16] The

---

[14] On the multilayered culture of the Portuguese Jews, see Swetschinski, *Reluctant Cosmopolitans*, 278–323; on their ethnicity, see Bodian, *Hebrews of the Portuguese Nation*; on their myths of origin and Jewish identity in Amsterdam, see Melammed, *A Question of Identity*, 69–80.

[15] Melammed, *A Question of Identity*, 72. A variant tradition recounts that a beautiful young woman travelling disguised as a man was incarcerated in England after being taken captive en route to Holland. No record of Maria Nunes's conversion to Judaism exists. Furthermore, she probably did not remain in Amsterdam. A Maria Nunes is recorded as having returned with her husband to Spain in 1612 (Koen, 'The Earliest Sources Relating to the Portuguese Jews in the Municipal Archives of Amsterdam'). On how Portuguese memory in Amsterdam was constructed, see R. Cohen, '*Memoria para os siglos futuros*'.

[16] Bodian, *Hebrews of the Portuguese Nation*, 43–4.

account concludes with the burgomasters acknowledging the commercial advantages that would accrue to Amsterdam if the Jews were admitted and agreeing 'to give them all the freedom in the world to live here, to observe [their] Law and religion freely and to maintain a house for [their] prayers'.[17]

A third account begins with the discovery by the Dutch authorities of a clandestine prayer group led by Jacob Tirado (James Lopes da Costa) or, in some versions, Moses Uri Halevi. The group was secretly observing Yom Kippur and was mistaken for Catholics holding an illegal service and arrested on charges of papist activities. When they protested that they were Jews, the arresting officer allegedly told them to pray 'to the God of Israel for the government of Amsterdam'.[18] The story concludes with the city officials permitting open Jewish worship and the founding of the first Jewish congregation in Amsterdam.[19]

Like all founding myths, these contain kernels of historical truth coloured by wishful thinking. They paint a heroic picture that matched the atmosphere of triumphant achievement associated with the inauguration of the Esnoga. Maria Nunes was a genuine person: her parents had been incarcerated by the Inquisition in Portugal, which was probably the reason for her flight; her name appears in the municipal archives in the late 1590s; and her marriage is recorded in the city registers in 1598.[20] In general, stories of shared oppression and liberation serve as important unifiers, especially among new communities seeking common elements to bind them together. In the case of the Portuguese Jews of Amsterdam, other motivations were also involved. Since the Conversos who flocked to the Netherlands were not Jews and had never been part of any Jewish community, it was important to create shared memories that were both Jewish and heroic in content. Hence the emphasis on escape from the Inquisition and hazardous journeys. At the same time, it was also essential to unite the community to Judaism in a more formal fashion. Hence the emphasis on circumcision, a rite that was particularly meaningful to these former Catholics, for whom it had been both proscribed and vilified. Circumcision and formal conversion were prerequisites for community membership prescribed in the *ascamot*. A famous etching by Romeyn de Hooghe, *Circumcision in a Sephardic Family* (1668), offers an outsider's testimony to the centrality of this joyous family event that was celebrated by the community at large. The presence of Christian onlookers in de Hooghe's painting also suggests the ease with which the Jews of Amsterdam shared this private religious ceremony with curious and sympathetic Christian acquaintances.

[17] R. Cohen, '*Memoria para os siglos futuros*'; Swetschinski, *Reluctant Cosmopolitans*, 168–70.

[18] Swetschinski, *Reluctant Cosmopolitans*, 169.

[19] See R. Cohen, '*Memoria para os siglos futuros*'; Vlessing, 'New Light on the Earliest History of the Amsterdam Portuguese Jews'; see also Cooperman, 'Amsterdam from an International Perspective'; Huusen, 'The Legal Position of Sephardi Jews in Holland'; Melammed, *A Question of Identity*.

[20] Vlessing, 'New Light on the Earliest History of the Amsterdam Portuguese Jews'; Koen, 'The Earliest Sources Relating to the Portuguese Jews in the Municipal Archives of Amsterdam'.

The details of the foundation myths include common occurrences on the journey from Iberia to Amsterdam. It was not exceptional to be captured at sea in that era of piracy and colonial warfare, and many Conversos had had harrowing escapes from the clutches of the Inquisition. The stories had a familiar ring that lent them a sense of legitimacy and could endow members of the community with a personal history and shared memories that many did not possess.

Tolerance, Intolerance, and Economics

The Netherlands at the end of the sixteenth century was not a religious haven that celebrated diversity and dissent. Conversos, like all non-Protestants, were barely tolerated, let alone welcomed. While the Netherlands and Calvinism were not synonymous, and Amsterdam was home to various Protestant denominations, Calvinism was the official form of Christianity. Dutch Calvinism was strict and moralizing, even though its followers tended to be practical and fairly moderate (towards non-Catholics, at least). The foundation myths of the Jewish community of Amsterdam acknowledge the reality of the sober, practical burgomasters and the bigoted clergy.

Each city in the Netherlands had control over its own immigration and religion. However, what one city decided regarding Jews was of more than passing interest to the others, since economic competition among the various cities was rife. A Jewish presence was accepted, in principle, in the northern Dutch cities of Alkmaar and Haarlem in 1604 and 1605 respectively, reflecting the first stirrings of a new spirit of mercantilism in which considerations of commercial well-being would eventually overcome medieval religious fanaticism. Rotterdam had already accepted a token Jewish presence. Amsterdam could scarcely afford to be left behind in admitting Portuguese Jewish merchants.[21] The first congregation in Amsterdam, Beit Ya'akov, was established between 1602 and 1604; the second, Neve Shalom, in 1608. Tentatively at first, the Conversos of Amsterdam began to acknowledge openly that they were Jews. Given the ongoing Eighty Years War between the Catholic Spanish Habsburgs and the Protestant Dutch, it was preferable for the Portuguese-speaking merchants of Vlooienburg to be regarded as Jews, that is, as common victims of Iberian cruelty, rather than as Spanish or Portuguese Catholics.

The prospect of commercial prosperity that Jewish settlement promised, enunciated in one version of their founding myth, reflects one facet of the new mercantilist thinking that played a greater role in allowing Jews to settle in Amsterdam than any enlightened toleration. Jews in Holland could trade with Conversos in Spain, Portugal, or their colonies, while the Dutch could not. Moreover, the Conversos' trade in commodities from the Americas, such as cacao, tobacco, and sugarcane, did not compete with local Dutch merchants. Perhaps, some speculated, the Converso merchants might

---

[21] Israel, *European Jewry in the Age of Mercantilisim*; id., *The Dutch Republic*, 506–8.

even help Protestant Amsterdam replace Catholic Antwerp as the trading centre of Europe. The duke of Tuscany had recently granted settlement and trading rights to Sephardim in the port of Livorno, which was rapidly emerging as an economic powerhouse in the Mediterranean and Atlantic trade, and it was obvious to foreign observers that the Portuguese Jews, like their brethren in Venice, played an important role in the city's trade with the Ottoman empire.

Positive expectations of the contribution that the Jews might make to Dutch commerce were not unrealistic. Their importance became even more obvious after the Dutch conquest of Brazil in 1630. The Jews of Amsterdam, in concert with their Brazilian kin, were pre-eminent in trade between the Netherlands and Brazil. By 1644 Portuguese Jews formed one-third of the European population of Brazil. Commercial, geopolitical, and religious considerations were thus intertwined in the minds of the Dutch authorities as they quietly permitted the Jews to assume a status similar to non-Calvinist Christians in Amsterdam. Jews also held a certain fascination in Protestant circles as the descendants of the biblical Israelites, and some sympathy as victims of Catholic persecution.[22]

The Jews were tolerated in Amsterdam on the proviso that their religious observances remained private and inconspicuous. One of the earliest arrivals, Jacob Tirado, held the first religious services in his house. In 1612, when the Jews were permitted to build a synagogue, the fiction was maintained that they were worshipping in private. By 1614 they had already acquired a cemetery in Ouderkerk, close to the city. They established a dowry society in 1615 and several charitable organizations. As they now had a population of over 200, two synagogues, and several social institutions, the city fathers could no longer ignore their legal status. In 1615 the city government established a commission to advise on whether the Jews should be officially permitted to settle and under what conditions. One of its leaders was Hugo Grotius (1583–1645), a distinguished Hebraist, prominent theologian, and recognized dramatist. He would later be recognized as the father of international law for his classic work, *On the Law of War and Peace*. In his *Remonstrance Concerning the Regulations to be Imposed upon the Jews* Grotius somewhat reluctantly counselled their admission. His work provides a barometer of the nascent attitudes of toleration of the Jews in a fascinating blend of medieval attitudes, philosemitism, Protestant Hebraism, and early Enlightenment ideas.

After duly cataloguing the 'crimes' that the Jews had allegedly committed throughout history, Grotius advocated admitting them to Holland, explaining that their anti-Christian behaviour was caused by the persecutions they had suffered for their religion. Moreover, Christian charity demanded love and forgiveness. Settling among adherents of the Dutch Reformed Church, he argued, might even hasten their conversion. Indeed, although they were misguided, in his view, their presence would benefit

---

[22] See B. Kaplan, 'Dutch Religious Toleration'.

Holland, including helping non-Jews learn Hebrew (an argument commonly made by seventeenth-century Protestants, who were keen to read their Old Testament in the original language[23]). To forestall the objections of those who feared that Judaism might somehow be imposed upon the country, Grotius wrote that Judaism, 'being most foreign, was the least likely religion to constitute a danger to "true belief"'.[24] Grotius then proceeded to set down forty-nine principles for regulating the Jews' status. While their presence was accepted, the boundaries of their activities and their community were ambiguous.

The Jews were granted official protection by a resolution of the States of Holland in 1619, with relatively few limitations. They could live strictly according to the law of Moses; however, dissidence of any kind was to be avoided and they were not to spread heretical beliefs among Christians. They were to refrain from circumcising non-Jews and from discussing religious questions with Christians. Nor were they to say or write anything disparaging Christianity. Sexual relations between Jews and Christians were strictly prohibited. While the number of Jews was to be limited, they were free to live anywhere in the city. They were not required to pay special discriminatory taxes nor to wear any distinguishing clothing or other marks. They could maintain their own sabbath, operate their own printing presses, and have their own houses of worship. In sum, within a relatively short time of their arrival, the Portuguese Jews of Amsterdam had attained a status that included many of the rights of citizens. They also confronted a few important limitations: they were barred from holding public office, bearing arms, joining any of the guilds, or passing on burgher rights to their children. These limitations did not prevent them from attaining conspicuous wealth and a sense of security. The primary concern of the authorities was the establishment of a stable religious and social order. With the right to live in Amsterdam now publicly proclaimed, the city became an even more powerful magnet for Jews. In 1615 a boatload arrived from Nantes; in 1617 seventy-three Sephardim expelled from Saint-Jean-de-Luz appeared. Groups of refugees from Germany also began to arrive in numbers.

The Hispanicity of the Portuguese Jewish Diaspora

Many of the Conversos arriving in the Netherlands had been part of Iberia's golden-age culture and had participated in its universities and salons. Others had ascended in the Church hierarchy in Spain or had served Portugal's monarchs and princes. Their values,

---

[23] Discussing doctrinal matters with Jews was frowned upon by the Reformed Dutch Church yet quite common among some Christian intellectuals. See Y. Kaplan, Méchoulan, and Popkin (eds.), *Menasseh ben Israel and his World*; Popkin, 'Some Aspects of Jewish–Christian Theological Interchanges in Holland and England'.

[24] Hugo Grotius, *Remonstrance Concerning the Regulations to be Imposed upon the Jews*, cited in Meijer, 'Hugo Grotius' *Remonstantie*', 97–8.

predictably, were shaped by Iberian elite society, including its emphasis on nobility and lineage. This typically Iberian sentiment was expressed in a sense of superiority over non-Portuguese Jews.[25] Their *ascamot* barred non-Portuguese Jews from burial in their cemetery (1647) (except in the case of mulatto converts, and then under specific circumstances); from receiving synagogue honours, such as being called up to the Torah (1644); or from attending their communal school (1657).[26] In 1697 Portuguese Jewish ethnic exclusivism reached the extreme of refusing to recognize as a member of the *nação* any Portuguese male who married a Jewish woman who was not a member of the *nação*. At the same time, membership in the *nação* was open to all Portuguese Conversos, whether or not they espoused Judaism. This ethnic solidarity was vividly expressed in the unique dowry society they created in 1615 for indigent Portuguese Jewish girls, the Santa Companhia de Dotar Orfans e Donzelas Pobres. It was one of their first institutions and was modelled on a similar society established by the Portuguese Jews in Venice in 1613. The principles of the society reflect the unique sense of identity of the western Sephardi diaspora. Recipients of the society's awards were selected annually from among Portuguese Converso and Jewish girls living in an area that stretched from Iberia to Germany. Eligibility was determined by Portuguese or Castilian descent on either the male or female side. This definition of Jewish ancestry differed from the traditional matrilineal definition of normative Judaism. In practice, Catholics of Converso background living in France or Iberia might be the recipients of funds. Although membership was limited to members of the *nação*, there were exceptions: as an Italian Jew, Saul Morteira, the leading rabbi of the Portuguese Jews in Amsterdam, was technically ineligible for membership, but the society accepted him on the grounds of his marriage to a Portuguese Jewish woman, his decades of service to the congregation, and the fact that he delivered his sermons in Portuguese. This made his daughter eligible for a dowry. But, they cautioned, it was to be understood that his non-Sephardi female relatives and offspring were not eligible for dowries from the society.[27]

The Sephardim of Amsterdam sought to replicate the lively cultural life of Iberia that they had been forced to abandon. Theatrical performances were at first performed in synagogues, then in warehouses and private houses. In 1676 a literary salon, the Academia de los Sitibondos (Academy of the Thirsty), was founded, followed by a second, the Academia de los Floridos (Academy of the Flowery or 'the Select'), in 1685. The logo of the Academia de los Sitibondos was a burning bush, with a motto drawn from Proverbs 20: 27: 'Es el alma candela del Señor' ("The soul of man is the candle of

---

[25] See Y. Kaplan, 'The Attitude of the Spanish and Portuguese Jews to the Ashkenazi Jews' (Heb.); id., 'The Self-Definition of the Sephardi Jews of Western Europe'.

[26] See Y. Kaplan, 'Wayward New Christians and Stubborn New Jews'.

[27] Bodian, *Hebrews of the Portuguese Nation*, 136–7; ead., 'The "Portuguese" Dowry Societies in Venice and Amsterdam'.

the Lord'). The two societies closely resembled contemporary literary salons in Lisbon, Madrid, and Seville. Their activities included poetry contests in Castilian, Latin, French, and Italian; theatrical pageants; and debates on themes such as 'Does love outweigh vengeance?' and 'Which is preferable, poverty with children or riches without them?' Members included intellectuals, the wealthiest merchants, and the most prominent leaders of the community. Women participated alongside men in the Academia de los Sitibondos but were barred from the Academia de los Floridos. One of the more unconventional women in the Academia de los Sitibondos, Isabel (Rebecca) Correa, was born in Spain and lived in Brussels and Antwerp before settling in Amsterdam. Her major poetic work, *El pastor fido poema* ('The Faithful Shepherd'), was not censured by the leaders of the community, despite its pagan themes. These cultural activities performed an important function beyond providing diversion. The literary societies, like the splendid mansions of the Portuguese Jewish elite, functioned as showcases for 'Portuguese culture' to the general as well as the Jewish public.[28]

Hispanic material culture remained a conspicuous part of the lifestyle of the Portuguese Jews long after their arrival in Amsterdam. Their homes boasted portraits of Spanish royalty, Spanish silverware, cabinetry, beds, and bed linen. Portuguese majolica with coats of arms and Iberian landscapes was conspicuously displayed in cupboards alongside Dutch delft pieces. Some of these items were brought to Amsterdam by the refugees; others were ordered from Portugal or purchased from shops in Amsterdam that catered specifically to an Iberian clientele.[29] Many Sephardim continued to sport Iberian fashions in clothing, hairstyles, and jewellery. Some of the material objects that Portuguese Jews displayed so proudly could also be found among Dutch Christians of the same economic background, creating similar domestic environments among Jews and non-Jews. The internationalism of both Christian and Jewish mercantile groups was evidenced in the acquisition and display of maps and globes and portraits of European potentates alongside genre paintings of Dutch landscapes in the public areas of their homes. In contrast to their concealed religious identity in Portugal, the Portuguese Jews now proudly displayed sabbath candlesticks, Hanukkah menorahs, and even their own Torah scrolls richly decorated with silver.[30] They hung etchings of the Esnoga in their parlours and embroidered family coats of arms on their prayer shawls. At the same time, their leisure pursuits mirrored those of the Iberian aristocratic and merchant class, including gambling.

The Jewish publishing houses in Amsterdam tended to produce fine books in Spanish and Portuguese, especially the classics of drama and poetry of the Iberian golden age, whereas the books on Jewish subjects that they published were quite basic.

---

[28] Bodian, *Hebrews of the Portuguese Nation*, 76–95; Swetschinski, *Reluctant Cosmopolitans*, 286–304; Israel, 'Gregorio Leti', 276–7.   [29] Levie Bernfeld, 'Matters Matter', 200.

[30] Ibid. 208 n. 70. A bequest of a Torah scroll with its ornaments specified that it was never to be sold and must remain in the synagogue (ibid.).

The libraries of educated Portuguese Jews contained French, Spanish, and Portuguese works with only a sprinkling of Judaica. Learned Jews, such as Manasseh ben Israel, corresponded actively with Protestant scholars in Spanish and Latin. Among the 159 books in the inventory of Spinoza's library, seventeen were in Spanish and included some of the great literary figures of the early modern period, such as Cervantes and De Quevedo. Specific publications peculiar to Amsterdam that appeared in Portuguese included the *ascamot* of the religious and charitable institutions of the community and the collected poetry of two Conversos burned alive by the Inquisition in 1655 and 1656.[31]

In its golden age, the Dutch republic developed a rich and highly visible culture, many elements of which were accessible to the Portuguese Jews. Inventories of Jewish estates and descriptions of Jewish leisure activities suggest that they adopted many aspects of the surrounding culture. It was not unusual for Jews and Christians to decorate the whitewashed walls of their homes with paintings or etchings having secular or even pagan themes as well as biblical ones. A painting of the prophet Elijah or of King Ahasuerus, or a dramatic depiction of the parting of the Red Sea, might be found on the wall of a parlour alongside depictions of Bacchus, Turkish galleys, or stormy seascapes. There is no evidence that the Jewish merchant class preferred biblical scenes over pagan or historical Dutch scenes or that the juxtaposition of Jewish, Spanish, and Dutch *objets d'art* was a manifestation of split identities.[32] The Portuguese Jews had many of the same tastes as the Christians of their class. They did not simply emulate their neighbours but lived comfortably in the same cultural milieu. The private collections of the Jewish merchant class included popular artists of the day such as Van Dyke, Vermeer, Titian, Rubens, and less well-known painters. Portuguese Jews commissioned portraits of themselves and their rabbis from local artists both Jewish and Christian. Even a rabbi's library might contain ancient classics and contemporary Spanish, Italian, and French literature. Probably most Amsterdam Portuguese Jews did not perceive any contradiction in their retention of Iberian tastes, their adoption of Dutch popular culture, and their simultaneous adherence to Judaism. It is only historians of a later period who regard this cultural mix as symptomatic of 'divided souls' or as a sign of the beginning of the process of secularization and a step towards the entry of Jews into the broader life of Europe.[33] What is remarkable is not the Jews' possession of such objects but, rather, the absence of any condemnation by the rabbinic and lay leadership of them. On the contrary, the lay leaders of the Jewish community were among the most avid consumers of the artefacts of Dutch Christian

---

[31] Den Boer, 'Amsterdam as "Locus" of Iberian Printing', 93; Offenberg, 'Spanish and Portuguese Sephardi Books Published in the Northern Netherlands before Menasseh Ben Israel'.

[32] Swetschinski, *Reluctant Cosmopolitans*, 322. On the persistence of Iberian cultural tastes and how they determined the tone of Portuguese Jewish life in Amsterdam, see id., 'The Portuguese Jews of Seventeenth-Century Amsterdam', 74.   [33] Baron, *A Social and Religious History of the Jews*, i. 205–12.

society, the proud bearers of what has been called by Swetschinski a 'patchwork' culture.[34]

Loyalty to the languages of Iberia endured in Amsterdam's Portuguese diaspora, just as Spanish shaped the identity of the Sephardim of the Ottoman empire. Until their emancipation in 1796, the Sephardim of the Netherlands generally did not speak Dutch among themselves, although their Dutch surnames and other signs of linguistic acculturation appear with increasing frequency in the eighteenth century.[35] However, language divided the Sephardim who went east after 1492 and those who remained in the west. The language of the eastern Sephardi diaspora, Ladino, gradually diverged from Castilian and became infused with Hebrew and Jewish traditions. The Portuguese Jews who arrived in Amsterdam and became the western Sephardi diaspora never spoke Ladino and had no proficiency in Hebrew. They had experienced the golden age of Iberian literary culture and were several generations removed from Jewish contexts. Their Hispanic identity was consequently different from that of their Ottoman cousins. It was more profoundly Iberian in many important linguistic and social respects.

Authority within the community resided in the hands of the *mahamad*, a group of lay leaders (*parnasim*) who rotated in and out of office. Like the secular government of regents, the *parnasim* formed an oligarchy that perpetuated its own rule. Although the Portuguese community was cosmopolitan, the *mahamad* sought to enforce religious and social conformity. It made liberal use of the ban, or ḥerem, and censored all material printed by members of the community. The *mahamad* acted on the premise that the continuing presence of the Jews in Amsterdam depended upon respect for sharply drawn boundaries that ensured a stable religious and social order. This premise guided the famous trials of dissidents such as de Prado and Spinoza.

Lacking a cadre of Portuguese religious leaders, the rabbis and teachers of the Portuguese Jewish community were generally imported from Italy or the Muslim world. They were employed by the *mahamad* and had to minister to a community that was usually more respectful of Jewish law in theory than in practice. The eastern and western Sephardi diasporas differed greatly in the respect and status they accorded their rabbis. The esteem in which rabbis were held in the eastern Sephardi diaspora was unmatched anywhere in western Europe. They could usually lay claim to an unbroken chain of Jewish learning, something that the rabbis of the Dutch community could not.

The attachment of Portuguese Jews to one another stood in stark contrast to their relations with Ashkenazim. Whereas the Amsterdam Sephardim recognized Conversos wherever they happened to reside, even those who were still practising Catholics, as kin, they distanced themselves socially and communally from the Yiddish-speaking Ashkenazi refugees from Poland and Germany who began crowding into the

---

[34] Swetschinski, *Reluctant Cosmopolitans*, 278–314.
[35] Baron, *A Social and Religious History of the Jews*, i. 67; Swetschinski, *Reluctant Cosmopolitans*, 278–85.

city in the seventeenth century. Despite their sense of superiority, however, the Sephardim recognized that they were fellow Jews in need of asylum and assistance and dutifully fulfilled their charitable obligations towards them while barring them from their social and religious gatherings. Even in their charitable activities, the Portuguese Jews retained a sense of exclusivism. Distinctions were drawn between Sephardim, *forasteiros* ('foreigners', usually Italian or Ottoman Jews), and *tudescos* (Germans). The term *tudesco* was applied to all Ashkenazim and was generally synonymous with 'pauper' or 'beggar'. They were only eligible for some of the charities, were barred from membership of the Portuguese synagogue, and, if one should marry a Portuguese Jew, the Ashkenazi partner was listed in the marriage rolls as *tudesco* or *tudesca* and not by their personal name. Membership in the Portuguese community was restricted to the Portuguese and Spanish Jews then living in the city or to future Portuguese immigrants, although other Jews were permitted to pray in the Portuguese synagogues. Synagogue honours were also restricted to members of the *nação*.[36]

The social distance between Ashkenazim and Sephardim was expressed in myriad ways. One of the first *ascamot* promulgated by the Kahal Kados de Talmud Tora, which emerged in 1639 out of the union of the three Portuguese congregations, entitled 'Regulation about the *Tudescos*', lamented and condemned 'the annoyance and discomfort caused by the *tudescos* who are in the habit of coming to this country' who 'loiter and beg for charity in the gates on Friday and the Sabbath. Because people give them donations, they stay and they live in this country, and if no solution is found, perhaps more will come in the future.'[37] Congregating outside the synagogue on sabbaths and holidays was thus strictly prohibited, as was begging for alms. In 1642 the charitable society Avodat Hesed was created, whose express role was to deal with poverty among German Jews. The society acknowledged the causes of the extreme misery of the Ashkenazim but also warned of the threat that Ashkenazi indignity could pose to all. The Sephardim considered Ashkenazi religious observances unruly, their occupations humiliating, and their general comportment undignified. They feared that these traits would undermine their own good name. In response, it was resolved to provide Ashkenazim with vocational training and instruction in the ways of 'polite Jewish society'.

The Ashkenazim's dependence on the Sephardim was religious as well as economic until 1635, when they founded their own synagogue. However, their increasing numbers meant that among the Ashkenazim poverty remained ubiquitous. While the Sephardim offered them lodging and monetary assistance and organized vocational education for them, they sought to limit their numbers in general and to minimize their visibility. *Ascamot* were promulgated several times to encourage poor Ashkenazim (and

---

[36] Swetschinski, *Reluctant Cosmopolitans*, 187–8.

[37] Kahal Kados de Talmud Tora, 'Regulation about the *Tudescos*', cited in Y. Kaplan, 'The Self-Definition of the Sephardic Jews of Western Europe', 136.

Sephardim) to settle as far away from Amsterdam as possible.[38] Newcomers were often dispatched peremptorily to Italy, Turkey, or the New World, where they formed a large proportion of Jewish settlers. As early as 1622 unwanted Sephardi paupers from Iberia had been encouraged to leave Amsterdam and were dispatched to Essequibo in Guiana. They were offered a partial stipend upon arrival in Amsterdam, on condition that they agreed to depart. By the eighteenth century the poor were dispatched primarily to Suriname, Barbados, Curaçao, and Jamaica.[39] They were barred from returning to Amsterdam for a period of time, sometimes as long as fifteen years, and threatened that there would be no further assistance if they did. The particularism of the Amsterdam Portuguese and their disapproval of the indigent resembles the attitudes of other corporate groups towards the poor in medieval and early modern times. Their reluctance to absorb the stranger—even in the case of co-religionists—represented a blending of their ethnic exclusivism and the negative attitudes towards the poor in general society. The practice of sending the indigent on to the New World was commonplace among British, French, and Dutch societies of the time.

The Portuguese Jews were able to set the terms of membership of their new community and to shape its institutions since there was no established community into which they were required to integrate. Divisions between Sephardim and Ashkenazim were not limited to Amsterdam but arose wherever the two groups came into contact. However, they were greatly exaggerated in Amsterdam by a combination of the Portuguese sense of inherent superiority and the profound socioeconomic rift between the two communities.

Religious Identity and Religious Leadership

The Portuguese Jews of Amsterdam did not describe themselves as Sephardim, although they were indeed part of the Iberian Jewish family. They were members of the *nação*, 'the (Portuguese Jewish) Nation', an ethnic as much as a religious group. This distinction was fundamental to their thinking and to the community they organized. Regardless of their actual practices, many Portuguese Conversos saw belief in the law of Moses as their defining characteristic. Catholic ideas of salvation and sin remained of paramount concern, even after they had left Catholicism behind, and interior conflicts were not unusual as they reinvented themselves as Jews in Amsterdam. Rabbis who had worked in Sephardi communities in North Africa, Italy, and the Ottoman empire were particularly well suited to meet the special concerns of the new

---

[38] Friedmann, 'Letters of Recommendation for Jewish Mendicants' (Heb.). In the *ascamot* of 1622, it was declared that only those who came from Spain and Portugal by sea would be recognized as eligible for assistance by the general charitable fund. On passage to America, see R. Cohen, 'Passage to the New World'.

[39] R. Cohen, 'Passage to the New World'; Levie Bernfeld, *Poverty and Welfare among the Portuguese Jews in Early Modern Amsterdam*, 44–60.

community. In their early years the Portuguese Jews turned to the rabbis of Venice and Salonica to help them resolve theological questions. Their earliest teacher, a somewhat transitional figure, was the Ashkenazi rabbi Moses Uri Halevi of Emden (1544–c.1628). Since he was the only learned Jew in the midst of Conversos, he became something of a jack of all trades, as the first ritual slaughterer, circumciser, teacher, and prayer leader. Another early leader was the merchant and diplomat Rabbi Samuel Palache of Morocco. Palache was an agent of the king of Fez in Amsterdam from 1609 until his death in 1616. He was a scion of a communally active family in Morocco. He brought his ritual artefacts with him when he accepted his diplomatic appointment and held clandestine prayer gatherings in his private home. He was responsible for the establishment of the second Portuguese congregation in Amsterdam, Neve Shalom. Another influential leader was Rabbi Joseph Pardo (d. 1619), who was born in Salonica and educated in Venice, where he served as rabbi of the Levantine community. Pardo's immersion in Sephardi traditions, familiarity with the special needs of ex-Marranos, and understanding of Venetian commercial and practical affairs made him an ideal leader for the Converso merchants in Amsterdam. Pardo's arrival in Amsterdam in 1608 marked a milestone for Beit Ya'akov, the first congregation in the city. Pardo reputedly played a pivotal role in establishing ritual norms in the congregation.[40] In 1616 Rabbi Isaac Uziel (d. 1622) arrived from North Africa to lead Neve Shalom. He headed a yeshiva in Amsterdam whose pupils included Manasseh ben Israel and Isaac Aboab de Fonseca. In the 1660s Rabbi Jacob Sasportas (1610–98) from Algeria, an early and vocal opponent of Shabetai Tsevi, guided the community during the frenzy that overtook Amsterdam during the Shabatean crisis. As members of the community, alongside millenarian Christians, prepared to depart for Palestine in response to the messianic movement, Sasportas raised a voice of caution.

The towering figure of the Amsterdam rabbinate was Saul Morteira (c.1596–1660). Morteira studied with León de Modena in Venice and accompanied the famous Marrano physician Elijah de Montalto to Paris in 1611, when he was appointed physician to Maria de Medici, the queen of France. When Montalto died in 1616, Morteira accompanied his body to Amsterdam for burial in the newly acquired Jewish cemetery of Ouderkerk. Morteira was prevailed upon to remain in Amsterdam, and served as the spiritual leader of the Beit Ya'akov congregation for decades, delivering hundreds of sermons in Portuguese and writing several polemical and apologetic treatises aimed at former Conversos. Many of Morteira's treatises were intended to counter Christological arguments that continued to trouble the Portuguese Jews.[41] He was also instrumental in the excommunication of Baruch Spinoza.

Venice played an important role in the transition of Conversos from Christianity to

[40] Bodian, *Hebrews of the Portuguese Nation*, 46.

[41] See Saperstein, *Exile in Amsterdam*, 253–374; id., 'The Treatment of "Heretical Views" in the Sermons of Saul Levi Morteira'.

Judaism and in the establishment and organization of the new Jewish community. It never completely lost its importance for Amsterdam's Jews, even after they surpassed it in wealth and scholarship. Venice served as the European collection and transfer point for charitable donations for the Land of Israel. Communication between the western and eastern Sephardi diasporas continued to pass through Venice well into the seventeenth century. The three synagogues founded in Amsterdam in the early seventeenth century were all based on the Venetian model of congregational association. The merger agreement of the Amsterdam congregations in 1639 states that the methods of enforcing the *mahamad*'s authority would be like those exercised in Venice.[42] However, the Portuguese Jews of Amsterdam formed a more homogeneous group than either the eastern Sephardi diaspora or the Sephardi community in Venice, and the synagogues did not remain separate institutions for long. In 1639 they joined together to form the Kahal Kados de Talmud Tora, a development which contrasts sharply with the fragmentation of congregational life among the Sephardim of the Ottoman empire. The *ascamot* of the Kahal Kados de Talmud Tora specified that there would be only one Portuguese synagogue in a city. In Hamburg, the three small Sephardi congregations united in 1652. Attempts to establish a breakaway synagogue in the daughter community of Curaçao were strongly opposed in Amsterdam, although the Jews of Curaçao enlisted the board of the Dutch West India Company in Amsterdam and the Dutch governor in support of a breakaway.[43] Similarly in New York, Congregation Shearith Israel remained the sole Spanish and Portuguese synagogue. The principle of one Portuguese community in a given locality is enunciated in the *ascamot* of the Jewish community of Recife even more emphatically. It prohibited the formation of a rival community 'even if they live in Parayba or any other place' in the Dutch colony of Brazil.[44]

Membership in the Kahal Kados de Talmud Tora was voluntary and restricted to those of Iberian background. The government of Amsterdam did not enforce membership or levy taxes on the congregation. Adoption of Judaism was an individual choice: in many cases it was the fulfilment of a long-suppressed desire; however, many Portuguese Conversos, for a variety of personal reasons, chose not to join the congregation but nevertheless maintained social as well as business contacts with its members, although their non-affiliation increased tensions within the community. The *mahamad* went to considerable lengths to persuade the 'fence sitters' to join, sometimes to no avail.

After the union of the three Portuguese congregations, the community was led by the *mahamad*, consisting of six *parnasim* and a *gabai* (treasurer), drawn from among the

---

[42] See Bodian, *Hebrews of the Portuguese Nation*, 191 n. 61; see also ead., 'Amsterdam, Venice and the Marrano Diaspora'. [43] Roitman, 'A Flock of Wolves instead of Sheep'; Surowitz Israel, 'Religious Authority'.

[44] Kahal Tsur Isra'el, Ascamah 9, cited in Bodian, 'The Escamot of the Spanish-Portuguese Jewish Community of London', 14 n. 13. On the far-reaching powers of the *mahamad*, see Swetschinski, *Reluctant Cosmopolitans*, 190–6.

wealthiest members of the Portuguese merchant class. Since the members of the *mahamad* chose their successors, it was a self-perpetuating institution. Eligibility for election to the *mahamad* was limited to married males who had resided in Amsterdam for the last three years and were preferably over the age of 40. If elected, a person was compelled to serve his term or face a significant fine and suspension of synagogue honours. The *mahamad* controlled every area of communal life in what Bodian has described as 'a deeply cherished aristocratic and patriarchal tradition', revealing continuity with the Iberian past of its members.[45]

Its first *ascamah* spells out the *mahamad*'s broad powers:

The Mahamad will have authority and superiority over everything. No person may go against the resolutions taken and made public by the said Mahamad nor sign papers to oppose it. Those who do will be punished with ḥerem [excommunication]. Therefore it is ruled that the Mahamad which serves every year has to be supreme in the governing of the Kahal and the *nação* and its dependencies. It can condemn disobedient persons to penalties it deems fit and make them ask forgiveness publicly from the *teva* [raised platform from which the Torah is read]. The Mahamad or whichever member of it is present in the synagogue (in case he finds it necessary to prevent the occurrence of discord) may also order (even under penalty of ḥerem) any person or persons of this Kahal to leave the synagogue, to keep silent, or to calm down, or not to leave their house until ordered. Neither in these cases nor in others ... will a father take the side of his son, nor a son the side of his father, nor a relative that of a relative. Above all they will see to it that the order of the Mahamad be obeyed and executed, for thus it behoves the good government, peace, and tranquillity of this Kahal Kados. May God bless her.[46]

In the minds of the Portuguese Jews, their right to live in Amsterdam depended on their 'good behaviour', and it was the *mahamad*'s role to ensure this good behaviour.[47] The Portuguese Jews were especially sensitive to appearances and repeatedly voiced concern that their neighbours should regard Judaism as a serious and upright tradition, possessed of 'proper decorum'. Towards this end, the *mahamad* prohibited young Jewish men from congregating on the city's bridges on the sabbath, gambling on the sabbath and fast days (apparently a favourite pastime of Portuguese Jews), and using snuff in the synagogue. The *ascamot* voice particular concerns about decorum during prayers, including their volume and tone. In deference to the strict Sunday observance of the Calvinists, the *mahamad* prohibited Jews from conducting business on Sundays or holding funeral processions on Sunday mornings. Some of the *ascamot* were designed to lend a bourgeois mien to the Jewish male's appearance, including the proper length of his beard. Artists' renditions reveal that Portuguese Jews bore a close resemblance to their Christian neighbours in dress and outward appearance. Yosef Kaplan avers that the concept of 'proper Judaism', or *bom judesmo*, a guiding principle in

---

[45] Bodian, 'The Escamot of the Spanish-Portuguese Jewish Community of London', 12.
[46] Kahal Kados de Talmud Tora, *Ascama* 1, cited in Swetschinski, *Reluctant Cosmopolitans*, 196.
[47] Y. Kaplan, 'The Social Functions of the Ḥerem'.

shaping the *ascamot*, represents the apologetic stance of a new and insecure community repeatedly concerned lest the behaviour of a few endanger the welfare of all. In the spirit of apologetic insecurity, the members of the *mahamad* declared in 1717: 'The members of the Mahamad would like to stress how important it is in safeguarding our position to avoid complaints and scandals, lest our neighbours come to hate us and make us appear in an unfavourable light. For it is by Divine grace and the good will of the Gentlemen of the government that our presence here is tolerated.'[48] Apologetics were intertwined, however, with specific Iberian notions of the superiority of the 'honourable name' of the House of Israel. These considerations of aesthetics and decorum, regardless of their origin, lent a unique dignity to the Portuguese Jewish community of Amsterdam.[49]

The favoured Jewish tool of social control, the *ḥerem*, or ban, was used liberally by the *mahamad*. The newness of the Amsterdam Jews to Judaism, their insecurity vis-à-vis their neighbours, and the conditional terms of their presence in Amsterdam meant that the *ḥerem* was imposed for deeds that might have gone unpunished in most medieval communities or in contemporary communities elsewhere.[50] An important distinction was made by the *mahamad* and the rabbis between public worship and private belief. As long as Jews adhered to prescribed rules of conduct, no serious enquiries were made into their beliefs. Although liberty of conscience existed, it was carefully contained. The *mahamad* was the arbiter of the morals and behaviour, including the religious behaviour, of the community, so that heterodoxy would not imperil the community's status as a tolerated minority. The *mahamad* was aware that the Jews' Calvinist neighbours did not condone any behaviour that might lead to nonconformity. The famous bans on Spinoza and Juan de Prado emerged in this self-consciously conformist atmosphere.

The Portuguese Jews took great pride in Christian interest in their synagogue, rituals, and customs. General guidebooks of the period pointed out the sites of Jewish interest in the city. The synagogues, in particular, merited special comment. John Evelyn, an English tourist, noted on his visit to a sabbath service on 21 August 1641:

> I procured to be brought to a Synagogue of the Jewes (it being then Saturday) whose ceremonies, ornaments, Lamps, Law and Scroles afforded matter for my wonder and enquiry. The women were secluded from the men, being seated above in certain Galleries by themselves, and having their heads mabbl'd with linen, after a fantastical and somewhat extraordinary fashion.[51]

Some Christian visitors were perplexed by the novelty of what they witnessed: the use

---

[48] See Y. Kaplan, '*Gente politica*'; id., 'The Self-Definition of the Sephardi Jews of Western Europe', 125.

[49] Y. Kaplan, '"Bom Judesmo"', 653 n. 11.

[50] Y. Kaplan, 'The Social Function of the Herem'; id., 'Deviance and Excommunication in the Eighteenth Century', 103.

[51] John Evelyn, *Diary*, cited in Y. Kaplan, 'For Whom Did Emanuel de Witte Paint His Three Pictures of the Sephardic Synagogue in Amsterdam?', 33 n. 18.

of prayer shawls, the separation of women in the gallery, and the raised *bimah*. They also noted the physical similarities between the Portuguese synagogues and the Calvinist churches, commenting that the synagogues were like 'the new Calvinist temples' in their simple layout, galleries, and the absence of figured decoration.[52]

The English traveller William Brereton commented in his travelogue on the inordinately lengthy prayer service and the lack of decorum: 'Here in this congregation, no good order, no great zeal and devotion here appearing; much time spent in singing and in talking.'[53] Brereton's comments resemble the famous reaction of Samuel Pepys, who was appalled by the lack of decorum and general hilarity that prevailed in the London Portuguese synagogue (probably during the Simhat Torah services).[54] In 1642 the Prince of Orange, Stadholder Frederick Henry, together with his son, William II, William's bride, Mary Stuart of England, and her mother, Queen Henrietta, wife of Charles I of England visited the Talmud Tora Synagogue, where they listened to a sermon by Manasseh ben Israel. In 1668 the duke of Tuscany attended synagogue services. King William III of England, former Prince of Orange, visited the synagogue in 1691, perhaps in recognition of the help that he had previously received from the Sephardim in the restoration of his dynasty and his accession to the throne. Not all visitors were dismayed by what they encountered in the synagogue. In the eyes of one French visitor, Gregorio Leti, 'the synagogue of the Portuguese seems to be a seat of noblemen, a well-made people, almost all civil, well dressed, rich, and who made a fine impression'.[55] The Portuguese Jews, ever sensitive to non-Jewish scrutiny, repeatedly attempted to ensure good manners in the synagogue. The presentation of an image of *bom judesmo* animated the regulation of synagogue services and public behaviour and guided the ordinances promulgated by the *mahamad*. The *ascamot* of the Kahal Kados de Talmud Tora provided that Jewish worship be dignified, good manners be exercised in public, and that dulcet tones be used and private conversations avoided during prayers. In the words of the *mahamad*, none should indulge in what they considered behaviour 'more appropriate to barbarians than to people of good breeding [*gente politica*]'.[56]

The *mahamad*'s concerns with good breeding presupposed an environment where Christians and Jews interacted on a fairly regular basis. Grotius had anticipated and welcomed such interactions. The terms and conditions of Jewish admission reflected

---

[52] See Wischnitzer, *The Architecture of the European Synagogue*, 82–3.

[53] William Brereton, *Travels in Holland, the United Provinces, England, Scotland and Ireland*, cited in Y. Kaplan, '*Gente politica*', 25 n. 13.

[54] Samuel Pepys, *Diary*, cited in Barnett, 'Mr. Pepys' Contacts with the Spanish and Portuguese Jews of London', 224–5.

[55] Gregorio Leti, *Il ceremonial historico e politico, opera utilissima a tutti gli Ambasciatori*, cited in Y. Kaplan, '"Bom Judesmo"', 653; see also Israel, 'Gregorio Leti'.

[56] Kahal Kados de Talmud Tora, *Ascama* 19, cited in Y. Kaplan, '"Bom Judesmo"', 653 n. 11; see id., '*Gente politica*'; Graizbord, 'Religion and Ethnicity among "Men of the Nation"'; Sutcliffe, 'Regulating Sociability'.

an interest in Jews and the Old Testament that permeated Dutch Protestant culture. Just as Christians visited the synagogues out of curiosity, Jews would visit the Calvinist churches, listen to their organ music, and remark upon their sermons. Such visits did not always lead to greater ecumenical understanding. In 1639, for instance, a near-riot occurred when Jewish visitors did not take off their hats in the church. The *mahamad* decided to ban such visits.

Portuguese Jews, their synagogues, and customs were popular subjects with some of the leading Dutch artists of the seventeenth century, and their works were purchased and displayed by both Jews and Christians. Jacob van Ruisdael, Romeyn de Hooghe, Emanuel de Witte, and Rembrandt all made etchings and engravings of Portuguese synagogues. According to Wischnitzer, the early Portuguese synagogue erected in 1639 resembled two recently constructed dissenters' churches in Amsterdam, the Church of the Remonstrants of 1629 and the Old Lutheran Church of 1632–3.[57] An exterior view of the synagogue by Romeyn de Hooghe, made after it had been converted into a wedding hall, is captioned *De Gewesene Kerk der Joden* (*The Former Church of the Jews*). Rembrandt also knew the synagogue well, calling it simply *The Synagogue* in an etching of 1646. Little in Rembrandt's etching identifies the building as a synagogue. The people gathered there, judging by their clothing and their features, are from diverse origins representing Sephardim, Levantini, and Ashkenazim. One man holds a fur pelt which he is apparently selling; perhaps Rembrandt is making an oblique comment on Jews and their worship in this representation.

Emanuel de Witte, one of the most famous painters of Dutch church interiors, was commissioned by the wealthy Portuguese merchant David de Abraham Cardozo to depict the Esnoga. Three different renditions of the synagogue by de Witte exist, two in the Rijksmuseum in Amsterdam and one in the Israel Museum in Jerusalem. De Witte depicted the Esnoga in faithful detail, showing a large interior with benches running along the side walls, illuminated by glass lamps and silver chandeliers. The men, women, and children are in contemporary dress and stand with their backs to the viewer. Prayer shawls can be seen covering the shoulders and hats of men who are confined to the front of the synagogue by a divider and are dressed in black (Plate 16). In another famous depiction of the synagogue, by Romeyn de Hooghe, a large crowd of elegant merchants and their families are represented.

Inauguration of the Esnoga

In 1670 Isaac Aboab de Fonseca, the rabbi of Amsterdam's Portuguese Jewish community, proposed to the *mahamad* that a new synagogue be erected, one that would reflect the community's growing prestige. It is not accidental that a new, resplendent Ashkenazi synagogue was then in the process of completion. The Ashkenazi

---

[57] Wischnitzer, *The Architecture of the European Synagogue*, 86.

community was growing rapidly, and its need for a more dignified and larger premises for community events was palpable. The Portuguese community turned to its most prominent members to set their own mark on the cityscape. Land was acquired directly across the canal from the new Ashkenazi synagogue, and a competition was held for the architectural design of the proposed edifice. The grand opening of the Esnoga took place in August 1675 with eight days of celebration, recalling the eight-day-long dedication ceremony of Solomon's temple and including patriotic sermons, the commissioning of artworks, and the composing of special poetry and music. The inauguration marked the climax of the visibility and affluence of the Portuguese Jewish presence in Amsterdam and a watershed in the life of its Jews. The grandeur of the new building was intended to accommodate the Portuguese Sephardim in a manner befitting their wealth and prestige and to herald the tolerance of the city of Amsterdam.

The Esnoga was, for many generations, the largest synagogue in Europe. It could seat over 1,000 men downstairs and several hundred women in the women's gallery. It was noteworthy for its ark of the Torah, a large cabinet almost 25 feet in height, topped by large tablets of the law with gold lettering, made of jacaranda wood from Brazil donated by Moses Curiel. Six hundred and fifteen members of the congregation donated to the building fund, along with several non-Jews. A series of prints in honour of the consecration was designed by Romeyn de Hooghe, official engraver at the court of the stadtholder, who was specially commissioned to commemorate the historic events. De Hooghe produced his etchings with more than one group of customers in mind: one of the prints, probably intended for a Dutch audience, contained the emblem of the city of Amsterdam in one corner. In another print, the Maid of Amsterdam is prominently seated in the top centre on a cloud, with a woman representing the United Provinces of the Netherlands to her left and an allegory of religious toleration to her right. Beside them is a figure holding a Torah scroll (Plate 17). Good will and patriotism abound in the various representations. De Hooghe also included his own patriotic poems among the multilingual inscriptions. These prints provide a visual record of the public fanfare surrounding the laying of the cornerstone by four of the most prominent members of the congregation: Moses Curiel (Geronimo Nunes da Costa), financial agent to the king of Portugal, David van Isaac de Pinto, Imanuel de Pinto, and Joseph Israel Nunes (Antonio Alvares). The prints depict an elegantly dressed crowd inside the building, including representatives of the government, magistrates, and many foreign and local visitors.

Romeyn de Hooghe also produced numerous prints of the Portuguese community for two prominent Jewish book publishers, David Castro Tartas and Joseph Athias. To celebrate and commemorate the dedication of the Esnoga, De Hooghe was commissioned by Athias to illustrate a commemorative booklet containing the sermons delivered at the inauguration. The illustrations were intended to evoke the dedication of the Temple of Solomon.

The Jerusalem Temple was a popular subject among the Jews, the biblically minded Protestants of the city, and the architect of the Esnoga, Elias Bouwman. A model of the Temple was brought to Amsterdam in 1642 by Rabbi Jehuda León, who served as a Hebrew teacher in the community. He displayed the model prominently in his home and wrote a multi-volume, illustrated work on the Temple that was widely read. Several details of his model were replicated in the design of the Esnoga. The model was widely viewed by Christians as well as Jews. Long lines of spectators threaded around his house, eagerly waiting to view the curiosity. Even William II, Prince of Orange, and his bride, Mary Stuart, went to see it.[58]

De Hooghe also produced a series of twenty prints depicting aspects of the synagogue, providing lively commentary on the Portuguese community, with gently humorous details characteristic of contemporary Dutch art. Thus, for example, liveried coachmen drive up to the synagogue, playful dogs frolic in the foreground of the sanctuary, and fashionable women clad in their sabbath finery chat in the balcony, as if at a theatrical performance. The worshippers wear typical Dutch outfits, including three-cornered hats, frock coats, and breeches: they might be any crowd of bourgeois or upper-class Amsterdam residents. The multilingual inscriptions in Latin, Spanish, and Portuguese on the etchings suggest that Christians as well as Jews purchased the works. One version of the print was probably commissioned by a Jew for Jewish consumption. It contains Spanish rather than Latin inscriptions and displays the names of the rabbi, Isaac Aboab, as well as members of the *mahamad*, the board of the Ets Haim Yeshiva, and the members of the board of the Bikur Holim society in several medallions. One version of the inauguration prints contains several poems, three of them composed by de Hooghe in Dutch and Latin, extolling the freedom the Jews enjoyed in Amsterdam and calling the synagogue 'the glory of the Amstel and its senate'.[59] At the top of one etching, four allegorical figures representing the Republic, Liberty of Conscience, Judea, and the High Priest holding a scroll of law are prominently displayed. In all likelihood, De Hooghe's prints served as the model for the famous set of paintings of the synagogue's interior that Emanuel de Witte created in 1680.

At least twelve professional Jewish artists worked in Amsterdam.[60] Their presence mirrors the important role that art played in Dutch bourgeois society. Portuguese Jews commissioned portraits from both Jewish and Christian artists, including Rembrandt's famous depictions of Manasseh ben Israel, Ephraim Bueno, and Jacob Sasportas. Probably those portraits that bore Latin inscriptions were intended to appeal to customers

---

[58] Stuart, 'The Portuguese Jewish Community in Seventeenth-Century Amsterdam'; Haley, *The Dutch in the Seventeenth Century*, 95.

[59] Nadler, *Rembrandt's Jews*, 145; Weinstein, 'Sepulchral Monuments of the Jews of Amsterdam', 226–8, 230.

[60] Swetschinski, *Reluctant Cosmopolitans*, 308–9.

outside the Jewish community. Perhaps as early as 1637 some of Rembrandt's prints may have attracted Jewish customers. Some of the portraits of Jews may have been intended to serve as frontispieces of books.[61]

The Amsterdam Printing Industry

After papal censorship crippled the printing industry in Venice, Amsterdam became the most important centre of Jewish publishing in the seventeenth century. Like those from Venice, the Amsterdam publications were noted for the quality of their printing and paper. Amsterdam's wide trade networks and general climate of intellectual tolerance aided in book production and distribution. The first Jewish printer in Amsterdam was Manasseh ben Israel. He began his career as a printer to supplement his income as a teacher. Other Amsterdam printers included Imanoel Benveniste and Uri Phoebus Halevi (grandson of the founder of the community). Many controversial works on religion, science, and philosophy in Spanish, Portuguese, French, German, Yiddish, Latin, Hebrew, and English were printed. The works in Spanish and Portuguese were for the domestic Sephardi market and dealt primarily with Jewish religion or Jewish communal life. Those in Latin were intended for a small but discerning market of Protestant scholars. The number of didactic and polemical works produced in the Jewish publishing houses should come as no surprise in light of the Sephardi interest in apologetic literature. One of the more original books to appear in Amsterdam was a Spanish work, *Confusion de confusiones* (1688) by Sephardi businessman Joseph Penso de la Vega. It contained the first explanation and critique of the stock market. Another series of publications and prints concerned the messianic career of Shabetai Tsevi. Etchings of Shabetai Tsevi and his prophet, Nathan of Gaza, and Hebrew, Spanish, and Portuguese editions of the prayer book composed by Nathan rolled off the Jewish presses. An extensive literature of sermons reflects the Jewish life unfolding in Amsterdam.[62]

In 1661 Joseph Athias was accepted into the Amsterdam printers' guild. His elaborate tombstone in the Ouderkerk cemetery reveals his pride in this accomplishment. Its decorative relief contains the image of a winged Mercury armed with a book and a staff. Athias held a monopoly on the printing of the Bible in English and was the largest supplier of English Bibles on the continent. He pioneered the use of copper plates for the printing of textiles and was the first Jew to advertise in a Dutch newspaper. He employed many Dutch typesetters, compositors, and printers. His printing house has been described as one of the most cosmopolitan workplaces in Amsterdam.[63]

The Jewish printing presses of Amsterdam catered to a diverse market of readers

---

[61] Zell, *Reframing Rembrandt*, 7–32.
[62] Saperstein, *Exile in Amsterdam*.
[63] See Swetschinski, *Reluctant Cosmopolitans*, 51, 153; Fuks and Fuks-Mansfeld, *Hebrew Typography in the Northern Netherlands*, i. 339–82.

in the Netherlands and abroad, Jewish as well as Christian. They published not only in Hebrew, Spanish, and Portuguese but also in Yiddish and even English. As in Venice and Ferrara, Jewish favourites, such as Bahya ibn Pakuda's *Ḥovot halevavot*, Judah Halevi's *Kuzari*, and Maimonides' 'Laws of Repentance' from his *Mishneh torah* appeared in Spanish translation. The Amsterdam community of 'new Jews' also required more basic works. Abraham Farar's book on the 613 commandments, *Declaracao das seiscentas e treze encomendancas da nossa sancta ley*, and Manasseh ben Israel's two-volume work, *Thesouro dos dinim* ('Treasury of the Laws'), were specially prepared and tailored to meet the needs of former Conversos. A Spanish translation of the Mishnah published in Venice in 1606 was reprinted in Amsterdam in 1663. Sermons by local rabbis were published in Portuguese, the language in which they were delivered. In addition, a number of Hebrew works were printed, probably specifically for a German or Polish Jewish readership already familiar with Judaism. The volume of secular works published by Amsterdam's Jewish printers testifies to a lively literary scene of poets and playwrights. The combination of polemical literature, basic Judaic texts, biblical works, and Hispanic and Lusitanian belles-lettres marks the intellectual profile of the Sephardi reader in Amsterdam.

Formal and Informal Education in Judaism

The Jews of Amsterdam hoped to reclaim their lost Judaic roots. They were 'potential' Jews in need of education. A *talmud torah* was established by the Neve Shalom and Beit Ya'akov congregations in 1616. By 1620 it had rented a house to serve as a school for the sons of the poor of the two congregations. In 1637 the directors of the *talmud torah* established a school of higher learning, the Ets Haim Yeshiva: its highest grade was taught by Saul Morteira. The *talmud torah* became a model educational arm of the Portuguese community. Spinoza began his studies there in 1639. Boys from wealthy as well as poor families were educated in the *talmud torah* while wealthy families also employed tutors (generally from among Polish Jews) at home for some secular subjects. Girls were not educated in the institution but received instruction from tutors. Some managed to reach a high degree of literacy and proficiency as poets. Jewish women with literary talents were also members of the Portuguese Jewish literary societies.

The excellence of the educational system in the Portuguese community is striking. Its high standards and unusual graded pedagogical system may have been influenced by the Jesuit or the Dutch Latin school systems or be simply due to the fact that the Portuguese Conversos lacked all prior Jewish educational experience and therefore drew on the educational systems that they knew best or observed in the Christian world.[64] The *talmud torah* offered graded instruction at several levels, included a variety

---

[64] Méchoulan and Nahon, introduction to Manasseh ben Israel, *The Hope of Israel*, 19.

of secular subjects, and was noted for its rigour and high standards. Its teachers were hired, supervised, and paid by the *mahamad*. Its level of Jewish instruction was particularly well regarded, even among Ashkenazi scholars who were accustomed to rigorous Jewish studies in their home communities. Its language of instruction was generally Spanish.

Informal Jewish educational opportunities were available on a regular basis. Initiation into Judaism and ongoing adult education formed an important part of the charitable work and social life in the community, and daily, weekly, or fortnightly attendance at study groups was commonplace. The community sometimes hired individual tutors for orphans and for those who were disabled or otherwise unable to attend school. Poor children were provided with an education by the community from the age of 5 until barmitzvah.[65] Members of the Portuguese Jewish community took pride in their education system even if they had little time or inclination to use it themselves. Education was not restricted to males or to the rich. As far as poor children's education was concerned, a charitable brotherhood or society existed to pay subsidies so that they would not be required to interrupt their studies to help support the family. The scholarships were determined by ability, diligence, and need.[66]

Men of Commerce and Men of Influence

The Conversos of Portugal were noted as 'men of commerce' wherever they settled in western Europe; however, they were not predominantly wealthy merchants. Their numbers included doctors, magistrates, brokers, butchers, labourers, craftsmen, and even a few pirates. A large proportion of members of the community were poor by the middle of the seventeenth century, lived on the communal dole, and had no independent means of support. Portuguese Jews as men of finance and international commerce have been the subject of a vast literature and will only be considered briefly here. Studies by Jonathan Israel and others suggest the pioneering nature of these businessmen as they fearlessly plied the seas in an age of mercantile rivalries and colonial warfare.[67]

'Commerce' and 'merchant' were extremely broad categories in the seventeenth century. Men of commerce might be engaged in sugar-refining and diamond-cutting, as well as importing sugar or diamonds. Since Jews were not permitted to engage in retailing or manufacturing in Amsterdam, international trade became their most important occupation, and many Portuguese Jewish merchants were linked in one fashion

---

[65] See Levie Bernfeld, *Poverty and Welfare among the Portuguese Jews in Early Modern Amsterdam*, 92, 171–95; see also ead., 'Financing Poor Relief in the Spanish–Portuguese Jewish Community in Amsterdam'.

[66] Swetschinski, *Reluctant Cosmopolitans*, 201.

[67] Israel, 'The Economic Contributions of Dutch Sephardi Jewry to Holland's Golden Age'.

or another to global trading networks that dealt in high-value colonial commodities. When trade embargoes were lifted in 1608 and twelve years of Spanish–Dutch truce ensued, the Jews of Amsterdam were in a strategic position to trade with the Iberian peninsula. The truce marked the golden age of Amsterdam in general, and of the Jews in particular. Since there were no merchants in Amsterdam who had had any dealings with Spain for decades, the Portuguese Jews had few rivals, and Dutch commercial opposition to the growth of the Portuguese Jewish community in Amsterdam was therefore minimal. The vast majority of Dutch freight contracts that have survived were signed by Jews. Italy sent silk, glass, and red coral to Amsterdam; wine, raisins, and syrup came from Spain.

The Portuguese Jewish diaspora consisted of a widely dispersed and interconnected community possessing close family and commercial ties. This profile, combined with the timing of their arrival as Dutch global trade was rapidly expanding, was fortuitous. Portuguese Jewish trade was confined to a few routes, such as Brazil and perhaps Guinea, and products, such as sugar, Brazil wood, cinnamon, tobacco, and diamonds, but these were critical to the Dutch and world economies.[68] During the tumultuous years from 1608 to 1648, the Portuguese Jews of Amsterdam dealt mainly in overseas trade with Portugal and its colonies. A large proportion of the European population who settled in Portuguese Brazil were Conversos, many related in one fashion or another to the Portuguese Jews of Amsterdam. At its peak, one-third of the Amsterdam Portuguese community was involved in the Brazil trade. When Portuguese Brazil fell to the Dutch in 1630, many of the Converso merchants were emboldened to abandon their Christian identity and openly espouse Judaism. They prospered during the short period of Dutch colonial rule (1630–54), especially under the benign regime of Governor Mauritz, and many Amsterdam Jews sought their fortune in the new colony. After Portuguese plantation owners rose against the Dutch in 1645 and Portuguese rule returned in 1654, the Jewish community of Brazil was forced to flee. Most returned to Amsterdam, but many settled on other islands in the Caribbean and a few ended up in New Amsterdam, which would become New York in 1664. Trade and personal connections formed during the sojourn in Brazil could continue to be exploited in their new homes. In 1655 Abraham Pereira obtained permission to refine sugar in Amsterdam. Several immigrants from Brazil were experts in sugar-refining. Within a decade of being ousted from Brazil, Jewish refugees were operating twenty sugar refineries in Amsterdam. Trade with Dutch Curaçao, especially in cacao and chocolate, also played a prominent part in the life of the Jewish community of Amsterdam during the second half of the seventeenth century, and the manufacture of chocolate emerged as a Sephardi speciality. Frequently only a few years separated the penniless 'dispatched' Jewish mendicant of Amsterdam from his emergence as a significant merchant in Dutch or British Caribbean possessions.

[68] See Israel, *European Jewry in the Age of Mercantilisim*, 513; id., *The Dutch Republic*, 504–8.

The Sephardi diaspora formed a natural trading network, solidified by global dispersal and strong kinship ties. Spain and Morocco were important Dutch trading partners. Although Spain and Holland were political and economic rivals and mired in warfare and economic blockades for decades, the Portuguese Jews in Amsterdam could rely upon their relatives in the Iberian peninsula to serve as agents and intermediaries in Spanish and Moroccan commerce. Portuguese Jews from Amsterdam were also heavily involved in the trade in diamonds and corals from the Far East via Lisbon.

The Portuguese community of Amsterdam reached its peak of 3,500 to 4,000 members and attained its greatest influence at the time of the inauguration of the Esnoga in 1675. Many of its leaders had held influential positions on the Iberian peninsula. The Portuguese physician and student of philosophy and theology Baltazar de Orobio became Isaac Orobio in Amsterdam. The former Dominican friar Vicente de Rocamora, born in Valencia, had been confessor to Infanta Maria (later Empress Maria of Austria). Rocamora arrived in Amsterdam in 1643 and initially attempted to join the Protestant Church. He later assumed the name Isaac de Rocamora and became a preacher in the Jewish community. Their new religious affiliation did not prevent the more ambitious of them from retaining their high rank in the diplomatic services of Spain or Portugal. Jeronimo Nunes da Costa became Moses Curiel and was awarded the title Agent of the Crown of Portugal in the United Provinces in 1645 in recognition of his service to Portugal; Manuel de Belmonte was knighted for his service to the Crown of Spain and was named Agent General and Resident [Consul General] of Spain in the United Provinces.

The handful of Portuguese grandees in Amsterdam startled their contemporaries with their extravagant lifestyles and continuing dedication to the Iberian monarchs. Most Sephardim had unpleasant recollections of the sufferings of family, friends, and acquaintances at the hands of the Inquisition, but some, especially the courtiers, were able to separate the monarchy from the Inquisition. Such complex loyalties were a common phenomenon among the Spanish and Portuguese Jews in Morocco as well. A hint of their luxurious lifestyles is preserved in several prints by Romeyn de Hooghe depicting the residences of the men who laid the foundation stones of the Esnoga: Manuel de Belmonte, Moses Curiel, and Imanuel and David de Pinto. The prints suggest the flurry of activity as elegant carriages arrive in front of the mansions, the canals bustle with river traffic, and people wash their laundry at the water's edge or examine their wares on the waterfront.

Belmonte's mansion (Plate 18) is the most impressive of the three, befitting his status as Resident of Spain in the United Provinces. In this capacity, he provided information to the Spanish on the many activities of Spain's rivals. At the same time he served on the *mahamad* of the Jewish community and was a guiding force in the establishment of its two literary societies. He was appointed a count palatine by the Holy Roman Emperor Leopold I, and in 1693 was made a baron by Charles II of Spain. Moses

Curiel served as the sole representative of the Portuguese in Amsterdam after 1669. He was an agent of the Crown of Portugal in the Netherlands from 1645 to 1697, while his brother Jacob acted as Portuguese agent in Hamburg. Curiel was granted exemption from extraordinary taxes by the States General in 1673 in recognition of his diplomatic services to the Dutch. He is remembered for his generous donations to the building fund for the Esnoga and for providing the ark. He also hosted the visit of William III to the synagogue in 1691.[69] Isaac de Pinto, like da Costa, grew rich through trade with the Iberian peninsula. In 1651 he arrived in Amsterdam after a harrowing escape from Portugal through Rotterdam. He and his son David became prominent members of the merchant class of Amsterdam. They were generous members of the Portuguese community.

Romeyn de Hooghe's prints capture a special moment of Sephardi self-realization. They exude a sense of confidence and pride in the accomplishments of the community and the reality of its integration into Dutch society. The sheer size of the houses, towering over the neighbourhood, proclaims, as it were, the right of the Portuguese Sephardim to dwell freely anywhere in Amsterdam. The residences, like the men themselves, mirror the aristocracy of Madrid or Lisbon more than the Calvinist *haute bourgeoisie* of Amsterdam.

Ouderkerk Cemetery

In that most traditional of Jewish sites, the *bet ḥayim* or cemetery, the Portuguese Jews of Amsterdam have left an enduring record of their creative interaction with the exciting culture of the seventeenth century. Approval for the cemetery not far from the city in 1614 marked a decisive stage in the institutional development of the community. Its bas-reliefs and statuary demonstrate the Sephardim's ability to integrate the several cultural spheres—Jewish, Dutch, Spanish, Portuguese—they inhabited. Ouderkerk is famous for its elaborate and unusual sepulchral sculpture and baroque monuments. It has been included among the tourist sites of Amsterdam for centuries. The pre-1800 part of the cemetery is of special artistic and historical interest. Its monumental tombstones and special atmosphere inspired one of the most famous Dutch artists of the seventeenth century, Jacob van Ruisdael, to depict the largest and oldest tombs in the cemetery, those of Rabbis Montalto and Uziel, with their elaborate raised marble slabs set amidst a mysterious landscape that includes a rainbow, an imaginary ruin, and a rushing stream (Plate 19). Romeyn de Hooghe also reproduced the Ouderkerk gravestones. In another print he depicted a grieving family disembarking from a funeral barge at Ouderkerk, which provided a wide audience with a visual representation of the Jewish custom of accompanying the coffin to the gravesite (Plate 20).

[69] Israel, 'Duarte Nunes da Costa', 31; see also Swetschinski, 'An Amsterdam Jewish Merchant-Diplomat'.

The decorative stones at Ouderkerk, like the finely etched Dutch representations of Jewish festivals in the synagogue, provide extraordinary visual confirmation of the complex cultural orientation of the Portuguese Jews of Amsterdam. Extravagant monuments and bas-reliefs mark the graves of the da Costas, the Suassos, the Belmontes, the de Pintos, the Teixieras, and the Guedallas. The elaborately carved marble stones constitute only a small proportion of those in the cemetery. Few Jews in Amsterdam, even in the Portuguese community, could afford such luxury, and fewer still would have commissioned such representations for their final statements on life. Nevertheless, the striking figured reliefs in Ouderkerk attest to a dimension of Sephardi life that was religiously Jewish yet remained sociologically Iberian.

An outdoor cemetery with separate carved stone monuments represented a radical departure from the funerary customs of Dutch Christian society. It was also totally alien to traditional Jewish funerary practices. This may be one reason why the cemetery evoked so much curiosity among Dutch artists and the broader public. The majority of Dutch citizens were buried anonymously, with only a few notables meriting individual monuments and statuary within a church. The poor were buried in unmarked communal graves. The Ouderkerk cemetery is similar to the Jewish cemeteries in the Sephardi diaspora in its horizontal tombstones; its elaborate statuary is unique in Jewish art.[70]

The stones in Ouderkerk are carved out of marble imported from Italy. In the second half of the seventeenth century, Amsterdam was the main importer of Italian marble, primarily from Livorno. The inscriptions are mainly in Portuguese, with a few in Spanish and the occasional Latin motto; those of rabbis are generally in Hebrew. They were usually commissioned from poets and scholars by the deceased before they died, although some may have been copied from books or from other cemeteries. Dates are given according to the Jewish calendar but written in Roman numerals.[71] The Portuguese Jews of Amsterdam established a style of funerary art that could be found wherever their influence dominated among Sephardim in the west.[72]

Iberian, Jewish, and Dutch Calvinist images exist in fascinating combination in the sculpture at Ouderkerk. There are traditional Jewish funerary motifs, common to both Ashkenazi and Sephardi communities, such as hands extended to perform the priestly benediction to mark the grave of a Cohen, a hand pouring water or oil from a jug into a basin to mark the grave of a Levite, an open book with a hand holding a quill to denote the grave of a scholar, and biblical tribal designations, such as the lion of Judah. There

---

[70] Ashkenazi tombstones rarely contained carvings except for the occasional indication of priestly or Levite lineage and a simple Hebrew epitaph, with the exception of the sixteenth- and seventeenth-century tombstones in the cemetery in Prague, which are decorated with armorial crests, figural emblems, and acrostics.   [71] Weinstein, 'Sepulchral Monuments of the Jews of Amsterdam'; ead., 'Stones of Memory'.

[72] On sepulchral art in Curaçao, see Emmanuel, *Precious Stones of the Jews of Curaçao*; on Suriname, see Ben-Ur and Frankel, *Remnant Stones*; on the tombstones in Jamaica, see Frankel, 'Testimonial Terrain'.

are also Christian Renaissance and Baroque images, including mortality motifs such as the winged hourglass, the skull and crossbones, flickering lamps, and a bearded Father Time wielding a scythe. Stones are decorated with wreaths of laurel, angels, putti, signs of the zodiac, and even the very Christian symbol of a single lamb. In the case of the skull and crossbones, some art historians have identified them as gravestones of pirates, although this is highly questionable even on the Caribbean graves, as the motif is common on Christian graves from the same era and appears on the tombs of people known to have no connection to piracy. Frankel suggests that the motif may have been derived from the book of Ezekiel and its description of the resurrection.[73]

The Sephardim employed heraldic seals long before the seventeenth century, such as those in Samuel Halevi Abulafia's synagogue in Toledo.[74] The seal of the chief rabbi in Portugal in the fifteenth century included a royal coat of arms. It is unclear whether the use of family crests on the tombstones of Ouderkerk and over the door lintels of Jewish homes was an emulation of their Dutch neighbours or an expression of the aristocratic pretensions they had adopted in Iberia and continued to display in the Netherlands. Unfortunately, the few surviving Jewish burial sites in Spain rarely contain imagery, and those medieval tombstones that have survived are extremely simple and devoid of decoration.[75]

The tombstones of Ouderkerk also record details of the lives of the deceased. The untimely death of a child is represented by an axe chopping down a young tree; a modest and pious woman's grave is decorated with doves, denoting innocence. Many gravestones depict scenes from the lives of the biblical figures whose names the deceased bore. The striking variety and frequency of biblical episodes from the lives of the patriarchs and matriarchs can be attributed to the fact that most Portuguese Jews of seventeenth-century Amsterdam were converts: upon conversion they adopted biblical names, especially those of the patriarchs and matriarchs. Of the 444 men on the tax register in 1674, 71 were named Isaac, as were 188 Jewish bridegrooms registered between 1598 and 1699.[76] The episodes depicted on the stones include Eve near the forbidden tree in the Garden of Eden (Gen. 3), the binding of Isaac (Gen. 22: 1–13), Abraham looking to the heavens (Gen. 22: 17), Rebecca coming from the well (Gen. 24), Jacob sleeping near the ladder with ascending angels (Gen. 29), the death of Rachel (Gen. 35), Joseph thrown into the pit (Gen. 37), and Moses carrying the tablets of the law (Exod. 24).[77] Daniel Swetschinski suggests that the biblical figures on Ouderkerk's tombstones might also represent an Iberian Jewish variant of Christian patron saints and that the angels and saints of Catholic statuary may have served as a source of inspiration for these former Catholics.[78]

---

[73] See Frankel, 'Testimonial Terrain', 137.
[74] See Chapter 2 above.
[75] Bango, *Remembering Sepharad*, 109–10.
[76] Swetschinski, *Reluctant Cosmopolitans*, 282–5, 321.
[77] Studemund-Halevy, 'The Persistence of Images', 145.
[78] Swetschinski, *Reluctant Cosmopolitans*, 312–13, 322.

Old Testament themes were popular in Dutch art in the seventeenth century.[79] Paintings and drawings containing stories from the Bible were displayed in the homes of Dutch Christians. Illustrated Bibles were especially coveted by both Catholics and Protestants. Protestants distinguished between 'pedagogical' images, whose prime function was to teach the lessons of Scripture, and 'decorative' images, whose beauty encouraged adoration or even idolatry and were therefore taboo. After their long conflict with Catholic Spain, the Dutch took Calvinist iconoclasm very seriously. The walls of their churches were painted white; the windows in the churches were of clear, not stained, glass; religious statuary was regarded as particularly undesirable. The synagogues of Amsterdam followed a similar pattern. Their facades and interiors were quite plain. Like the Protestants, the Jews had long differentiated between the decorative presence of sculpture in their houses of worship (which was taboo) and painted or carved depictions of heroic scenes from religious or biblical history. Just as the inclusion of monumental relief figures of a historical nature was not considered idolatrous in the Calvinist houses of worship, by extension perhaps, the Portuguese Jews may have reasoned that the inclusion of monumental sculpture and bas-reliefs in their cemetery was acceptable.

One of the sources of the imagery in the Ouderkerk cemetery was Bible illustrations. In the early seventeenth century a flood of artists, calligraphers, and sculptors from the southern Netherlands, Antwerp in particular, arrived in Amsterdam, drawn to the new affluence of its growing class of burghers and clergy. They were trained in the Baroque tradition, which included depicting figures drawn from history and the Bible. This new art soon gained great popularity, even amongst the otherwise austere Dutch. Many of the Ouderkerk tombstone images can be traced directly to etchings in illustrated Old and New Testaments. Book illustrations lent themselves easily to tombstone decoration. Some may have been inspired by the monuments in the new town halls and plazas being built throughout the Netherlands, as public funds multiplied in Holland's age of mercantile expansion. The stonecutters of Amsterdam who produced the gravestones of Ouderkerk had experience in creating the civic monuments that celebrated victories in the protracted wars of independence of the northern Netherlands, and in decorating Dutch churches during the seventeenth-century heyday of Protestant church construction.[80] They may have been trained by sculptors who arrived among the refugee artists from Antwerp.

The wealthiest Portuguese Jewish merchants may have personally selected the designs for their tombstones from illustrations in their art and rare book collections. Other designs were culled from choir stalls, tapestries, and Greek mythology. Some rich Portuguese Jewish merchants in the Dutch colonies of Curaçao and Suriname had their tombstones shipped to the Caribbean. The old Portuguese cemetery of Curaçao was a miniature Ouderkerk, a reminder of Iberian and Dutch cultural hybridity in the

---

[79] Kiers and Tissink, *The Golden Age of Dutch Art*.   [80] Weinstein, 'Stones of Memory', 91–7.

New World.⁸¹ Occasionally, interment with a decorative marble stone would take place in Curaçao and a second stone, equally elaborate, would be commissioned and placed in the family plot in Ouderkerk.

Manasseh ben Israel

Manasseh ben Israel (1604–57) was probably the most famous Jew in Europe in the seventeenth century. He enjoyed friendships and intellectual exchanges with Protestant thinkers in the Netherlands and England, and his range of writings in diverse languages is enormous. His conversations with Protestant theologians mark an early step in the long process of dissolving some of the barriers that separated Jews and Christians. As a Portuguese Converso in his youth, and a product of Amsterdam's Ets Haim Yeshiva, he was equipped with some of the intellectual tools to carve out this new social position. In a portrait by the Jewish artist Salom Italia painted in 1642, Manasseh is portrayed with a skull cap, a flat linen collar, and a dark narrow scarf over his garment (Plate 21). The portrait bears a Latin inscription that proclaims 'We seek by travelling: Manasseh ben Israel, Jewish Theologian and Philosopher'; in the upper left corner is a small badge depicting a pilgrim with a staff, which Manasseh ben Israel used as his printer's logo, and the upper right-hand corner contains a table with a candle and an open book with the Hebrew inscription 'Your word is a lamp to my feet.' Beneath the portrait, Italia reproduced a Latin poem emphasizing Manasseh ben Israel's modesty and his Dutch and Portuguese connections.⁸²

Manasseh ben Israel was born Manoel Dias Soeiro, probably in the Portuguese colony of Madeira off the coast of Africa, and spent his early years in either Lisbon or La Rochelle, France. His childhood was typical of many Portuguese Conversos. His father was summoned several times before the Inquisition on suspicion of Judaizing and suffered torture and confiscation of his property. The family fled to Amsterdam, where young Manoel was circumcised and became Manasseh. The family adoption of the surname Ben Israel reflected the sense of spiritual rebirth and renewal as a 'son of Israel' that Conversos commonly experienced upon their escape from Portugal and formal entry to Judaism. Manasseh repeatedly expressed his appreciation of the freedom he acquired in the Netherlands, referring to himself as a Lusitanian by birth but Batavian in spirit.⁸³

---

⁸¹ Salomon, 'The Fidanques'. Monuments ordered by the illustrious family of Joseph Fidanque were captured by Barbary pirates in the Canary Islands and replacements ordered. The Curaçao tombstones were photographed by Isaac Samuel Emmanuel in 1941 to illustrate *Precious Stones of the Jews of Curaçao*, a celebratory volume he prepared in honour of the community that he served as rabbi.

⁸² The standard biography of Manasseh Ben Israel is C. Roth, *A Life of Menasseh ben Israel*. It has been superseded by Steven Nadler's lively and human portrait in *Menasseh ben Israel: Rabbi of Amsterdam*.

⁸³ Méchoulan and Nahon, introduction to Manasseh ben Israel, *The Hope of Israel*, 24.

Manasseh was a precocious child, completing his first book, a Hebrew grammar, at the age of 17. In 1622, while still in his teens, he was appointed assistant rabbi of Neve Shalom, the smallest of the three Portuguese congregations in Amsterdam. His modest salary compelled him to take up work as a printer in 1627.[84] When the three Portuguese congregations merged in 1639 and formed the Kahal Kados de Talmud Tora, Manasseh was assigned a subordinate role as preacher of monthly sermons and Hebrew teacher. He had hoped for a more prestigious position, and apparently resolved at this point to go into business. Frequently at odds with the synagogue's most important leader, Saul Morteira, and frustrated by what he considered a meagre income and a lack of appreciation of his talents, Manasseh entered into a partnership with his brother in the trade with Brazil and briefly contemplated emigration to the Portuguese Jewish outpost of Recife. His work as a printer helped him to survive the serious financial reverses he suffered when the Brazilian trade with the Netherlands collapsed in the 1650s. It also provided an outlet for his considerable literary talent. He unsuccessfully sought employment in 1651 as a Judaica librarian to Queen Christina of Sweden, thereafter turning his attention to his dream of Jewish ingathering in his final years. Repeatedly frustrated, Manasseh never obtained the wide acclaim in Jewish intellectual circles that he did in Christian ones.

Like other Sephardim, Manasseh was obsessed with lineage and pedigree. He was extremely proud of his wife's Abravanel ancestry and repeatedly reminded his sons of their noble and aristocratic origins. His was the first Hebrew printing house in Amsterdam, and his first publication in 1626/7 was a pocket-size prayer book. In the course of his career, his publishing house produced forty-four Hebrew titles and twenty-six vernacular titles, as well as many of his own works. He produced the Bible and prayer book in Spanish. His primer on Jewish rituals, composed in collaboration with Saul Morteira, served as an introductory text for Conversos entering Judaism. The majority of his personal works were published simultaneously in Latin and Spanish, for both Christians and Jews. Manasseh began to attend the famous Frankfurt Book Fair in 1634, where he reached a broader audience, producing an Ashkenazi prayer book for the German Jewish market. He later dedicated his famous kabbalistic treatise *Nishmat ḥayim* (1651) to the German emperor, Leopold.

Manasseh's oeuvre reflects his wide knowledge: his works are studded with allusions to Hebrew, Greek, and Latin literature and the writings of the Church Fathers, and include a book on resurrection, the kabbalistic work *Nishmat hayim*, a volume on the divine nature of the law of Moses, and several political tracts. He exchanged more than 300 letters with Christians. Many of his works were aimed at explaining Judaism to

---

[84] On Hebrew printing in Amsterdam, see Fuks and Fuks-Mansfeld, *Hebrew Typography in the Northern Netherlands*; Swetschinski, *Reluctant Cosmopolitans*, 150–3; Bloom, *The Economic History of the Jews in Amsterdam*.

Jews or defending it before Christians. So vigorous were his arguments that the rabbi of Amsterdam's Beit Yisrael congregation, Joseph Delmedigo, described him as 'the ornament of scholars and the glorious diadem of our people in the eyes of the nation, who writes learned works, the likes of which have never been seen in any lands or peoples; and their theologians consult him daily to hear his learning'.[85] In a similar vein, Pierre Daniel Huet, bishop of Avranches and no friend of the Jews, reported that Manasseh was 'a Jew of the first order. . . . I have had long and frequent conversations with him on religious subjects. He is an excellent man, conciliatory, moderate, sensible to reason, free from numerous Jewish superstitions and the empty dreams of the kabbalah.'[86] His good friend, the theologian Gerardus Johannes Vossius, described him as a learned and pious man, adding wistfully, 'I for my part (and I would say this of few, not only of that sect but of any other) consider him a man of true worth, albeit he lives in darkness.'[87] The great seventeenth-century jurist Hugo Grotius was also among Manasseh's friends: he would turn to Manasseh for clarification of points of Hebrew translation and biblical interpretation.[88]

While not a profound thinker, Manasseh was recognized as a fine orator. Christians as well as Jews flocked to hear his sermons. Most accounts of his life recall the visit of the stadtholder, Frederick Henry, Prince of Orange, to the Talmud Tora Synagogue on 22 May 1642, a day on which Manasseh was officiating.[89] The symbolism of the royal visit could scarcely have been lost on Manasseh and his congregation. As ex-officio head of the court, commander-in-chief of the army and navy of the Dutch republic, and defender of the Dutch Reformed Church, the stadtholder was, in effect, extending his protection to the Jews.

Manasseh's life spanned the most dynamic years of Amsterdam's development. By the 1620s the city had undergone a major economic transformation. His close neighbours included Rembrandt and the family of Spinoza. Two artistic projects brought Rembrandt into close contact with Manasseh in around 1635, when the already famous artist turned to his neighbour and friend for exegetical input on a monumental painting he was executing of Belshazzar's feast (Dan. 5). The painting's mystical atmosphere and inclusion of Hebrew letters has called forth a flood of commentaries by Rembrandt scholars about the relationship of the two and the degree of influence that Manasseh had on the artist.[90] Shortly afterwards, Rembrandt completed his portrait of Manas-

---

[85] Joseph Delmedigo, *Sefer elim*, cited in Nadler, *Rembrandt's Jews*, 109.

[86] Pierre Daniel Huet, *Huetania*, cited ibid.

[87] Gerardus Johannes Vossius, letter to Anthony van der Linden, cited in Zell, *Reframing Rembrandt*, 65 n. 28; see C. Roth, *A Life of Menasseh ben Israel*, 121.

[88] See Méchoulan and Nahon, introduction to Manasseh ben Israel, *The Hope of Israel*, 28.

[89] C. Roth, *A Life of Menasseh ben Israel*, 66–7; Méchoulan and Nahon, introduction to Manasseh ben Israel, *The Hope of Israel*, 16.

[90] Zell, *Reframing Rembrandt*, 59–64.

seh (Plate 22). Manasseh commissioned a series of illustrations for his *Piedra gloriosa* on the messianic promises in the book of Daniel from Rembrandt in 1655. Art historians have been especially intrigued by the impact that the execution of the four illustrations for the *Piedra gloriosa* had upon Rembrandt's oeuvre, some seeing it as a turning point in his spiritual and artistic development. Execution of the work required an enormous degree of co-operation between the two men. The text also contained Manasseh's speculations on the place of both Jews and non-Jews in the messianic era.[91]

Manasseh first gained recognition among Christian scholars in 1632 when he published his *Conciliador*, a work that attempted to reconcile the contradictory passages of the Bible, explaining and vindicating the Torah. It was originally published in Spanish and translated into Latin in 1633 by his pupil Dionysius Vossius, and was replete with Christian sources. While intended for doubting former Conversos, it struck a chord among a broad circle of Christian theologians. Thereafter, much of Manasseh's writing in Latin was addressed to a Christian audience. His ease in handling Christian sources facilitated dialogue with Protestant scholars. Interfaith dialogue was taken seriously in the Netherlands, as Protestant messianic notions included the conversion of the Jews to Christianity. For many Jews and Dutch and English Protestants the link between the dispersion of the Jews, the dawn of the messianic era, and the Puritan revolution was clear. According to Jewish messianic tradition, one of the prerequisites for redemption was Jews inhabiting all four corners of the world, and the recently discovered natives of the New World were held by many to be Jews. Although Jews and Christians disagreed on whether the messianic advent would mark the first or the second coming of the messiah, they both expected it to occur in the middle of the seventeenth century.

In 1644 a Portuguese Converso, Antonio (Aaron Levi) de Montezinos, arrived in Amsterdam with a wondrous account of his travels in South America in which he identified the natives of the Andes as the remnants of the tribe of Reuben, one of the ten Lost Tribes of Israel. Manasseh was among the crowd in the synagogue who listened rapturously to Montezinos's account. If remnants of ancient Israel were to be found in America, it followed, according to some believers, that the Jewish global dispersal was almost complete and the End of Days was approaching. Montezinos's identity as a Converso, a victim of the Inquisition's round-ups of 1639, and an adventurer in the New World struck a familiar and sympathetic chord among Amsterdam's Portuguese Jews. Probably the germ of Manasseh's mission to Oliver Cromwell to plead for the readmission of the Jews into England crystallized as he absorbed Montezinos's message. In 1650 Manasseh composed an extremely influential tract, *Miqweh Israel, Esto es esperanza de Israel*, in Spanish and Latin, translated into English as *The Hope of Israel*. Montezinos's claim of the Jewish identity of the Andean tribe was incorporated within a broader messianic tract and received an enthusiastic reception in

[91] Ibid. 72–85.

England. It was already believed in some Protestant circles that 1665/6 would see the advent of the messiah. Messianic excitement was simultaneously careering out of control among the Jews of Amsterdam and elsewhere as accounts of Shabetai Tsevi's claims emanated from the Ottoman empire. Amsterdam's Jewish printing houses responded to Shabetai Tsevi's drama with a rash of tracts and portraits of the putative messiah on his throne, and his prophet, Nathan of Gaza. Some Jewish merchants even set out for the Land of Israel in anticipation of the End of Days. Arguments about allowing the return of the Jews to England were not confined to theologians and millenarians. Some were receptive to the idea on practical, moral, political, or economic grounds.

On 2 September 1655 Manasseh set out for England armed with a persuasive set of arguments for the readmission of the Jews to England, in a treatise to Oliver Cromwell entitled *A Humble Address*.[92] Success would provide a sorely needed additional refuge for Marranos and would complete the requisite dispersion of the Jews to usher in the messianic era. Manasseh's *Humble Address*, borrowing freely from Simone Luzzatto's *Discorso circa il stato de gl'Hebrei*, offered historic proofs from Livorno and Venice of the economic advantages that accrued to a city that permitted Jewish residence.[93] But the public debate on the readmission of the Jews galvanized the forces of antisemitism. Anti-Jewish pamphlets appeared and rumours began to spread, including the unlikely claim that, should the Jews be readmitted, they planned to purchase St Paul's Cathedral and convert it into a synagogue. They were also accused of plotting to acquire the Bodleian Library in Oxford.

Despite Cromwell's positive attitude, the opposition to Jewish readmission carried the day, and no formal authorization of admission was promulgated. Little could Manasseh have foreseen that the defeat of his petition to Cromwell was a blessing in disguise, since all the laws enacted under Cromwell were overturned during the restoration of the Stuarts. As no decree readmitting the Jews had been promulgated, no such decree could be annulled. Portuguese Jews therefore continued to enter England unofficially. Those already living in London succeeded in leasing land for their first synagogue in December 1656. A few months later, they acquired a formal burial ground. Not long after this, a Marrano was admitted to the Stock Exchange as a licensed broker without being required to take a Christian oath. Through these informal steps, the Jews re-entered England, although it would be another 200 years before the last political barriers to Jewish emancipation were removed.

---

[92] Manasseh's mission has been reviewed in many of the standard books on the history of the Jews of England, but they have generally neglected to point out its special Portuguese Jewish resonances and depicted it within the broader context of Puritan thought and the arguments on Jewish resettlement (see C. Roth, *A Life of Menasseh ben Israel*, esp. 176–287; D. Katz, *Philosemitism and the Readmission of the Jews to England*; see also Schorsch, 'From Messianism to Realpolitik').

[93] Ravid, '"How Profitable the Nation of the Jewes Are"'; id., *Economics and Toleration in Seventeenth-Century Venice*.

Portuguese precedent reached across the English Channel. The *ascamot* of the new community in London were modelled on those of Amsterdam (which had been modelled on those of Venice). In 1664 Jacob Sasportas was brought from Amsterdam to serve as rabbi, thereby strengthening the already significant ties of the western Sephardi diaspora. Finally, in 1665 the congregation of Spanish and Portuguese Jews in London, the Kahal Kadosh Sha'ar Hashamayim, acquired a site fronting on Bevis Marks and Heneage Lane, where the synagogue, commonly known as Bevis Marks, still stands today.

Manasseh left for home a disappointed man. He died on 20 November 1657. He did not live to see these landmark decisions nor did he understand his influence in encouraging the Marranos of London to emerge from their clandestine existence. His simple grave at Ouderkerk cemetery bears the laconic inscription: 'He is not dead; for in heaven he lives in supreme glory, while on earth his pen has won him immortal remembrance.'

From Portuguese Nation to Spanish and Portuguese Congregation

During the 1660s and 1670s Portuguese Jewish immigration to Amsterdam from the Iberian peninsula tapered off. The Netherlands was no longer a magnet for Sephardi merchants as England gained ascendancy over Holland and the Dutch economy began to languish. The latest arrivals were more observant than their predecessors, including Sephardim from Morocco, émigrés from Italian ghettos, and a growing number of Jews from the declining Ottoman empire. By the end of the seventeenth century the 3,500 Sephardim of Amsterdam were an ethnically diverse congregation, no longer a kinship group. A subtle marriage of Sephardi diasporas had occurred which finally lent a sense of Jewish legitimacy to the Portuguese neophytes and their descendants. Elsewhere, the gulf between the eastern and western Sephardim was also diminishing.

Historians have tended to read modern issues into past narratives, intrigued by the formative seventeenth century in the Portuguese community of Amsterdam.[94] Whether in the careers of the dissidents Spinoza and de Prado or in the uncontrolled exuberance with which the Jews of Amsterdam greeted the career of Shabetai Tsevi, observers sometimes see the Portuguese community's flirtation with new patterns of thought as providing the foundations for Jewish modernity. It remains unclear, however, how central these dissidents were to the community's self-identity.

[94] See Baron, *A Social and Religious History of the Jews*, vol. xv. Yerushalmi claims that 'the secular culture of many Dutch and Italian Jews anticipated the Berlin Haskalah of the eighteenth century and was, in some respects, more naturally acquired, mature, and more broadly based. . . . Against the backdrop of an age which produced a number of significantly "modern" developments in Jewry, [the Marrano migrants] stand out as perhaps the first modern Jews' (Yerushalmi, *From Spanish Court to Italian Ghetto*, 43–4); for a contrasting view, see Y. Kaplan, 'The Portuguese Community of Amsterdam in the Seventeenth Century'; for the distinctions between pre-modern and modern Jewry, see J. Katz, *Tradition and Crisis*; id., *Out of the Ghetto*.

Amsterdam's Jews have been called a 'brand plucked from the fire'.[95] They faced an unprecedented challenge in adjusting to Jewish customs and the formalities of an organized community. Their spiritual leaders well understood that Jews who had learned about their heritage from a Christian text were going to be different from Jews who had grown up in a Jewish community. They would need help reintegrating and might balk at the strictures of Judaism. Amsterdam's leaders were less concerned about what Jewish congregants believed privately than with what they said and how they behaved publicly. At the same time, many Conversos returned to Judaism with great zeal and high expectations. Some, naturally, would be more interested in theology than in ritual, and some would feel compelled to express their religious doubts regardless of the social consequences. Individualism and freedom of thought, hallmarks of modernity, were tentatively tested among some Portuguese Jews of Amsterdam.

Some observers contend that the economic dynamism of the Portuguese introduced a new image of the Jew to Christian Europe. Unlike the later, modernizing Jews of Germany, the Jews of Amsterdam did not set out on their uncharted journey self-consciously seeking to restructure Jewish life either economically or religiously. They sought to recapture a heritage which their ancestors had been forced to relinquish, while making the most of the opportunities available to them in an age of economic expansion. In this respect, they were extraordinarily successful. Their prior cultural interests endured even as they measured the boundaries of their new identities.

In the final analysis the Portuguese community of Amsterdam, never large in numbers, provided the template for the re-establishment and expansion of Jewish life in western Europe and the Atlantic world. Its synagogues provided the architectural and organizational model for the Portuguese synagogues in London, New York, and Curaçao. One of its leaders, Manasseh ben Israel, was the embodiment of the enlightened Jew for a generation of European Protestants who sought not just converts but also friendships with Jews. From some of their friendly exchanges, a new sense of the humanity of the Jews, rather than a view of the Jew as a theological abstraction, would emerge, although they probably did not alter the largely conversionist hopes that much.

The Portuguese Jews did not strive to bend Judaism to their unique needs as former Christians. Instead, many simply 'fell away', while others began the long process of separating the secular and profane areas of life from its religious dimensions, which would become the hallmark of modernity. In some respects, most of Amsterdam's Portuguese Jews became 'modern' Jews without ever having been medieval Jews. Their concern with their image in the eyes of their neighbours strikes a thoroughly modern, apologetic note. They pioneered living in a situation of quasi-toleration that pre-dated the Jewish movement for toleration in the west by more than a century. Their *ascamot*

---

[95] Yovel, *Spinoza and Other Heretics*, i. 38.

demonstrate little interest in establishing an all-encompassing Jewish community. Trade, business, and commerce were separate from family, worship, and the synagogue.

The union of Portuguese, Spanish, Moroccan, Italian, and Ottoman Jews into one community in Amsterdam in the late seventeenth and early eighteenth centuries prefigures the current federated nature of many Sephardi communities. No longer unified by a common Hispanic origin or cultural orientation, then, as now, Sephardim were bound together by the romance, the myth, and the memory of a heroic past in Sepharad. They performed a balancing act of religiosity and materialism, with devotion to family and kin at its core. Neither language nor geography embraces the totality of what was a long and intricate journey in cities of splendour on many continents.

CONCLUSION

▪

Si nevi'im no somos, de nevi'im venimos
[We may not be prophets, but we are descended from them]

Ya basta mi nombre ke es abravanel
[It suffices that my name is Abravanel]

LADINO PROVERBS

THE YEAR 1492 marked the end of one form of Jewish life and the beginning of another for the Jews of the Iberian peninsula, but they had already become masters of diaspora life. Prior to 1492 their poets sang poignantly of exile from the Land of Israel; however, they also seem to have been quite comfortable in their life in Spain. After 1492 they experienced a second exile, this time from Sepharad, their Iberian homeland. Like all other Jews, Sephardim collectively mourned the loss of Zion; as Sephardim they also collectively mourned the loss of Spain. They participated in many cultures, yet their diasporic language, Ladino, together with their shared history, bound them to other Sephardim in ways that estranged them from non-Sephardi Jews.

The deportation of the Jews from their ancient homeland to Babylon in 586 BCE produced the first diaspora in history, although the term was not applied to Jewish settlements outside the Land of Israel until Hellenistic times. In Babylonia, the Jews constructed a home in exile, established new sacred places, and produced new sacred books. In the process, they reinvented themselves while forging the tools for survival outside the homeland: worship in the synagogue and study in the *beit midrash* substituted for the sacrifices in the Temple. This first experiment of Jewish life lived elsewhere served as the prototype for subsequent diasporas. One of the guiding principles of diasporic existence, first enunciated by the prophet Jeremiah, was to 'seek the welfare of the city where I have sent you into exile, and pray to the Lord on its behalf, for in its welfare you will find your welfare' (Jer. 29: 7).

The word 'diaspora' has been applied since Graeco-Roman times to many groups sharing a common geographical and ethno-cultural origin who are dispersed outside their land of origin. The Jews identified with their ancestral home in the Land of Israel, yet simultaneously demonstrated an uncanny ability to adapt to new and foreign host cultures. More often than not, they found themselves poised between two poles. While planting local roots, they nevertheless retained hopes for the ultimate ingathering of their scattered people. Jewish life unfolded between exile and return. Some Jewish diasporas were ephemeral, others more enduring. Some diasporas were exceptionally creative, others merely derivative. But, regardless of the cultural level, Jewish communities tended to relate to each other through shared memories and common traditions and laws. Rabbinic Judaism evolved in large measure as an expression of the existential challenges and contradictions of the diasporic condition.

Jeremiah also instructed the displaced Jews 'to build houses and dwell in them, plant gardens and eat the fruit of them' (Jer. 29: 5). Nowhere was the reality of diaspora as a verdant garden more vivid, both literally and poetically, than in Andalusia. Spain was exile, but an exile of a special order. Jewish life on the Iberian peninsula exhibited a unique sense of attachment to place. The presence of trilingual tombstone inscriptions in Latin, Greek, and Hebrew from the fourth century testifies to Jewish immersion in the surrounding Graeco-Roman culture. At the same time, the presence of the menorah as a tombstone motif suggests that they still nurtured an identification with Jerusalem. They lived, as it were, on two planes simultaneously—the historical and the eschatological. Though ensconced in their surroundings, their daily prayers, festivals, and myriad customs reminded them of their glorious past somewhere else and of their future destined to unfold at some indeterminate date in Jerusalem. While this double consciousness of being simultaneously immersed in yet outside the culture of the host society may have been disorienting, it also served as a source of enormous creative energy. When Judah Halevi sang 'My heart is in the East and I am in the far West', he echoed the keen Sephardi awareness of being embedded in both Sepharad and Jerusalem. His pilgrimage to the Land of Israel in 1141 was not simply a voyage in imitation of the Christian Spanish pilgrimage to Santiago de Compostela that had captured the hearts of Castilians in his day, but was perceived by Halevi as a return to a home in ruins and a mother in mourning. Halevi's dual poetic connections were no simple matter. They involved a complex sense of dislocation entwined with rootedness in both Spain and the Land of Israel.

Spain has correctly been viewed as a diaspora within a diaspora, or a double diaspora, different from other diasporas in several fundamental ways. On the most obvious level, the Jews of Spain form one of the two major divisions of the Jewish people but the only division to be identified with a specific piece of geography. Few diasporas were as long-lived. Jews lived in Spain at least as long as they lived in ancient Israel: from perhaps as early as the time of Paul (first century) until 1492. But it was not just the longevity of residence, nor the intensity of assimilation, nor the final tragic chapter of life on Iberian soil that set Spain apart. Other diasporas also experienced great flowerings and violent ends. Spain continued to shape the self-definition of its exiles for hundreds of years after the Expulsion. The Ladino language that evolved in the Ottoman empire out of the linguistic traditions of the exiles of 1492 and their heirs served to unify a transnational diaspora that stretched through the Balkans to the Middle East and linked Jews in Sarajevo and Salonica, Rhodes and Rhodesia.

Even the afterlife of Spain was unique. The place of Spain in Jewish memory and identity assumed unanticipated and novel forms. On the simplest level, being from Spain or Portugal or having ancestors who were originally from Spain or Portugal made one Sephardi. Yet what Spain was and what its Jews had accomplished there assumed quasi-mythical proportions. Before long it was not clear what was diaspora and what was homeland, who belonged and who did not. Romaniote Jews had never lived in Spain, yet they became part of a greater Sephardi diaspora in Istanbul. Portuguese Jews in Amsterdam had been Catholic for over a century, yet remained Portuguese and Jewish in the eyes of their Old Christian neighbours and in their own consciousness.

Unlike other Jewish communities in pre-modern times, Sephardim engaged in almost all fields of knowledge in Muslim and Christian Spain: Hebrew language and poetry, science, philosophy, statecraft, biblical and talmudic commentary, art, astronomy, music, and more. Their versatility on Iberian soil in both the secular and religious spheres was prodigious. The Jews of Spain recognized that their accomplishments in Iberia were exceptional, took enormous pride in them, and attributed them to their superior lineage. They developed 'historical' theories to explain their virtuosity, drawing inspiration from the sharp debates on lineage and pedigree that circulated among the Muslims in Spain and the race-conscious culture of late medieval Christian Spain. Alongside their consciousness of pedigree, the Sephardim also acquired a sense of honour that coloured their relationships with the other Jews whom they encountered after leaving Iberia.

Sephardi Jewry was unique because Spain was unique. The Iberian peninsula was the sole territory in Europe where Christians, Jews, and Muslims had coexisted on the same soil for hundreds of years. Among the fruitful results of this coexistence was a remarkable interaction of cultures, not only on the battlefield but also in people's books and in their minds. Sephardi multilingualism facilitated their emergence as intermediaries of cultures. They wrote in the vernaculars of Spain and translated and transformed the fruits of other cultures into the Jewish canon. Paradoxically, leaving Spain intensified the Sephardi attachment to their Iberian past, also complicating their prior multilingualism.

It is not clear what being Sephardi signified prior to 1492. No political entity known as Spain existed before then, and the Jews of Iberia tended to identify themselves as Catalan, Aragonese, Navarese, Portuguese, or, on a provincial or local level, as Saragossan, Murcian, Valencian, Tortosan, or Toledan. Spain only became unified on the eve of the Expulsion, and Sephardim thereafter defined themselves in relation to a country that did not exist when they dwelt there. It is not clear what Maimonides meant when he referred to himself in his correspondence as Moshe ben Maimon Hasefaradi when he was living in twelfth-century Egypt. Was Sepharad simply a geographical designator or did it also imply a set of skills, a mental outlook, and a social stance? Localized loyalties continued among the exiles from Iberia for at least a century after the Expulsion, as they continued to identify with a specific Iberian city, province, or kingdom, only gradually relinquishing these past identities for a sense of belonging to a Sephardi diaspora. To be Sephardi after 1600 meant to be connected in some way to Jewish memories of Spain, to a noble extended family, and to a bygone golden age of Jewish creativity. The Iberian associations ranged from the scintillating at one end of the spectrum to the most tragic autos-da-fé at the other. It also meant belonging to a diaspora that was global and transnational. In this sense, Sephardim were the first modern Jews.

BIBLIOGRAPHY

ABRAVANEL, ISAAC, *Ma'ayanei hayeshuah* [commentary on Daniel] (Stettin, 1860).
—— *Yeshuot meshiḥo* [on the messiah] (Königsberg, 1861).
ADELMAN, HOWARD TZVI, 'Custom, Law and Gender: Levirate Union Among Ashkenazim and Sephardim in Italy after the Expulsion from Spain', in Raymond Waddington and Arthur Williamson (eds.), *The Expulsion of the Jews 1492 and After* (New York, 1994), 107–25.
—— 'Italian Jewish Women', in Judith Baskin (ed.), *Jewish Women in Historical Perspective* (Detroit, 1991), 135–58.
—— 'Jewish Women and Family Life, Inside and Outside the Ghetto', in Robert C. Davis and Benjamin Ravid (eds.), *The Jews of Early Modern Venice* (Baltimore, Md., 2001), 143–65.
—— 'Rabbis and Reality: The Public Roles of Jewish Women in the Renaissance and Catholic Restoration', *Jewish History*, 5 (1991), 27–40.
—— 'Success and Failure in the Seventeenth Century Ghetto of Venice', Ph.D. thesis (Brandeis University, 1985).
ADLER, ISRAEL, *La Pratique musicale savante dans quelques communautés juives en Europe aux XVIIe–XVIIe siècles*, 2 vols. (Paris, 1966).
AL-HARIZI, JUDAH, *The Book of Taḥkemoni*, ed. David Simha Segal (London, 2001).
ALCOY I PEDROS, ROSA, 'The Artist of the Marginal Decorations of the "Copenhagen Maimonides"', *Jewish Art*, 18 (1992), 129–39.
ALFONSO, ESPERANZA, 'Uses of Exile in Poetic Discourse: Some Examples from Medieval Literature', in Ross Brann and Adam Sutcliffe (eds.), *Renewing the Past: Reconfiguring Jewish Culture* (Philadelphia, 2004), 31–49.
ALLONY, NEHEMIAH, 'The Kuzari of R. Judah Halevi in the Light of the *Shu'ubiyya*' (Heb.), *Bitzaron*, 65/3 (1974), 105–13.
—— 'The Reaction of Moses ibn Ezra to '*Arabiyya*', *Bulletin of the Institute of Jewish Studies*, 3 (1975), 19–40.
ALMOSNINO, MOSES BEN BARUCH, *Extremos y grandezas de Constantinople* (Istanbul, 1509).
AMADOR DE LOS RÍOS, RODRIGO, *Toledo* (Madrid, 1905).
AMARILLO, ABRAHAM S., 'The Great Talmud Torah of Salonica' (Heb.), *Sefunot*, 13 (1971), 275–308.
ARBEL, BENJAMIN, 'Venice and the Jewish Merchants of Istanbul in the Sixteenth Century', in Ariel Toaff and Simon Schwartzfuchs (eds.), *The Mediterranean and the Jews: Banking, Finance, and International Trade (XVI–XVIII Centuries)* (Ramat Gan, 1989), 39–56.
ASHTOR, ELIYAHU, *The Jews of Moslem Spain*, 3 vols. in 2 (Philadelphia, 1992).
ASSIS, YOM TOV, *The Golden Age of Aragonese Jewry: Community and Society in the Crown of Aragon, 1213–1327* (Oxford, 1997).
—— 'Poor and Rich in Jewish Society in Mediterranean Spain' (Heb.), *Pe'amim*, 46–7 (1991), 115–38.
ASSIS, YOM TOV, 'Sefarad: A Definition in the Context of a Cultural Encounter', in Carlos Carrete Parrondo et al. (eds.), *Encuentros and Desencuentros: Spanish Jewish Cultural Interaction throughout History* (Tel Aviv, 2000), 29–37.

ASSIS, YOM TOV, 'Sexual Behaviour in Mediaeval Hispano-Jewish Society', in Ada Rapoport-Albert and Steven J. Zipperstein (eds.), *Jewish History: Essays in Honour of Chimen Abramsky* (London, 1988), 25–59.

AVITSUR, SHEMUEL, 'The Woollen Textile Industry in Salonica' (Heb.), *Sefunot*, 12 (1971), 145–68.

AYALON, YARON, *Natural Disasters in the Ottoman Empire: Plague, Famine, and Other Misfortunes* (Cambridge, 2015).

BAER, MARC D., *Dönme: Jewish Converts, Muslim Revolutionaries, and Secular Turks* (Stanford, Calif., 2010).

—— 'The Great Fire of 1660 and the Islamization of Christian and Jewish Space in Istanbul', *International Journal of Middle Eastern Studies*, 36 (2004), 159–81.

BAER, YITZHAK, *A History of the Jews in Christian Spain*, trans. Louis Schiffman, 2 vols. (Philadelphia, 1961–6).

—— 'The Messianic Movement in Spain in the Period of the Expulsion' (Heb.), *Me'asef tsiyon*, 5 (1933), 61–78.

BAGBY, ALBERT I., JR., 'The Jew in the *Cantigas* of Alfonso X, El Sabio', *Speculum*, 46 (1971), 670–88.

BANGO, ISIDRO G., *Remembering Sepharad: Jewish Culture in Medieval Spain* (Madrid, 2003).

BAR HEBRAEUS, GREGORY (ABU L FARAJ), *The Chronology*, trans. E. A. Wallis Budge (London, 1932).

BARGEBUHR, FREDERICK P., 'The Alhambra Palace of the Eleventh Century', *Journal of the Warburg and Courtauld Institutes*, 19 (1956), 192–258.

BARNETT, RICHARD, 'Mr. Pepys' Contacts with the Spanish and Portuguese Jews of London', in Aaron Mirsky, Avraham Grossman, and Yosef Kaplan (eds.), *Exile and Diaspora: Studies in the History of the Jewish People Presented to Professor Haim Beinart* (Jerusalem, 1991), 224–30.

BARON, SALO W., 'Plenitude of Apostolic Powers and Medieval Jewish Serfdom', in id., *Ancient and Medieval Jewish History*, ed. Leon A. Feldman (New Brunswick, NJ, 1972), 284–307.

—— *A Social and Religious History of the Jews*, 2nd edn., 18 vols. (Philadelphia and New York, 1952–83).

BARTON, THOMAS W., *Contested Treasure: Jews and Authority in the Crown of Aragon* (University Park, Pa., 2015).

BARZILAY, ISAAC, 'John Toland's Borrowings from Simone Luzzatto', *Jewish Social Studies*, 31 (1969), 75–81.

BASHAN, ELIEZER, 'The Attitude of Eighteenth- and Nineteenth-Century Moroccan Rabbis to the Duty of Settling in the Land of Israel' (Heb.), in *Vatiqin: Studies in the History of the Yishuv in Memory of Rabbi Yosef Yitzchak Rivlin* [Vatikin: meḥkarim betoledot hayishuv: lezikhro shel r. yosef yitsḥak rivlin, asor lefetirato, 1963–73], ed. Yehoshua Kaniel and H. Z. Hirschberg (Ramat Gan, 1975), 35–46.

BASOLA, MOSES, *In Zion and Jerusalem: The Itinerary of Rabbi Moses Basola 1521–1523* (Jerusalem, 1999).

BATTERMAN, MICHAEL, 'Bread of Affliction, Emblem of Power: The Passover Matzah in Haggadah Manuscripts from Christian Spain', in Eva Frojmovic (ed.), *Imaging the Self, Imagining the Other: Visual Representation and Jewish–Christian Dynamics in the Middle Ages and Early Modern Period* (Leiden, 2002), 53–89.

—— 'The Emergence of the Spanish Illuminated Haggadah Manuscript', Ph.D. thesis (Northwestern University, 2000).

BEINART, HAIM, 'A Prophesying Movement in Cordova in the Years 1499–1502' (Heb.), *Zion*, 44 (1979), 190–200.

BEN ISRAEL, MANASSEH, *The Hope of Israel*, ed. Henry Méchoulan and Gérard Nahon (Oxford, 2004).

BEN-MENAHEM, NAPHTALI, 'The Works of Rabbi Moses Almosnino' (Heb.), *Sinai*, 10 (1946–7), 268–85.

BEN-NAEH, YARON, 'The City of Torah and Learning: Salonica as a Centre of Learning in the Sixteenth and Seventeenth Centuries' (Heb.), *Pe'amim*, 80 (1999), 60–82.

—— 'Honor and Its Meaning Among Ottoman Jews', *Jewish Social Studies*, 11/12 (2005), 19–50.

—— and GIACOMO SABAN, 'Three German Travellers on Istanbul Jews', *Journal of Jewish Studies*, 12 (2013), 37–51.

BEN-UR, AVIVA, and RACHEL FRANKEL, *Remnant Stones: The Jewish Cemeteries and Synagogue of Suriname* (Cincinnati, 2009).

BENAYAHU, MEIR Z., 'Devotional Practices of the Kabbalists of Safed in Meron' (Heb.), *Sefunot*, 6 (1962), 9–40.

—— *Moses Almosnino of Salonica: His Life and Work* [Mosheh almosnino de saloniki: ḥayav umifaloh] (Tel Aviv, 1996).

BENBASSA, ESTHER, and ARON RODRIGUE, *The Jews of the Balkans: The Judeo-Spanish Community, 15th to 20th Centuries* (Oxford, 1995).

BENMELECH, MOTI, 'History, Politics, and Messianism: David ha-Reuveni's Origin and Mission', *AJS Review*, 35 (2011), 35–60.

BENTOV, HAIM, 'Methods of Study of Talmud in the Yeshivas of Salonica and Turkey after the Expulsion from Spain' (Heb.), *Sefunot*, 13 (1971), 7–102.

BERGER, DAVID, *The Jewish–Christian Debate in the High Middle Ages: A Critical Edition of the Nitzahon Vetus* (Philadelphia, 1979).

BLAND, KALMAN, *The Artless Jew: Medieval and Modern Affirmations and Denials of the Visual* (Princeton, NJ, 2001).

BLOCH, JOSHUA, 'Early Hebrew Printing in Spain and Portugal', in C. Berlin (ed.), *Hebrew Printing and Bibliography* (New York, 1976), 7–53.

—— 'Venetian Printers of Hebrew Books', *Bulletin of the New York Public Library*, 37/9 (Feb. 1932), 71–92.

BLOOM, HERBERT I., *The Economic Activities of the Jews of Amsterdam in the Seventeenth and Eighteenth Centuries* (Port Washington, NY, 1937).

BOCCATTO, CARLA, 'Aspetti della condizione femminile nel ghetto di Venezia (secolo XVII): I testamenti', *Italia*, 10 (1993), 105–35.

BODIAN, MIRIAM, 'Amsterdam, Venice and the Marrano Diaspora', in Jozeph Michman (ed.), *Dutch Jewish History*, vol. ii: *Proceedings of the Fourth Symposium on the History of the Jews of the Netherlands* (Jerusalem, 1989), 47–66.

—— 'The Escamot of the Spanish-Portuguese Jewish Community in London, 1664', *Michael*, 9 (1985), 9–26.

—— *Hebrews of the Portuguese Nation* (Bloomington, Ind., 1997).

BODIAN, MIRIAM, 'Liberty of Conscience and the Jews in the Dutch Republic', *Studies in Christian–Jewish Relations*, 6 (2011), 1–9.

—— '"Men of the Nation": The Shaping of Converso Identity in Early Modern Europe', *Past and Present*, 143 (1994), 48–76.

—— 'The "Portuguese" Dowry Societies in Venice and Amsterdam: A Case of Communal Differentiation within the Marrano Diaspora', *Italia*, 6 (1987), 30–61.

BONAZZOLLI, VIVIANA, 'Ebrei italiani, portoghesi, levantini sulla piazza commerciale di Ancona intorno alla metà del Cinquecento', in Gaetano Cozzi (ed.), *Gli ebrei e Venezia* (Milan, 1987), 727–70.

BONFIL, ROBERT, 'A Cultural Profile', in Robert C. Davis and Benjamin Ravid (eds.), *The Jews of Early Modern Venice* (Baltimore, Md., 2001), 169–90.

BORNSTEIN-MAKOVETSKY, LEAH, 'The Jewish Community in Istanbul in the Mid-Sixteenth Century: Its Sephardi and Romaniot Personalities and Sages' (Heb.), *Michael*, 9 (1985), 145–54.

—— 'Structure, Organization, and Spiritual Life of the Sephardi Jews in the Ottoman Empire from the Sixteenth to the Eighteenth Centuries', in Richard David Barnett and W. M. Schwab (eds.), *The Sephardi Heritage*, vol. ii: *The Western Sephardim* (Grendon, Northants, 1989), 314–48.

BRANN, ROSS, 'The Arabized Jews', in Maria Rosa Menocal, Raymond P. Scheindlin, and Michael Sells (eds.), *The Literature of al-Andalus* (Cambridge, 2000), 435–54.

—— *The Compunctious Poet: Cultural Ambiguity and Hebrew Poetry in Muslim Spain* (Baltimore, Md., 1991), 365–81.

—— 'How Can My Heart Be in the East? Intertextual Irony in Judah ha-Levi', in Benjamin H. Hary, John Hayes, and Fred Astren (eds.), *Judaism and Islam: Boundaries, Communication and Interaction* (Leiden, 2000), 365–80.

BRAUDE, BENJAMIN, 'The Rise and Fall of Salonica Woollens, 1500–1650: Technology Transfer and Western Competition', *Mediterranean Historical Review*, 6 (1991), 216–36.

BREMER, ANN, *Judah Halevi and His Circle of Hebrew Poets in Granada* (Leiden, 2005).

BULLIET, RICHARD W., *Conversion to Islam in the Medieval Period: An Essay in Quantitative History* (Cambridge, Mass., 1979).

BUNIS, DAVID M., 'Distinctive Characteristics of Jewish Ibero-Romance, circa 1492', *Hispania Judaica Bulletin*, 4 (2004), 105–37.

—— 'The Language of the Spanish Jews: A Historical Survey' (Heb.), in Haim Beinart (ed.), *The Sephardi Legacy* [Moreshet sefarad] (Jerusalem, 1992), 694–713.

BURDELEZ, IVANA, 'The Role of Ragusan Jews in the History of the Mediterranean Countries', *Mediterranean Historical Review*, 6 (1991), 190–7.

BURNS, ROBERT I. (ed.), *Emperor of Culture: Alfonso X the Learned of Castile and his Thirteenth Century Renaissance* (Philadelphia, 1990).

CALIMANI, RICCARDO, *The Ghetto of Venice* (Milan, 1995).

CANTERA BURGOS, FRANCISCO, *Sinagogas españolas: Con especial studio de la Córdba y la Toledana de El Tránsito* (Madrid, 1955).

—— and JOSE MARIA MILLAS VALLICROSA, *Las inscripciones hebraicas en España* (Madrid, 1956).

CAPSALI, ELIYAHU, *Seder eliyahu zuta* [history of the Ottoman empire], 3 vols., ed. Aryeh Shmuelevitz, Meir Benayahu, and Shlomo Simonsohn (Jerusalem, 1976–83).

CARLEBACH, ELISHEVA, *Between Ashkenaz and Sepharad: Jewish Messianism in Ashkenaz and Sepharad* (New York, 1998).

CARPENTER, DWAYNE, *Alphonso X and the Jews: An Edition of and Commentary on 'Siete Partidas' 7.24, 'De los Judios'* (Berkeley, Calif., 1986).

—— 'The Portrayal of the Jew in Alfonso the Learned's Cantigas de Santa Maria', in Bernard D. Cooperman (ed.), *In Iberia and Beyond: Hispanic Jews Between Cultures* (Newark, Del., 1998), 15–42.

CHAZAN, ROBERT, *Barcelona and Beyond* (Berkeley, Calif., 1986).

—— *Medieval Stereotypes* (Cambridge, 2005).

COHEN, AMNON, 'Ritual Murder Accusations against Jews during the Days of Suleiman the Magnificent', *Journal of Turkish Studies*, 10 (1986), 73–8.

—— and BERNARD LEWIS, *Population and Revenue in the Towns of Palestine in the Sixteenth Century* (Princeton, NJ, 1978).

COHEN, GERSON D., 'The Blessing of Assimilation in Jewish History', in Neil Gilman (ed.), *Jewish History and Jewish Identity* (New York, 1997), 145–56.

—— 'Messianic Postures of Ashkenazim and Sephardim', in Marc Saperstein (ed.), *Essential Papers on Messianic Movements and Personalities in Jewish History* (New York, 1992), 202–33.

COHEN, JEREMY, *The Friars and the Jews: The Evolution of Medieval Anti-Judaism* (Ithaca, NY, 1982).

—— *Living Letters of the Law: Ideas of the Jew in Medieval Christianity* (Berkeley, Calif., 1999).

COHEN, JULIA PHILLIPS, *Becoming Ottoman: Sephardi Jews and Imperial Citizenship in the Modern Era* (Oxford, 2014).

COHEN, MARK R., 'Leone da Modena's Riti: A Seventeenth Century Plea for Social Toleration of Jews', *Jewish Social Studies*, 34 (1972), 287–321.

—— 'Sociability and the Concept of *Galut* in Muslim–Jewish Relations in the Middle Ages', in Benjamin H. Hary, John Hayes, and Fred Astren (eds.), *Judaism and Islam: Boundaries, Communication and Interaction* (Leiden, 2000), 37–51.

COHEN, ROBERT, '*Memoria para os siglos futuros*: Myth and Memory on the Beginnings of the Amsterdam Sephardi Community', *Jewish History*, 2 (1987), 67–72.

—— 'Passage to the New World: The Sephardi Poor of Eighteenth-Century Amsterdam', in Lea Dasberg and Jonathan N. Cohen (eds.), *Neveh Ya'akov: Jubilee Volume Presented to Dr. Jaap Meijer on the Occasion of his Seventieth Birthday* (Assen, 1982), 31–42.

COLE, PETER, 'Solomon ibn Gabirol: An Andalusian Alphabet', in Solomon ibn Gabirol, *Selected Poems*, trans. Peter Cole (Princeton, NJ, 2001), 7–37.

COOPERMAN, BERNARD D., 'Amsterdam from an International Perspective: Tolerance and Kehillah in the Portuguese Diaspora', in Yosef Kaplan (ed.), *The Dutch Intersection: The Jews and the Netherlands in Modern History* (Leiden, 2008), 1–18.

—— 'Portuguese Conversos in Ancona: Jewish Political Activity in Early Modern Italy', in id. (ed.), *In Iberia and Beyond: Hispanic Jews Between Cultures* (Newark, Del., 1998), 298–352.

—— 'Trade and Settlement: The Establishment and Early Development of the Jewish Communities of Leghorn and Pisa (1591–1626)', Ph.D. thesis (Harvard University, 1977).

—— 'Venetian Policy towards the Levantine Jews in its Broader Italian Context', in Gaetano Cozzi (ed.), *Gli ebrei e Venezia* (Milan, 1987), 65–84.

CORYAT, THOMAS, *Crudities* [1611] (Glasgow, 1905).

CURIEL, ROBERTA, and BERNARD COOPERMAN, *The Venetian Ghetto* (New York, 1989).

DAVID, ABRAHAM, *To Come to the Land: Immigration and Settlement in 16th-Century Eretz-Israel* (Tuscaloosa, Ala., 1999).

DAVID, JOSEPH, 'The Reception of the *Shulhan Aruch* and the Formation of Ashkenazic Identity', *AJS Review*, 26 (2002), 251–76.

DE MEDINA, SAMUEL, *She'elot uteshuvot meharashdam* [responsa], 4 vols. (Salonica, 1594–7).

DECTER, JONATHAN P., 'Before Caliphs and Kings', in Jonathan Ray (ed.), *The Jew in Medieval Iberia* (Boston, Mass., 2012), 1–32.

—— *Iberian Jewish Literature: Between al-Andalus and Christian Europe* (Bloomington, Ind., 2007).

DEN BOER, HARM, 'Amsterdam as "Locus" of Iberian Printing in the Seventeenth and Eighteenth Centuries', in Yosef Kaplan (ed.), *The Dutch Intersection: The Jews and the Netherlands in Modern History* (Leiden, 2008), 87–110.

DESCARTES, RENÉ, *Correspondance*, vol. i: *Avril 1622 – Février 1638*, Œuvres de Descartes, ed. Charles Adam and Paul Tannery (Paris, 1897).

DI LEONE LEONI, ARON, *The Hebrew Portuguese Nations in Antwerp and London at the Time of Charles V and Henry VIII: New Documents and Interpretations* (Jersey City, NJ, 2005).

DIMITROVSKY, HAYYIM, 'New Documents Regarding the "Semicha" Controversy in Safed' (Heb.), *Sefunot*, 10 (1966), 113–92.

DODDS, JERRILYN, *Al-Andalus: The Art of Islamic Spain* (New York, 1992).

—— *Architecture and Ideology in Early Medieval Spain* (University Park, Pa., 1990).

—— 'The Arts of al-Andalus', in Salma Khadra Jayyusi (ed.), *The Legacy of Muslim Spain*, 2 vols. (Leiden, 2000), ii. 599–618.

—— 'Mudéjar Tradition and the Synagogues of Medieval Spain: Cultural Identity and Cultural Hegemony', in Vivian Mann, Thomas F. Glick, and Jerrilynn Dodds (eds.), *Convivencia: Jews, Muslims, and Christians in Medieval Spain* (New York, 1992), 113–31.

—— 'The Mudéjar Tradition in Architecture', in Salma Khadra Jayyusi (ed.), *The Legacy of Muslim Spain*, 2 vols. (Leiden, 2000), ii. 592–8.

—— MARIA ROSA MENOCAL, and ABIGAIL KRASNER BALBALE, *The Arts of Intimacy: Christians, Jews and Muslims in the Making of Castilian Culture* (New Haven, Conn., 2008).

DOZY, REINHART, *Histoire des Musulmanes d'Espagne*, 3 vols. (Leiden, 1932).

DRORY, RINA, *The First Contacts between Jewish and Arabic Literature in the Tenth Century* [Reshit hamaga'im shel hasifrut hayehudit im hasifrut ha'aravit beme'ah ha'asirit] (Tel Aviv, 1988).

—— 'Literary Contacts and Where to Find Them: On Arabic Literary Models in Medieval Jewish Culture', *Poetics Today*, 14/2 (1993), 277–302.

ECKER, HEATHER, *Caliphs and Kings: The Art and Influence of Islamic Spain* (Washington DC, n.d.).

EFRON, JOHN M., *German Jewry and the Allure of the Sephardic* (Princeton, NJ, 2016).

ELDEM, EDHEM, 'Istanbul: From Imperial to Peripheralized Capital', in Edhem Eldem, Daniel Goffman, and Bruce Masters, *The Ottoman City Between East and West: Aleppo, Izmir, and Istanbul* (Cambridge, 1999), 135–206.

ELIAV-FELDON, MIRIAM, 'Invented Identities: Credulity in the Age of Prophecy and Exploration', *Journal of Early Modern History*, 3/3 (1999), 203–32.

ELIOR, RACHEL, 'Messianic Expectations and Spiritualization of Religious Life in the Sixteenth Century', in David B. Ruderman (ed.), *Essential Papers on Jewish Culture in Renaissance and Baroque Italy* (New York, 1992), 283–98.

EMMANUEL, ISAAC SAMUEL, *Histoire des Israélites de Salonique*, 3 vols. (Paris, 1936).

—— *Precious Stones of the Jews of Curaçao: Curaçaon Jewry 1656–1957* (New York, 1957).

EPSTEIN, MARC M., *Dreams of Subversion in Medieval Jewish Art and Literature* (University Park, Pa., 1997).

—— *The Medieval Haggadah: Art, Narrative and Religious Imagination* (New Haven, Conn., 2011).

EPSTEIN, MARK ALAN, *The Ottoman Jewish Communities and Their Role in the Fifteenth and Sixteenth Centuries* (Freiburg, 1980).

ESTOW, CLAIRE, *Pedro the Cruel of Castile, 1350–1369* (Leiden, 1995).

FEINGOLD, AARON J., *Three Jewish Physicians of the Renaissance* (New York, 1994).

FIERRO, MARIBEL, *Abd al-Rahman III* (Oxford, 2005).

FINE, LAWRENCE, 'Benevolent Spirit Possession in Sixteenth-Century Safed', in Matt Goldish (ed.), *Spirit Possession in Judaism: Cases and Contexts from the Middle Ages to the Present* (Detroit, 2005), 101–23.

—— *Physician of the Soul, Healer of the Cosmos: Isaac Luria and His Kabbalistic Fellowship* (Stanford, Calif., 2003).

FINKELSTEIN, LOUIS, *Jewish Self-Government in the Middle Ages* (New York, 1924).

FISCHEL, WALTER, *Jews in the Economic and Political Life of Medieval Islam* (London, 1937).

FLEISCHER, EZRA, 'On Dunash ben Labrat, His Wife, and His Son' (Heb.), *Meḥkerei yerushalayim*, 5 (1984), 189–202.

FOSTER, ELISA ANNE, 'The Writing on the Wall: The Presence of Arabic Inscriptions in the Synagogue El Tránsito', MA thesis (Southern Methodist University, 2004).

FRANKEL, RACHEL, 'Testimonial Terrain: The Cemeteries of New World Sephardim', in Jane S. Gerber (ed.), *The Jews in the Caribbean* (Oxford, 2013), 131–42.

FRIEDENWALD, HARRY, *The Jews and Medicine: Essays*, 2 vols. (Baltimore, Md., 1944).

—— and HENRY E. SIGERIST, 'Biography of Lusitanus', in eid., *Jewish Luminaries in Medical History* (Baltimore, 1946), 35–7.

FRIEDMANN, MENACHEM, 'Letters of Recommendation for Jewish Mendicants: A Comment upon the Problem of Jewish Vagrancy in Eighteenth-Century Germany' (Heb.), *Michael*, 2 (1973), 34–51.

FUKS, LEO, and RENA G. FUKS-MANSFELD, *Hebrew Typography in the Northern Netherlands, 1585–1815*, 2 vols. (Leiden, 1984–7).

The Gazelle: Medieval Hebrew Poems on God, Israel, and the Soul, ed. Raymond P. Scheindlin (Philadelphia, 1991).

GERBER, JANE S., *Jewish Society in Fez, 1450–1700: Studies in Communal and Economic Life* (Leiden, 1980).

—— *The Jews of Spain: A History of the Sephardic Experience* (New York, 1992).

—— 'The Links Between Morocco and Palestine', in Ronald A. Brauner (ed.), *Shivim: Essays in Honor of the Seventieth Birthday of Ira Eisenstein* (New York, 1976), 119–28.

—— 'Pride and Pedigree: The Development of the Myth of Sephardic Aristocratic Lineage', in Brian M. Smollett and Christian Wiese (eds.), *Reappraisals and New Studies of the Modern Jewish Experience: Essays in Honor of Robert M. Seltzer* (Leiden, 2015), 85–104.

—— 'Those Who Walk in the Court of Our Master the King: The Sephardic Courtier Tradition Revisited', in Carsten Schapkow, Shmuel Shepkaru, and Alan T. Levenson (eds.), *The Festschrift Darkhei Noam: The Jews of Arab Lands* (Leiden, 2015), 128–50.

GERBER, JANE S., 'Toward an Understanding of the Term "The Golden Age" as a Historical Reality', in Aviva Doron (ed.), *The Culture of Spanish Jewry* (Tel Aviv, 1991), 15–22.

—— 'The World of Samuel Halevi: Testimony from the El Tránsito Synagogue of Toledo', in Jonathan Ray (ed.), *The Jew in Medieval Iberia* (Boston, Mass., 2012), 33–59.

GIBB, HAMILTON A. R., *Studies on the Civilization of Islam* (Boston, Mass., 1962).

GLATZER, MORDECHAI, 'Early Hebrew Printing', in Leonard S. Gold (ed.), *A Sign and a Witness: 2,000 Years of Hebrew Books and Illuminated Manuscripts* (New York, 1988), 80–92.

GLICK, THOMAS F., *Islamic and Christian Spain in the Early Middle Ages* (Leiden, 2005).

—— 'Moriscos and Marranos as Agents of Technological Diffusion', *History of Technology*, 17 (1995), 113–25.

—— 'Reading the *Repartimentos*: Modeling Settlement in the Wake of Conquest', in Mark D. Meyerson and Edward D. English (eds.), *Christians, Muslims and Jews in Medieval and Early Modern Spain* (Notre Dame, Ind., 1999), 20–39.

—— 'Science in Medieval Spain: The Jewish Contribution in the Context of Convivencia', in Vivian Mann, Thomas F. Glick, and Jerrilynn Dodds (eds.), *Convivencia: Jews, Muslims, and Christians in Medieval Spain* (New York, 1992), 83–112.

GOITEIN, SHELOMO DOV, *A Mediterranean Society: The Jewish Communities of the Arab World as Portrayed in the Documents of the Cairo Geniza*, 6 vols. (Berkeley, Calif., 1967–93).

—— 'A Report on Messianic Troubles in Baghdad in 1120–21', in Marc Saperstein (ed.), *Essential Papers on Messianic Movements and Personalities in Jewish History* (New York, 1992), 189–201.

GOLDISH, MATT, *Jewish Questions: Responsa on Sephardic Life in the Early Modern Period* (Princeton, NJ, 2008).

GOLDMAN, ISRAEL, *The Life and Times of Rabbi David ibn Abi Zimra* (New York, 1970).

GOLDZIHER, IGNAZ, *Muslim Studies* [1889–90], 2 vols., trans. C. R. Barber and S. M. Stern (London, 1967).

GOODBLATT, MORRIS, *Jewish Life in Turkey in the XVIth Century as Reflected in the Legal Writings of Samuel de Medina* (New York, 1952).

GRABAR, OLEG, *The Alhambra* (Cambridge, Mass., 1978).

—— *The Mediation of Ornament* (Princeton, NJ, 1992).

GRAIZBORD, DAVID, 'Religion and Ethnicity among "Men of the Nation": Toward a Realistic Interpretation', *Jewish Social Studies*, NS 15 (2008), 32–65.

—— *Souls in Dispute: Converso Identity in Iberia and the Jewish Diaspora, 1580–1700* (Philadelphia, 2004).

GRAYZEL, SOLOMON, *The Church and the Jews in the XIIIth Century*, 2 vols. (Philadelphia, 1933–89).

GRENDLER, PAUL F., 'The Destruction of Hebrew Books in Venice, 1568', *Proceedings of the American Academy for Jewish Research*, 45 (1978), 103–30.

GROSS, HENRI, 'La Famille juive des Hamon', *Revue des Études Juives*, 56 (1908), 1–26; 57 (1909), 55–78.

HACKER, JOSEPH R., 'The Intellectual Activity of the Jews of the Ottoman Empire during the Sixteenth and Seventeenth Centuries', in Isadore Twersky and Bernard Septimus (eds.), *Jewish Thought in the Seventeenth Century* (Cambridge, Mass, 1987), 95–135.

—— 'The Ottoman Policy towards the Jews and Jewish Attitudes towards the Ottomans during the Fifteenth Century', in Benjamin Braude and Bernard Lewis (eds.), *Christians and Jews in the Ottoman Empire: The Functioning of a Plural Society*, 2 vols. (New York, 1982), i. 117–25.

—— 'The Sephardim in the Ottoman Empire in the Sixteenth Century: Community and Society', in Haim Beinart (ed.), *The Sephardi Legacy*, 2 vols. (Jerusalem, 1992), ii. 109–33.

—— 'Sixteenth-Century Jewish Internal Censorship of Hebrew Books', in Joseph R. Hacker and Adam Shear (eds.), *The Hebrew Book in Early Modern Italy* (Philadelphia, 2011), 109–20.

—— 'The Sürgün System and Jewish Society in the Ottoman Empire during the Fifteenth and Sixteenth Centuries', in A. Rodrigue (ed.), *Ottoman and Turkish Jewry: Community and Leadership* (Bloomington, Ind., 1992), 1–65.

HALEY, KENNETH. H. D., *The Dutch in the Seventeenth Century* (London, 1972).

HARRÁN, DAN, 'Jewish Musical Culture: León Modena', in Robert C. Davis and Benjamin Ravid (eds.), *The Jews of Early Modern Venice* (Baltimore, Md., 2001), 211–30.

—— *Salamone Rossi: Jewish Musician in Late Renaissance Mantua* (Oxford, 1999).

—— 'Was Rabbi León Modena a Composer?', in David Malkiel (ed.), *'The Lion Shall Roar': León Modena and His World* (Jerusalem, 2003), 195–228.

HARRIS, JULIE, 'Polemical Images in the Golden Haggadah', *Medieval Encounters*, 8/2–3 (2002), 105–20.

HARVEY, L. P., 'The Alfonsine School of Translators: Translations from Arabic into Castilian Produced under the Patronage of Alfonso the Wise of Castile, 1252–1284', *Journal of the Royal Asiatic Society of Great Britain and Ireland*, 109/1 (1977–8), 109–117.

Hebrew Poems from Spain, ed. David Goldstein (Oxford, 2007).

HEYD, URIEL, 'Blood Libels in Turkey in the Fifteenth and Sixteenth Centuries' (Heb.), *Sefunot*, 5 (1961), 135–49.

—— 'The Jewish Communities of Istanbul in the Seventeenth Century', *Oriens*, 6 (1953), 299–314.

—— 'Moses Hamon, Chief Jewish Physician to Sultan Suleyman the Magnificent', *Oriens*, 16 (1963), 152–70.

—— *Ottoman Documents on Palestine, 1552–1615: A Study of the Firman according to the Mühimme Defteri* (Oxford, 1960).

—— 'Turkish Documents Concerning the Reconstruction of Tiberias in the Sixteenth Century' (Heb.), *Sefunot*, 10 (1966), 193–210.

HEYDECK, JUAN JOSEPH, *Inscripciones hebreas de la Sinagoga Toledana de R. Samuel ha-Levi* (Toledo, 1975).

HILLENBRAND, ROBERT, '"The Ornament of the World": Medieval Córdoba as a Cultural Centre', in Salma Khadra Jayyusi (ed.), *The Legacy of Muslim Spain*, 2 vols. (Leiden, 2000), i. 112–35.

HOROWITZ, ELLIOTT, 'Processions, Piety and Jewish Confraternities', in Robert C. Davis and Benjamin Ravid (eds.), *The Jews of Modern Venice* (Baltimore, 2001), 231–48.

—— 'Speaking of the Dead: The Emergence of the Eulogy among Italian Jewry of the Sixteenth Century', in D. Ruderman (ed.), *Preachers of the Italian Ghetto* (Berkeley, Calif., 1992), 129–62.

HUUSSEN, AREND, JR., 'The Legal Position of Sephardi Jews in Holland, circa 1600', in Jozeph Michman (ed.), *Dutch Jewish History*, vol. iii: *Proceedings of the Fifth Symposium on the History of the Jews of the Netherlands* (Jerusalem, 1993), 19–41.

IBN DAUD, ABRAHAM, *Sefer ha-Qabbalah: The Book of Tradition*, trans. Gerson D. Cohen (Philadelphia, 1967).

IBN EZRA, MOSES, *Kitāb al-Muḥāḍara wa al-Mudhākara* (Arab.); Heb. trans. B. Z. Halper, *Shirat yisra'el* (Leipzig, 1924); bilingual edn. Abraham S. Halkin, *Sefer ha'iyunim vehadiyunim* (Jerusalem, 1975).

IBN GABIROL, *Vulture in a Cage: Poems by Solomon ibn Gabirol*, trans. Raymond P. Scheindlin (Brooklyn, NY, 2016).

IBN GARCIA, *Risala*, in *The Shu'ubiyya in al-Andalus: The Risala of Ibn Garcia and Five Refutations*, trans. James T. Monroe (Berkeley, Calif., 1970).

IBN HAWKAL, *Kitab surat al-ard* [on geography], ed. J. H. Kramers (Leiden, 1938).

IBN VERGA SOLOMON, *Shevet yehudah* [on persecutions of Jews], ed. Abraham Shohat (Jerusalem, 1947).

IBN ZUR, JACOB, *Leshon limudim* [letters and responsa] (Constantinople, 1542).

—— *Mishpat utsedakah beya'akov* [responsa], 2 vols. (Alexandria, 1894).

IDEL, MOSHEH, 'Enquiries into the Doctrine of the Book of Meshiv' (Heb.), *Sefunot*, 17 (1983), 185–206.

—— 'Solomon Molkho as Magician' (Heb.), *Sefunot*, 18 (1985), 193–219.

—— 'Spanish Kabbalah after the Expulsion', in Haim Beinart (ed.), *The Sephardi Legacy*, 2 vols. (Jerusalem, 1992), ii. 155–78.

INALCIK, HALIL, 'Foundations of Ottoman–Jewish Cooperation', in Avigdor Levy (ed.), *Jews, Turks, and Ottomans* (Syracuse, NY, 2002), 3–14.

—— *The Ottoman Empire: The Classical Age 1300–1600* (London, 1973).

ISRAEL, JONATHAN, 'Duarte Nunes da Costa (Jacob Curiel) of Hamburg, Sephardi Nobleman and Communal Leader (1585–1664)', *Studia Rosenthaliana*, 21 (1987), 14–34.

—— *The Dutch Republic: Its Rise, Greatness, and Fall, 1477–1806* (Oxford, 1995).

—— 'The Economic Contribution of Dutch Sephardi Jewry to Holland's Golden Age, 1595–1713', *Tijdschrift voor Geschiedenis*, 96 (1983), 505–35.

—— *European Jewry in the Age of Mercantilism, 1570–1750* (Oxford, 1989).

—— 'Gregorio Leti (1631–1701) and the Dutch Sephardi Elite at the Close of the Seventeenth Century', in Ada Rapoport-Albert and Steven J. Zipperstein (eds.), *Jewish History: Essays in Honour of Chimen Abramsky* (London, 1988), 267–84.

—— 'The Republic of the United Netherlands until 1750: Demography and Economic Activity', in J. C. H. Blom, Rena G. Fuks-Mansfeld, and Ivo Schöffer (eds.), *The History of the Jews in the Netherlands* (Oxford, 2007), 85–115.

The Jew in the Medieval World: A Source Book 315–1791, ed. Jacob Marcus [1960], rev. edn., ed. Marc Saperstein (New York, 1999).

Jewish Mystical Testimonies, ed. Louis Jacobs (New York, 1978).

Jewish Texts on the Visual Arts, ed. Vivian Mann (Cambridge, 2009).

Jewish Travellers, 2nd edn., ed. Elkan N. Adler (New York, 1966).

KAPLAN, BENJAMIN, 'Dutch Religious Toleration: Celebration and Revision', in R. Po-Chia Hsia and H. F. K. van Nierop (eds.), *Calvinism and Religious Toleration in the Dutch Golden Age* (Cambridge, 2002), 10–16.

KAPLAN, YOSEF (ed.), *An Alternative Path to Modernity: The Sephardi Diaspora in Western Europe* (Leiden, 2000).

—— 'Amsterdam, the Forbidden Lands, and the Dynamics of the Sephardi Diaspora', in id. (ed.), *The Dutch Intersection: The Jews and the Netherlands in Modern History* (Leiden, 2008), 33–85.

—— 'The Attitude of the Spanish and Portuguese Jews to the Ashkenazi Jews in Seventeenth-Century Amsterdam' (Heb.), in Shmuel Almog et al. (eds.), *Transition and Change in Modern Jewish History: Essays in Honor of Shmuel Ettinger* (Jerusalem, 1988), 389–412.

—— '"Bom Judesmo": The Western Sephardic Diaspora', in David Biale (ed.), *Cultures of the Jews: A New History* (New York, 2002), 639–669.

—— 'Court Jews before the Hofjuden', in Vivian Mann, Richard Cohen, and F. Backhaus (eds.), *From Court Jews to the Rothschilds: Art, Patronage, and Power* (New York, 1996), 11–26.

—— 'Deviance and Excommunication in the Eighteenth Century: A Chapter in the Social History of the Sephardi Community of Amsterdam', in Jozeph Michman (ed.), *Dutch Jewish History*, vol. iii: *Proceedings of the Fifth Symposium on the History of the Jews of the Netherlands* (Jerusalem, 1993), 103–15.

—— 'For Whom Did Emanuel de Witte Paint His Three Pictures of the Sephardic Synagogue in Amsterdam?', in id. (ed.), *An Alternative Path to Modernity*, 29–51.

—— *From Christianity to Judaism: The Life and Works of Isaac Orobio de Castro* (Oxford, 1989).

—— '*Gente politica*: The Portuguese Jews of Amsterdam vis-à-vis Dutch Society', in Chaja Brasz and Yosef Kaplan (eds.), *Dutch Jews as Perceived by Themselves and by Others* (Leiden, 2001), 21–40.

—— 'The Portuguese Community of Amsterdam in the Seventeenth Century between Tradition and Change', in Abraham Haim (ed.), *Society and Community: Proceedings of the Second International Congress for Research of the Sephardi and Oriental Jewish Heritage, 1984* (Jerusalem, 1991), 141–71.

—— 'The Self-Definition of the Sephardi Jews of Western Europe and Their Relation to the Alien and Stranger', in Benjamin R. Gampel (ed.), *Crisis and Creativity in the Sephardic World, 1391–1648* (New York, 1997), 121–45.

—— 'The Social Functions of the Herem in the Portuguese Jewish Community of Amsterdam in the Seventeenth Century', in id. (ed.), *An Alternative Path to Modernity*, 108–43.

—— 'The Struggle Against Travellers to Spain and Portugal in the Western Sephardi Diaspora' (Heb.), *Zion*, 64 (1999–2000), 65–100.

—— 'The Travels of Portuguese Jews from Amsterdam to the "Lands of Idolatry" (1644–1724)', in id. (ed.), *Jews and Conversos: Studies in Society and the Inquisition* (Jerusalem, 1981), 197–224.

—— 'Wayward New Christians and Stubborn New Jews: The Shaping of a Jewish Identity', *Jewish History*, 8 (1994), 27–41.

—— HENRY MÉCHOULAN, and RICHARD H. POPKIN (eds.), *Menasseh ben Israel and His World* (Leiden, 1989).

KATZ, DAVID, *Philosemitism and the Readmission of the Jews to England, 1603–1655* (Oxford, 1982).

KATZ, JACOB, *Out of the Ghetto: The Social Background of Jewish Emancipation* (Cambridge, Mass., 1973).

—— *Tradition and Crisis: Jewish Society at the End of the Middle Ages* (New York, 1961).

KAYSERLING, MEYER, *Geschichte der Juden in Portugal* (Leipzig, 1867).

KEFADAR, CEMAL, *Between Two Worlds: The Construction of the Ottoman State* (Berkeley, Calif., 1995).

KIERS, JUDKE, and FIECKE TISSINK, *The Golden Age of Dutch Art* (London, 2000).

KLEIN, ELKA BETH, *Jews, Christian Society, and Royal Power in Medieval Barcelona* (Ann Arbor, Mich., 2006).

KOEN, E. M., 'The Earliest Sources Relating to the Portuguese Jews in the Municipal Archives of Amsterdam', *Studia Rosenthaliana*, 4 (1970), 25–42.

KOGMAN-APPEL, KATRIN, 'Coping with Christian Pictorial Sources: What Did Jewish Miniaturists not Paint?', *Speculum*, 75 (2000), 816–58.
—— 'The Sephardic Picture Cycles and the Rabbinic Tradition: Continuity and Innovation in Jewish Iconography', *Zeitschrift für Kunstgeschichte*, 60 (1997), 451–82.
KRAMER, MARTIN (ed.), *The Jewish Discovery of Islam: Studies in Honor of Bernard Lewis* (Tel Aviv, 1999).
LARSSON, GÖRAN, *Ibn Garcia's Shu'ubiyya Letter: Ethnic and Theological Tensions in Medieval al-Andalus* (Boston, Mass., 2003).
LASKER, DANIEL J., *Jewish Philosophical Polemics against Christianity in the Middle Ages*, 2nd edn. (Oxford, 2007).
LASOCKI, DAVID, *The Bassanos: Venetian Musicians and Instrument Makers in England, 1531–1665* (Aldershot, 1995).
LAWEE, ERIC, *Isaac Abarbanel's Stance Toward Tradition: Defense, Dissent, and Dialogue* (Albany, NY, 2001).
—— 'The Messianism of Isaac Abarbanel, Father of the (Jewish) Messianic Movements of the Sixteenth and Seventeenth Centuries', in Matt Goldish and Richard H. Popkin (eds.), *Millenarianism and Messianism in Early Modern European Culture* (Dordrecht, 2001), 1–39.
LEHMANN, MATTHIAS, *Emissaries from the Holy Land: The Sephardic Diaspora and the Practice of Pan-Judaism in the Eighteenth Century* (Stanford, Calif., 2014).
LEIBOWITZ, JOSHUA O., 'Amatus Lusitanus', *Encyclopedia Judaica* (Jerusalem, 1972), ii. 795–98.
Letters from the Land of Israel [Igerot erets yisra'el: shekatvu hayehudim hayoshevim ba'arets le'aḥehem shebagolah miyemei galut bavel ve'ad shivat tsiyon shebeyamenu], ed. Abraham Ya'ari (Tel Aviv, 1953).
Letters of Jews through the Ages, 2 vols., ed. Franz Kobler (London, 1953).
LEVIE BERNFELD, TIRTSAH, 'Financing Poor Relief in the Spanish–Portuguese Jewish Community in Amsterdam in the Seventeenth and Eighteenth Centuries', in Jonathan I. Israel and Reinier Salverda (eds.), *Dutch Jewry: Its History and Secular Culture* (Leiden, 2002), 63–102.
—— 'Matters Matter: Material Culture of Dutch Sephardim (1600–1750)', *Studia Rosenthaliana*, 44 (2012), 149–72.
—— *Poverty and Welfare among the Portuguese Jews in Early Modern Amsterdam* (Oxford, 2012).
LEVY, AVIGDOR, *The Sephardim in the Ottoman Empire* (Princeton, NJ, 1992).
LEWIS, BERNARD, *Islam in History: Ideas, People, and Events in the Middle East* (New York, 1973).
—— *Istanbul and the Civilization of the Ottoman Empire* (Norman, Okla., 1963).
—— *The Jews of Islam* (Princeton, NJ, 1984).
—— *The Middle East and the West* (Bloomington, Ind., 1965).
El Libro de los Acuerdos: Being the Records and Accompts of the Spanish and Portuguese Synagogue of London from 1663 to 1681, trans. Lionel D. Barnett (Oxford, 1931).
LOEWE, RAPHAEL, *Ibn Gabirol* (London, 1989).
LÓPEZ DE AYALA, PEDRO, *Crónica del rey don Pedro*, ed. Constance L. Wilkins and Heanon M. Wilkins (Madison, Wisc., 1985).
LOWRY, HEATH, 'When Did the Sephardim Arrive in Salonica? The Testimony of the Ottoman Tax Registers, 1478–1613', in Avigdor Levy (ed.), *The Jews of the Ottoman Empire* (Princeton, NJ, 1994), 203–13.

MAIMONIDES, MOSES, *Epistle to Yemen*, in *Crisis and Leadership: Epistles of Maimonides*, ed. Abraham Halkin and David Hartman (Philadelphia, 1985), 91–207.

MALKIEL, DAVID (ed.), *'The Lion Shall Roar': León Modena and His World* (Jerusalem, 2003).

—— *Reconstructing Ashkenaz: The Human Face of Franco-German Jewry 1000–1250* (Stanford, Calif., 2009).

MANN, JACOB, 'Messianic Movements during the First Three Crusades' (Heb.), *Hatekufah*, 23 (1925), 243–61; 24 (1928), 335–58.

—— *Texts and Studies in Jewish History and Literature*, 2 vols. (New York, 1972).

MARCUS, IVAN, *The Rituals of Childhood: Jewish Acculturation in Medieval Europe* (New Haven, Conn., 1996).

MARKOVA, ALA, 'El Tratado de astrolabio de Mosé Almosnino en un manuscrito de Leningrado', *Sefarad*, 51 (1991), 437–46.

MARX, ALEXANDER, 'The Expulsion of the Jews from Spain: Two New Accounts', *Studies in Jewish History and Booklore* (New York, 1944), 77–106.

MATRAN, ROBERT, 'Foreign Merchants and the Minorities in Istanbul during the Sixteenth and Seventeenth Centuries', in Benjamin Braude and Bernard Lewis (eds.), *Christians and Jews in the Ottoman Empire: The Functioning of a Plural Society*, 2 vols. (New York, 1982), i. 127–37.

Medieval Iberia: Readings from Christian, Muslim, and Jewish Sources, ed. Olivia Remie Constable (Philadelphia, 1997).

MEIJER, JACOB, 'Hugo Grotius' *Remonstrantie*', *Jewish Social Studies*, 17 (1955), 91–104.

MELAMMED, RENÉE LEVINE, *A Question of Identity: Iberian Conversos in Historical Perspective* (Oxford, 2004).

Memoirs of My People through a Thousand Years, ed. Leo W. Schwarz (Philadelphia, 1943).

MENOCAL, MARÍA ROSA, 'Culture in the Time of Tolerance: Al-Andalus as a Model for Our Time', *Yale Law School Occasional Papers*, 1 (2000), available at Yale Law School website, visited 18 Nov. 2018.

—— *The Ornament of the World* (Boston, Mass., 2002).

METZGER, THÉRÈSE, and MENDEL METZGER, *Jewish Life in the Middle Ages* (Secaucus, NJ, 1982).

MODENA, LEÓN DE, *The Autobiography of a Seventeenth-Century Venetian Rabbi: León Modena's Life of Judah*, ed. Mark R. Cohen (Princeton, NJ, 1988).

—— *She'elot uteshuvot ziknei yehudah* [responsa], ed. Shlomo Simonsohn (Jerusalem, 1955).

MOLCHO, ISAAC, 'Moses Almosnino: Liberator of the Community of Salonica in the Sixteenth Century' (Heb.), *Sinai*, 4 (1940–1), 245–56.

MOLCHO, MICHAEL, 'The "Communities" (Synagogues) in Salonica' (Heb.), in *Salonica* [Zikhron saloniki: gedulatah veḥurvatah shel yerushalayim debalkan], ed. David A. Recanati (Jerusalem, 1975), 173–84.

—— 'The Talmud Torah School' (Heb.), in *Salonica* [Zikhron saloniki: gedulatah veḥurvatah shel yerushalayim debalkan], ed. David A. Recanati (Jerusalem, 1975), 60–6.

MONROE, JAMES T., 'Zajal and Muwashshah: Hispano-Arabic Poetry and the Romance Tradition', in Salma Khadra Jayyusi (ed.), *The Legacy of Muslim Spain*, 2 vols. (Leiden, 2000), i. 398–419.

MURPHEY, RHOADS, 'Jewish Contributions to Ottoman Medicine, 1450–1800', in Avigdor Levy (ed.), *Jews, Turks, and Ottomans* (Syracuse, NY, 2002), 61–74.

NAAR, DEVIN E., 'Fashioning the "Mother of Israel": The Ottoman Jewish Historical Narrative and the Image of Jewish Salonica', *Jewish History*, 28 (2014), 337–72.

NADLER, STEVEN, *Rembrandt's Jews* (Chicago, 2003).

NARKISS, BEZALEL, *Hebrew Illuminated Manuscripts* (New York, 1976).

NAVARRO, ANGELES, 'Moses ibn "Ezra": El poema de los dos exilios', *Sefarad*, 61 (2001), 381–93.

NIELSEN, BRUCE, 'Daniel von Bombergen, a Bookman of Two Worlds', in Joseph R. Hacker and Adam Shear (eds.), *The Hebrew Book in Early Modern Italy* (Philadelphia, 2011), 56–76.

NORA, PIERRE (ed.), *Realms of Memory: Rethinking the French Past*, 3 vols., ed. Lawrence D. Kritzman, trans. Arthur Goldhammer (New York, 1996–8).

Notes and Documents from the Turkish Archives: A Contribution to the History of the Jews in the Ottoman Empire, ed. Bernard Lewis (Jerusalem, 1952).

OFFENBERG, ADRI K., 'Spanish and Portuguese Sephardi Books Published in the Northern Netherlands before Menasseh Ben Israel (1584–1627)', in Jozeph Michman (ed.), *Dutch Jewish History*, vol. iii: *Proceedings of the Fifth Symposium on the History of the Jews in the Netherlands* (Jerusalem, 1993), 77–90.

OMER, MORDECHAI, *The Synagogue of Samuel Halevy (El Tránsito)* (Tel Aviv, 1992).

ORFALI, MOISES, 'Dona Gracia Mendes and the Ragusan Republic', in Elliot Horowitz and Moises Orfali (eds.), *The Mediterranean and the Jews: Society, Culture and Economy in Early Modern Times* (Ramat Gan, 2002), 175–201.

PATTON, PAMELA A., *Art of Estrangement: Redefining Jews in Reconquest Spain* (University Park, Pa., 2012).

The Penguin Book of Hebrew Verse, ed. and trans. T. Carmi (New York, 1981).

POLIAKOV, LÉON, *Jewish Bankers and the Holy See from the Thirteenth to the Seventeenth Century* (London, 1977).

POPKIN, RICHARD H., 'Some Aspects of Jewish–Christian Theological Interchanges in Holland and England, 1640–1700', in Johannes van den Berg and Ernestine G. E. van der Wall (eds.), *Jewish–Christian Relations in the Seventeenth Century: Studies and Documents* (Leiden, 1988), 3–32.

PRIOR, RICHARD, 'Jewish Musicians at the Tudor Court', *Musical Quarterly*, 69 (1983), 253–65.

PROCTOR, EVELYN S., *Alfonso X of Castile: Patron of Literature and Learning* (Oxford, 1951).

—— 'The Scientific Works of the Court of Alfonso X of Castile: The King and his Collaborators', *Modern Language Review*, 40 (1945), 12–29.

PULLAN, BRIAN, 'The Inquisition and the Jews of Venice: The Case of Gaspare Ribiero, 1580–81', *Bulletin of the John Rylands Library of Manchester*, 62 (1979), 207–31.

—— *The Jews of Europe and the Inquisition of Venice, 1550–1670* (Oxford, 1983).

—— *Rich and Poor in Renaissance Venice* (Cambridge, Mass., 1971).

—— '"A Ship with Two Rudders": "Righetto Marrano" and the Inquisition in Venice', *Historical Review*, 20 (1977), 25–58.

PUTNAM, GEORGE HAVEN, *Books and Their Makers during the Middle Ages*, 2 vols. (New York, 1897; repr. 2004).

RAVID, BENJAMIN, 'An Autobiographical Memorandum by Daniel Rodriga, "Inventore" of the "Scala of Spalato"', in Ariel Toaff and Simon Schwartzfuchs (eds.), *The Mediterranean and the Jews: Banking, Finance, and International Trade (XVI–XVIII Centuries)* (Ramat Gan, 1989), 189–214.

—— 'Between the Myth of Venice and the Lachrymose Conception of Jewish History: The Historical Experience of the Jews of Venice', in Barbara Garvin and Bernard D. Cooperman (eds.), *Memory and Identity: The Jews of Italy* (Bethesda, Md., 2000), 151–92.

—— 'Daniel Rodriga and the First Decade of the Jewish Merchants of Venice', in Aaron Mirsky, Avraham Grossman, and Yosef Kaplan (eds.), *Exile and Diaspora: Studies in the History of the Jewish People Presented to Professor Haim Beinart* (Jerusalem, 1991), 203–23.

—— *Economics and Toleration in Seventeenth-Century Venice: The Background and Context of the 'Discorso' of Simone Luzzatto*, American Academy for Jewish Research Monograph Series, 8 (Jerusalem, 1978).

—— 'The Establishment of the Ghetto Vecchio of Venice, 1541: Background and Reappraisal', in Malka Jadendorf and Avigdor Shinan (eds.), *Proceedings of the Sixth World Congress of Jewish Studies*, 2 vols. (Jerusalem, 1973–5), ii. 153–67.

—— 'The First Charter of the Jewish Merchants of Venice, 1589', *AJS Review*, 1 (1976), 187–222.

—— 'From Yellow to Red: On the Distinguishing Head-Covering of the Jews of Venice', *Jewish History*, 6 (1992), 179–210.

—— '"How Profitable the Nation of the Jewes Are": The Humble Addresses of Menasseh ben Israel and the Discorso of Simone Luzzatto', in Jehuda Reinharz and Daniel Swetschinski (eds.), *Mystics, Philosophers, and Politicians: Essays in Jewish Intellectual History in Honor of Alexander Altmann* (Durham, NC, 1982), 159–80.

—— 'The Legal Status of the Jewish Merchants of Venice, 1541–1638', Ph.D. thesis (Harvard University, 1973).

—— 'Moneylending in Seventeenth-Century Jewish Vernacular Apologetica', in Isadore Twersky and Bernard Septimus (eds.), *Jewish Thought in the Seventeenth Century* (Cambridge, Mass, 1987), 257–83.

—— 'New Light on the Ghetti in Venice', in Daniel Carpi (ed.), *Shlomo Simonsohn Jubilee Volume: Studies on the History of the Jews in the Middle Ages and the Renaissance* (Tel Aviv, 1993), 149–76.

—— '"On Sufferance and Not As of Right": The Status of the Jewish Community of Early Modern Venice', in David Malkiel (ed.), *'The Lion Shall Roar': León Modena and His World* (Jerusalem, 2003), 17–60.

—— 'The Prohibition against Jewish Printing and Publishing in Venice and the Difficulties of León Modena', in Isadore Twersky (ed.), *Studies in Medieval Jewish History and Literature* (Cambridge, Mass., 1979), 135–53.

—— 'The Religious, Economic, and Social Background and Context of the Establishment of the Ghetto of Venice', in Gaetan Cozzi (ed.), *Gli ebrei e Venezia* (Milan, 1987), 211–59.

—— 'The Socioeconomic Background of the Expulsion and Readmission of the Venetian Jews, 1571–1573', in Frances Malino and Phyllis Cohen Albert (eds.), *Essays in Modern Jewish History: A Tribute to Ben Halpern* (Rutherford, NJ, 1982), 27–45.

—— 'A Tale of Three Cities and their *Raison d'Etat*: Ancona, Venice, Livorno, and the Competition for Jewish Merchants in the Sixteenth Century', *Mediterranean Historical Review*, 6 (1991–2), 141–5.

—— 'The Third Charter of the Jewish Merchants of Venice, 1611', *Jewish Political Studies Review*, 6 (1994), 83–134.

—— 'The Venetian Government and the Jews', in Robert C. Davis and Benjamin Ravid (eds.), *The Jews of Early Modern Venice* (Baltimore, Md., 2001), 3–30.

RAVID, BENJAMIN, 'Venice, Rome, and the Reversion of Conversos to Judaism: A Study in Ragione di Stato', in Pier Cesare and Ioly Zorattini (eds.), *L'identità dissimulata: Guidaizzanti iberici nell'Europa Cristiana dell'età moderna* (Florence, 2000), 151–93.

RAY, JONATHAN, *After Expulsion: 1492 and the Making of Sephardic Jewry* (New York, 2013).

—— 'Beyond Tolerance and Persecution: Reassessing our Approach to Medieval "Convivencia"', *Jewish Social Studies*, NS 11 (2005), 1–18.

—— 'Images of the Jewish Community in Medieval Iberia', *Journal of Medieval Iberian Studies*, 1 (2009), 195–211.

—— 'The *Reconquista* and the Jews: 1212 from the Perspective of Jewish History', *Journal of Medieval History*, 40 (2014), 159–75.

—— *The Sephardic Frontier: The Reconquista and the Jewish Community in Medieval Iberia* (Ithaca, NY, 2006).

RECANATI, DAVID A. (ed.), *Salonica* [Zikhron saloniki: gedulatah veḥurvatah shel yerushalayim debalkan] (Tel Aviv, 1972).

REMIE CONSTABLE, OLIVIA, *Trade and Traders in Muslim Spain: The Commercial Realignment of the Iberian Peninsula, 900–1500* (Cambridge, 1994).

REUBENI DAVID, *Sipur david reuveni* [diary], ed. Aaron Ze'ev Aescoly (Jerusalem, 1993).

RODRIGUE, ARON, 'Difference and Tolerance in the Ottoman Empire', interview by Nancy Reynolds, *Stanford Humanities Review*, 5 (Fall 1995), 81–92.

—— *French Jews, Turkish Jews: The Alliance Israélite Universelle and the Politics of Jewish Schooling in Turkey 1860–1925* (Bloomington, Ind., 1990).

ROITMAN, JESSICA, 'A Flock of Wolves instead of Sheep: The Dutch West India Company, Conflict Resolution, and the Jewish Community of Curaçao in the Eighteenth Century', in Jane S. Gerber (ed.), *The Jews in the Caribbean* (Oxford, 2013), 85–106.

ROSENBERG, SHALOM, 'Exile and Redemption in Jewish Thought in the Sixteenth Century: Contending Conceptions', in Bernard D. Cooperman (ed.), *Jewish Thought in the Sixteenth Century* (Cambridge, Mass., 1983), 399–430.

ROSENFELD, MOSHE N., 'The Development of Hebrew Printing in the Sixteenth and Seventeenth Centuries', in Leonard S. Gold (ed.), *A Sign and a Witness: 2,000 Years of Hebrew Books and Illuminated Manuscripts* (New York, 1988), 92–101.

ROTH, CECIL, 'A Hebrew Elegy on the Martyrs of Toledo, 1391', *Jewish Quarterly Review*, 39 (1948), 123–50.

—— *History of the Jews of Venice* (Philadelphia, 1930).

—— *The House of Nasi: Doña Gracia* (Philadelphia, 1947).

—— 'Las inscripciones historica de la Sinagoga del Tránsito de Toledo', *Sefarad*, 8 (1948), 3–22.

—— *A Life of Menasseh ben Israel* (Philadelphia, 1945).

—— *The Sarajevo Haggadah* (London, 1963).

ROTH, NORMAN, 'Jewish Collaborators in Alfonso's Scientific Work', in Robert I. Burns (ed.), *Emperor of Culture: Alfonso X the Learned of Castile and his Thirteenth Century Renaissance* (Philadelphia, 1990), 59–71.

—— 'Jewish Reactions to the 'Arabiyya and the Renaissance of Hebrew in Spain', *Journal of Semitic Studies*, 28 (1983), 63–84.

—— 'Jewish Translators at the Court of Alfonso X', *Thought*, 60/239 (Dec. 1985), 439–55.

—— 'The Jews and the Muslim Conquest of Spain', *Jewish Social Studies*, 38 (1976), 147–58.

—— *Jews, Visigoths and Muslims in Medieval Spain* (Leiden, 1994).

—— 'New Light on the Jews of Mozarabic Toledo', *AJS Review*, 2 (1986), 189–220.

—— 'Two Jewish Courtiers of Alfonso X Called Zag (Isaac)', *Sefarad*, 43 (1983), 75–85.

ROZANES, SALOMON, *History of the Jews in the Ottoman Empire* [Divrei yemei yisra'el betogarmah], vol. i (Tel Aviv, 1930); vols. ii–iv: *History of the Jews in Turkey and the Near East* [Korot hayehudim beturkiyah ve'artsot hakedem] (Sofia, 1937–9).

ROZEN, MINNA, 'Collective Memories and Group Boundaries: The Judeo-Spanish Diaspora between the Lands of Christendom and the World of Islam', *Michael*, 14 (1997), 35–52.

—— *A History of the Jewish Community in Istanbul: The Formative Years, 1453–1566* (Leiden, 2002).

—— 'Public Space and Private Space among the Jews of Istanbul during the Sixteenth and Seventeenth Centuries', *Turcica*, 30 (1998), 331–46.

RUBEN, MIRI, *Gentile Tales: The Narrative Assault on Late Medieval Jews* (New Haven, Conn., 1999).

RUDERMAN, DAVID B., *Early Modern Jewry: A New Cultural History* (Princeton, NJ, 2010).

—— 'The Hebrew Book in a Christian World', in Leonard S. Gold (ed.), *A Sign and a Witness: 2,000 Years of Hebrew Books and Illuminated Manuscripts* (New York, 1988), 101–13.

—— 'Hope against Hope: Jewish and Christian Messianic Expectations in the Late Middle Ages', in id. (ed.), *Essential Papers on Jewish Culture in Renaissance and Baroque Italy* (New York, 1992), 299–323.

RUGGLES, D. FAIRCHILD, *Gardens, Landscape, and Vision in the Palaces of Islamic Spain* (University Park, Pa., 2003).

SABAR, SHALOM, 'The Beginnings of *Ketubbah* Decoration in Italy', *Jewish Art*, 12–13 (1986–7), 96–110.

Sabbath and Festival Prayer Book, ed. and trans. Morris Silverman (New York, 1947).

SAENZ-BADILLOS, ANGEL, 'Hebrew Philology in Sefarad: The State of the Question', in Nicholas de Lange (ed.), *Hebrew Scholarship in the Medieval World* (Cambridge, 2001), 38–59.

SALOMON, HERMAN P., 'The Fidanques, Hidalgos of Faith', *American Sephardi*, 4 (1970–1), 15–36.

—— and ARON DI LEONE LEONI, 'Mendes, Benveniste, de Luna, Micas, Nasci: The State of the Art (1532–1558)', *Jewish Quarterly Review*, 88 (1998), 135–211.

SAPERSTEIN, MARC, *Exile in Amsterdam: Saul Levi Morteira's Sermons to a Congregation of 'New Jews'* (Cincinnati, 2005).

—— *Jewish Preaching, 1200–1800: An Anthology* (New Haven, Conn., 1989).

—— 'Martyrs, Merchants and Rabbis: Jewish Communal Conflict as Reflected in the Responsa on the Boycott of Ancona', *Jewish Social Studies*, 43 (1981), 215–28.

—— *Moments of Crisis in Jewish–Christian Relations* (London, 1989).

—— 'The Treatment of "Heretical Views" in the Sermons of Rabbi Saul Morteira of Amsterdam', in Daniel Frank and Matt Goldish (eds.), *Rabbinic Culture and Its Critics* (Detroit, 2008), 313–34.

SARNA, NAHUM M., *Exploring Exodus: The Origins of Biblical Israel* (New York, 1986).

Sarra Copia Sulam: Jewish Poet and Intellectual in Seventeenth Century Venice, ed. and trans. Don Harrán (Chicago, 2009).

SCHECHTER, SOLOMON, 'Safed in the Sixteenth Century: A City of Legists and Mystics', in Judah Goldin (ed.), *The Jewish Expression* (New Haven, Conn., 1976), 258–321.

SCHEINDLIN, RAYMOND P., 'Moses ibn Ezra', in Maria Rosa Menocal, Raymond P. Scheindlin, and Michael Sells (eds.), *The Literature of al-Andalus* (Cambridge, 2000), 252–64.
—— 'Rabbi Moses ibn Ezra on the Legitimacy of Poetry', *Medievalia et Humanistica*, NS 7 (1976), 101–15.
—— (ed.), *Wine, Women and Death: Medieval Hebrew Poets on the Good Life* (Philadelphia, 1986).
SCHIRMANN, JEFIM, 'The Function of the Hebrew Poet in Medieval Spain', *Jewish Social Studies*, 16 (1954), 235–52.
—— 'Samuel Hanagid: The Man, the Soldier, the Politician', *Jewish Social Studies*, 13 (1951), 99–126.
SCHMELZER, MENAHEM, 'Hebrew Manuscripts and Printed Books among the Sephardim before and after the Expulsion', in Benjamin R. Gampel (ed.), *Crisis and Creativity in the Sephardic World, 1391–1648* (New York, 1997), 257–66.
SCHOLEM, GERSHOM, 'On the Knowledge of Kabbalah before the Expulsion' (Heb.), *Tarbiz*, 24 (1955), 167–206.
SCHORSCH, ISMAR, 'From Messianism to Realpolitik: Menasseh ben Israel and the Readmission of the Jews to England', *Proceedings of the American Academy for Jewish Research*, 45 (1978), 187–208.
—— 'The Myth of Sephardic Supremacy', *Leo Baeck Institute Yearbook*, 34 (1989), 47–66.
SED-RAJNA, GABRIELLE, 'Hebrew Illuminated Manuscripts from the Iberian Peninsula', in Vivian Mann, Thomas F. Glick, and Jerrilynn Dodds (eds.), *Convivencia: Jews, Muslims, and Christians in Medieval Spain* (New York, 1992), 133–56.
—— 'Hebrew Manuscripts of Fourteenth-Century Catalonia and the Workshop of the Master of St. Mark', *Jewish Art*, 18 (1992), 117–39.
—— 'Toledo or Burgos?', *Journal of Jewish Art*, 2 (1975), 6–21.
SEGRE, RENATA, 'Sephardi Settlements in Sixteenth-Century Italy: A Historical and Geographical Survey', in Alisa Meyuhas Ginio (ed.), *Jews, Christians and Muslims in the Mediterranean World after 1492* (London, 1992), 112–37.
SEPTIMUS, BERNARD, *Hispano-Jewish Society in Transition: The Career and Controversies of the Ramah* (Cambridge, Mass., 1982).
—— 'Piety and Power in Thirteenth-Century Catalonia', in Isadore Twersky (ed.), *Studies in Medieval Jewish History and Literature* (Cambridge, Mass., 1979), 197–230.
SHATZMILLER, JOSEPH, 'Travelling in the Mediterranean in 1563: The Testimony of Eliahu of Pesaro', in Ariel Toaff and Simon Schwartzfuchs (eds.), *The Mediterranean and the Jews: Banking, Finance, and International Trade (XVI–XVIII Centuries)* (Ramat Gan, 1989), 237–48.
SHATZMILLER, MAYA, *The Berbers and the Islamic State: The Marinid Experience in Pre-Protectorate Morocco* (Princeton, NJ, 2000).
SHAW, STANFORD J., *The Jews of the Ottoman Empire and the Turkish Republic* (New York, 1991).
SHIDELER, JOHN C., *A Medieval Catalan Noble Family: The Montcadas, 1000–1230* (Berkeley, Calif., 1983).
SHMUELEVITZ, ARYEH, *The Jews of the Ottoman Empire in the Late Fifteenth and Sixteenth Centuries: Administrative, Economic, Legal and Social Relations as Reflected in the Responsa* (Leiden, 1984).
SHULVASS, MOSES A., *The Jews in the World of the Renaissance* (Leiden, 1973).
—— 'A Story of the Misfortunes which Afflicted the Jews in Italy' (Heb.), *Hebrew Union College Annual*, 22 (1949), 1–29.

SICROFF, ALBERT A., *Les Controverses des statuts de 'pureté de sang' en Espagne du XVe au XVIIe siècle* (Paris, 1960).

SNOW, JOSEPH, 'The Central Rôle of the Troubadour *Persona* of Alfonso X in the *Cantigas de Santa Maria*', *Bulletin of Hispanic Studies*, 56 (1979), 305–16.

SONCINO, JOSHUA, *Naḥalah leyehoshua: vehu she'elot uteshuvot* [responsa] (Istanbul, 1731).

STEIN, SARAH ABREVAYA, 'Sephardic and Middle Eastern Jewries since 1492: The Sephardic Mystique/the Sephardic Mistake', in Martin Goodman (ed.), *The Oxford Handbook of Jewish Studies* (Oxford, 2002), 327–62.

STERN, GREGG, *Philosophy and Rabbinic Culture* (Oxford, 2009).

STILLMAN, NORMAN, *The Jews of Arab Lands: A History and Source Book* (Philadelphia, 1979).

STOW, KENNETH, 'Ethnic Rivalry or Melting Pot? The *Edot* in the Roman Ghetto', *Judaism*, 41 (1992), 286–96.

—— and SANDRA DEBENEDETTI STOW, 'Donne ebree a Roma nell'eta del ghetto affetto, dependenz, autonomia', *La rassegna mensile di Israel*, 52 (1986), 107–16.

STRACHAN, MICHAEL, *The Life and Adventures of Thomas Coryate* (Oxford, 1962).

STUART, SHANA L., 'The Portuguese Jewish Community in Seventeenth-Century Amsterdam: Images of Commemoration and Documentation', Ph.D. thesis (University of Kansas, 1992).

STUDEMUND-HALEVY, MICHAEL, 'The Persistence of Images: Reproductive Success in the History of Sephardi Sepulchral Art', in Yosef Kaplan (ed.), *An Alternative Path to Modernity: The Sephardi Diaspora in Western Europe* (Leiden, 2000), 125–49.

SUROWITZ ISRAEL, HILIT, 'Religious Authority: A Perspective from the Americas', in Jane S. Gerber (ed.), *The Jews in the Caribbean* (Oxford, 2013), 107–18.

SUTCLIFFE, ADAM, 'Regulating Sociability: Rabbinical Authority and Jewish–Christian Interaction in Seventeenth-Century Amsterdam', in Daniel Frank and Matt Goldish (eds.), *Rabbinic Culture and Its Critics* (Detroit, 2008), 289–312.

SWETSCHINSKI, DANIEL, 'An Amsterdam Jewish Merchant-Diplomat: Jeronomio Nunes da Costa alias Mosheh Curiel (1620–1697), Agent of Portugal', in Lea Dasberg and Jonathan N. Cohen (eds.), *Neveh Ya'akov: Jubilee Volume Presented to Dr. Jaap Meijer on the Occasion of his Seventieth Birthday* (Assen, 1982), 3–30.

—— 'The Portuguese Jews of Seventeenth-Century Amsterdam: Cultural Continuity and Adaptation', in Frances Malino and David Sorkin (eds.), *Essays in Modern Jewish History in Honor of Ben Halpern* (New York, 1982), 56–80.

—— *Reluctant Cosmopolitans: The Portuguese Jews of Amsterdam* (Oxford, 2000).

TAGGIE, BENJAMIN, 'Samuel ha-Levi Abulafia and the Hebraic Policy of Pedro I of Castile (1350–69)', *Fifteenth-Century Studies*, 5 (1982), 191–208.

TISHBY, ISAIAH, 'Acute Apocalyptic Messianism', in Marc Saperstein (ed.), *Essential Papers on Messianic Movements and Personalities in Jewish History* (New York, 1992), 259–86.

—— *Messianism in the Time of the Expulsion from Spain and Portugal* [Meshiḥiyut bedor gerushei sefarad ufortugal] (Jerusalem, 1985).

TOLAND, JOHN, *Reasons for Naturalizing the Jews in Great Britain and Ireland On the Same Footing with all other Nations, Containing also a Defence of the Jews Against all vulgar Prejudices in all Countries* [1714] (n.p., 2012).

TOLEDANO, HAIM HENRY, *The Sephardic Legacy* (Scranton, Pa., 2010).

USQUE, SAMUEL, *Consolations for the Tribulations of Israel*, ed. and trans. Martin A. Cohen (Philadelphia, 1967).

VARLIK, NUKHET, 'Plague, Conflict, and Negotiation: The Jewish Broadcloth Weavers of Salonica and the Ottoman Central Administration in the Late Sixteenth Century', *Jewish History*, 28 (2014), 261–88.

VILNAY, ZEV, *Legends of Galilee, Jordan and Sinai* (Philadelphia, 1978).

VLESSING, ODETTE, 'New Light on the Earliest History of the Amsterdam Portuguese Jews', in Jozeph Michman (ed.), *Dutch Jewish History*, vol. iii: *Proceedings of the Fifth Symposium on the History of the Jews of the Netherlands* (Jerusalem, 1993), 43–75.

VRYONIS, SPEROS, JR., 'The Ottoman Conquest of Thessaloniki in 1430', in id. (ed.), *Continuity and Change in Late Byzantine and Early Ottoman Society* (Washington DC, 1986), 281–32.

WASSERSTEIN, DAVID, 'Jewish Elites in al-Andalus', in Daniel Frank (ed.), *The Jews in Medieval Islam* (Leiden, 1995), 101–10.

WEINBERGER, LEON, *Samuel ibn Nagrela* (Tuscaloosa, Ala., 1973).

WEINSTEIN, ROCHELLE, 'Sepulchral Monuments of the Jews of Amsterdam in the Seventeenth and Eighteenth Centuries', Ph.D. thesis (New York University, 1979).

—— 'Stones of Memory: Revelations from a Cemetery in Curaçao', in Martin A. Cohen and Abraham J. Peck (eds.), *Sephardim in the Americas: Studies in Culture and History* (Tuscaloosa, Ala., 1993), 81–140.

WERBLOWSKY, R. J. ZWI, *Joseph Caro: Lawyer and Mystic* (Philadelphia, 1980).

WIMMER, YEHUDIT, 'Jewish Merchants in Ragusa as Intermediaries between East and West in the Sixteenth and Seventeenth Centuries' (Heb.), in Minna Rozen (ed.), *The Days of the Crescent: Chapters in the History of the Jews in the Ottoman Empire* [Perakim betoledot hayehudim ba'imperia ha'othmanit] (Tel Aviv, 1996), 73–150.

WISCHNITZER, RACHEL, *The Architecture of the European Synagogue* (Philadelphia, 1984).

YA'ARI, ABRAHAM, *Hebrew Printing in the Middle East* [Hadefus ha'ivri be'artsot hamizrah] (Jerusalem, 1936).

YARDENI, MYRIAM, *Anti-Jewish Mentalities in Early Modern Europe* (Lanham, Md., 1990).

YEHUDA, ABRAHAM SHALOM, 'David Reuveni, His Origins, Language, and Identity' (Heb.), *Hatekufah*, 34–5 (1950), 599–625.

YERUSHALMI, YOSEF HAYIM, 'Exile and Expulsion in Jewish History', in Benjamin R. Gampel (ed.), *Crisis and Creativity in the Sephardic World, 1391–1648* (New York, 1997), 3–22.

—— *From Spanish Court to Italian Ghetto: A Study in Seventeenth Century Marranism and Jewish Apologetics* (New York, 1971).

—— *Haggadah and History* (Philadelphia, 1975).

—— 'Messianic Impulses in Joseph ha-Kohen', in Bernard Cooperman (ed.), *Jewish Thought in the Sixteenth Century* (Cambridge, Mass., 1983), 460–87.

—— 'The Re-education of Marranos in the Seventeenth Century', in David Myers and Alexander Kaye (eds.), *The Faith of Fallen Jews* (Waltham, Mass., 2014), 157–74.

—— *Zachor: Jewish History and Jewish Memory* (Seattle, 1982).

YOVEL, YIRMIYAHU, *The Other Within. The Marranos: Split Identity and Emerging Modernity* (Princeton, NJ, 2009).

—— *Spinoza and Other Heretics*, 2 vols. (Princeton, NJ, 1989).

YUVAL, ISRAEL J., *Two Nations in Your Womb: Perceptions of Jews and Christians in Antiquity and the Middle Ages*, trans. Barbara Harshav and Jonathan Chapman (Berkeley, Calif., 2006).

ZELL, MICHAEL, *Reframing Rembrandt: Rembrandt, the Jews, and the Christian Image in Seventeenth-Century Amsterdam* (Berkeley, Calif., 2002).

ZIMMELS, HIRSCH JAKOB, *Ashkenazim and Sephardim* (London, 1958).

ZORATINNI, IOLY, 'The Inquisition and the Jews in Sixteenth Century Venice', in *Proceedings of the Eighth World Congress of Jewish Studies*, Division B: *History* (Jerusalem, 1981), 83–91.

ZUMTHOR, PAUL, *Daily Life in Rembrandt's Holland* (Stanford, Calif., 1994).

INDEX

A
Aaron (Haroun) ben Battas 11, 19–20
Abd al-Rahman I Emir of Cordoba (756–88) 11
Abd al-Rahman II Emir of Cordoba (822–52) 11
Abd al-Rahman III caliph of Cordoba (912–61) 10
  embellishment of Cordoba 12, 13
  'the golden age of Spain' 14–15
  and Hasdai ibn Shaprut 16, 20–1
  knowledge of Greek 21
Aboab de Fonseca, Rabbi Isaac 239
Abrabanel, Abraham 153–4
Abraham Alfaquim 63
Abraham of Ankara 177
Abravanel, Benvenida 95
Abravanel, Don Isaac 92–3
Abu Ishaq ibn Khafaja (d. 1139) 38
Abu Mansur al-Thaʼalibi 29
Abu Saʻd Ibrahim al-Tustari 19
Abulafia, Samuel Halevi 77–8, 80–5
Abulafia family 77
Academia de los Floridos 228–9
Academia de los Sitibondos 228–9
Academia degl'Impedita 159
adoption of Judaism 235
Adret, Solomon ibn 150
agriculture 11
Akrish, Isaac ben Abraham 194
Al-Harizi, Judah 101
  Taḥkemoni 48
Alcazar of Seville 81, Plate 8
alcohol 32
Alfasi, Isaac, *Sefer hahalakhot* 150
Alfonsine Tables 63–4
Alfonsine translations 61–3

Alfonso VI of León and Castile (1065–1109) 50
Alfonso VII of León and Castile (1126–57) 50
Alfonso X of Castile (r. 1252–84):
  Cantigas de Santa Maria 64–8
  conquest of Murcia 65
  contradictory attitudes towards Jews 49, 64
  discriminatory papal legislation 67
  intellectual energy 60–4
  Jewish courtiers 66
  Las siete partidas 53–4, 61, 65, 79
  as 'royal troubadour' 64
Alfonso XI of Castile (r. 1312–50) 77
Alhambra (Granada) 14, 80, 81, 84, Plate 7
Alkabetz, Solomon (c.1505–c.1576) 86, 110, 111, 112–15
  'Lekhah dodi' 113–15
Alkmaar (Netherlands) 225
Almohads 44, 49
Almoravids 43–4
Almosnino, Moses ben Baruch (c.1510–c.1580) 192–3
  Crónica de los reyes otomanos 193
  Extremos y grandezas de Constantinopla 192
Amador de los Rios, Rodrigo 79
Amarzigh language (Berber) 26
Amatus Lusitanus (Joao Rodrigues de Castelo Branco) 204–5, 206
  Curationum medicinalium centuriae septem 205
America, *see* New World
Amsterdam 214–58
  Ashkenazi refugees 216
  Ashkenazi synagogue 239–40
  Breestraat 217

canals 215
Iberian Marrano 220
individualism and freedom of thought 257
Jewish artists 241–2
languages 217, 222
patterns of identity 217
population 215
Portuguese Conversos 167–8, 216–17, 222
printing and publishing 229–30, 242–3, 252
refugees from Antwerp 216
religious freedom 215
return to Judaism 222
Sephardi settlers 215–16
Sephardim and Conversos 231–2
Sephardim from Morocco 256
shipbuilding 216
stonecutters 250
synagogues 226, 235, 257
talmud torah 243–4
tolerance 225–7
trade 216
as the trading centre of Europe 226
union of Jewish communities 257–8
see also Jews of Amsterdam; Netherlands; Portuguese Jews of Amsterdam
Ancona:
  boycott (1556) 205–11
  Conversos 132, 205–8
  Levant trade 126
  Levantine Jews 133
  messianic preaching 97
  Portuguese Jews 138
Ancona–Ragusa trade link 136
Andalusia:
  centre of civilization 11

Andalusia (*cont.*):
   independence and cultural autonomy 23
   industries 11, 12
   Jewish poetry and Arab culture 36
   Jewish refugees from 49, 53
   Jewish sense of rootedness 45
   re-establishing culture 58–9
   as a verdant garden 260
'Andalusian style' of writing 45
aniconic-style illuminated manuscripts 69
anti-Christian behaviour 226
anti-Jewish accusations:
   blood libel 65
   host desecration 65
anti-Jewish legislation 49, 66
anti-Jewish sentiments 52–3
anti-Jewish stereotypes 138–9
anti-Jewish violence 65–6
Antwerp 142–4, 205, 216, 217, 220, 226
apocalypse 88–9
Arabic culture:
   Andalusian Jewish poetry 36
   assertions of superiority 26–7, 28, 29
   calligraphy 81–2
   classics 62
   decline in influence 52
   gardens 38
   poets and poetry 25, 28–31, 38, 58
   sophistication and refinement 69
   Spanish Golden Era 28–31
Arabic inscriptions:
   Alhambra 80, 84 n.72
   Christian Spain 80
   El Tránsito Synagogue 78–9
   Mudéjar style of art 79–80
Arabic language 28, 30, 31, 59
'arabiyya–shu'ubiyya controversy 26–7
Arabization 26–9
Arabized Christians (Mozarabs) 10

Arabized Jewish communities 53
'Arabness' pseudo-genealogies 27
arabophone (Jewish dialects of Arabic) 26
Aramaic 31
Arghun Khan 20
aristocratic lineage 9
art:
   Amsterdam 250
   as a pedagogical tool 72–3
   traditional artistic styles 71, Plate 4
   Venice ghetto 159–62
   see also illuminated manuscripts
ascamot (community regulations):
   Amsterdam 236–7
   Bevis Marks synagogue (London) 256
   Kahal Kados de Talmud Tora 232, 235, 238
   not applying to commerce 217
   in Portuguese 222
   Venetian ghetto 167–8
Asher ben Yehiel, Rabbi (c.1250–1327) 72
Ashkenazi rites 73
Ashkenazim:
   in Amsterdam 167, 216
   boycott of Ancona (1556) 208, 210
   depicting the human form 71
   Istanbul 181
   poverty 232–3
   refugees in Istanbul 212–13
   Safed (Galilee) 105
   and Sephardim 73–4, 167, 231–3
   in Spain 49, 59
   synagogue in Amsterdam 239–40
   tudescos (Germans) 167, 232
   Venice 130, 165
astrology 63–4, 88
astronomy 63–4
Athias, Joseph 240, 242
Atlantic colonies, *see* New World
Avodat Hesed charitable society 232
Azulai, Abraham 86

B
Babylon exile 259
Baer, Yitzhak 17–18, 77, 84
   History of the Jews of Christian Spain 18
   The Jews of Christian Spain 51
Bagby, Albert 64
Baghdad 15, 23, 90
ballasteros (crossbowman) 55
Banu Wattas (Fez) 19–20
Bar Hebraeus, *The Chronography* 20
Barbados 233
Barrios, Daniel Levi de, *Triompho de govierno popular* 215
Basola, Moses 100, 104–5, 208
Bassano family 162
Batterman, Michael 75
battle of Lepanto (1573) 135
Bayezid II, sultan (r. 1481–1512) 176
Beatrice de Luna, *see* Nasi, Gracia Mendes
begging 232
Beit Ya'akov congregation 225, 234, 243
Beit yosef (Karo) 112
Belgrade 180
Belmonte, Manuel de 246
Benjamin of Tudela (c.1167) 101
Benveniste, Imanoel 242
Benveniste family 142, 198–9
Berab, Jacob (1474–1541) 110–11
Berbers 27
'Bergonzi affair' (1636) 163
Bible:
   Andalusian Jewish poetry 36–7
   apocalyptic date 89
   Christological readings 75
   date of the redemption 88
   Hebrew poetry 30–1
   illustrated 70, 250
   Old and New Testament themes in art 249–50
   printing in English 242
   story of Joseph (Genesis) 16
biblical citations:
   Gen. 22 75
   Exod. 16: 14 37

INDEX

Exod. 20: 4–5 71
Deut. 23: 20–1 163–4
Deut. 30: 1–10 89
Isaiah 2: 2–4 89
Jer. 29: 5 260
Jer. 29: 7 259
Amos 9: 9–15 89
Obad. 1: 20 7
Proverbs 20: 27 228–9
Ruth 4: 11–12 153–4
Esther 1: 6 36
Esther 2: 21 16–17
Esther 10: 3 17
Dan. 5 253
biblical figures on tombstones 249
biblical names 222, 249
bimah 140, 238, Plate 12
blasphemy 131
blood libel 65, 204
blood purity laws 202–3, 219
Boccato, Carla 158
bom judesmo 238
Bomberg, Daniel (1483–1553) 148–50
   Bomberg Babylonian Talmud, *Pe'ah* 1a Plate 14
Bonifaccio, Baldassare 157
Bonifacio di Ragusa 121
books, *see* printing and publishing
Bosphorus 174
Bouwman, Elias 241
boycott of Ancona (1556) 205–11
Brazil 226, 245, 252
Breestraat, Amsterdam 217
Brereton, William 238
British Levant Company 191
Buda (Hungary) 178
Bulan, king of Khazars 22
Bursa 180, 209
Byzantium 21

C

Cairo *geniza* 25
Calabrians 181
caliphs 14
Calle de los Judìos (Cordoba) 46
Calvinism 225, 239, 250

Campanton, Rabbi Isaac 198
Campiello delle Scuole (Venice) 140
Campo del Ghetto Nuovo (Venice) 168–9
canals 215
Canano, Giambattista 205
Cantigas de Santa Maria (Alfonso X) 61, 64–8, Plate 1
canton ('corner') 140
cantorial music 160
Capsali, Eliyahu, *Seder eliyahu zuta* 176, 197
Cardozo, David de Abraham 239, Plate 16
Carpenter, Dwayne 65
Castile:
   debates on philosophy and rationalism 59
   discriminatory dress 67–8
   economic reconstruction 57
   Hebrew illuminated manuscripts 68
   Muslim and Jewish occupations 57
Castilian 62–3, 201, 231
   see also Ladino; Spanish language
Castilian identity 48–9
Castro Tartas, David 240
Catalan Bible (Duke of Sussex) Plate 5
Catalonia 68
Catholic Reconquest 44–5
Catholics, salvation and sin 233
Cebà, Ansaldo 156–7
cemeteries, *see* Ouderkerk Cemetery
censorship 150–2
centres of Jewish learning 15
charity and charities 109
   see also *monti di pietà*
Charles V, Holy Roman Emperor 143, 145, 220
charters (*fueros*):
   Levantine Jews 129, 133
   Livorno 138
   Spain 49, 53

Venice 124, 125 n.2
Christian Spain:
   Arabic inscriptions 80, 82
   cross-cultural borrowing and cultural fusion 69
   ecclesiastical policies 66
   eucharistic imagery 74–5
   Jewish culture 49–50, 58
   Jewish economic status 6
   Jewish migration into 43, 52
   Jewish refugees 50
   Jews after Reconquest 49–50, 52
   Muslim rebellions 52
Christians:
   anti-Jewish literature 64–8
   clothing 180
   coexisting with Jews and Muslims 53, 261
   confronting Jews 53
   Eucharist 65, 74–5, 76
   Feast of Corpus Christi 76
   fraternizing with Jews 154–5
   Greek 180
   illuminated manuscripts 68–9
   interest in synagogues 237–8
   internationalism of mercantile groups 229
   Manasseh ben Israel's writings 254
   messianism 87–8, 93
   moneylenders 164
   Muslim Spain 10
   onlookers to circumcisions 224
   Ottoman colonization policies 177–8
   Palestine 121
   printing presses 201
   publishing houses 148
   sürgün (forced population transfers) 177
   symbols and artistic motifs 69
   transubstantiation, doctrine 65, 76
Christological readings 75
chroniclers 101
The Chronography (Bar Hebraeus) 20
circumcision 221, 224

Circumcision in a Sephardic Family (Hooghe) 224
Clement VII, Pope 94
cloth production, *see* textile industry
clothing:
  discriminatory 67–8
  distinctive 67–8, 127, 130, 180
  Muslim Spain 80
  Sephardim 130, 138–9
  Spanish synagogue 138–9
  women's 155
'The Coming of Spring' (Moses ibn Ezra) 33
Commentary on the Torah (Rashi) 200
commerce 217, 244–5
commercial agents (*fattori*) 173
commercial banks 164
commercial prosperity 225
community regulations, see *ascamot*
Conciliador (Manasseh ben Israel) 254
Confusion de confusiones (Penso de la Vega) 242
Congregation Shearith Israel (New York) 235
congregations, see *kehalim*
Consolation for the Tribulations of Israel (Usque) 145–6
Constantine VII of Byzantium 21
Constantinople, siege and fall (1453) 175
  see also Istanbul
conversion, forced 197
Converso courtiers 17–18
  see also Jewish courtiers
Conversos 161–2
  adoption of Judaism as heresy 131
  Amsterdam 216–17, 218, 220–1, 225
  Ancona 132, 205–8
  Beatrice de Luna (Gracia Mendes Nasi) 141
  Christian publishing houses 148

  cultural identities 183
  disappearing into Christian society 221
  hopeful message of Reubeni 95–6
  'how-to' books to return to Judaism 201
  Iberia's golden-age culture 227–8
  identity 197
  and the Inquisition 218–20, 220
  Jewish marriages in Venice 154
  leaving Iberia 136–7, 183, 218–19
  in medicine 202
  merchants 132, 225–6
  in Netherlands were not Jews 224
  Ottoman empire 132, 183–4
  Portuguese Brazil 245
  possession of Hebrew books 142
  returning to Judaism 221–2
  subterranean and perilous world 144
  with tainted blood 219
  trade with the Americas 225
  Venice 137, 148
  see also Portuguese Conversos
converts:
  to Islam 213
  Portuguese Jews 249
convivencia 7
Copia Sulam, Sara 154, 156–8, 159
  Manifesto 157
copperplate printing 242
Cordoba:
  academy of learning 23
  cultural life 12
  great mosque 12–13
  intellectual centre 14–15
  Jews as guards 10
  libraries 12
  Reconquest 45–6
  Sephardi civilization 9, 45
  social elitism and poetry 28
  synagogue 46–7
  Umayyads 11
  weaving 12

  yeshiva 18
  zenith 11–12
Cordoba caliphate (929–1031) 9, 10, 13, 20–1, 42–3
Cordovero, Moses (1522–70) 110
Cori (Rome) 101–2, 120
Correa, Isabel (Rebecca) 229
Correggio, Giovanni Mercurio da 88
Coryate, Thomas (1577–1617) 130, 138–9
'council of sages' (Safed, Galilee) 105
Council of Trent (1475) 164
Counter-Reformation 150–2
counts as protector of the Jews 57
courtiers 25
  see also Jewish courtiers
creation theories 117
credit 164
Cromwell, Oliver 166, 254, 255
Crónica de los reyes otomanos (Almosnino) 192, 193
cross-cultural borrowing 69
crusaders 49, 52
cultural change 10
cultural exchanges 8, 58–60, 85, 154–9
cultural fusion 69
Cum nimis absurdum papal bull (1555) 120, 151, 206
Curaçao 233, 235, 250–1
Curationum medicinalium centuriae septem (Amatus Lusitanus) 205
Curiel, Moses (Jeronimo Nunes da Costa) 246–7
customs and rituals 181
Cyprus 135, 178–9

D

Damascus 100
al-Dar'i, Moses 89
David, Abraham 105–6
debates 25
debts 164
Declaracao das seiscentas e treze encomendancas da nossa sancta ley (Farar) 243

'decorative' images 250
decorative ritual objects and
    sacred texts 72
*Dedication of the Portuguese
    Synagogue in Amsterdam*
    (Hooghe) 240, Plate 17
    see also synagogues: Esnoga
deism 21
Delmedigo, Joseph 253
depictions of Jews 66
deportations:
    Babylon (586 BCE) 259
    Ottoman empire 177, 180
Dernschwam, Hans 174, 181–2
Descartes, René 216
devshirme system 177–8
dhimmis ('protected people') 8–9,
    179–80, 184
diaspora 259–60
    see also Sephardi diaspora
Dieulosal, Isaac 87
dignity 197
Dioscorides (Greek physician),
    De materia medica 21
diplomats 21, 57
Discorso circa il stato de gl'Hebrei
    (Luzzatto) 124, 165–6
discrimination 221
discriminatory Jewish dress 67–8
dissidents 218
distinctive clothing 67, 127, 130,
    138–9, 180
'divided souls' 230–1
Dodds, Jerrilynn 69, 79
domestic life 73–4
Dönmeh sect 213
dowry society 226, 228
Dresnitz, Shelomoh 116
Dunash ben Labrat 18, 25, 32–3
    'Reply to an Invitation to a
        Feast' 37
Duran (Profiat), *Ma'aseh efod* 48
Dutch Curaçao 245
Dutch golden age 230–1
Dutch republic, *see* Netherlands
Dutch Sephardi radicalism 218

E
Edirne (Turkey) 180

education 243–4
Egypt 19, 178
El Tránsito Synagogue (Toledo)
    77–85, Plates 7–9
    Arabic inscriptions 81–2, Plate
        10
    dedicatory plaque 79, 83
    Hebrew inscriptions 79, 82–3,
        84, Plate 10
    inscriptions and decorations
        77, 78–9
elders (*muqaddamin*) 50–1
Eliezer Azikri, Rabbi (1533–1600)
    113
Elijah of Pesaro 100–1
Elizabeth I, Queen 223
Emden 223
Emek habakhah (Hakohen) 197
End of Days 88, 91, 99
England 255–6
English Bibles 242
Epistle to Yemen (Maimonides) 91
Ercole II, duke of Ferrara 133, 206
Essequibo (Guiana) 233
Ets Haim Yeshiva 243
European culture 198
Evelyn, John 237
exiles:
    family ties 182–3
    poetic themes 42–3, 44, 259
Exodus story 73, 74
exotic Jewish kingdoms 98
Expulsion from Spain (1492):
    exile from Iberia 259
    Jewish messianic and mystical
        traditions 92
    Portuguese Conversos 218–19
    Safed in the Galilee 99
    unification of Spain 261
expulsions of Jews:
    for debts and as scapegoats 164
    from Ferrara 146
    Jewish settlement patterns
        86–7
    portents of redemption 87
*Extremos y grandezas de
    Constantinopla* (Almosnino)
    192

F
family crests 249
famine 164
Fano, Azariah da 141
Farar, Abraham, *Declaracao* 243
Farissol, Abraham 88
Fatimids 19
Ferdinand I, Grand Duke of
    Tuscany 138
Ferdinand III, King of Castile and
    León 67
Ferrara 132, 133–4, 137, 145–6
Ferrizuel, Joseph 50
Ferrizuel family 50
Fez 130, 147
Fleischer, Ezra 25
forasteiros ('foreigners') 232
France 220, 221
Franciscan banks 164
Frankel, Rachel 249
Frankfurt am Main 130
Frankfurt Book Fair 252
Frederick Henry, Prince of
    Orange and Stadholder 238,
    253
fulling mills 189–90
*Funeral at the Portuguese Jewish
    Cemetery in Ouderkerk aan de
    Amstel* (Hooghe) Plate 20
funerary motifs 248–9

G
gaba'im (treasurers) 235–6
gambling 155
gematria (textual computations)
    89
Genoese 57
Gerardus Johannes Vossius 253
German Jews, *see* Tedeschi;
    tudesco
De Gewesene Kerk der Joden (de
    Hooghe) 239
ghettoizations 151
ghettos:
    Papal States 151
    Ragusa 173
    Venice 126–7
    see also Jewish quarters;
        Venetian ghetto

Giorgi, Francesco, *De harmonia mundi* 94
Glick, Thomas 63
golden ages:
   Amsterdam 245
   Dutch republic 230
   Iberia 227–8
   Spain 15, 29–47
Golden Horn (Istanbul) 174
Grabar, Oleg 80
Granada 57, 66, 69
graves and gravestones 247–9
Greek Christians 180
Greek classics 62
Greek Jews 177, 180
Greek language 21
Grotius, Hugo 226, 238, 253
   On the Law of War and Peace 226
   Remonstrance Concerning the Regulations to be Imposed upon the Jews 214, 226–7
Guidobaldo II, duke of Urbino 206, 208
Gundissalinus, Dominicus 61

H
Haarlem 225
Habib, Jacob ibn 198
Habib, Rabbi Levi ibn 111, 197
Hacker, Joseph 184
Haggadot 73, 76
   illuminations 73, 75–7, Plate 6
al-Hakam II, Caliph of Cordoba (961–76) 11, 15
Hakohen, Joseph 96–8
   Emek habakhah 197
   History of the Kings of France and of the Ottoman Turkish Sultans 93
Halevi Abulafia, Samuel 50, 63, 77–8, 80–5
Halevi, Aron 223
Halevi, Jacob 159
Halevi, Judah 31, 260
Halevi, Rabbi Moses Uri 223, 224
Halevi, Uri Phoebus 242
Halley's Comet (1456) 87
Hamburg 235
Hamon, Isaac 204

Hamon, Joseph (grandfather) 203
Hamon, Joseph (grandson) 204
Hamon, Moses 103, 203–4
Hamon family 203–4
Hamon Synagogue 204
De harmonia mundi (Giorgi) 94
Hasdai ibn Shaprut (915–70) 15–16, 18–19, 20–5, 31, 89–90
Haskoy (Istanbul) 195
Hebrew belles-lettres 58
Hebrew books:
   for Christians 149–50
   Conversos in possession of 142
   and the Inquisition 151
   pre-censorship 151
   printing 148–9, 151–2, 201
   publishing in Venice 127, 146–8, 151
Hebrew illuminated manuscripts 68–71
Hebrew inscriptions 79, 82–3, 84, Plate 10
Hebrew language 30, 217, 221
Hebrew names 222
Hebrew poetry and poets 25, 29–47
   and the Almoravids 44–5
   Arab culture 36–8
   and exile 42–3
   experimenting with Arabic poetics 30
   grey hairs 40
   improvisation and spontaneity 41
   light-hearted verse 42
   linguistic virtuosity 38–9
   lion imagery 35
   miserliness of courtiers 39–40
   multilingualism 31–2
   music 38
   poetic forms 31
   Sephardi poets 29, 31
   themes 32
   and wars 39
   wine poems 32–6
   women 25–6
Hekim Yakub (Jacobo) 203
Helena, empress 21

Henry VIII, King 161–2
heraldic seals 249
ḥerem (ban) 237
Herengracht with the Baron Belmonte House (Hooghe) Plate 18
Ḥisba Manual (Ibn Abdun) 43–4
Hispanic identity 231
Hispanic Judaism 168
Hispanic material culture 229
Historia de' riti hebraici (Modena) 141, 152
History of the Jews of Christian Spain (Baer) 18
History of the Kings of France and of the Ottoman Turkish Sultans (Hakohen) 93
Holland, *see* Netherlands
Holocaust memorial (Venice ghetto) 169
homens de nação (Conversos) 214
homoerotic themes in poetry 37
Honorius III, Pope 67
Honorius IV, Pope 67
honour 196–7
Hooghe, Romeyn de:
   Circumcision in a Sephardic Family (1668) 224
   De Gewesene Kerk der Joden 239
   Dedication of the Portuguese Synagogue in Amsterdam 240, Plate 17
   depicting luxurious lifestyles 246
   Esnoga 240–1, Plate 17
   Funeral at the Portuguese Jewish Cemetery in Ouderkerk aan de Amstel Plate 20
   Herengracht with the Baron Belmonte House Plate 18
   Sephardi self-realization 247
host desecration, accusations of 65–6
host societies 217, 260
House of Este 146
Hroswitha of Gandersheim 11
Huet, Pierre Daniel, bishop of Avranches 253
A Humble Address (Manasseh ben Israel) 255

Hungarian Jews 175–6, 178
hymns, penitential (*seliḥot*) 33

I
Iberian elite society 228
Iberian Jewish acculturation 9
Iberian Marrano 220
Ibn Abdun, Muhammad, *Ḥisba Manual* 43–4
Ibn Abi Zimra, Rabbi David 196
Ibn Daud, Abraham (1089–1164) 15, 51, 58, 61
  Sefer ha-Qabbalah 23, 24
Ibn Ezra, Abraham 40–1, 44
Ibn Ezra, Judah 51–2
Ibn Ferrizuel, Solomon 50
Ibn Gabirol, Solomon 34, 41, 42
  'The Kingly Crown' 3
  Mekor ḥayim 39
Ibn Hawkal (chronicler) 11–12
Ibn Khalfun, Isaac 39–40
  'A Present of Cheese' 40
Ibn Killis, Ya'qub 19
ibn Leb, Rabbi Joseph 186, 211
Ibn Nagrela, Samuel 20, 31, 39, 83–4
ibn Nahmias, David 199, 200
Ibn Nahmias, Samuel 199
Ibn Tumart, Muhammad (c.1080–c.1128) 89
Ibn Verga, Solomon, *Shevet yehudah* 197
iconography 50
identities:
  and forced conversions 197
  Iberian Jews 261
illuminated manuscripts 68–7
immortality of the soul 220
'infidels' 52
Innocent IV, Pope 46
Inquisition:
  attacking Hebrew books 151
  and Conversos 218–20
  free from in England 161
  messianic agitation 92
  in Portugal 219, 220
  in Venice 131
inscriptions:
  El Tránsito Synagogue 79, 82–3, 84, Plate 10

gravestones 248–9
medieval Spain 80–2
Interior of the Portuguese Synagogue Amsterdam (Witte) Plate 16
international trade 244–5
internationalism 229
Iran 19
Isaac ben Sid 63, 64
Isaac (court of Sultan Mahmud of the Ghaznavid dynasty) 19
Isaac (Gen. 22) 75
Islam:
  Almoravids 43–4
  converts to 213
  dhimmis 8–9
  heterodox movements 88
  Judaism's messianic traditions 87, 89
  and the rise of the Jews 19
Islamic architecture 81
Islamic scientific knowledge 60
Israel Hasofer 70
Israel, Jonathan 216, 244
Israelite slavery 73
Isserles, Rabbi Moses 112
Istanbul 171–213
  approaching by ship 173–4
  census (1455) 175
  cosmopolitan city 172
  discriminatory housing policies 194–5
  economic revival 174
  fires 193–5
  Golden Horn 174
  Iberian immigrants 172
  Islamization 194–5
  medical college 203
  sürgünlis and refugees 175–7
  see also Ottoman empire
Istanbul Jewry:
  boycott of Ancona (1556) 208, 209–10
  division of 181
  Ottoman tax registers 175
  population 181–4
  resettled in Haskoy 195
Italian Jews:
  boycott of Ancona 208

diversity of customs 140
migrating to Palestine 176
Salonica 180–1
settlements 164
Italy:
  marble 248
  textile industry 190–1

J
Jacob ben Asher 49, 59
Jacob ben Makhir ibn Tibbon 61
jahiliyya 30
Jamaica 233
janissary corps 177
Jeremiah (prophet) 259, 260
Jerusalem 101, 103
A Jew and a Christian playing chess Plate 3
Jewish ancestry 228
Jewish artists 50, 69, 241–2
The Jewish Cemetery (Ruisdael) 247, Plate 19
Jewish courtiers 15–20
  and Alfonso X 66
  Egypt and North Africa 19
  envoys to the Muslim courts 50–1
  intervening with monarchs 58
  privileged classes 51
  protector of his people 21–2
  Reconquest and intergroup relations 57
  as a redeemer 83
  refinement and purity of language 18
  roles 15
  and royal sponsors 83
  shaping Sephardi life and history 77–8
  shuttling between Pedro and Muhammad V 81
  and the *taifas* 19
  Toledo 56
  toleration 19
Jewish culture:
  Christian Spain 49–50, 58
  Venetian ghettos 152
Jewish merchants 126, 229
Jewish Museum of Venice 169

Jewish mystical texts 59
Jewish population:
  Jerusalem 10
  Ottoman empire 181–4
  Safed (Galilee) 105–6
  Salonica 187
  Toledo 54–5
Jewish quarters 55, 130
  see also ghettos; Venetian ghetto
Jewish self-expression 9
Jewish self-perception 223–5
Jews:
  cultural symbiosis 8
  depictions of in Alfonso's court 66
  distinctive clothing 127, 130, 180
  expelled to clear debts 164
  funerary practices 248
  as guards 10
  historical and eschatological lives 260
  resettlement in Istanbul 176
  as royal asset 66–7
  as scapegoats 164
  as scribes 69
  secret 143
  social fragmentation 196
Jews of Amsterdam:
  adjusting to Jewish customs 257
  economic dynamism 257
  education 243–4
  foundation myths 223–5
  Jewish life 220
  messianic excitement 255
  'proper decorum' 236
  publishing houses 229–30
  rabbis from Venetian ghettos 167–8
  recapturing a heritage 257
  rules of conduct 237
  trade with Brazil 226
  trade with the Iberian peninsula 245
  union of Jewish communities 257–8
  see also Amsterdam; Portuguese Jews of Amsterdam

Jews of Ancona 207
  see also Ancona
Jews of Andalusia, see Andalusia
Jews of Buda 178
Jews of Bursa 209
The Jews of Christian Spain (Baer) 51
Jews of Cori 101–2, 120
Jews, German, see Tedeschi; tudesco
Jews, modern:
  Marranos 256 n.94
  Portuguese Jews of Amsterdam 217, 256
  Sephardim 262
Jews and Muslims playing dice Plate 2
Jews of the Near East (Mustaribim) 105
Jews, Portuguese, see Portuguese Jews
Jews of Sicily 181
Jews of Toulouse 21–2
Jiménez de Rada, Rodrigo, archbishop of Toledo 60
jizya poll tax 179
Joao III, King of Portugal 96
Joao Rodrigues de Castelo Branco (Amatus Lusitanus) 204–5
Joseph (biblical figure) 16
Joseph, king of the Khazars 22
Joseph, king of the Lost Tribes of Israel 94
Judah ben Asher, Rabbi 72
Judah Halevi 31, 40, 50, 260
Judah ben Moses Cohen 61–2
Judah ibn Tibbon (1120–c.1190) 24
Judaism:
  adoption of by Conversos 234–5
  Conversos' Christianized version 220
  messianic doctrine 87–8
  mystical and rationalist approaches 49
  ordination, rabbinic 110–11
  'proper Judaism' (*bom judesmo*) 236–7
  quasi-neutrality 22

  rabbinic courts 54
  rabbinic Judaism 259–60
  rabbinic leadership 54, 100
  rabbinic scholars (*gaonim*) 23
  rabbis 231, 233–4
Judaizing 131
juderías (*judiarias*) 53
Julius III, Pope 133, 151, 206

K

kabbalism 94–5, 115, 199
Kahal Gerush 209
Kahal Kados de Talmud Tora 232, 235, 238
Kahal Kadosh Sha'ar Hashamayim 168, 256
Kahal Portugal 209
Kaplan, Yosef 236–7
Karaites 181, 182, 194
Karo, Joseph (1488–1575) 104, 111–13, 115, 197
  Beit yosef 112
  Magid mesharim 112
  Shulḥan arukh 112, 150
Kasmuna (wife of Dunash ben Labrat) 25–6
  'Will her love remember his graceful doe' 26
kehalim (congregations) 105–9
  Aragonese 108, 187
  Ashkenazi 188, 209–10
  being assigned to 195
  Catalan 188
  Iberian 194
  independence and customs 106–7
  Italian 183
  linguistic criteria 108
  Lisbon 187
  organization 108, 184, 185–6
  Ottoman taxation 185, 186, 187
  printing prayer books 200
  Romaniotes of Istanbul 186
  Safed (Galilee) 107 (Table 3.2)
  scholars 196
  Sephardi 182, 183, 186, 187, 197
  Sicilian 183, 188
kendi gelen (refugees from Europe) 175–6

INDEX

Ketubah, Abraham, son of
  Abrabanel, to Dona Gracia
  Plate 15
ketubot (marriage contracts)
  152–4, Plate 15
  Ashkenazi 153
Khazars 18–19, 22–3
Kimhi, David 28
'The Kingly Crown' (Ibn Gabirol)
  39

L

La Seniora (Hageveret), *see* Nasi,
  Gracia Mendes
Ladino 199–202, 213, 231, 260
Ladino proverbs 171, 259
Laguna, Andres 174
Land of Israel 22, 100–2
languages:
  Amarzigh (Berber) 26
  in Amsterdam 217, 231
  Arabic 28, 30, 31, 59
  arabophone (Jewish dialects of
    Arabic) 26
  Castilian 62–3, 201, 231
  congregational affiliation 108
  in eastern caliphate 26
  in eastern Sephardi diaspora
    231
  Greek 21
  Hebrew 30, 217, 221
  Ladino 199–202, 213, 231, 260
  Latin 60–3, 242
  in Muslim Spain 28, 30
  Portuguese 217, 222, 229–30,
    242
  Romance languages 31
  Spanish 217, 222, 229–30, 242
  of Spanish Jews 31, 59, 261
  xenoglossia 112
Lapidary (*Lapidario*) 62
law codes 112
  see also charters (*fueros*); *Las siete
    partidas* (Alfonso X)
law of Moses 221
lay leaders (*parnasim*) 231, 235–6
leaven (*ḥamets*) 73
'Lekhah dodi' ('Come, My
  Beloved', Alkabetz) 113–15

León, Rabbi Jehuda 241
Leti, Gregorio 238
Levantine Jews (Levantini):
  charters 129, 133, 137, 145
  customs 140
  Ghetto Vecchio 134
  Sephardim in Venice 128
Levita, Elijah 148
Lewis, Bernard 181
libraries:
  Cordoba 12
  loss of 70, 201
  Salonica 198–9
Libro de ajedrez, dados y tablas 66,
  Plates 2, 3
Libro de la alcora 64
Libro de las estrellas fijas 64
Libro grande (1604) 169
light-hearted verse 42
lion imagery 35
Lisbon 95
literacy 63
literary rivalry 25
literary societies 228–9
liturgical poetry 33
Livorno 126, 138, 226, 248
London 168, 223, 256
Longhena, Baldassare 140
Lopes, Miguel 223
Lopes Pereira, Manuel 223
Loredan (Venetian patrician) 129
Lost Tribes of Israel 98–9, 254
Low Countries, *see* Netherlands
Lucena, Juan de 147 n.41
Lucena, Spain 28
lunar eclipses 64
Lupo family of musicians 162
Luria, Isaac, Rabbi (1534–72) 102,
  108, 115–18, 122–3
Lurianic kabbalah 123, 147
Luther, Martin 87
luxurious lifestyles 246
Luzzatto, Simone 127
  Discorso circa il stato de gl'Hebrei
    124, 165–6

M

Ma'aseh efod (Duran) 48
Ma'ayanei hayeshuah (Abravanel)
  92–3

Madinat al-Yahud (Toledo) 55
Madinat al-Zahra (Andalusia)
  13–14
Maghrebi Jews 102, 105
Magid mesharim (Karo) 112
magidic phenomenon 123
mahamad 231, 235–9, 244
Maimonidean controversy 59
Maimonides, Moses 45, 261
  Epistle to Yemen 91
  Mishneh torah 71, 91, 200
Maleha, Don Cag de la 66
Manasseh ben Israel (Manoel Dias
  Soeiro) 98–9, 251–6, 257
  Conciliador 254
  correspondence with
    Protestant scholars 230
  A Humble Address 255
  Miqweh Israel 254
  Nishmat ḥayim 252
  petition to Oliver Cromwell
    166, 254, 255
  portrait by Rembrandt 253–4,
    Plate 22
  portrait by Salom Italia 251,
    Plate 21
  as a printer 242
  sermons 238, 253
  Thesouro dos dinim 243
The Manifesto of Sarra Copia Sulam
  (Copia Sulam) 157
Mantua 132
al-Maqqari, Ahmed Mohammed
  (1591–1632) 12
marble 248
Maria Nunes 224
Marranism 219, 220
Marranos:
  expelled from Venice 145
  knowledge of Hebrew 221
  in London 223
  Lupo brothers 162
  as modern Jews 256 n.94
  Portugal 220
  as 'Portuguese'
    ('Jew'/'Judaizer') 219
  and Reubeni 95–6
  in Spain 219
  Spanish Jews fearing 146

marriage:
    ceremonies 152–3
    contracts (*ketubot*) 152–4,
        Plate 15
    endogamous 222
Maslama al-Majriti (astronomer)
    12
Masoretic texts 71
Massignon, Louis 38
De materia medica (Dioscorides) 21
Matsah: Kaufmann Haggadah
    Plate 6
matsah (unleavened bread) 73, 75
    n.52, 76
medicine 202–5
Medina, Samuel de 188, 189–90,
    197, 198, 213
Mediterranean basin 15
Mehmet II the Conqueror,
    Ottoman sultan 175–6, 203,
    204
Mekor ḥayim (Ibn Gabirol) 39
'men of commerce' 244
    see also Portuguese Conversos
Menahem ben Aaron ibn Zerah
    17
Menahem ibn Saruq 18, 25
Mendes, Francisco 142–3
Mendes family 142–6
Menocal, Maria Rosa 79
menorah 75
mercantilism 225, 229
'merchants' 244–5
Merida, Spain 28
messianic pretenders 88, 89, 90,
    91, 98
messianism 87–99
    Amsterdam 253–5
    Ancona 97
    and the Crusades 91
    dates 89
    downtrodden communities 91
    Expulsion from Spain (1492) 92
    Jewish and Protestant traditions
        254
    Jews and Christians 93
    Muslim–Christian campaigns
        94

mysticism 88–9
Ottoman Jewry 212–13
predictions 89
rural Jews 92
Sephardi diaspora 22–3
women 90
    see also Molkho, Solomon
    (Diogo Pires); Reubeni,
    David
micrography 71
Middle Eastern Jews 88, 100
midrashic interpretations 70
militant messianism 94
minhagim (communal customs)
    196
Miqweh Israel (Manasseh ben
    Israel) 254
Mishneh torah (Maimonides) 71,
    91, 200
Mizrahi, Rabbi Eliyahu 177
Modena, Rabbi León de 127, 234
    bankruptcy 155
    Beit yehudah 151–2
    'Bergonzi affair' (1636) 163
    Historia de' riti hebraici 141, 152
    as a musician 159–61
    openness to change 168
    plague 162
    Sara Copia Sulam 157, 158
    sermons 140, 141
Molkho, Solomon (Diogo Pires)
    93, 96–8
monarchs as protectors of the
    Jews 57, 66–7
moneylending 55, 57, 162–6
Montalto, Elijah de 234, 247
Montezinos, Antonio de (Aaron
    Levi) 254
monti di pietà 164–5, 166
Mordechai (Esther 2: 21) 16–17
Moretto, Giorgio 131
Morocco 102, 167, 246
Morteira, Rabbi Saul 167, 228, 234,
    243, 252
Moses al-Dar'i 89
Moses ben Hanoch 23
Moses Curiel (Jeronimo Nunes da
    Costa) 246–7

Moses ibn Ezra (c.1055–c.1138) 28,
    29, 36, 38, 42–3, 45
    'The Coming of Spring' 33
Moses Uri Halevi (1544–c.1628)
    234
Moshe ben Maimon Hasefaradi,
    see Maimonides, Moses
Mozarabs (Arabized Christians)
    10
Mudéjar architecture 81
Mudéjar styles of art 79–81,
    Plate 4
Mudéjares (Muslims in Christian
    Spain) 10, 53
Muhammad V, Nasrid king
    (1354–91) 80, 81
multilingualism 31, 59, 261
music and musicians 38, 159–62
Muslim prayer rugs (*sajjada*) 72
Muslim Spain:
    Arabic 28
    ethnic hypersensitivity 10
    hierarchies 27
    internecine struggles 9–10
    Jews leaving 51
    pseudo-genealogies 27
Muslims:
    clothing 180
    Mudéjares (Muslims in
        Christian Spain) 10, 53
    new Muslims 9–10
    occupations 57
    rebellions in Christian Spain 52
    refugees from Reconquest 52
    Safed (Galilee) 105–6
    Tiberias 121
Mustaribim (Jews of the Near
    East) 105
al-Mu'tamid ibn Abbad 43
muwashshah poetic forms 31
mysticism:
    and the Expulsion from Spain
        92
    and messianism 88–9
    mystical techniques 53–4, 116
    and the sabbath 113
    in Safed (Galilee) 111, 115–16
    Salonica 199
    Venetian ghetto 126

N

nação (the 'Nation') 214, 228, 233
  see also Portuguese Jews
Nagrela, Samuel ibn 28, 34, 35–6
Nahmanides Synagogue
  (Jerusalem) 122
Naples 147, 181
Nasi, Gracia Mendes (Doña Nasi)
  141–6
  in Antwerp as a secret Jew 143
  boycott of Ancona (1556) 209,
    210
  changing name 174
  in Ferrara as a Jew 145–6
  Istanbul (1553) 174–5
  Jews of Ancona 206–7
  journey to Istanbul 172–3
  and Moses Hamon 203–4
  Ragusa 173
  and Suleiman the Magnificent
    103
  Tiberias 119
  in Venice 141–2, 145
Nasi, Joseph (Don Joseph) 103,
  119–20, 209
Nasrid kingdom of Granada 57,
  66, 69
Nathan of Gaza 242
Netherlands:
  admitting Jews 226–7
  art and artists 239, 250
  Calvinism 225
  Christian funerary customs
    248
  Dutch golden age 230–1
  global trade 225–6, 245–6
  immigration and religion 225
  languages 231
  Protestant culture 238–9
  religious tolerance 215, 220
  trade with Conversos 225
  trade with Spain and Morocco
    246
  see also Amsterdam
Neve Shalom congregation 225,
  234, 243
New World:
  Inquisition 219–20
  messianism 87
  sending poor to 233
New York 235
Nishmat ḥayim (Manasseh ben
  Israel) 252
noble ancestry 26, 27–8, 45
North Africa 19
Nunes, Maria 223
Nunes da Costa, Jeronimo (Moses
  Curiel) 246–7

O

Obadiah of Bertinoro, Rabbi 103
occupations 55–6, 57
Old and New Testament themes
  in art 249–50
On the Law of War and Peace
  (Grotius) 226
Order of the Knights of Calatrava
  78
Orobio de Castro, (Baltazar) Isaac
  222, 246
Ottoman empire:
  colonization policies 177–8
  commerce 128
  contracting of the empire 212
  and Conversos 132, 183–4
  defeat at Lepanto (1573) 135
  deportations 175, 177
  disdain for non-Muslims 184
  eastern Sephardi diaspora 211
  economy 189
  expansion into Europe 94
  fall of Constantinople 175–6
  Jews, Christians, and Muslims
    living together 186
  landholding system 212
  manuscripts printed in Venice
    147
  Palestine 103
  place of refuge 220
  printing industry 199–200
  revolts 212
  Sephardi group identity 195–7
  'Silver Age' 211–13
  sürgün (forced population
    transfers) 121, 175, 177–9, 180,
    196
  tax-paying religious collectives
    184
  tax registers 187
  wars with Venice 121, 135
  wealthy and poor areas 187
  see also Istanbul
Ottoman Jewry:
  boycott of Ancona (1556) 209,
    210–11
  communal associations 172
  decline 212–13
  fractionalization 167
  fragmentation on ethnic lines
    195–6
  heterogeneity 181–2
  kehalim 184, 187, 196
  population 181–4
  Portuguese Jews 187–8
  Sephardi civilization 211
  Sephardi doctors 203
  Sephardi refugees 171–2
  Sephardicization 187
  taxation 184–5, 186
Ouderkerk Cemetery 226, 247–51,
  Plate 20
  see also Portuguese Jews of
    Amsterdam

P

Padua 155
Palache, Rabbi Samuel 234
Palestine 100, 101, 102–3, 118–19,
  167
Palestinian charities 109
papal policies:
  burning the Talmud 150–1
  separating Jews from Christians
    66, 151
  see also ghettos
paper-manufacturing 12
Pardo, Rabbi Joseph (d. 1619) 234
parnasim (lay leaders) 231, 235–6
Passover 73–5
  Haggadot 72, 74
  Seder 73–4
patron–retainer relationships 18
Paul IV, Pope 151, 206
pawnbroking 163
'pedagogical' images 250
Pedro I, King of Castile
  (r. 1350–69) 77–8, 79, 81

Penso de la Vega, Joseph,
    Confusion de confusiones 242
Pepys, Samuel 238
Pereira, Abraham 245
Perelheim, Zadok 214
periodization 10
persecutions 226
Persians 27
Pesaro 206-9
pharmacology 21
Philip II, King of Spain 216
physicians 16, 202, 202-3
Piedra gloriosa (Rembrandt) 254
pietism 59
pilgrimages 100
Pinto, David de 246
Pinto, Isaac de 214, 247
Pires, Diego, *see* Molkho,
    Solomon
plagues 162-4, 191
poetry 29-30
    Arabic gardens 38
    'arabiyya-shu'ubiyya
        controversy 27
    break-up of caliphate of
        Cordoba 42-3
    exile 42-3
    in Hebrew belles-lettres 58
    homoerotic themes 37
    improvisation and spontaneity
        41
    light-hearted verse 42
    'paradise lost' 38
    social settings 37
    spectacle of ruins 37-8
    war 39
    wine poems 32-6
    see also Hebrew poetry and
        poets
polyphonic music 160
Ponentine Jews 128-9, 137
    see also Portuguese Conversos
population:
    Amsterdam 215
    Andalusia 11
    Ottoman Jewry 181-4
    Safed (Galilee) 105-6
    Salonica 180-1, 187
    Toledo 54-5

Portugal:
    emigration to America 219
    forced conversions (1497)
        218-19
    trade with Jews of Amsterdam
        245
    union with Spain 136-7, 219
Portuguese Conversos:
    adopting Judaism 221
    in Amsterdam 167-8, 216-17,
        222, 235
    in Brazil 245
    cosmopolitanism 222-3
    education 243
    Ferrara expelling 146
    and the Inquisition 220
    'men of commerce' 244
    Ponentine Jews 128-9
    refugees from Spain 218-19
    religious identity 233
    transnational trading network
        222
    Venice 128-9, 131-2, 137
    see also Conversos; Manasseh
        ben Israel
Portuguese Inquisition 219, 220
'Portuguese' as 'Jew' / 'Judaizer'
    219
Portuguese Jews:
    affluent lifestyle 155
    in Amsterdam 215-16
    of Ancona 206
    Bevis Marks synagogue,
        London 256
    cemeteries 250-1
    Christian interest in synagogue
        237
    congregational arguments 188
    cultural identities 183
    designs for tombstones 250
    diaspora 227-33, 245
    divide with Tunis Jews 167
    divisions with Spanish refugees
        146
    England 255
    exclusivism 228, 232
    former Conversos 105
    immigration to Amsterdam
        256

    manners in synagogues 238
    Ottoman empire 187-8
    portraits 241-2
    trade with Brazil 226, 245
Portuguese Jews of Amsterdam:
    adopting biblical names 249
    bet ḥayim (cemetery) 247
    as Catholics 261
    communities 214-15
    community 214-15
    converts 249
    culture of the host society
        217-18
    display of religious identity 229
    Dutch artists 239
    education 243-4
    founding myths 224
    Hispanic identity and culture
        229, 231
    homogeneous group 235
    Iberian tastes 230-1
    immigration 256
    individualism and freedom of
        thought 257
    merchants 216, 225
    as 'modern' Jews 217, 256
    nação ('the Nation') 233
    particularism 233
    'proper decorum' 236
    rabbis 231, 233-4
    right to live in 236
    rights of citizens 227
    trade 245
    union of congregations 235-6
    western Sephardi diaspora 231
    see also Amsterdam; Ouderkerk
        Cemetery
Portuguese language 217, 222
Portuguese language books
    229-30, 242
portugueses de la nación hebrea 214
power relationships 49
Prague 130
prayer books 200, 242
printing and publishing:
    Amsterdam 242-3, 252
    books 24, 200
    complete texts 200-1

with copper plates 242
didactic and polemical works
    242
early modern Jewish culture
    150
Hebrew books 147, 148–9,
    151–2, 201
movable type 147
Ottoman empire 199–202
secular works 243
Venice 146–50
privileged classes 51
see also Jewish courtiers
Profiat Duran, *Ma'aseh efod* 48
'proper decorum' 236
proselytizing 66, 75
Protestantism 221, 250
pseudo-genealogies 27
Pumbedita talmudic academy
    (Iraq) 23
puns and riddles in poetry 42
'purity of blood' statutes 218

Q
Qasr al-Yahud (Toledo) 55
Quran 29

R
Rabd al-Yahud (Toledo) 55
Ragusa 173
ram's horn (*shofar*) 75
Rashi (Solomon ben Isaac),
    Commentary on the Torah,
    Haftorah and Five Megillot 200
Rashi script 149, 201, Plate 14
Raymond, archbishop of Toledo
    (1125–51) 60
Reconquest:
    crusading fervour 52–3
    intergroup relations 57
    religious identities 44–5
redemption 87–8, 117, 123
refugees 49, 52, 53, 145
'Regulation about the *Tudescos*'
    232
religious freedoms 220
Rembrandt van Rijn 217, 241–2
    Belshazzar's feast (Dan. 5) 253
    Piedra gloriosa 254

portrait of Manasseh ben Israel
    253–4, Plate 22
The Synagogue 239
Remonstrance Concerning the
    Regulations to be Imposed upon
    the Jews (Grotius) 214, 226–7
'Reply to an Invitation to a Feast'
    (Dunash ben Labrat) 37
Reubeni, David 93–8
Rhodes 178
rich/poor gap 68
Rocamora, Vicente de 246
Rodriga, Daniel 135–8
Romance languages 31
Romaniote Jews:
    boycott of Ancona 210
    communal organization 184
    Istanbul 181, 182, 186, 194
    Sephardi *kehalim* 187, 194, 261
    sürgün policy 179
rosh hagolah (exilarch) 23
Rossi, Salomone, 'Songs of
    Solomon' 160–1
Roth, Norman 28
royal favour 50–1
royal lineage 28
royal patronage 16–17, 58
Ruderman, David 87, 149
Ruisdael, Jacob van, *The Jewish*
    Cemetery 247, Plate 19
rules of conduct 237
rural Jews 92

S
Sa'adyah Gaon 25
Saba, Abraham 200
sabbath 115, 139
Sa'd al-Dawla 20
Safed (Galilee) 99–118
    background 101
    charity 109
    community relations 106–7
    'council of sages' 105
    decline of Jewish community
        121–2
    harmony and tranquillity 103–4
    'holy cities' of the Land of
        Israel 122
    imminent redemption 110

Jewish deportees to Cyprus
    178–9
journey to 101–3
kabbalists 109–18, 115
kehalim 107 (Table 3.2)
messianism 116
mystics 110–18
population 105–6, 106
    (Table 3.1)
rapid development 104
Sephardi exiles 97
synagogues 122
taxation 107
textile manufacture 103
Torah study 105
Said al-Andalusi 15
St Mark's Basilica (Venice) 126
Salom Italia, portrait of Manasseh
    ben Israel 251, Plate 21
Salonica 171–213
    boycott of Ancona (1556) 208
    census (1478) 180
    destruction of Jewish
        community 199
    European culture 198
    Italian Jewish immigrants 180
    Jewish community 187
    kehalim 186, 187
    libraries 198–9
    'a mother of Judaism' 211
    mysticism 96–7, 199
    plagues 191
    population 180–1
    printing 199–200
    refugees 171
    scholarship 197–9
    Sephardi immigrants 180–1
    Sephardi rabbis 171–2
    talmud torah 198
    textiles 172, 186, 189–92
salvation and sin 233
Sancho IV, King of Castile 63
Sanhedrin (supreme court) 110–11
Santa Companhia de Dotar
    Orfans e Donzelas Pobres
    228
Sarajevo 180
Sarajevo Haggadah 76

Sarpi, Fra Paolo 137
Sasportas, Rabbi Jacob 234, 256
Schechter, Solomon 111
scientific treatises 63–4
Scuola Canton (Venice) 139–40
Scuola Grande Spagnola (Venice) 140, Plate 13
Scuola Grande Tedesca (Venice) 139–40
Scuola Italiana (Venice) 139–40
Scuola Levantina (Venice) 140, Plates 11, 12
Sea of Galilee 120
sea voyages 101–2
secular courts 54
secular works 243
  see also poetry
Seder eliyahu zuta (Capsali) 176, 197
Sefer hahalakhot (Alfasi) 150
Sefer hameshiv 92
Sefer ha-Qabbalah (Ibn Daud) 23, 24
Sefer nitsaḥon yashan 76–7
Selim I, sultan of the Ottoman empire 178
Selim II, sultan of the Ottoman empire 121, 178
separatism 196
'Sepharad' 7, 8, 261–2
Sephardi art 50
Sephardi civilization 45, 211
Sephardi courtiers 17
  see also Jewish courtiers
Sephardi cultural identity 10
Sephardi diaspora 97, 146, 246, 256, 262
  eastern 211, 231
  western 215, 218–23
Sephardi history 8
Sephardi leadership 23–4
Sephardi poets 29, 31
  see also Hebrew poetry and poets
Sephardi rites 73, 188–9
Sephardi women 139, 202
Sephardim:
  Amsterdam 228–9

appearance of term 53
and Ashkenazim 59, 165, 167, 232
asylum in Istanbul 176
commerce with or in the Ottoman empire 128
complex loyalties 246
Cordoba shaping Sephardi civilization 45
cultural expression 202
clothing 130, 138–9, 180
distinctive Jewish subgroup 10
exclusivism 232
fields of knowledge in Muslim and Christian Spain 261
first modern Jews 262
Hamburg 235
honour and dignity 196–7
Iberian aesthetic tastes 154
identity 195–7
loss of libraries and material culture 201
marriage customs 153
messianic activism 88
multilingualism 261
mysticism 92, 115
noble ancestry 26, 45
opposition to in Venice 136
Ottoman economy 189
Ottoman empire 181–2
Passover Haggadot 73–4
refugees going to Salonica 171–2
replicating cultural life of Iberia 228–9
Safed (Galilee) 105
self-consciousness 9
self-realization 247
sending paupers to Guiana 233
superiority 28
synagogues in Venice 140–1
textiles 103, 189
tsaḥut halashon 45
uniqueness 261
Shabateans 118
Shabetai Tsevi 98, 212, 242, 255
Shevet yehudah (Ibn Verga) 197
Shimon bar Yohai 92, 118

shipbuilding 216
Shomrim Laboker 169
Shulḥan arukh (Karo) 112, 150
shu'ubiyya 27
Las siete partidas (Alfonso X) 53–4, 61, 65, 79
  and antisemitic doctrines 65
Sinan (Ottoman architect) 174
social control 237
Sokollu, Mehmet (vizier) 121
Solomon ibn Ferrizuel 50
Solomon ben Isaac, *see* Rashi
Soncino, Eliezer 200
Soncino, Gershom 147, 200–1
Soncino, Rabbi Joshua 208–10
'Songs of Solomon' (Rossi) 160–1
South American Indians 98–9, 254
South Carolina 166
Spain:
  cultural autonomy 23
  culture blending Islamic and Gothic 69–70
  diaspora within a diaspora 260
  Dutch trading partners 246
  emigration from 219
  golden era 29–47
  individual morality 54
  Jewish burial sites 249
  Jewish–Christian confrontation 53
  in Jewish memory 260–1
  Jewish neighbourhoods 53–4
  Jewish quarters 130
  refugees from Portuguese Inquisition 219
  self-definition of its exiles 260
  trading with Jews of Amsterdam 245
  unification 261
  union with Portugal 136–7, 219
Spalato (Split) 136
Spanish Conversos 223
Spanish–Dutch truce (1608) 245
Spanish Hebrew poetry 29, 41–2
Spanish Inquisition 219
Spanish Jewish courtiers 18–19
Spanish Jews:
  accomplishments in Iberia 261

burial sites 249
emigration to Jerusalem 101
exile 44–5
fearing Marranos 146
messianic agitation 92
noble ancestry 27–8
occupations 57
role in Muslim Spain 10
as royal treasure 52
Spanish language 217, 222
  see also Castilian
Spanish language books 229–30, 242
Spanish refugees 146
Spanish synagogue (Venice) 138–9
Spinoza, Baruch (Benedict de) 230, 234, 243
stone monuments 248
stonecutters 250
sugar-refining 245
Suleiman the Magnificent, sultan (r. 1520–66) 103, 104, 119, 174, 207, 211
sultans 202–3
sumptuary restrictions 179
Sura talmudic academy (Iraq) 23
sürgün (forced population transfers) 121, 175, 177–9, 180, 195–6
sürgünlis 175, 177, 178, 196
Suriname 233
Swetschinski, Daniel 249
The Synagogue (Rembrandt) 239
synagogues:
  Amsterdam 226, 235, 257
  Bevis Marks (London) 256
  changing 187
  chaotic services 139
  charity chests 109
  Christian interest in 237–8
  construction of in Spain 79
  Cordoba 46–7
  Esnoga 223, 224, 239–42, Plate 16
  lack of decorum 238
  music 160
  Muslim artefacts in 71–2
  Portuguese exclusivism 232

Safed (Galilee) 122
Sephardi Jews 140–1
social life 186
sumptuary restrictions 179
Talmud Tora 238, 253
Tedeschi 139–40
Toledo 66
Venetian model of congregational association 235
Venice 138–41
women 186
see also El Tránsito Synagogue

T
Taḥkemoni (Al-Harizi) 48
taifas (independent Muslim kingdoms) 14, 19
Taitatzak, Rabbi Joseph 97, 197
Talmud 149, 150–1
  Babylonian 23, 249
  Bomberg Babylonian Talmud, *Pe'ah* 1a Plate 14
  burning (papal policy) 150–1
  Jerusalem 119, 149
talmud torah 198, 243–4
tax-collectors 56, 77–8
tax farmers 57, 66
taxation in the Ottoman empire 184–5
Tedeschi (German Jews in Venice) 128, 129–30, 139–40
Tedeschi synagogues 140
Temple of Jerusalem 75, 76, 240–1, Plate 5
textile industry:
  cloth production 191
  plague carriers 191
  Safed (Galilee) 103
  Salonica 172, 186, 189–92
  Sephardi refugees 103
  Tiberias 120
  weaving 12, 103
Thesouro dos dinim (Manasseh ben Israel) 243
Tiberias 119–21
tikun olam doctrine (Luria) 117
Tirado, Jacob (James Lopes da Costa) 167, 224, 226

Toland, John 166
Toledan Jews:
  Arabized community 53
  artists 50
  courtiers 56
  defenders of the city 55
  identity 50
  Jewish quarter 55, 55–6
  population 54–5
  refugees 49
  taxpayers 55
Toledo 48–85
  Ashkenazi and Sephardi traditions 59
  Bab al-Yahud gate 55
  Christian, Mudéjar, and Sephardi relations 53
  cultural crossroads 48
  gap between rich and poor 56
  Hebrew illuminated manuscripts 68–71
  hybrid cultural world 59, 69
  ideological debates 59–60
  Muslim prayer rugs 72
  occupations 55–6
  as a place of asylum 51–2
  Qasr al-Yahud 55
  Rabd al-Yahud/Madinat al-Yahud district 55
  reconstruction 7
  scientific knowledge 60
  synagogues 66
  translation activities 60, 61–3
tombstones 249–50, 260
Torah:
  Ladino translation 200
  study in Safed 105
Toulouse 21–2
Trani, Rabbi Moses 107–8
translation activities:
  intermediary languages 62
  Muslim Spain 21
  new words 62
  Ottoman empire 200
  Toledo 60, 61–3
  vernacular languages 62–3
travel conditions 103
travel literature 101

Triompho de govierno popular, y de la antiguedad holandesa (de Barrios) 215
tsaḥut halashon ('purity of the language') 45
tudesco (Ashkenazim in Amsterdam) 167, 232
Tudor court (England) 161–2
Tunis 167

U
Umayyad caliphate 11, 100
Union of Utrecht (1570) 215
United Provinces of the Netherlands, *see* Netherlands
unleavened bread (*matsah*) 73, 75 n.52, 76
urbanization 11
Uri Phoebus Halevi 242
Usque, Samuel 211
 Consolation for the Tribulations of Israel 145–6
usury 163–4, 165
 'Utility of the Jews' 162–6
Uziel, Rabbi Isaac (d. 1622) 234, 247

V
Valladolid *cortes* decree (1322) 58
Venetian ghetto 127–35
 accommodation 129, 132–3
 charters 125 n.2
 contemporary descriptions 130–1
 curfews 127
 daily life 169
 decree creating 124–5
 demolishing 127–8
 diverse communities 129
 gambling and duelling 155
 Ghetto Nuovissimo 125, 133, 158
 Ghetto Nuovo 125, 134, 158
 Ghetto Vecchio 125, 133, 134, 140, 158
 languages 169
 lieu de mémoire 168
 model of self-governance 167–8
 music and art 159–62

population of refugees 129
Portuguese Conversos 128–9, 131–2
protection from mobs 131
refuge to Sephardim 168
renewing Sephardi life 169–70
restrictions on Jews 128
shaping Sephardi history 126–7
tourist attraction 138, 169
training teachers and rabbis 167
see also Jewish quarters
Venetian Jews:
 Ashkenazim 130
 cultural expression 152
 distinctive clothing 130
 diverse community 125
 diversity of customs 140
 economic role 165–6
 fraternizing with Christians 154–5
 Hebrew book production 127, 146–52
 illuminated *ketubot* 154
 Italianized 154
 loyalties 135
 model of congregational association 235
 moneylenders 165
 organized communal structure 125
 Sephardim 129–30, 135
 settlement of Sephardim in Ragusa 173
 status 127, 134–5
 synagogues 138–41
 Tedeschi 129–30
 western and eastern Sephardi diasporas 235
 wills 158–9
 women 155
Venice 124–70
 burning Hebrew books 150–1
 charters 124, 125 n.2, 137–8
 commercial supremacy 126
 David Reubeni 94
 expelling Marranos 145
 Inquisition 131
 monti di pietà 165

opposition to Sephardim 136
papal censorship 150–1, 242
plague 162–3
and the Salonica textile industry 190
Sephardim and Mediterranean geopolitics 135
signs of wealth 125–6
as a transit point 161
violence, insecurity, and licentiousness 155
wars with Ottoman empire 121, 135
vigils 113
Visigothic persecutions 10
Vital, Hayim (1542–1620) 113, 115, 118, 122
Vlooienburg (Amsterdam) 225

W
'warriors of the faith' (crusaders) 52
wars 39
weaving, *see* textile industry
'Will her love remember his graceful doe' (Kasmuna) 26
William II Prince of Orange 238, 241
William III, King of England and Prince of Orange 238, 247
wills 158–9
Wischnitzer, Rachel 239
Witte, Emanuel de 239
 Interior of the Portuguese Synagogue Amsterdam Plate 16
women:
 Academia de los Sitibondos 229
 assets 158–9
 clothing and modesty 155
 messianic agitation 92
 messianic movements 90, 92
 poets 25–6
 prayer 155–6
 restrictions on in Padua 155
 Sephardi 139, 202
 synagogues 186
 wives 102

woollen broadcloth 191
worshipping in private 226

Y
Yahya, Guedalia 198
Ya'qub ibn Killis 19

Yehuda ben Moses Cohen 63
Yemen 91

Z
zajal (strophic poetic form in colloquial dialect of Andalusia) 31

Zarco, Judah 86
al-Zarkali (astronomer) 63
Zohar 92, 110

www.ingramcontent.com/pod-product-compliance
Lightning Source LLC
Chambersburg PA
CBHW041411300426
44114CB00028B/2988